THEORETICAL AND EMPIRICAL FOUNDATIONS OF RATIONAL-EMOTIVE THERAPY

THE BROOKS/COLE SERIES IN COUNSELING
PSYCHOLOGY
John M. Whiteley, University of California at Irvine
Arthur Resnikoff, Washington University
Series Editors

COUNSELING ADULTS
Editors: Nancy K. Schlossberg, University of Maryland
Alan D. Entine, State University of New York at Stony Brook

CAREER COUNSELING
Editors: John M. Whiteley, University of California at Irvine
Arthur Resnikoff, Washington University

APPROACHES TO ASSERTION TRAINING
Editors: John M. Whiteley, University of California at Irvine
John V. Flowers, University of California at Irvine

COUNSELING WOMEN
Editors: Lenore W. Harmon, University of Wisconsin—Milwaukee
Janice M. Birk, University of Maryland
Laurine E. Fitzgerald, University of Wisconsin—Oshkosh
Mary Faith Tanney, University of Maryland

THEORETICAL AND EMPIRICAL FOUNDATIONS OF
RATIONAL-EMOTIVE THERAPY
Editors: Albert Ellis, Institute for Rational-Emotive Therapy
John M. Whiteley, University of California at Irvine

THEORETICAL AND EMPIRICAL FOUNDATIONS OF RATIONAL-EMOTIVE THERAPY

EDITED BY

ALBERT ELLIS

INSTITUTE FOR RATIONAL-EMOTIVE THERAPY

JOHN M. WHITELEY

UNIVERSITY OF CALIFORNIA AT IRVINE

BROOKS/COLE PUBLISHING COMPANY

Monterey, California
A Division of Wadsworth, Inc.

Acquisition Editor: *Claire Verduin*
Project Development Editor: *Ray Kingman*
Production Editor: *Fiorella Ljunggren*
Interior Design: *Laurie Cook*
Cover Design: *Sharon Marie Bird*
Typesetting: *Linda Andrews, Ashland, Oregon*

Printed in the United States of America

10 9 8 7 6 5 4 3 2 1

Much of the material in this book originally appeared in *The Counseling
Psychologist*, the official publication of the Division of Counseling
Psychology of the American Psychological Association.

Library of Congress Cataloging in Publication Data

Main entry under title:

Theoretical and empirical foundations of rational-
     emotive therapy.

   (Brooks/Cole series in counseling psychology)
   Includes index.
   1. Rational-emotive psychotherapy. I. Ellis,
Albert, 1913–   II. Whiteley, John M
RC489.R3T47   616.8'914   79-11083
ISBN 0-8185-0336-X

SERIES FOREWORD

The books in the Brooks/Cole Series in Counseling Psychology reflect the significant developments that have occurred in the counseling field over the past several decades. No longer is it possible for a single author to cover the complexity and scope of counseling as it is practiced today. Our approach has been to incorporate within the Brooks/Cole Series the viewpoints of different authors having quite diverse training and perspectives.

Over the past decades, too, the counseling field has expanded its theoretical basis, the problems of human living to which it addresses itself, the methods it uses to advance scientifically, and the range of persons who practice it successfully—from competent and skillful paraprofessionals to doctoral-level practitioners in counseling, psychology, education, social work, and psychiatry.

The books in the Brooks/Cole Series are intended for instructors and both graduate and undergraduate students alike who want the most stimulating in current thinking. Each volume may be used independently as a text to focus in detail on an individual topic, or the books may be used in combination to highlight the growth and breadth of the profession. However they are used, the books explore the many new skills that are available to counselors as they struggle to help people learn to change their behavior and gain self-understanding. Single volumes also lend themselves as background reading for workshops or in-service training, as well as in regular semester or quarter classes.

The intent of all the books in the Brooks/Cole Series is to stimulate the reader's thinking about the field, about the assumptions made regarding the basic nature of people, about the normal course of human development and the progressive growth tasks that everyone faces, about how behavior is acquired, and about what different approaches to counseling postulate concerning how human beings can help one another.

John M. Whiteley
Arthur Resnikoff

PREFACE

This book represents a comprehensive treatment of rational-emotive therapy (RET) both as a theory of personality and as an approach to therapy. Included are four original articles by Dr. Albert Ellis and the July 1977 issue of *The Counseling Psychologist,* which was entirely devoted to rational-emotive therapy.

Section 1 deals with the theoretical underpinnings of RET, first as a theory of personality and then as the basis for the theory and practice of psychotherapy, thus providing the reader with the necessary background for approaching the rest of the book. Ellis' article on research data supporting the clinical and personality hypotheses of RET and other modes of cognitive-behavior therapy represents an introductory chapter to Section 2. This article is followed by a series of commentaries by professionals of very different points of view. These reviews are, in turn, followed by a rejoinder entitled "Elegant and Inelegant RET" by Dr. Ellis, which concludes the book.

This volume is intended for use by undergraduates and graduate students, interested laypersons, practicing professionals, and participants in in-service training programs.

John M. Whiteley

CONTENTS

THEORETICAL AND EMPIRICAL FOUNDATIONS OF RATIONAL-EMOTIVE THERAPY

RATIONAL-EMOTIVE THERAPY AS A NEW THEORY OF PERSONALITY AND THERAPY

1

Rational-Emotive Therapy

ALBERT ELLIS
Institute for Rational-Emotive Therapy

DEFINITION

Rational-emotive therapy (RET), a theory of personality and a method of psychotherapy, takes two main forms. In its general, or inelegant, form it employs, for theoretical and practical reasons, a large variety of cognitive, affective, and behavioral methods of personality change and is synonymous with cognitive behavior modification (as viewed by Michael Mahoney and Donald Meichenbaum), with cognitive therapy (as presented by Aaron T. Beck), with multimodal therapy (as defined by Arnold A. Lazarus), and with general, or broadspectrum, behavior therapy (as seen by Cyril M. Franks). In its more specific, or elegant, form it emphasizes cognitive restructuring, or philosophic disputing, in accordance with its A-B-C theory of emotional disturbance and personality change. This theory holds that, when a highly charged emotional Consequence (C) follows a significant Activating Experience or Event (A), A may importantly contribute to but only partially "causes" C. Rational-emotive theory hypothesizes that emotional difficulties, or Consequences, are largely created ("caused") by B—people's Belief System about A.

Elegant RET, following the leads of philosophers such as Epictetus and Marcus Aurelius and psychotherapists such as Alfred Adler and George Kelly, contends that, when undesirable emotional Consequences occur at point C, these Consequences (such as severe anxiety, depression, hostility, or inadequacy feelings) can almost invariably be traced to people's irrational Beliefs (iB's). It also holds that these irrational Beliefs can be most effectively Disputed (at point D) by using the logico-empirical method of science. When disturbed individuals do this kind of Disputing—and thereby change or eliminate their absolutistic, illogical, and antiempirical thinking—their undesirable emotional and behavioral Consequences (that is, their neurotic symptoms) ameliorate or disappear and eventually cease to reoccur. Elegant RET, perhaps more than any other system of psychotherapy, emphasizes the philosophic Disputing of clients' self-defeating Beliefs. Thus it is highly disputational and reeducational. Its cognitive restructuring is done in conjunction with a variety of other emotive and behavioral methods, because the system holds that cognitions, emotions, and behaviors all significantly interact and have a reciprocal cause-and-effect relationship. RET is therefore a comprehensive method of psychological treatment that is pronouncedly cognitive but that also stresses and utilizes affective and behavioral modes of basic personality change.

HISTORY

Rational-emotive therapy (RET) was formulated by Albert Ellis, a clinical psychologist, at the beginning of 1955. Ellis had been a pioneer sex therapist and a marriage and family counselor. Later he was trained as a psychoanalyst and for several years practiced psychoanalysis and psychoanalytically oriented therapy. In the course of these years he came to see psychoanalysis as woefully inefficient because of its neglect of the philosophic sources of disturbance, its obsession with irrelevant historical material, and its neglect of behavioral methods of change. This view of psychoanalysis led Ellis back to philosophy and science, whose findings he amalgamated with modern humanistic thinking to create a new system of therapy, RET, which he started to practice. This system emphasized that people:

1. Condition themselves to feel disturbed (rather than being conditioned by their parents and other external sources);

2. Have the biological as well as cultural tendency to think crookedly and to needlessly upset themselves;

3. Have the uniquely human tendency to invent disturbing beliefs and to disturb themselves about their disturbances; and

4. Have an unusual capacity to change their cognitive, emotive, and behavioral processes so that they can (a) choose to react differently from the way they usually do, (b) refuse to upset themselves about almost anything that may occur, and (c) train themselves so that they can semiautomatically remain minimally disturbed for the rest of their lives.

THE TECHNIQUE OF RATIONAL-EMOTIVE THERAPY

RET therapists almost invariably utilize a number of cognitive, affective, and behavioral methods of therapy. They do so quite consciously, on theoretical as well as practical grounds. However, unlike many "eclectic" therapists, they don't use unselectively almost any procedure that works with a given client, nor do they emphasize symptom removal, as do classical behavior therapists. Instead, they strive for the kind of profound personality change that tends to accompany radical philosophic restructuring.

Emotively, RET therapists use several procedures, including the following. They fully accept their clients no matter how poor their behavior, and they practice and teach an unusual degree of tolerance and unconditional positive regard. They use many affective techniques, such as the well-known shame-attacking and risk-taking exercises. They employ the rational-emotive imagery originated by Dr. Maxie C. Maultsby, Jr. (1975). They use verbal vigor in their encounters with clients, in order to maximize their efficacy in uprooting their clients' self-sabotaging ideas and behaviors. They clearly distinguish between clients' appropriate (goal-achieving) and inappropriate (self-defeating) feelings and show clients how to enhance and practice the former and how to minimize the latter. At times they use special emotive methods, such as rational humorous songs, to help clients change their disturbed thoughts and feelings.

Behaviorally, rational-emotive therapists use almost all the regular behavior-therapy methods, particularly operant conditioning, self-management principles, systematic desensitization, instrumental conditioning, biofeedback, relaxation methods, and modeling. They especially favor *in vivo* desensitization and have pioneered various assertion training, skill training, and activity homework assignments. In using both emotive and behavioral methods, RET practitioners don't just try for symptom removal but also strive to help clients effectuate a profound philosophic as well as behavioral change.

Cognitively, RET (especially in its elegant mode), shows clients, quickly and forthrightly, what it is that they keep telling themselves to make themselves emotionally upset. Then it teaches them how to deal with these self-statements so that they no longer believe them and, instead, acquire a sensible, reality-based philosophy. In this respect, RET hypothesizes that "emotional" disturbances almost invariably include a strong element of absolutistic or *must*urbatory thinking. If clients fully acknowledge and surrender their shoulds, oughts, musts, demands, commands, and necessities; if they forego their childish grandiosity; and if they stick rigorously to wanting, wishing, and preferring instead of direly needing, they can eliminate most of these disturbances (Ellis & Abrahms, 1978).

More concretely, RET shows clients that they have one or more major irrational Beliefs (iB's) which stem from their innate tendency to think crookedly and from the exacerbation of this tendency by their social and cultural learning (Ellis, 1962, 1971, 1973, 1977a; Ellis & Grieger, 1977; Ellis & Harper, 1975). These basic irrationalities can be reduced to the following three main forms of *must*urbation, which virtually all humans hold to some degree but which disturbed individuals hold more intensely, extensively, and rigidly.

Irrational Idea No. 1: "I MUST be competent, adequate, and achieving, and I MUST win the approval of virtually all the significant people in my life. It is *awful* when I don't. I *can't stand* failing in these all-important respects. I am a *rotten person* (R.P.) when I don't do what I must do to act competently and to win others' approval." When people strongly hold this irrational Belief and its many correlates and subheadings, they tend to make themselves feel inadequate, worthless, anxious, and depressed and to develop phobias, obsessions, compulsions, inhibitions, and similar disturbances.

Irrational Idea No. 2: "Others MUST treat me kindly, fairly, and properly when I want them to do so. It is *terrible* when they don't. I *can't bear* their acting obnoxiously toward me. They are damnable, worthless people when they don't do what they MUST do to treat me satisfactorily." When people have this irrational Belief and its correlates, they tend to make themselves feel intensely and persistently angry, condemning, bigoted, violent, feuding, warring, vindictive, and even homicidal. They can also become grandiose and depressed.

Irrational Idea No. 3: "I need and MUST have the things I really want. The conditions under which I live and the world around me MUST be well ordered, positive, certain—just the way I want them to be. I MUST gratify my desires easily and immediately, without having to deal with too many difficulties or hassles. It is *horrible* when conditions are not this way. I *can't tolerate* their being uncomfortable, frustrating, or merely not ideal. The world is a rotten place and life is hardly worth living when things are not as they *should be* in this respect." When people devoutly believe this irrational idea and its correlates, they make themselves angry, self-pitying, and depressed. They whine, inwardly or externally, and have abysmally low frustration tolerance, along with its concomitants of avoidance, goofing, lack of discipline, and procrastination.

The rational-emotive therapist quickly and efficiently tries to show clients that they have one, two, or all three of these irrational Beliefs (iB's) and perhaps many of their corollaries and subheadings. The therapist also tries to teach clients that their emotional problems and neurotic behaviors are the direct and indirect results of such Beliefs. In all likelihood these Beliefs will not weaken, let alone disappear for good, until the person clearly sees and acknowledges these Beliefs, actively and cognitively Disputes them, forces himself or herself to emote differently while undermining them, and uses a number of behavioral approaches to change the actions that accompany and reinforce these absolutistic, self-sabotaging Beliefs. Rational-emotive therapists use mainly the cognitive restructuring methods of science and philosophy to help uproot their clients' disturbance-creating ideas. But they also employ and teach a number of other cognitive techniques, such as the use of positive self-coping statements, thought stopping, cognitive diversionary methods, semantic and linguistic analysis, self-monitoring procedures, the analysis of false attributions and expectancies, didactic instruction, skill training, and effective methods of problem solving.

APPLICATIONS

Although Albert Ellis originated RET as a method of individual psychotherapy, he soon developed a group-therapy procedure. This procedure involves training all group members to use RET with one another (as well as with their friends and associates outside the group), so that they become skilled at talking themselves out of their own irrationalities and at doing their *in vivo* homework assignments. Group RET also includes a good many shame-attacking and risk-taking exercises, active confrontation, role playing and behavior rehearsal, verbal and nonverbal feedback, and other active-directive procedures.

RET favors large-scale group processes—lectures, workshops, live public demonstrations, seminars, courses, and so forth. It strongly encourages several bibliotherapy and self-help procedures, including the reading of books and pamphlets; the use of recordings, films, radio, and TV presentations, as well as that of charts, signs, and posters; vicarious therapy; the regular filling out of rational self-help forms; and various other psychoeducational methods. RET has also been successfully applied in the classroom by teaching schoolchildren some of the RET principles. Such teaching is done as part of the regular school program and is carried out by teachers especially trained in RET rather than by psychologists or psychotherapists.

Although RET is a relatively new form of psychotherapy, it has already inspired a large number of written and recorded applications and has led to the publication of hundreds of articles, pamphlets, books, and dissertations in a number of fields. There have been studies on the application of RET to the treatment of clinical problems such as anxiety, depression, hostility, character disorder, and psychosis; to sex, love, and marriage problems; to child rearing and adolescence; and to assertion training and self-management (DiGiuseppe, Miller, & Trexler, 1977; Ellis, 1977b, 1980; Murphy & Simon, in press). In non-clinical areas, RET-oriented authors have published materials on law and criminality, political science, executive leadership, religion, literature, child rearing, philosophy, music, and many other fields.

RET has also achieved outstanding success and popularity in the field of self-help books. Some notable therapeutic writings in this area have been authored by Wayne Dyer, Albert Ellis and Robert A. Harper, Paul Hauck, Maxie Maultsby, Jr., John Powell, and Howard Young. In addition, RET materials have been incorporated into literally hundreds of other books and pamphlets on assertion training, self-management, personal adjustment, and do-it-yourself therapy. RET principles and techniques have also been embodied (with or without due credit) into many forms of psychotherapy and personality-training procedures. Considering the enormous impact that acknowledged and unacknowledged RET principles have had on the public, there is little question that rational-emotive therapy is one of the most influential forms of treatment of the 20th century.

REFERENCES

DiGiuseppe, R., Miller, N., & Trexler, L. Outcome studies of rational-emotive therapy. *The Counseling Psychologist,* 1977, 7(1), 43-50.

Ellis, A. *Reason and emotion in psychotherapy.* New York: Lyle Stuart, 1962. (Paperback edition: New York: Citadel Press, 1977.)

Ellis, A. *Growth through reason.* Palo Alto, Calif.: Science and Behavior Books, 1971. (Also, Hollywood, Calif.: Wilshire Books, 1971.)

Ellis, A. *Humanistic psychotherapy: The rational-emotive approach.* New York: Julian Press, 1973. (Also, McGraw-Hill Paperbacks, 1973.)

Ellis, A. *How to live with—and without—anger.* New York: Reader's Digest Press, 1977. (a)

Ellis, A. Rational-emotive therapy: Research data that support the clinical and personality hypotheses of RET and other modes of cognitive-behavior therapy. *The Counseling Psychologist,* 1977, 7(1), 2-42. (b)

Ellis, A. *A comprehensive bibliography of materials on rational-emotive therapy and cognitive-behavior therapy.* New York: Institute for Rational-Emotive Therapy, 1980.

Ellis, A., & Abrahms, E. *Brief psychotherapy in medical and health practice.* New York: Springer, 1978.

Ellis, A., & Grieger, R. *Handbook of rational-emotive therapy.* New York: Springer, 1977.

Ellis, A., & Harper, R. A. *A new guide to rational living.* Englewood Cliffs, N.J.: Prentice-Hall, 1975. (Also, Hollywood, Calif.: Wilshire Books, 1975.)

Maultsby, M. C., Jr. *Help yourself to happiness.* New York: Institute for Rational Living, 1975.

Murphy, R., & Simon, W. *An annotated bibliography of research on rational-emotive therapy and cognitive-behavior therapy.* New York: Institute for Rational Living, in press.

Toward a New Theory
of Personality

ALBERT ELLIS
Institute for Rational-Emotive Therapy

Unless I delude myself seriously, in the past several years I have developed a new theory of personality—one that significantly differs from the views of other personality theorists, particularly those who have originated schools of psychotherapy, such as Adler (1927/1974), Freud (1965), Jung (1954), Reich (1949), and Rogers (1961). First, I am going to state why I think that virtually all the existent theories of personality come to clearly wrong conclusions about the ways in which humans function and the reasons why they function in these ways. Then I shall get on to outlining my own theory of personality, which developed, of course, from my theory and practice of rational-emotive therapy (Ellis, 1958, 1962, 1971b, 1973a, 1976b, 1977a; Ellis & Abrahms, 1978).

WHY PERSONALITY THEORISTS ALMOST
INVARIABLY GO WRONG

Personality theorists, even when they have an excellent theory of personality change, almost invariably go wrong and lead themselves and their readers up the garden path because, fundamentally, they think crookedly. Their innate tendency to think and to act irrationally—which, as I shall state later, is by and large part of the human condition—leads them astray in innumerable respects, including their theorizing about personality. Consequently these theorists come up with some highly brilliant and often quite plausible views of "human nature," which nevertheless contain almost incredible logical errors and nearly insurmountable prejudices. For that is the way in which practically all humans think: badly, inefficiently, and bigotedly. Scientists, and their personality theories, represent no exception to this general (but not invariant) rule.

What are some of the "natural," or innate, tendencies toward crooked thinking that lead personality theorists astray? Here are a few of them.

Attribution of special reasons to events and behaviors. Humans tend to attribute special reasons to various events and behaviors. Because they feel comfortable (the Gestalt psychologist would say that they feel "completed" or that they have effected "closure") with these reasons, they then wrongly believe that they have "proved" the validity of their "explanations." Primitive people pray for rain and, when eventually it does rain, they see their prayers as the "cause" of the rain. Meteorologists observe a certain kind of cloud formation or pressure system before it rains and, when the rain comes, say that this formation or system "caused" the downpour. We may dismiss the primitives' "explanation" for the rain as just belief in magic, for their prayers are hardly the cause of the rain. But the meteorologists, too, think crookedly. The cloud formation or the pressure system is only one part of an enormously complex system of events, ranging from conditions at the North Pole to conditions at the equator, all of which contribute in varying degrees to the cloud formation and to the pressure system and therefore have some "causal" connection with the downpour. Meteorologists know about these many other "causes" but put them out of their minds or, at least, fail to explain them to the public when they talk about what "caused" the rain. And we, the public, hardly think of these complex causes at all. Even if someone did indeed try to "explain" these causes to us, we would tend to edit them out. For we, too, enjoy simple explanations—of the rain or of anything else—and we don't want to bother ourselves with all the complex factors that constitute the "causal" conditions of some event.

So with personality theories. If I murder someone and you want to explain the cause of my act, you are likely to focus on one or two outstanding "influences" —for example, that my mother taught me the value of aggression or that some early religious teachings led me to believe in the philosophy of an eye for an eye. Certainly these "influences" *may* have affected me. But it seems most likely that, out of a hundred children whose mothers or whose early religious teachings favored aggression, very few will murder someone later in life! In fact, it is unlikely that any of them will. Therefore, if I murdered someone, countless things might have contributed to my act. There might have been, for example, my innate tendency to demand that things go my way; my rebellion against social teachings, which oppose murder; my low frustration tolerance when someone balks me; my being particularly sensitive, for one reason or another, to my victim's insults; and my accidentally happening to have a gun or knife available when I experienced extreme hostility toward the person I eventually killed. Considering all these possible "influences" or "causes"—and heaven knows how many more there are!—your "explanation" of my act hardly seems a very good one, even though it may have *some* mild degree of credibility.

My theory of personality—the rational-emotive therapy (RET) theory— holds that any special reason for personality development or disturbance rarely, if ever, seems to exist. If I murder someone, especially if I commit the crime more than once (and thus have the "trait" of a murderer in addition to having done the "act" of murdering), I do so for many reasons, several of which have great importance but none of which probably has crucial or sufficient importance. As a confirmed murderer, I probably have a strong innate predisposition toward responding with intense hostility to cruelty or injustice; I have learned that, under certain conditions, murder is justified; I firmly believe, for whatever reason, that I can get away with murder or even that I will benefit from it; I have low tolerance to frustration; I find it difficult to relate to others, perhaps because of some problems I had in my early interpersonal relations; I think and act in absolutistic, *must*urbatory ways; and so on. Any one of these tendencies or conditions could help "make me" a confirmed murderer, and the combination of several of them could significantly increase the probability of my turning into one.

But, again, no particular innate or acquired set of conditions ensures that I shall end up as a murderer, although many such sets will significantly contribute to this outcome. Accident or chance may also play an important role. If I murder only once during my lifetime, I may do so partly because I happen to have easy access to a gun. If I hadn't, I might have never killed. But even if I murder several times, my doing so the first time largely or partly by accident may set in motion a series of other less accidental events that may contribute to my turning into a confirmed murderer. Thus, after accidentally killing the first time, I may berate myself so savagely for it that I may develop a compulsive need to keep killing. Had I not, by semiaccident, committed the first murder, I might never have, under almost any conditions, driven myself, by my own overweening guilt and self-downing, to commit the subsequent ones. So my "trait" of murdering might originally stem from significant accidental sources.

In sum, almost all humans tend to attribute "special" causes to the origin or development of personality traits, when the "real" causes seem to arise out of multifaceted, often obscure, and partly accidental conditions.

Illogical thinking about special reasons for behavioral patterns. Once we tend to invoke special reasons, particularly dramatic reasons, for certain behaviors, we usually tend to feel so comfortable with them that we dogmatically convince ourselves of their truth and ignore evidence that contradicts our hypotheses. Such reasons seem to "fit" beautifully the observed facts of personality functioning, so that our satisfaction in such a good fit helps convince us of these reasons' indubitable truth. Even when we finally surrender them for another set of "explanatory" reasons, we frequently do so not because the new reasons fit better the facts but because they fit better our preconceived esthetic notions of "good fit." Our new explanations feel better than the old ones; so we decide that they *are* (and will in all probability always remain) better.

In other words, as soon as we construct a theory about almost anything that seems to nicely or esthetically fit observed data, we easily convince ourselves of the truth of this theory by ignoring some of the data that don't fit, by falsifying some of the data that fit poorly, and by ignoring or failing to seek theories that fit the data more accurately or elegantly. In the realm of personality theories, where (as explained above) explanations or reasons for a given behavior appear multifaceted and almost invariably insufficient, the temptation to settle for special reasons for a certain behavior—and to ignore all kinds of nonspecial reasons—is perhaps greater than usual.

Environmentalist prejudices. The great majority of psychologists seem to fall in the "do-gooder" category. They fondly hope not merely to understand but to help people change their dysfunctional and self-defeating behaviors. They realize that the basic way to achieve their goal is to resort to some kind of learning or behavior modification—getting people to learn how they can change themselves just as they presumably learned in the first place how to act the way they now do. Psychologists also realize that some behaviors (for example, breathing and walking) have such strong inherited or instinctive tendencies behind them that people have great difficulty changing these behaviors.

Because of their do-goodism and their inclination to draw wrong conclusions from irrational premises, most personality theorists begin with the assumption that "we must help people change their disordered personality traits," go on to the empirical observation that "we find it very difficult to help them when these traits seem solidly rooted in their inherited predispositions," and wind up with the illogical conclusion that "such traits must therefore have arisen from learning rather than from hereditary tendencies."

These are not the only forms of illogical thinking that occur in this connection. There are many others:

1. Because people have great difficulty making certain personality changes, they believe that it is impossible to make them.

2. Because a behavior originated in some learned tendency, it has no innate component; therefore, one can easily unlearn it or relearn it.

3. Because a personality trait or behavior is rooted in a hereditary predisposition, one cannot change it.

4. Because a person has learned to behave badly, he or she has no responsibility for having learned such behavior or for continuing it, and the only way to change the behavior is to change environmental conditions.

5. Because others (for example, one's parents) conditioned a person to behave in some defeating manner, certain helping others (for example, teachers or therapists) must externally recondition the person to behave differently.

6. Because the environment significantly contributes to dysfunctional behavior, it is only by making significant changes in environmental conditions that one can have the ability to change the malfunctioning.

7. Because virtually all human behavior is based, to a greater or lesser degree, on learning, learning constitutes the main or even the only important element in the behavior. Consequently, the person must have external conditioning or reinforcement to modify the behavior.

From the above list we can see that, as a result of a combination of compulsive do-goodism and several other forms of cognitive slippage, the weight of environmental factors in the formation and changing of personality traits tends to get enormously exaggerated. Note that almost all systems of psychotherapy fall victim to this kind of exaggeration in their personality theories.

Overemphasis on dramatic incidents from the past. We have a tendency, probably mostly innate, to dramatize certain incidents in our lives, especially so-called "traumatic" incidents, and then to affectively remember them for months or years to come. Thus, we can vividly and often spontaneously recall how we urinated in our underwear at the age of 4 or made a "fool" of ourselves in class or in a game at the age of 6. Because of the dramatic effect of these remembrances (especially when they are called to mind after years of forgetfulness), we often make the following wrong conclusions about them and about the original events preceding them:

1. The original occurrence, because it immediately led to pronounced feelings such as shame or guilt, *caused* these feelings.

2. Forgetting about these events, and consequently having no bad feelings about them, is *always* the result of deliberate suppression or repression of memory and affect.

3. Because recalling these "traumatic" events sometimes reduces or eliminates the shame or guilt about them, the recall itself (rather than what I tell myself today *about* the original happenings and *about* my part in them) has curative effects.

4. If a therapist asks me to recall an early event in my life and I choose one of these traumatic events, the therapist assumes that the particular happening, as well as my reaction to it at the time, has invariably an important connection with my general life-style today and tells a great deal about my personality.

5. If I reacted dysfunctionally to an early event that I now dramatically remember, I will indubitably react the same way to such an event today, for we have a general tendency to react similarly to the same event throughout our lives.

Our tendency to dramatize early events in our lives and to continue to dramatize them, in many instances, years later certainly indicates something about our personalities. But psychotherapists and personality theorists tend to overemphasize this "something" and to make all-encompassing conclusions about it, some of which are often unwarranted. Just as we make false "observations" and conclusions about dramatic events, as in the case of a staged uproar in a college class, so do we and our psychological observers make similarly false "observations" and conclusions about past dramatic events in our lives. Where such events had *some* importance, we tend to make them *all*-important. Moreover, since many or most of us experience real satisfaction in reviewing our past histories—what seems more interesting than our *own* acts and feelings?—we foolishly expend much time and energy talking to ourselves or to our therapists about our pasts, when we would do ourselves much more good by thinking about our present and future existences. This is why some woefully inefficient systems of psychotherapy such as psychoanalysis continue to have immense popularity (Ellis, 1962, 1969).

Overgeneralization and other forms of crooked thinking. People have an exceptionally strong tendency, most probably innate, to generalize adequately and to overgeneralize inadequately about other people and events. Many psychologists, such as Beck (1976), Ellis (1962), and Kelly (1955), have pointed this out. The same tendency was observed by Alfred Korzybski (1933), the great general semanticist, and by a good many of his followers (Bourland, 1965–1966, 1968; Hayakawa, 1965). Because of this tendency, we seem to make certain valid observations about human personality, but then we go on to make certain overgeneralized, hence partly false, conclusions about these observations. This is especially true for those who theorize about personality. Here are some of these overgeneralizations, which can be added to those listed earlier.

1. Because we strongly desire certain things—such as approval and success— we *need* or *must have* those things if we are to achieve any significant degree of happiness.

2. Because dreams often reveal our underlying wishes and anxieties, all dreams consist of wish fulfillments or indicate deep-seated fears. Therefore, all dreams have enormous significance in understanding someone's personality.

3. Because dreams and free associations sometimes reveal material of which we have little or no awareness, dreams and free associations constitute the royal road to the unconscious and give highly accurate information about it.

4. Because we sometimes represent or symbolize sex organs in our dreams, free associations, or literary productions by objects such as guns, knives, or keyholes, every time we dream or write about one of these objects we are in fact dreaming or writing about sex organs.

5. Because some individuals make themselves feel inferior or inadequate as a result of some physical or mental deficiencies, such deficiencies always lead to feelings of inferiority.

6. Because many women require sexual intercourse to achieve full or better orgasms, all women require it. Those who achieve orgasm in noncoital or extravaginal ways have serious sex and general personality problems.

7. Because the intense feelings that often accompany an intimate interpersonal relationship frequently enhance happiness, everyone needs a good one-to-one love relationship in order to lead a "normal" or "healthy" existence.

These and literally scores of other overgeneralizations and nonempirical conclusions contribute to false views of personality on the part of lay people and psychologists alike. The human tendency to jump from "some people do this some of the time" to "therefore virtually all people do this all of the time" and from "a minority of individuals under certain conditions act this way" to "the majority of (or all) people under almost all conditions act this way" leads to numerous instances of erroneous views of personality.

Hereditarian biases. Many psychological professionals, for one reason or another, have hereditarian biases and consequently overemphasize the importance of innate influences on personality. It seems, for example, that the well-known psychologist Cyril Burt for many years faked data in support of his theories about the relative importance of genetic as opposed to environmental factors in determining intelligence (Evans, 1976).

This bias toward heredity leads to a number of false conclusions. For example:

1. Because heredity represents a strong element in virtually all human behavior, it is the almost exclusive determinant of behavior.

2. If certain peoples or groups (say, Italians, Jews, or Chinese) have an innate tendency to act in a certain way, virtually all members of those groups act in that way.

3. When a personality trait has strong hereditary influences behind it, people who have that trait find it virtually impossible to significantly change it or eliminate it.

4. If one personality trait such as sexual interest or intelligence has strong hereditary determinants, all other personality traits, from introversion to a liking for jazz, must have equally strong innate determinants.

These kinds of hereditarian prejudices, coupled with a tendency to overgeneralize, lead to many false conclusions about human personality. On the one hand, as shown above, environmentalists overemphasize the significance of cultural and learned factors in human behavior. On the other hand, hereditarians overemphasize the significance of innate factors. The former tend to forget that environmental learning itself has to rest on an inborn basis, because, in order to learn anything, we clearly must be born with a tendency to learn, to listen, and to respond to social conditioning (Ellis, 1976a). The latter tend to forget that, no matter what tendencies we are born with, we start learning (including self-learning) immediately after birth. Therefore, all behavior includes a combination of learned and innate factors. Both sets of theorists, neglecting to look at the other side of the fence, espouse a one-sided view of personality by exaggerating the significance of either the inherited or the acquired aspects of behavior.

Autism and grandiosity. We tend to take an autistic and grandiose view of ourselves and the world. We imply, if not directly hold, that the universe revolves around us and that, at least to some extent, it runs in accordance with our wishes and goals. Therefore, we don't accept the fairly obvious fact that there seems to exist no intrinsic purpose in the world itself and that the universe has no interest, concern, or love for us. We exist and it exists. Although our existence depends on the world in which we live, we have no intentional, interpersonal, or necessary connection with it. The universe can easily remain extant without humans (and presumably for trillions of years in the past it has done so, and it will do so again for trillions of years to come), and there is no evidence that it exists *for* humans—although most of us seem to think that it does.

Because of this autistic view, both lay people and professional psychologists seem loath to accept the deep influence of accident, purposelessness, and unintentionality on human personality. This reluctance results in the tendency we discussed earlier of explaining behavior in terms of special reasons and often in semimystical, transpersonal, and religiously oriented views of personality that have little or nothing to do with reality.

Self-rating and its effects. We almost invariably rate ourselves as well as our deeds, acts, and performances. We start with the values of being alive and happy, and we rationally and appropriately rate our acts and traits on the basis of how well such acts and traits permit us to stay alive and enjoy ourselves. But then, irrationally and inappropriately, we jump to give ratings or report cards to our total selves, our very essences, our entire personhoods. This approach, as I have shown elsewhere, has no sensible empirical or practical justification (Ellis, 1957, 1971a, 1972, 1975; Ellis & Abrahms, 1978; Ellis & Harper, 1975). But that doesn't stop most of us from continuing to rate ourselves as well as our deeds!

Personality theorists are human beings and, as such, make the same error; they continually extoll the value of self-esteem, self-confidence, and self-regard. They don't seem to see that, even if we have self-esteem, we usually harm ourselves, for we remain preoccupied with rating ourselves positively or negatively rather than with changing our dysfunctional behaviors so that we can *enjoy* life more. And they don't see that, when we rate ourselves as "good" or "adequate," we strongly imply that we can also see ourselves as "bad" or "inadequate"; consequently, we live on the verge of anxiety.

As a result of the human tendency to rate the total person as well as individual acts, personality theory has an enormous "self-esteem" or "self-worth" literature. Most of it seems quite misleading, for humans, as such, do not actually have "worth" or "value." They merely have aliveness and (potential or actual) pleasure or satisfaction. And their intrinsic, or essential, value, to which personality theories are constantly referring, differs little from mythical entities such as "spirit" and "soul."

Absolutistic and mus*turbatory thinking.* As I show in several of my writings (Ellis, 1973b, 1976b, 1977a; Ellis & Grieger, 1977), people tend to take probabilistic views (for example, "I like others' approval and would probably be happier if I got more of it") and escalate them into absolutes and musts ("I must have others' approval and cannot feel happy at all without it"). This absolutistic view leads people astray. It seems to also lead astray many personality theorists, who promulgate *musts* by the dozen instead of more realistic *it-would-seem-better-ifs*. Some *musts* that these theorists iterate over and over again in their writings include:

1. You must have a happy, secure childhood in order to achieve a happy adult existence.

2. If you have an emotional problem, you must go for prolonged, intensive therapy to help yourself; no other method will work.

3. In order to accomplish anything or to change your behavior you must have the help of specific reinforcers such as money or love.

4. All of your dysfunctional or self-defeating behaviors result from your irrational ideas and from no other sources.

5. In order to function well sexually, you must have prolonged intercourse leading to orgasm for you and your partner.

6. You must feel terribly anxious about the knowledge that eventually you are going to die.

7. When people treat you unfairly or frustrate you, you must feel overt or covert hostility toward them.

Defensiveness and resistance to change. Many personality theorists, pretty much like most other humans, tend to resist change. Once they have produced a theory, they construct defenses against acknowledging that the theory has faults and that they had better revise it or abandon it. As a consequence, they ignore evidence that contradicts their views. These theorists keep claiming that their theories explain practically all aspects of human personality and not just a limited number of these aspects. They give specious answers to the objections that other critics raise against their ideas and avoid probing into new areas in which they might discover evidence that confutes their views. They excoriate the notions of other personality theorists who have significant contributions to make. They reach conclusions that do not gibe with the evidence that they themselves turn up in regard to their own hypotheses and cling to views that have long outlived their usefulness and no longer have heuristic value. Even when they privately see some flaws in their own theories, they refuse to acknowledge these flaws publicly.

For reasons like these—most of which, you may note, involve ego bolstering and grandiosity—many personality theorists unduly limit themselves and promulgate views that never had, or at least no longer have, a high degree of validity.

THE A-B-C THEORY OF HUMAN BEHAVIOR AND PERSONALITY CHANGE

As the foregoing points indicate, most contemporary theories of personality, particularly those promulgated by psychotherapists, show woeful inadequacies, and many of them have little likelihood of proving true. Can, then, a better-rounded and more valid theory of personality arise out of clinical data? I think so, as I indicated in my own writings on rational-emotive therapy (RET), where I described a theory of personality based on clinical data and supported by experimental findings (Ellis, 1977b). Here are some of the main elements of such a theory.

RET has included from its very beginning a basic theory of personality change that also implies a theory of personality itself. I have called this the A-B-C theory of human behavior. Over the years I have accumulated evidence of the validity of this theory in the form of countless case histories. These individuals came to see me (and other rational-emotive therapists) in a state of near despair. They emerged from these consultations more than just improved. Their main symptoms were gone; they had reached a new understanding of how they themselves had created their symptoms; and they were ready to face the world and live a better and more joyous existence.

In addition to clinical validity, the A-B-C theory of personality change has shown an unusual degree of experimental backing. In my article on research data that support RET and other modes of cognitive-behavior therapy (Section 2 of this book), I review literally hundreds of articles and monographs. All this literature shows that, when an individual feels various emotional and behavioral Consequences at point C after having experienced certain unpleasant Activating

Events at point A, A does *not* really cause C, although it may contribute significantly to it (Ellis, 1977b). My comprehensive summary and review of the research literature shows that it is B (the individual's Belief System) that more directly and importantly than A leads to ("causes") C. My review also shows that, if B changes significantly, C (the emotional or behavioral Consequences) also undergoes almost immediate vital changes. My associates DiGiuseppe, Miller, and Trexler (in Section 2 of this book) and Murphy and Simon (in press) have also comprehensively reviewed clinical outcome studies. In these studies some subjects experienced RET (experimental group) and other subjects experienced no form of psychotherapy (control group). Then the experimenters made statistical comparisons between the experimental (RET) group and the control group. In almost all the studies under investigation, the subjects who had received RET showed more significant behavior changes than the control subjects.

When people, after having undergone some unpleasant Activating Event or Experience at point A, feel anxious or depressed at point C, they almost invariably conclude that A caused C. They say "No wonder I feel depressed. My wife (husband) just left me" or "Of course I feel anxious. I'm about to take this important exam, and it's quite likely that I'll fail." For most people—clients and personality theorists alike—the connection between A and C seems evident, even obvious.

But I reject this view and, over the last two decades, have taught thousands of clients to reject it too. The stimulus does not explain the reaction. This kind of thinking is a form of S-R thinking. My own conceptualization, following that of Woodworth (1958), is expressed in the S-O-R (or A-B-C) theory. To quote Woodworth (1958), "The O inserted between S and R makes explicit the obvious role of the living and active organism in the process; O receives the stimulus and makes the response." My personality-change hypothesis makes B, the individual's Belief System, the crucial issue. A does not determine C; rather, B does! Let's say that two people who have acted pretty much the same way during their lifetimes are (at point A) called bastards by someone. One of them (at point C) ignores the insult or laughs at it; the other person, instead, feels very upset and gives the culprit the beating of his life. How can we explain these radically different Consequences in terms of A (the Activating Event)? We cannot. But the explanation is readily available if we turn to B, the two people's Belief Systems *about* A.

Up to the present time, I have largely taken B as a "fact"—namely, that some people do indeed have one kind of mind set and other people have other kinds of sets. And I have maintained over and over again that both types of people—particularly those who bring on themselves highly dysfunctional Consequences at C—can definitely change their B's (Belief Systems) and thereby bring about radically different Consequences (such as feelings of displeasure but *not* of emotional disturbance). Showing people how they can change their irrational Beliefs that directly create their disturbed emotional Consequences constitutes the essence of RET. As Kelly (1955) and Raimy (1975) have shown, it also constitutes the essence of virtually all psychotherapy.

I have no intention of repeating the salient points of rational-emotive therapy (RET) here, since I have done so and in much detail elsewhere (Ellis, 1961, 1962, 1973a, 1973b, 1976d, 1977b; Ellis & Grieger, 1977; Ellis & Harper, 1961, 1975). The issue I want to discuss here is, instead, how people develop their Belief Systems—both their rational Beliefs (rB's) and their irrational Beliefs (iB's). How does it come about that Johanna has such a healthy attitude toward herself, others, and life in general and behaves so sanely, sensibly, and success-fully, while her brother, John, behaves so self-defeatingly, neurotically, and un-successfully? In the following pages I shall attempt to explain the development of an individual's Belief System. I shall try to show in much more detail than I have previously done the origins and the growth of Johanna's and John's Beliefs —what we commonly call their "personality."

Hereditary Influences on Personality

Although almost all contemporary schools of psychotherapy and personal-ity formation take a different view, it seems probable that the main influence on human personality comes from hereditary sources. Actually, as briefly noted above, it seems almost impossible to deny this, since just about all environmental influences on personality formation essentially depend on heredity. Humans seem unusually teachable or changeable or conditionable as compared to the so-called "lower" animals. But their teachability, mediated through their un-usually large and specially wired cerebral cortex, represents one of the essences of their humanity. Animals remain much more driven by fairly clear-cut in-stincts. Humans, instead, have what Maslow (1954) called "instinctoid" tenden-cies—strong predispositions to act in certain ways but predispositions that nonetheless can get radically modified by environmental and educational in-fluences.

My RET-oriented theory of personality says that probably 80% of the variance in human behavior rests largely on biological bases and 20% or so on specific environmental training. We find a good illustration of this view in what I call our iB's (irrational Beliefs), which spark our emotional and behavioral disturbances. At first blush, as I have wrongly said myself in the past (Ellis, 1961, 1962), these beliefs may appear to stem primarily from cultural learning —from our imbibing the crazy standards that our parents, schools, religions, and other socializing agents teach us from early childhood on. Most of us end up largely subscribing to these standards, even though many of them are obviously insane and inane and clearly do much more harm than good. Do not our per-sonalities, then, get set mainly by our cultures?

Yes—and no! Our "normal" standards certainly do seem to be set by cultural proscriptions. Here we are, in the Western world, wearing much too much clothes even when the temperature reaches 90 degrees, allowing ourselves to love intensely only one member of the other sex at a time, and trying to win the approval of many people whom we hate or in whom we have no real interest. Pretty crazy, eh?

Definitely. But, before indicting our culture for our madness, let's consider a very cogent point. Our culture mainly teaches us standards, not perfectionistic musts or absolutes *about* these standards. Thus, the culture tells us that it is *desirable* or *preferable* to wear a certain amount of clothes even in hot weather, to fall in love with only one person at a time, and to seek the approval of people we don't like all that much. But it is we who, largely because we turn preferences into absolute musts, convince ourselves that we *have to* do these "preferable" things, that we must see it as *awful* and *horrible* (rather than merely damned annoying) if we don't, and that we must rate ourselves as thoroughly *rotten persons* (R.P.'s) if we fall below the cultural standards.

Moreover, just as we take senseless cultural standards like those just mentioned and make them into necessities and absolutistic shoulds, we take sane and sensible cultural rules and turn them into (often not so sane) absolute musts. Thus, if our culture teaches us that we had better wear warm clothes in winter, we tend to add that we must—yes, must!—wear the nicest, most fashionable, outstanding clothes, even at the risk of finding them uncomfortable and over-priced. If our culture tells us that being in love is a pleasant state to be in, we convince ourselves that we have to love and win the love of the most special person in the world and that the two of us must keep loving each other madly forever! If our culture informs us of the advantages of having other people approve of us (so that they will give us jobs, act companionably, do us favors, and so on), we tell ourselves and the universe that virtually everyone we meet, including perfect strangers whom we'll never encounter again, must like us, or else we cannot stand ourselves at all!

This kind of *must*urbation—admittedly encouraged but not demanded by our society—seems largely innate. Just about all of us frequently engage in it, even though we soon note its pernicious results. We demand guarantees; we insist that we have to do well, that others must treat us considerately, and that the world around us must be one that lets us get everything we want immediately and easily. Just about all children frequently think this way, and virtually no adults stop this kind of crazy thinking. Our "commandingness" and our gran-diose whining when we don't get exactly what we want precisely when we want it seem pandemic—and incredibly human.

What we call personality, however, does not consist merely of our silly demandingness. It also includes our wishing, wanting, and desiring, which are essentially healthy ingredients that give purpose and meaning to life. If we had no desires, we would hardly survive. But, even if we did, would it really be worth it? Desiring, seeking, striving, and yearning are the essence of living.

But where do most of our desires come from? Almost certainly, they originate in our biological predispositions. We naturally enjoy eating, and we like certain kinds of food more than others. We crave sexual arousal and orgasm. We enjoy certain odors. We like to handle things, to play sports, to build, to create something artistic. We appreciate certain kinds of sights and scenes. In all these sensory pursuits, we learn specific cultural standards, and we generally follow them. In our society, for example, we eat beef but not grasshoppers; we copulate in private rather than in public; and we play tennis and golf more than we practice archery.

But just about all of our culturally taught pursuits rest on a pronounced biological basis. In other words, because of the biological predisposition of our human species, we naturally like and want certain things and we dislike and avoid other things. For example, we like, enjoy, and feel comfortable consorting with other people. And we also like, enjoy, and feel comfortable—at least to a certain degree—having a variety of people around and changing our friends, partners, and lovemates from time to time. Our desire for both security and novelty seems built into our very nature. And, although the degree of preference for sameness or novelty varies from person to person, most of us enjoy, at different times, both familiarity and variety.

The list of the things that most of us—in fact, practically all of us—like and enjoy and whose opposites we also seem to like from time to time is endless. Here are just a few examples. We like to learn new things (ways of eating, dressing, traveling, playing games, having sex, and so on), and we have trouble unlearning old things even when we want to do so (giving up foods that no longer agree with us, wearing new clothes when our old ones wear out, or changing sex patterns that prove unsatisfactory). We enjoy many kinds of activities (walking, running, swimming, and even fighting), and we often have difficulty getting going when we want to do so (getting up in the morning, starting to write a term paper, or dressing to go out to a party). We plan things for the future (saving our money for a car, going to college for four years to get a bachelor's degree, and making wedding arrangements six months in advance of the wedding date), and we act very shortsightedly and go for the pleasures of the moment that sabotage our goals (overeating when we want to lose weight, squandering our money when we would like to buy a car, or staying in a job we hate because of the effort involved in getting a new one). We are very suggestible (accepting beliefs in gods, demons, panaceas, specious cures, and so on), and we resist acting on factual information that would help us live more enjoyably (smoking in spite of the fact that it may have pernicious effects on our health or driving at 75 miles an hour when we know that such a high speed may well result in a serious accident).

We learn to act vigilantly in the face of real dangers (looking before we cross the street, watching what we eat, and dressing warmly in cold weather). But we also often act very carelessly (taking too many chances when crossing the street, eating junk foods that taste good, and dressing lightly in cold weather because warmer clothes feel uncomfortable). And we also act overvigilantly or overcautiously (crossing the street too slowly, fanatically avoiding many good foods as "harmful," and worrying about dressing properly even after we have taken due precautions about the cold weather). We realize that we live in a social group and act politely and modestly toward most other members of that group. But we frequently act as if the world revolved around us and as if everyone else should put us at the center of their attention and serve only our best interests—in sum, practically deify us. We often compromise our desires (taking a disadvantageous or boring job because it pays well, or doing "asinine" work at school in order to get a degree). Simultaneously, we sometimes go to uncompromising extremes (either working compulsively at a boring job or accepting the job and then refusing to do practically any of the work involved in it.)

We plot, scheme, and plan to do many things and spend hours or even days working out all the details (finishing a novel or completing a financial deal). We also do many things automatically and unthinkingly (tying our shoelaces, typing a letter, and working for 20 or more years at a job we don't like). We easily forget many things, including important things, we would like to remember (keeping appointments or refraining from smoking after we have promised ourselves to quit). But we also obsessively keep in mind many things we would like to forget about (a tune we have heard on the radio or in a film, the remembrance of a harmful event that we still feel terrified about). We engage in a good deal of wishful thinking (believing that someone who obviously doesn't love us will fall in love with us or thinking that we will get promoted when we consistently come late for work and soldier on the job). But we also refuse to acknowledge that we can get many of the things we really want (that we can get a compatible mate if we keep looking for one and can get through school if we will attend classes regularly).

We frequently rant and rave against injustices and keep them forever in mind, even to our own disadvantage. But we also do not acknowledge or ignore many gross injustices (political corruption and inheritance rules and laws). Often we even contribute to making the world more unjust (favoring an employee whom we find physically attractive or excusing a relative who acts badly and unjustly toward others). We tend to condemn ourselves for our errors, to feel guilty, to down our entire existence, and to consider ourselves, after we have made a "serious" mistake, undeserving of virtually any present or future happiness. But we also ignore many of our worst errors, rationalize and pretend that we have not made them, and refuse to make any real efforts to correct our misdeeds. We frequently pursue excitement for its own sake, even when the pursuit can clearly harm us (gambling large sums of money, driving our cars too fast, or taking hard drugs). At the same time, we foolishly put up with all kinds of needless monotony and boredom (whiling away an entire weekend doing virtually nothing, staying at a job far below our abilities, because we can easily fulfill its requirements, or remaining with boring companions when we could find much more interesting ones).

In sum, we have biological (as well as sociological) tendencies to act in contradictory ways. We strongly desire opposite and opposing things, sometimes at different times and sometimes simultaneously. We have what seem quite healthy wants and preferences—and quite unhealthy needs and commands. We frequently go from one self-defeating extreme to another. Yet, we also act, on many or most occasions, in a reasonably well-balanced, compromising, and realistic manner.

Assuming that most of us want to survive and survive in a fairly happy (or, at least, satisfied) way, we cannot very well have strong biological predispositions to go against these goals, for the human race would then die out. If, as I tell my audiences when I lecture, you had strong innate tendencies to eat poisonous foods, to drive your car at 90 miles an hour, and to stick a knife in your friends and associates, you most probably wouldn't live to attend my talk or to read this book. So, as a human, you practically have to act "sanely" most of the time. But you also can get away with a great deal of "insanity"! You can, as many people seem to do, live into your 80s while chainsmoking, overeating, driving too fast, and taking too many other needless risks. Still, the more insanely you behave, the less likely you are to survive and survive well.

Perhaps I am belaboring the importance of the biological basis of human behavior in general and of irrationality in particular. If I do so, it is partly because those who support the environmentalist view have dominated the literature, particularly the therapeutic literature, during the last half century. Freud himself had strong biological leanings; but virtually all his main followers, including Berne (1964), Fromm (1941, 1947), Horney (1965), and Sullivan (1947), have emphasized and overemphasized so-called cultural and early childhood conditioning. And yet, as I pointed out in my paper "The Biological Basis of Human Irrationality" (Ellis, 1976a), we have many reasons for strongly suspecting that disturbed or self-defeating behavior is based in large part on innate (as well as acquired) tendencies. Here is a brief summary of my arguments in that paper.

1. All the major human irrationalities seem to exist, in one form or another, in virtually all of us.

2. Just about all the irrationalities and disturbances that we witness today in our society have held rampant sway in just about all social and cultural groups we have investigated historically and anthropologically.

3. Many of the irrational behaviors that we engage in, such as procrastination and lack of self-discipline, go counter to almost all the teachings of our parents, peers, and mass media.

4. It is not only the ignorant, the stupid, and the severely disturbed who subscribe to and act upon the common irrationalities. The highly intelligent, the educated, and the relatively "normal" also hold and enact irrational beliefs.

5. So many people hold highly irrational beliefs and so often engage in self-defeating behaviors that it is quite hard to uphold the hypothesis that these beliefs and behaviors are due entirely to learning. Even if we hypothesize that, essentially, self-defeating behavior is learned, some obvious questions arise. Why do people allow themselves to get taken in so badly by the teachings of their culture? And, once they have imbibed these teachings during their youth, why don't they teach themselves how to give them up later?

6. When people—even bright and competent people—surrender their irrationalities, they frequently tend to adopt other and often opposite irrationalities. The devoutly religious often turns into a rabid atheist, and the right-wing extremist frequently winds up as a left-wing extremist.

7. Many of those who seem least afflicted by irrational thoughts and behaviors or who have given up their disturbed ways of behaving revert to them, and sometimes seriously so, on many occasions.

8. People manifestly opposed to various kinds of irrational approaches often fall prey to those very irrationalities. Agnostics exhibit zealous and absolutistic thoughts and feelings, and highly religious individuals act quite immorally.

9. Insight into our irrational behaviors only partially, if at all, helps us change them. You may know full well about the harmfulness of smoking, yet, you smoke more than ever!

10. No matter how hard and how long people work at overcoming their irrational thoughts and behaviors, they find it exceptionally difficult to do so. To some degree, they always remain quite fallible in this respect (Ellis, 1962; Ellis & Abrahms, 1978; Ellis & Harper, 1975; Hauck, 1973; Maultsby, 1975).

11. It seems reasonably clear that certain irrational ideas stem from personal, nonlearned (or even antilearned) experiences and that we creatively, albeit crazily, *invent* these ideas. We insist, for example, that we'll madly love someone *forever,* even though most of the available evidence and the teaching we receive conclusively prove that infatuation or in-lovedness rarely lasts for a long period of time.

12. Must and non sequiturs seem native to human thinking. Because you feel that so-and-so is a great person and that you would greatly enjoy his or her loving you, you foolishly and absolutistically conclude "This person *must* love me. Life without him (her) is awful, unbearable. If I can't gain his (her) love, I'm a totally worthless person!" These illogical conclusions often *seem* and *feel* right despite their obvious invalidity.

13. As Korzybski (1933) and his followers have shown, overgeneralization seems to characterize the human condition. Virtually all humans overgeneralize some or much of the time.

14. Some forms of irrationality or self-defeatism exist in many lower animals as well as in humans and seem biologically rooted. In his review of the literature on specious reward (the seeking of immediate rather than long-term gratification) Ainslie (1975) shows that such behavior is exhibited by animals as well as by men and women.

15. There is some evidence that people often find it easier to learn self-defeating than nondefeating behaviors. Thus, people very easily overeat but have great trouble sticking to a sensible diet.

Don't misinterpret my views of human nature because of this long list of human follies. True, I do think that irrationality and emotional disturbance have distinct biological roots. But I quite agree with many humanistic psychologists—especially, Friedman (1975), Maslow (1962), and Rogers (1977)—that we also have strong innate tendencies to act rationally, self-fulfillingly, and self-actualizingly. The fact remains, however, that we have strong inborn tendencies to defeat ourselves and that there is an immense amount of evidence of experimental, clinical, anecdotal, anthropological, sociological, and historical nature to prove it.

I have collected for many years factual evidence of the biological bases of human-personality development, and citing it even briefly here would vastly exceed the scope of this article. The following is a list of a few major references only: Chess, Thomas, and Birch (1965), Eysenck (1967), Frazer (1959), Garmezy

(1975), Kety (1967), Lévi-Strauss (1970), Meehl (1962), Oltman and Friedman (1965, 1966), Osborn (1968), Rimland (1964), Rosenthal (1970), Rosenthal and Kety (1968), Seligman (1971), Slater and Cowie (1971), and Thomas and Chess (1977).

Let me say a final word on the importance of hereditary, or biological, factors in human personality. Take a single aspect of personality—for example, responding impulsively to sexual arousal. For almost half a century, one of my female friends has quickly and intensely got aroused by what she considers "attractive" members of either sex and has gone to bed with many of them within an hour or two of first meeting them. Yet, she was reared by her parents as a highly conventional middle-class Protestant and was taught the virtues of marital fidelity.

What makes her react in such an unconventional way? Many things, some of which are doubtlessly of cultural nature. Generally, she goes for males who would normally rate as "attractive" in our society. She has married two of them and lived for long periods of time with two others. She is partial to "exciting" men—like those portrayed in the movies she saw during her childhood and teens. She loves intelligent, highly educated people—as her parents strongly encouraged her to do. She rarely divorces sex from love completely, just as the great majority of women in her culture rarely do. She allows her mates to somewhat dominate her, perhaps adhering to the pattern her father had set with her mother and that most women of her generation followed.

On the other hand, this woman appears to have her own unique bents, which make her rebelliously acultural. She has a high degree of sexual responsiveness, can get aroused quickly, has orgasms by the dozens, and feels sexually interested literally 365 days a year. She has great physical energies, which drive her to do very active and exciting things—such as run out to a bar at midnight after having worked hard for 12 or more hours. She has esthetic and emotional responsiveness to various nonsexual stimuli—a colorful sunset, a touch of the hand, a musical composition, a good and well-prepared meal, and many other things that would move others only mildly. She has superior intelligence and gets easily bored when she is with dull people or even with bright people who have become too familiar. These rebelliously individualistic traits are accompanied by other traits, seemingly innate, that make her act the way she has for many years, particularly in the sexual area.

More specifically, this is the scenario when this woman picks up a new sex partner and quickly ends up in bed with him or her. (1) She feels sexy. (2) She deliberately goes out in search of a partner. (3) She sees one whom she considers physically attractive. (4) She talks to him or her for a while and judges how intelligent this person seems. (5) If the person seems satisfactory, she gets into a high state of emotional and sexual arousal. (6) She takes the risk of letting the other person know that she likes him or her and would like to go to bed with him or her soon. (7) She knows the danger of coming on too fast and having the other person consider her promiscuous, but she decides to take the chance. (8) She plots and schemes, sometimes in an involved manner, to go home with her chosen partner. (9) When she gets there, she makes overt sex passes and takes her clothes off. (10) She goes through a range of noncoital sex acts, all of which she thoroughly enjoys—kissing, embracing, mutual oral-genital stimulation, but not anal relations, which she has tried several times and found quite painful. (11) She experiences several orgasms. If her partner is so inclined, she spends most of the night having sex and starts all over again in the morning. (12) For the next few days she has almost obsessive thoughts about her new partner and thinks all the time of having sex with him or her—and generally does. (13) This intense sexual activity is accompanied by deep emotional involvement on her part until she gets bored with her partner—from a few weeks to a few months later.

All of the above 13 behaviors—and many more I could list—seem to have a learned or cultural component. But all of them also seem to be rooted in distinctly innate predispositions. This woman *easily,* and against much of her childhood training, feels sexy, makes unusual efforts to fulfill her sex urges, and charges into new relationships. When for some reason she is blocked from fulfilling her urge, as occasionally has occurred during the past 30 years that I have known her, she quickly feels very frustrated and disorganized. And, typically, she soon does something to make sure that her frustrations end.

She acts the way she does easily and naturally. She gets great satisfaction from fulfilling her wants and feels a great deal of pain when she is kept from so doing. She doesn't behave the way she behaves on a purely instinctive basis (since she makes clear-cut choices with regard to partners as well as activities in context with them). She returns to her endeavors time and again, even when she knows that the odds are against her or that the relationship is not good for her. In so doing, she keeps going against much of her parental and cultural upbringing. Throughout, she essentially, although not wholly, remains her unique, individual self. I therefore conclude that her innate tendencies to act, think, and emote in certain sex-love ways are probably more powerful determinants of her behavior than her early or later societal upbringing and conditioning.

Multiplicity of Origins and Maintainers of Personality.

My RET-oriented theory of personality recognizes the existence of a multiplicity of factors that originate and maintain our personalities. As emphasized throughout this discussion, environmental as well as innate influences drive us to act the way we do. The following are some of these influences:

1. Relationships with other people;
2. Specific teachings by others, including parents, teachers, clergymen, and peers;
3. Teachings by the mass media (books, newspapers, radio, TV, films, popular songs, and magazines);
4. Group influences (peers, social classes, community organizations and groups, political institutions, and religious organizations);
5. Biological and innate desires and urges;

6. Many kinds of reinforcers or rewards, such as money, success, physical pleasures, and inner feelings of satisfaction;

7. Many kinds of penalizers, such as disapproval, poverty, material frustrations, physical pains, and inner feelings of anxiety and depression;

8. Self-ratings, including rating oneself as a "good person" for doing one kind of act or having one kind of trait and as a "bad person" for doing another kind of act or for having another kind of trait;

9. Self-observation—noting how one behaves and the usual consequences of that behavior;

10. Modeling after others—particularly after outstanding people, real or imaginary;

11. Identification with certain groups or individuals and consequent acceptance or imitation of their behavior;

12. Formulation of goals, purposes, and ideals and attempts to achieve them;

13. Magical or mystical notions, such as belief in perfection, in utopia, in gods and devils, and in a heaven-centered or hell-centered afterlife;

14. Gullibility and suggestibility to the teachings and persuasions of others and of the mass media;

15. Yearning for freedom and individuality.

These are only a few of the major influences on personality. All of them seem to have both innate and acquired aspects. A most important thing to note in this connection is that many of these influences contradict other influences and that some of them are self-contradictory. Thus, relationships with others and group influences are frequently in conflict with certain key reinforcers, such as money and success, and with other strong urges, such as the yearning for freedom and individuality. Also, relationships with others have their contradictory aspects. We often love some people and want their love. But we also try to dominate them and have them do what we want them to do. The same is true of our self-rating tendencies. We observe our ineffectual traits, and we wisely try to change them so we can lead a more satisfactory existence. At the same time we savagely berate ourselves for having such traits, thus sabotaging our own attempts to change them and interfering with our own happiness and well-being.

Because the human personality is subject to so many different kinds of influences and because these influences are often in conflict with one another, our behavior generally turns out to display both consistencies and inconsistencies. The consistencies probably stem from the prevalence of one influence over another. Let's take the case of the woman I mentioned earlier. She acts quite promiscuously in the sexual arena, most of the time feels sexually aroused, follows her own individualistic bents, goes for immediate physical satisfaction, lets herself go along with some of her innate drives and feelings, doesn't put herself down for acting unconventionally, formulates clear-cut goals and determinedly tries to effectuate them, and generally follows what we might call her "inner" inclinations. But not always! She happens to head a department in a large university, wants to inherit a sizeable fortune from her aged parents, and knows that, if she acts too unconventionally, she risks missing out on a good deal of what she wants in life.

Consequently, before she picks up a man and goes to bed with him, she also takes into account considerations such as how he is likely to respond, how the other bar customers will react to her picking him up and going off with him, what unpleasant consequences may result from her action (will he fail her sexually? will she end up with some venereal disease?), and what possible repercussions her behavior will have on her professional status and on her relationships with certain people.

This means that my friends's actions on a given evening, and her promiscuity in general, have many determinants—past, present, and future. Even though, unlike most women in our culture, she lets social and superstitious influences affect her in relatively small ways, she does not merely do her own thing and let her actions be guided solely by her biological inclinations or moods of the moment. Nor does virtually anyone in any culture. Our actions reflect a very complicated pattern of biological and sociological influences. Therefore, we act one way today and quite differently tomorrow. And even when we are fairly consistent, we do so for many reasons and in spite of many counterreasons. Our personality "traits" have almost innumerable "causes." These causes operate statistically most of the time but hardly all of the time. They differ significantly, literally from day to day. And sometimes they change for long periods of time or permanently. (For example, my friend once lived with another woman for two years and during that time remained completely monogamous and had little desire for other women or men.) These various causes can affect one's life lightly, or they can obsessively and compulsively take over (at least for a while) practically one's whole existence.

"Explanations" of personality are generally quite shaky and specious and are rarely backed up by solid and unequivocal evidence. In my friend's case, for example, one psychotherapist "explained" to her that her promiscuity originated in the puritanical teachings of her parents, against which she rebelled. Another therapist insisted that her behavior stemmed from her parents' overpermissiveness during her childhood and adolescence, when they trusted her so much that they allowed her to date whomever she wanted and to come home at all hours. One psychologist friend of hers was certain that her hatred of her father drove her into the arms of both men and women. Another psychologist friend contended that her love and lust for her father made her seek men just like him and that, when she realized that they were not what she was looking for, impelled her to go sulkingly after women.

These and similar "explanations" of someone's personality almost always seem plausible—just as different theories of personality usually have some face validity. But they obviously cannot all be true, since most of them contradict one another. Moreover, how can we truly validate or invalidate them? No matter how much evidence we have that favors any given explanation, we never have all the facts and can always think of an alternative reason that also seems related to whatever facts we know. We can easily find five or more "answers" for the existence of the same trait, and have no accurate way of knowing which one, two, or all of these answers truly account for the personality factors we seek to explain.

Is theorizing about personality, then, a rather hopeless and futile pursuit? To some extent, yes. For we probably won't for the present—and perhaps never will—arrive at precise and satisfactory hypotheses that cover all or most of the observed data. In my friend's case, for example, her promiscuous behavior, unusual in our society, may largely result from her innate tendencies toward high sexuality and emotional independence. And if we could accurately measure both of these tendencies (which, as yet, we cannot) and found that most women who have them turn out, no matter what their upbringing, to act significantly more promiscuously than most women who don't have them, we might well conclude that we have some (statistical) determinants of female promiscuity in our society. But, even then, we would have omitted many other possible determinants, such as high energy level, puritanical rearing, and a dominating father.

Moreover, even if we could prove that, in general, innate tendencies toward high sexuality and emotional independence favor women's promiscuity, we would hardly know why this particular woman behaves that way. Perhaps she felt rejected by the first man she ever fell in love with and, since that time, has consciously or unconsciously determined to have many partners rather than a single one in her life. Perhaps, in spite of her high sexuality, she allows her guilt over wanting to copulate with her father to interfere with her pleasure with other men and, therefore, must keep seeking new partners to try to reach the orgasmic heights that she never really lets herself experience. Perhaps . . .

As you can see, the possibilities are endless. Innumerable "psychodynamic" explanations for her behavior may easily occur to us, and, with a little cleverness, virtually all of them can sound convincing. And every single one of them may have virtually no validity. After all, with her particular kind of hormones and her innate drive for emotional independence, she might have wound up behaving promiscuously under almost any kind of environmental conditions. We'll never, never know.

What does all this mean? It means that we can, and probably had better, keep exploring for improved, more data-based "explanations" of human personality. But, at least for the present, let's not take any of them too seriously. Many possible reasons for the existence of certain behaviors and traits exist, and several seem pertinent in the case of almost any trait we can think of.

The RET Theory of Personality Change.

If it is indeed almost impossible at the present time for anyone to come up with a valid theory of personality, is it also impossible for someone to come up with an effective theory of personality change? I don't think so. I take the stand that methods of changing human personality may have relatively little relationship to theories explaining the origin and development of personality.

Also, while the creation and natural growth of personality is governed by so many factors that tracking them down and determining which of them seems paramount leads to almost insurmountable difficulties, the factors that contribute to personality change are far fewer and can be more clearly understood. Finally, barring some kind of desert-island experiments, controlled studies of personality development lead to partial and inconclusive results. But experiments in helping humans change some of their personality traits, particularly their self-defeating traits, seem very amenable to controlled experimentation and may produce fairly definitive results.

The first of the above propositions seems the most important one. For, even if we never quite pin down exactly how a person's self-sabotaging traits arise and develop, we may often work out effective techniques for helping the person change those traits. Thus, in the case of my friend, if she finds her promiscuous behavior defeating and wants to make herself relatively monogamous, we don't have to know the origins of her promiscuity or the details of her development in this regard. Not that we wouldn't, as therapists, benefit from such knowledge; for well we might. But, without it, we can figure out some highly effective means of helping her change. And, if we forget about fully understanding why she got the way she did, we may actually save time and energy and help her *more* than if we insist on discovering some of the origins of her promiscuity.

Strange? Not really. In the field of electronics, for example, we still seem to know relatively little about the ultimate source of electricity, we still have incomplete explanations for it, and even our definition of the term is somewhat imprecise. And, yet, we can effectively produce it, conduct it, change it, and apply it. Whether it originates in cosmic forces, in the sun, or with "god" doesn't really seem to matter too much. We still can create it on earth and utilize it—and change its manifestations.

Anyway, the fact remains that, while we still know comparatively little about the origins or the development of personality and may know little more about it for some time to come, we can experiment with modes of changing behaviors and traits and discover some highly effective ones. These include cognitive, emotive, and behavioral techniques of change—all utilized in RET. For the RET theory of change holds that, no matter how humans originally get certain personality characteristics and no matter what developmental processes they go through in connection with these characteristics, they can almost always significantly change them—with much hard work and effort.

Some of the main theories of personality change that RET endorses include the following:

1. Because people largely create their emotional problems by accepting and inventing irrational and illogical ideas, they also have the capacity to understand and change (or eliminate) their irrational Beliefs (iB's), their inappropriate emotions, and their self-sabotaging behaviors.

2. The basic, most elegant, and longest-lasting ways to help bring about change are cognitive awareness and philosophic restructuring—deliberately

and consciously finding one's irrational Beliefs and disputing them in a logico-empirical manner.

3. Even when change appears to have been effected mainly by emotive and behavioral procedures, it is the underlying cognitive reorganization that really motivates and to a large extent directly "causes" these changes. Therefore, even when emotive and behavioral experiences contribute importantly to disturbed thoughts and feelings, philosophic reconstruction works best, or at least seems to contribute significantly, in changing such thoughts and feelings.

4. Perhaps for biological reasons, we find it easy to behave dysfunctionally and to return to self-defeating behaviors after we have taught ourselves to function more effectively for a while. Therefore, we'd better interrupt and keep interrupting our disturbed behaviors with strong counterbeliefs, dramatic emotive moves, and determined and consistently practiced behavioral changes. Force and persistence remain important elements in changing ourselves and in remaining changed.

5. No one therapeutic method seems likely to work too well with anyone or everyone. Most people had better use a variety of cognitive, emotive, and behavioral methods and experimentally determine which work better for them. Therapists, too, may utilize a number of techniques, and use them somewhat selectively, with their clients. But this hardly means that all therapy methods are equally effective.

6. As I said many times before, we have innate as well as acquired tendencies to make ourselves disturbed (or to get "conditioned" by others to act in a disturbed fashion). These tendencies are strong, and, if we want to change them, usually we have to work very hard. This means that effort, work, and practice are the main ingredients of therapy (Ellis, 1962). And the main resistance to therapy is the human tendency to look for easy ways out, to shirk responsibility and effort, and to have low frustration tolerance (LFT). Whatever "causes" an individual to acquire personality problems, his or her low frustration tolerance often constitutes the main block to the minimization or elimination of these problems. Therapy that doesn't fully take into account the importance of LFT and doesn't effectively help the client to overcome it may easily prove ineffective.

7. Philosophic restructuring to change our dysfunctional personalities (no matter how the dysfunctions originated or developed) involves the following steps: (a) fully acknowledge that we create, to a lesser or greater degree, our own disturbances; (b) see clearly that we do have the ability to change these disturbances significantly; (c) understand that what we usually call "emotional problems" stem mainly from irrational Beliefs; (d) clearly perceive these beliefs and (e) see that we must dispute them, using the logicoempirical methods of science; (f) also see that we'd better work hard in emotive and behavioral ways to counteract these beliefs and the dysfunctional feelings and actions to which they lead; (g) reuse and repractice rational-emotive-behavioral methods of uprooting and changing disturbed Consequences for the rest of our lives.

Other RET Hypotheses on Personality and Personality Change

I have now outlined some of the essential elements of RET theory of personality and personality change. A good many more are discussed in my article "Rational-Emotive Therapy: Research Data That Support the Clinical and Personality Hypotheses of RET and Other Modes of Cognitive-Behavior Therapy" (in Section 2 of this book). As shown there, these RET-oriented personality hypotheses have a good deal of controlled research studies behind them that tend to made them seem valid.

As can easily be seen, some of the elements of RET personality theory overlap with those of other theories and forms of therapy. But they also have a unique flavor of their own, and they fit nicely into the rational-emotive system of psychotherapy, constituting a natural part of the system's main structure. And this structure, as I have tried to show in the preceding discussion, includes some specific rational-emotive views of personality and personality change that, for the most part, are different from the views upheld by other psychological systems.

REFERENCES

Adler, A. *Understanding human nature.* Greenwich, Conn.: Fawcett, 1974. (Originally published, 1927.)

Ainslie, G. Specious reward: A behavioral theory of impulsiveness and impulse control. *Psychological Bulletin, 1975, 82,* 463–496.

Beck, A. T. *Cognitive therapy and the emotional disorders.* New York: International Universities Press, 1976.

Berne, E. *Games people play.* New York: Grove Press, 1964.

Bourland, D. D., Jr. A linguistic note: Writing in E-prime. *General Semantics Bulletin,* 1965–1966, *32-33,* 111–114.

Bourland, D. D., Jr. The semantics of a non-Aristotelian language. *General Semantics Bulletin, 1968, 35,* 60–63.

Chess, S., Thomas, T., & Birch, H. G. *Your child is a person.* New York: Viking, 1965.

DiGiuseppe, R. A., Miller, J., & Trexler, D. A review of rational-emotive psychotherapy outcome studies. *The Counseling Psychologist, 1977, 7*(1), 64-72.

Ellis, A. Rational psychotherapy and individual psychology. *Journal of Individual Psychology, 1957, 13,* 38–44.

Ellis, A. Rational psychotherapy. *Journal of General Psychology, 1958, 59,* 35–49.

Ellis, A. *The folklore of sex* (Rev. ed.). New York: Grove Press, 1961.

Ellis, A. *Reason and emotion in psychotherapy.* New York: Lyle Stuart, 1962. (Also, New York: Citadel, 1977.)

Ellis, A. A cognitive approach to behavior therapy. *International Journal of Psychiatry, 1969, 8,* 896–900.

Ellis, A. *Growth through reason.* Palo Alto, Calif.: Science and Behavior Books, 1971. (Also, Hollywood, Calif.: Wilshire Books, 1971.) (a)

Ellis, A. *Rational-emotive therapy and its application to emotional education.* New York: Institute for Rational Living, 1971. (b)

Ellis, A. Psychotherapy and the value of a human being. In J. W. Davis (Ed.), *Value and valuation: Axiological studies in honor of Robert S. Hartman.* Knoxville: University of Tennessee Press, 1972, 117–139. (Also, New York: Institute for Rational Living, 1972.)

Ellis, A. Are cognitive-behavior therapy and rational therapy synonymous? *Rational Living,* 1973, *8*(2), 8–11. (a)

Ellis, A. *Humanistic psychotherapy: The rational-emotive approach.* New York: Julian Press, 1973. (Also, McGraw-Hill Paperbacks, 1973.) (b)

Ellis, A. *How to live with a "neurotic" at home and at work* (Rev. ed.). New York: Crown, 1975.

Ellis, A. The biological basis of human irrationality. *Journal of Individual Psychology,* 1976, *32,* 145–168. (a)

Ellis, A. Healthy and unhealthy aggression. *Humanitas,* 1976, *12,* 239–254. (b)

Ellis, A. *RET abolishes most of the human ego.* New York: Institute for Rational Living, 1976. (c)

Ellis, A. *Sex and the liberated man.* New York: Lyle Stuart, 1976. (d)

Ellis, A. *How to live with–and without–anger.* New York: Reader's Digest Press, 1977. (a)

Ellis, A. Rational-emotive therapy: Research data that support the clinical and personality hypotheses of RET and other modes of cognitive-behavior therapy. *The Counseling Psychologist,* 1977, *7*(1), 2–42. (b)

Ellis, A., & Abrahms, E. *Brief psychotherapy in medical and health practice.* New York: Springer, 1978.

Ellis, A., & Grieger, R. *Handbook of rational-emotive therapy.* New York: Springer, 1977.

Ellis, A., & Harper, R. A. *Creative marriage.* New York: Lyle Stuart, 1961. (Paperback edition, under the title *A guide to successful marriage,* Hollywood: Wilshire Books, 1971).

Ellis, A., & Harper, R. A. *A new guide to rational living.* Englewood Cliffs, N.J.: Prentice-Hall, 1975. (Also, Hollywood, Calif.: Wilshire Books, 1975.)

Evans, P. The Burt affair . . . Sleuthing in science. *APA Monitor,* December 1976, *1,* 4.

Eysenck, H. J. *The biological basis of personality.* Springfield, Ill.: Thomas, 1967.

Frazer, J. G. *The new golden bough.* New York: Criterion Books, 1959.

Freud, S. *Standard edition of the complete psychological works of Sigmund Freud.* London: Hogarth, 1965.

Friedman, M. *Rational behavior.* Columbia: University of South Carolina Press, 1975.

Fromm, E. *Escape from freedom.* New York: Rinehart, 1941.

Fromm, E. *Man for himself.* New York: Rinehart, 1947.

Garmezy, N. *Vulnerable and invulnerable children: Theory, research and intervention.* Washington: American Psychological Association, 1975.

Hauck, P. A. *Overcoming depression.* Philadelphia: Westminster, 1973.

Hayakawa, S. I. *Language in action.* New York: Harcourt Brace & World, 1965.

Horney, K. *Collected works.* New York: Norton, 1965.

Jung, C. G. *The practice of psychotherapy.* New York: Pantheon, 1954.

Kelly, G. *The psychology of personal constructs.* New York: Norton, 1955.

Kety, S. S. Current biochemical approaches to schizophrenia. *New England Journal of Medicine,* 1967, *276,* 325–331.

Korzybski, A. *Science and sanity.* Lancaster, Penn.: Lancaster Press, 1933.

Lévi-Strauss, C. *The savage mind.* Chicago: University of Chicago Press, 1970.

Maslow, A. H. *Motivation and Personality.* New York: Harper, 1954.

Maslow, A. H. *Toward a psychology of being.* Princeton, N.J.: Van Nostrand, 1962.

Maultsby, M. C., Jr. *Help yourself to happiness.* New York: Institute for Rational Living, 1975.

Meehl, P. Schizotaxia, schizotype, and schizophrenia. *American Psychologist,* 1962, *17,* 827–838.

Murphy, R., & Simon, W. *An annotated bibliography of research on rational-emotive therapy and cognitive-behavior therapy.* New York: Institute for Rational Living, in press.

Oltman, J. E., & Friedman, S. Report on parental deprivation in psychiatric disorders. *Archives of General Psychiatry,* 1965, *12,* 46–55.

Oltman, J. E., & Friedman, S. Report on parental deprivation in psychiatric disorders, II. In affective illness. *Diseases of the Nervous System,* 1966, *27,* 239–244.

Osborn, F. *The future of human heredity.* New York: Weybright & Talley, 1968.

Raimy, V. *Misunderstandings of the self: Cognitive psychotherapy and the misconception hypothesis.* San Francisco: Jossey-Bass, 1975.

Reich, W. *Character analysis.* New York: Orgone Institute Press, 1949.

Rimland, B. *Infantile autism.* New York: Appleton-Century-Crofts, 1964.

Rogers, C. R. *On becoming a person.* Boston: Houghton-Mifflin, 1961.

Rogers, C. R. *Person-centered psychology.* New York: Harper & Row, 1977.

Rosenthal, D. *Genetic theory and abnormal behavior.* New York: McGraw-Hill, 1970.

Rosenthal, D., & Kety, S. S. (Eds.). *The transmission of schizophrenia.* Elmsford, N.Y.: Pergamon, 1968.

Seligman, M. E. P. Phobias and preparedness. *Behavior Therapy,* 1971, *2,* 307–320.

Slater, E., & Cowie, V. *Psychiatry and genetics.* London: Oxford University Press, 1971.

Sullivan, H. S. *Conceptions of modern psychiatry.* Washington: Wm. Alanson White Foundation, 1947. (Also, New York: Norton, 1961.)

Thomas, A., & Chess, S. *Temperament and development.* New York: Brunner/Mazel, 1977.

Woodworth, R. S., *Dynamics of behavior.* New York: Holt, 1958.

The Theory of
Rational-Emotive Therapy

ALBERT ELLIS

Institute for Rational-Emotive Therapy

A BRIEF HISTORY

Technically, I first developed rational-emotive therapy (RET) in 1955, after I had broken away from my previous training and practice as a psychoanalyst. I had experimented with various forms of neoanalytic psychotherapy, including Ferenczi's (1952) technique of forming a deep emotional relationship with one's clients to compensate them for the early love they presumably "needed" and of which their parents had deprived them. Actually, however, I had developed some of the main principles and practices of RET by working out some of my own problems 20 years before that time, when I wasn't even studying for or thinking of becoming a therapist.

During my youth, as I have noted in a biographical essay (Ellis, 1972b), I had my own emotional problems and consequent inhibited behavior. One of these problems was a terror of speaking in public. To overcome this fear, I adopted a cognitive-philosophic approach combined with an *in vivo* desensitizing and active-directive set of homework assignments commanding myself to speak and speak in public no matter how uncomfortable I felt at first about doing so. With this cognitive-behavior methodology, I just about completely conquered some of my own worst blocks.

Nonetheless, I still believed in the efficacy of the psychoanalytic approach to therapy, was convinced that psychoanalysis was a "deeper" avenue to the unraveling and treatment of emotional disturbance, received training as an analyst, and practiced this mode of therapy for a number of years. As my faith in classical analysis waned—largely because it didn't work too well and was much too expensive for my clients to afford—I modified my approach considerably. I began to use more and more a psychoanalytically oriented method of psychotherapy (on a once-a-week sit-up-and-face-the-client basis) and less and less the orthodox psychoanalytic approach (on a several-times-a-week client-on-the-sofa basis).

Even that, however, didn't bring about the kind of efficient therapeutic results I wanted. Although I found psychoanalytically oriented counseling and therapy more effective in many respects than classical analysis (Ellis, 1957b), I still had the feeling that this approach was woefully inefficient and sometimes seemed to help people get worse instead of better. Also, having been trained in the *science* of psychology, I was somewhat allergic from the start to the basically unscientific (or antiscientific) outlook that seems to be an integral part of psychoanalysis. Even when, early in the game, I was still calling myself a "psychoanalyst," I quarreled with this outlook and wrote several papers attempting to reform it (Ellis, 1950).

As a result of a considerable amount of self-searching and experimentation with my clients, I ultimately came to the conclusion that I had become quite disillusioned with anything even slightly resembling psychoanalytic treatment. During the early 1950s I began to refer to myself as a "psychotherapist" instead of a "psychoanalyst" and, somewhat belligerently, tried to convince my friends and professional associates that, while "psychotherapy" was good and beneficial, "psychoanalysis" was bad and harmful. Around the beginning of 1955 I had developed enough confidence in what I was doing to give a name to my newly developed technique: rational psychotherapy. A few years later, when it appeared that this name was arousing misunderstanding and undue opposition on the part of many professionals (who wrongly identified it with 18th-century rationalism), I consulted with my first associate in the new mode of treatment, Robert A. Harper, and we agreed to change the name to rational-emotive therapy (RET).

In the beginning RET was largely a set of procedures developed on pragmatic grounds. As I realized that many of the psychoanalytic techniques I was using didn't work or were actually iatrogenic, I substituted other methods for them. In this endeavor, I was guided by a great deal of reading and a decade of practice in the field of psychology; by my own experiments with myself, as noted above; and, most fortunately and somewhat accidentally, by the fact that, long before I was a psychologist, my hobby had been philosophy. Although I never had a single college or graduate course in this important area, I had become deeply involved in it at the age of 16 and had read, during the next few years, virtually every major philosophic book ever written and innumerable secondary sources. To satisfy my long-standing aspirations to be a writer, I began working at a book on the philosophy of human happiness, focusing on those aspects of philosophy that dealt specifically with this area. I was especially interested in the writings of Epictetus, Marcus Aurelius, and other Stoics; of Spinoza, Erasmus, Voltaire, Schopenhauer, and other, latter-day philosophers who extended the practical, hard-headed thinking of the Stoics; and of 20th-century philosophers, such as John Dewey, Bertrand Russell, A. J. Ayer, Hans Reichenbach, and Ludwig Wittgenstein, who scientifically ripped up much of the obscurantist philosophy of the past and humanistically applied what was developed to some of the everyday problems of present-day living.

I found, mainly by my own clinical experimentation, that the more I forgot about psychodynamic psychology and the more I entered with my clients into the realm of speculative and practical philosophy, the quicker and the better my clients seemed to cope with their emotional problems and to make often remarkable changes in their thinking and behaviors. For, like Adler (1927, 1929, 1964) and Frankl (1966), I discovered that we human beings are largely goal-seeking and evaluating animals and that we run our lives more by purposes and ideals than by the conditioning we receive in early childhood. We seem to be born with a tendency to creatively *invent* certain ways of looking at ourselves, others, and the universe. We then construct our emotions and behaviors in accordance with the premises and philosophies (or, as George Kelly would say, personal constructs) that we have invented. We don't do our inventing or creative thinking in a vacuum, since we are raised in a social environment and, to a large degree, learn what to think *about*—for example, sex and marriage customs, political systems, and economic processes. But we bring ourselves and our special cognitive styles to these processes. It is largely the way we react to the conditions around us, rather than the conditions themselves, that leads to our "personality traits" and to our disturbances.

All of this was originally said by Epictetus (1899), and was transmitted to us in *The Encheiridion*. In the first century A.D., Epictetus said that humans "are disturbed not by things but by the views that they take of them." It was this ancient truth that I kept rediscovering, as I saw client after client, first for psychoanalytically oriented and then for nonanalytic therapy. In the beginning I worked pragmatically, by a sort of trial-and-error process. I saw that certain techniques—such as showing people that, when they failed, they *could* do better and explaining to them some problem-solving techniques that would help them do better—were fairly effective. But I also found that other techniques—such as showing people that, even if they did poorly, they didn't have to denigrate *themselves* and their *total* selves just because their *behavior* was ineffectual— helped them much more. So I used the more elegant rather than the less elegant rational approaches to help my clients improve.

After a while I began to realize that certain general principles were involved in RET. Karen Horney (1965) had coined the phrase "the tyranny of the shoulds" to explain how humans idealize and thereby disturb themselves. I saw that she was correct but that she had not gone far enough in attributing neurotic symptoms to absolutistic, overgeneralized thinking and that she had done little to apply her great insight to therapeutic procedures. Therefore, although I continued with my experimentation in cognitive-behavioral forms of treatment, I also applied myself to the development of an integrated theory of psychotherapy and personality. This theory was meant to enable me to understand more of what I was doing, to help my clients more quickly and thoroughly, and to communicate RET teachings to other professionals (Ellis, 1958, 1962, 1971, 1973, 1974, 1977a, 1977b, 1977c, 1978a, 1978d).

From the start, RET frankly espoused active-directive treatment methods. Consequently it immediately engendered violent opposition from almost all the other major therapeutic schools of the mid-1950s. Psychoanalytic, Rogerian, and existentialist therapists were horrified because the new theory abjured their indirect, passive, and highly cautious ways. Experiential and feeling-oriented therapists foamed at the mouth because the approach was "too intellectual" and "unemotional." Hans Eysenck (1964) included it as a form of behavior therapy in one of his early books on this subject; but most other behavior therapists, particularly of the Skinnerian and Wolpean variety, found it abhorrent because of its profound interest in cognitive mediating processes rather than in overt behaviors only (Rachlin, 1977).

This opposition failed to shake my belief in RET, since I had almost always used it on myself to overcome any latent or manifest feelings of anxiety or depression, and, therefore, I knew it worked. I had been working especially at one of the central RET theses—that it is highly desirable but hardly necessary for an individual to have the approval of significant others. Consequently, I refused to tell myself that RET was a wormy (meaning highly unpopular) form of treatment and that I was a worm for espousing it, in spite of the tremendous amount of flak about the "simplistic, overintellectual, and too directive" aspects of rational-emotive therapy that began to erupt soon after I gave my first paper on it at the American Psychological Association convention in Chicago in 1956 and after my publications on it began to appear in 1957. Instead, I constantly lectured, demonstrated, wrote, and recorded RET presentations at the Institute for Rational-Emotive Therapy in New York and in many other parts of the world, and, in the face of almost overwhelming opposition, I pigheadedly refused to make myself feel depressed, guilty, or ashamed.

For a combination of reasons, in the 1960s a notable change started to occur in psychology and psychotherapy. This change was sparked in part by RET; most of it, however, seemed to occur quite independently. Cognitive psychology, which had had its origins a quarter of a century before in the work of Jean Piaget (1952, 1954) and his coworkers, started to come into its own with a vengeance. The psychological shelves began to fill with fine research studies that seemed to show fairly conclusively that humans don't live by bread alone but also, and more importantly, by what they *think about* bread, cheese, wine, and other aspects of living. Consequently, from then on, virtually every new issue of innumerable psychological journals has included one or more significant research studies that empirically back some of the main RET hypotheses about personality and personality change (Ellis, 1977a; Murphy & Simon, in press).

In the 1960s something even more interesting happened. The very climate of psychotherapy began to change profoundly as a result of new developments in encounter groups, assertion training, and skill training. The encounter movement—which, ironically enough, had originated in the highly passive methods of sensitivity training—grew in popularity and thoroughly endorsed active-directive methods of group therapy (Schutz, 1967). Several schools of psychotherapy—especially Gestalt therapy (Perls, 1969)—attracted many adherents by emphasizing direct confrontation and by forcing clients to stay in the present rather than obsessing themselves with their pasts. Other forms of therapy, such as transactional analysis (Berne, 1961, 1964), began to strongly stress cognitive and instructional methods of treatment. Existential and humanistic therapy espoused procedures largely based on direct dialogue between therapist and client, on human values, and on philosophical analysis (Frankl, 1966; May, 1969). An influential group of therapists led by Jay Haley (1963, 1976) and Paul Watzlawick (Watzlawick, Beaven, & Jackson, 1967; Watzlawick, Weakland, & Fisch, 1974) began to stress a highly directive problem-solving approach to therapy. All these significant changes in the psychotherapeutic scene of the 1960s reflected in varying degrees the main positions that RET had begun to espouse in the mid-1950s.

To make things almost complete, the late 1960s witnessed an exceptionally important change in behavior therapy too. Outstanding authorities such as Albert Bandura (1969) and Cyril Franks (1969) observed that humans do not merely act after being confronted with an environmental stimulus but that they cognize and interpret that stimulus. Instead of the Watsonian view of stimulus-response (S-R), these new-style behavior therapists began to adopt a Woodworthian view of stimulus-organism-response (S-O-R). Following their lead and often inspired by RET-oriented cognitive-emotive-behavior therapy, a good many psychologists working in the field of behavior modification began to conduct controlled experiments that showed fairly definitively that humans influence their emotions and behaviors by what they tell themselves. These experiments also indicated that, if people can change with the help of therapists or experimenters their self-defeating cognitive statements, they can significantly change their feelings and their actions.

Also in the 1960s—and independently of my own clinical work and theorizing—Aaron T. Beck (1967, 1976), another psychoanalytically trained therapist, reached the conclusion that the common psychological symptom of depression is largely caused by cognitive overgeneralization and other forms of crooked thinking and constructed a highly cognitive form of therapy that parallels RET. Influenced by the Ellis and Beck formulations, as well as by the personal construct theory of George Kelly (1955), many experimenters and clinicians have developed a theoretical and practical school of cognitive-behavior therapy that is now one of the most important in the field. Some of the most prominent workers in this area include Davison and Neale (1975), Goldfried and Davison (1976), Goldfried and Merbaum (1973), Kanfer (Kanfer & Goldstein, 1975), Lazarus (1971a, 1971b, 1976), Mahoney (1974, 1977b), Meichenbaum (1977a), and Rimm and Masters (1974).

As a result of this recent clinical and experimental work, RET has become one of the most popular schools of psychotherapy and represents an essential part—and also the cognitive restructuring core—of the cognitive-behavior therapy movement. Most of the recent texts on behavior therapy, as well as many of the self-help books that show readers how to apply behavior-modification principles to their own lives, include a section on RET or some closely related form of cognitive restructuring. Following my own lead, a good many authors have written clinical texts applying RET to various kinds of problems. Among these authors are Church (1975), Diekstra and Dassen (1976), Hauck (1972), Lange and Jakubowski (1976), Lembo (1976), Morris and Kanitz (1975), Tosi (1974), and Wolfe and Brand (1977).

Rational-emotive therapy, because it can be stated in clear and simple form and thus made available to the average reader, has inspired a number of popular self-help books. Some of the best-known publications in this area are those written by Blazier (1975), Ellis (1957a, 1965a, 1965b, 1973, 1976a, 1977c), Ellis and Harper (1961a, 1975), Ellis, Wolfe, and Moseley (1966), Goodman and Maultsby (1974), Grossack (1974, 1976), Hauck (1973, 1974, 1975), Kranzler (1974), Lembo (1974, 1977), Little (1977), Maultsby (1975), Maultsby and Hendricks (1974), McMullen and Casey (1975), Powell (1976), Thoresen (1975), and Young (1974).

Just as Freudian psychology and philosophy have directly or indirectly influenced many writers who do not directly give it credit, so RET philosophy and practice have been incorporated into the writings of many authors who fail to fully acknowledge its impact. Incidentally, these writers also fail to acknowledge some of RET's most significant ancestors, such as Epictetus and Marcus Aurelius. Some of the authors who have incorporated RET principles in their work but who have not officially acknowledged doing so are L. S. Barksdale, Wayne Dyer, William Glasser, Haim Ginott, Ken Keyes, Roy Masters, and Manuel Smith. In view of the profound influence that RET writings have had on the public during the last two decades, it seems fair to say that rational-emotive therapy is one of the most influential systems of the 20th-century.

BASIC THEORETICAL FORMULATIONS

Like cognitive behavior modification, multimodal therapy, and what is often called eclectic therapy, RET includes many different kinds of procedures. Therefore, it is rarely done in a monolithic, one-sided manner. Even its somewhat unique method of disputing irrational beliefs can be, and often is, employed in a variety of ways. For example, I usually start logico-empirical disputing during the very first session of psychotherapy and as quickly as possible teach my clients to actively and vigorously look for and debate their own *must*urbatory ideas. A good many other RET practitioners, instead, are much more hesitant in this respect and, at the beginning, spend a considerable amount of time building a good degree of rapport with their clients and sometimes getting much more background material from them than I myself would choose to get. Yet, these less active-directive RETers follow the basic rational-emotive theory and wind up with their clients pretty much the same way as I would do.

Also, some RET professionals do a great deal more lecturing and talking during the first few sessions of therapy than I might do, while I do more challenging and questioning, as well as teaching of scientific methodology, than they might do. So there need not be uniformity of therapeutic style or approach in RET—any more than in the styles or approaches of different individuals working with basic psychoanalytic theory. Nonetheless, there are some general theoretical principles to which most rational-emotive therapists or those who use a good proportion of RET technique would tend to subscribe. These principles, which underlie therapeutic strategy in most instances, are along the following lines.

Hedonism

Virtually all humans are basically hedonistic, since they seem to have a strong biological tendency to try to stay alive and to achieve a reasonable degree of happiness (including relative freedom from pain). Hedonism, or happiness-seeking, is a choice rather than an absolute necessity, since a few individuals (albeit damned few!) seem to deliberately choose to be fairly unhappy or in pain throughout their lives—for example, those who wear hair shirts on earth on the supposition that they will later achieve happiness in heaven. But the vast majority of people choose to be happy. Therefore, it seems likely that it is our innate predisposition as humans to make this kind of fundamental choice.

Long- and short-range hedonism. People can decide to seek short-range hedonism—"Let me go for immediate and easy gratifications. Life is short, and who knows how long I'll be here!" They can also decide to focus on long-range hedonism—"Since in all probability I'll live for 75 years or so and since I want to be happy during most of my life and not just at the moment, let me discipline myself somewhat, put off many immediate gratifications in favor of future gains, and try to ration my happiness over my earthly existence." If people consciously choose to have a short and merry life and gracefully accept the consequences of that decision—for example, the fact that they may get lung cancer tomorrow because of the endless cigarettes they keep smoking today—that is their prerogative, and their behavior is not necessarily irrational. If, however, people choose immediate gratification over future happiness and then demand that they have the latter as well as the former and whine and wail when things don't turn out that way, that is not rational behavior, since they are not accepting the logical consequences of their choices. Also, if people consciously choose long-range happiness but then stubbornly refuse to follow the disciplined kind of existence that would actually accord them this goal, they are being self-contradictory and hence irrational.

Most humans, or at least most of those who come for psychotherapy, really do seem to be motivated by long-range rather than short-range hedonism. However, since so many of them sabotage their own goals by behaving in ways that virtually assure that they will get mainly short-range gains, RET helps them clarify their "real" goals, shows them that they are responsible for their choices and actions, and helps them become more efficient long-range hedonists. Practically all schools of psychotherapy are somewhat similar to RET in this respect. But rational-emotive therapy makes a special effort to show clients what their short-range and long-range goals are and to help them make a conscious and determined choice of one set of goals or the other, accepting the consequences of their own choices. This means that, since most clients seem to want (but not consistently follow) long-range hedonistic paths, RET tries to help them do so.

Criteria of Rationality.

RET posits no absolutistic or invariant criteria of rationality, unlike some authorities who call themselves "rational" or "reality" therapists—for example, Maultsby (1975) and Glasser (1965)—and who at times seem to do just that. The term *rational*, as used in RET, refers to people's (1) setting up or choosing for themselves certain basic values, purposes, goals, or ideals and then (2) using efficient, flexible, scientific, logico-empirical ways of attempting to achieve such values and goals and to avoid contradictory or self-defeating results.

This is an important point and one that is frequently misinterpreted by RET's critics. RET therapists are often accused of trying to persuade all their clients to adopt the kind of behavior that they themselves consider rational. False! RET therapists do *not* select clients' values, goals, and purposes or show them what their basic aims and choices *should* be. As a therapist, I try to determine, as quickly as feasible, what a client's basic values are. Usually I have little trouble in doing this, for the simple reason that these basic values are common to most people. As I noted in the previous section, almost all the individuals I see, whether they are fully conscious of it or not, choose to survive and to be reasonably happy while they are alive. Most of them, moreover, want to be happy when they are by and with themselves, as well as when they are with others. They also try to achieve happiness by relating intimately to a few others in the community in which they live, by involving themselves in some steady vocational and economically remunerating pursuit, and by engaging in recreational, esthetic, and creative activities.

As soon as I discover what my clients' basic goals and values are and how clients think, emote, and behave in ways that interfere with the achievement of these goals, I show them how they can rationally—that is, more efficiently—get more of what they want and less of what they don't want out of life. I don't *give* them "rational" goals; but I may often suggest that, *if* they have this desire (say, to be less anxious and depressed), *then* they had better give up this other demand (expect that every significant person they encounter will inordinately love them at all times). Or, *if* their goal is to lose 30 pounds and keep them off their bodies for the rest of their days, *then* they'd better rationally become long-range rather than short-range hedonists as far as food is concerned and had better use certain behavioral techniques to control their eating.

Antiabsolutism and Antimusturbation

Rational-emotive therapists have a scientific and logical approach because, as philosophers and psychologists have discovered over the centuries, the rules of science and logic usually (not always!) provide people with a higher probability of achieving their goals and purposes in an efficient and rational manner. This doesn't exclude that some bigoted, dogmatic, absolutistic, grandiose, and anti-scientific individuals can get what they want or lead happy and long lives. Some of these individuals, as history tells us, obviously do. Nonetheless, the fact is that, when people resort to absolutistic or *must*urbatory ways of thinking and behaving, they almost always defeat their own ends and wind up by getting a great many things they don't want and relatively few things they do want.

Take, for example, one of my clients, who has the basic goal of being a fine novelist and of making a living for herself by writing salable novels and/or teaching creative writing to college and graduate students. If this is her desire and she is willing to get the proper credentials (such as a master's or a doctor's degree in literature) to implement the teaching part of it, there is a good chance that she will get what she wants. Suppose, however, that she has the strong belief that she *must* be able to write a great novel easily and on the very first try and also that she *has to* get a fine teaching job without going to the trouble of obtaining proper academic credentials. Unless I can help her see that *it would be nice* if she were able to get what she wants easily and without any hassles but that that's just not the way things are, her absolutistic thinking will in all probability stop her from achieving her goals.

In sum, the basic theory of RET holds that human desires, wishes, and preferences are usually good and self-helping, because they add to existence and give us a purposeful and interested outlook. The theory also holds, however, that, as soon as we raise these desires to absolutistic, *must*urbatory needs, commands, and insistences, we usually interfere with getting our wishes fulfilled and defeat our own ends. This is not to say that absolutistic thinking always leads to poor results, for occasionally it motivates people to achieve their goals and feel happier than they otherwise would be. On these occasions, therefore, we may call this way of thinking "rational" or "constructive." The probability is high, however, that it will lead to self-destructive emotions, such as anxiety, despair, self-downing, hostility, and low frustration tolerance and to self-sabotaging actions, such as inertia, procrastination, and frantic decision making.

Human Fallibility

A cardinal RET principle, and one that is derived from much empirical observation, is that we are human and thus fallible and that it is most unlikely that we will ever be anything else. We have distinct limitations, which we can sometimes transcend and with which we can usually live. One aspect of our human nature is that we continually aspire to "higher," transcendental, or omniscient states of consciousness and being. Often we delude ourselves that we have actually reached such states and that we have gone beyond the material universe into the realm of pure spirit. No evidence exists that we have ever done this, and the chances are slim that we ever will. RET, therefore, fully accepts people as fallible humans and tries to help them accept themselves as creatures who now and forever will probably make continual and innumerable errors, who will for the most part lead rather average and unnotable lives, and who can acknowledge this state of affairs and still live happily and self-acceptingly.

Mortality

Although it is certainly possible that humans may some day arrange to live indefinitely and although it is also possible that some kind of meaningful "life" after death actually exists, the fact is that we now invariably sooner or later die and that no convincing evidence for any kind of immortality or after-life does exist. Therefore, a major RET assumption is that, at least for the time being, we probably will not live forever and that, if we want to survive and enjoy our lives as long as possible, we'd better assume that this is our only life and make the most of it while it lasts. Our behaving during our lifetime *as if* we were going to be immortal doesn't make very good sense when the overwhelming probability is that we will not.

THERAPEUTIC FORMULATIONS

RET is interested not so much in constructing a theory of personality that will explain exactly why humans behave the way they do in practically all respects as it is in constructing a theory of personality change. The central goal of this latter theory is to find some principles and methods of helping people change their irrational and dysfunctional thoughts, feelings, and behaviors so that they will be able to get more of what they want and less of what they don't want. RET assumes that, whatever the ultimate sources or causes of personality are and whether or not we presently have any comprehensive theory about these basic sources, we still can observe how people maintain their malfunctioning traits and how they can significantly change them.

Another way of stating this point is to say that RET has not yet constructed and provided the field of psychology with a totally satisfactory theory of personality formation and maintenance; nor, for that matter, do I think that any other school of psychotherapy has. In fact, as I noted in the preceding article, such a theory may be a virtual impossibility in the present state of our psychological knowledge. We simply don't know whether we shall ever be able to formulate a truly valid theory of personality. Nonetheless, enough is presently known (and more is becoming known almost every day) to build, at least tentatively, a theory of personality change. RET attempts to construct such a theory, as well as a practice to implement it. The theory emphasizes the following concepts.

Biological Predispositions

We humans seem to be born with a strong predisposition to think, feel, and act in a fairly rational, self-preserving, and self-actualizing way—as Maslow (1962) and Rogers (1961, 1977) have shown and as I have noted in various of my writings (Ellis, 1962, 1971, 1973). But we also have powerful predispositions or innate tendencies to behave irrationally and self-defeatingly (Ellis, 1962, 1976b, 1977c; Ellis & Grieger, 1977). By this I mean that we are easily and "naturally" rational, in that we have strong biological tendencies to think, to think about our thinking, to be creative, to love, to learn by our mistakes, and to change ourselves enormously when we perceive that we are not getting some of the results we want to get. But we also tend to be short-range hedonists, to avoid thinking things through, to procrastinate, to be suggestible and super-stitious, and to be perfectionistic and grandiose (Ellis & Knaus, 1977).

RET doesn't depend on this theory of innate predispositions to be effec-tive as a therapy. It would work just about as well even if we subsequently dis-covered that human behavior stems almost 100% from environmental learning rather than largely from the innate tendency to easily pick up x (for example, self-sabotaging responses) and to have difficulty in picking up y (for example, self-helping responses). For RET's theory of personality change, as noted earlier, doesn't necessarily depend on the validity of its theory of personality formation. However, my personal clinical experience during the last 35 years has convinced me of the importance of explaining certain aspects of personality formation to my clients. If I explain to them not only that they have learned (or taught them-selves) to have certain neurotic symptoms but that they also have strong bio-logical tendencies to learn *that* kind of behavior rather than *another* kind, they understand more clearly why they act the way they do and are more realistic and determined about changing their disturbed patterns of living.

RET, therefore, tends to espouse (although not dogmatically) a biologically oriented as well as learning-oriented theory of human disturbance for at least two important reasons. One is that the facts of modern psychology seem to confirm quite clearly such a view (Ellis, 1976b, 1977c; Ellis & Grieger, 1977). The other is that bringing these facts to the attention of clients often tends to help them work harder to get over their innately predisposed *and* their environ-mentally acquired symptoms.

Cultural Influenceability

Having acknowledged our innate predisposition to act more easily in one way than in another, RET also theorizes that one of our main innate tendencies is that of being influenceable, particularly during our early childhood, by our family members, by our close associates and teachers, and by our culture in gen-eral. RET also emphasizes that people have wide individual differences and that some of them seem to be significantly more influenceable or vulnerable than others (Garmezy, 1975). However, rational-emotive theory hypothesizes that virtually all humans add enormously to their innate emotional disturbability and irrationality by letting themselves be overinfluenced by societal teachings. A high degree of suggestibility or gullibility (or what B. F. Skinner [1971] might call "reinforceability") is inherent in the human condition. Because of this suggestibility, environmental teaching and control wield a powerful influence over almost all of the people almost all of the time.

One of the most trenchant and efficacious of these influences is psycho-educational or psychotherapeutic persuasion. If we were stuck with innate ideas (for example, the idea that we *must* do perfectly well and *have to* be universally loved), we would retain these ideas all our lives and almost certainly defeat ourselves forever. Fortunately, on the basis of our grim experiences in life and our natural tendencies to observe ourselves and to change some of our dysfunctional behaviors when we become aware of them, we can figure out how to make ourselves less disturbed and help ourselves function more efficiently. Also, we can receive help from others—teachers, preachers, writers, and psychotherapists—to achieve these goals. This is obviously a basic tenet of all psychotherapies, and RET is no exception. Rational-emotive therapy has a great deal of faith in people's ability to learn, during individual- or group-therapy sessions, more about how they are needlessly upsetting themselves and what they can do to stop doing so. To a very large degree, therefore, even though RET heavily emphasizes the innate tendencies of humans to be disturbed, it also stresses their natural abilities to learn in therapy and to free themselves from their disturbances.

Interaction of Thoughts, Feelings, and Actions

As I pointed out in some of my earliest writings on RET (Ellis, 1962; Ellis & Harper, 1961a, 1961b), humans almost invariably seem to think, feel, and act interactionally and transactionally. Their thinking significantly affects (and in some ways practically creates) their feelings and behaviors; their emotions have a very important effect on their thoughts and actions; and their acts distinctly influence their thoughts and feelings. If, in the course of psychotherapy, we help people change any one of these modalities, we simultaneously help them modify the others. RET, right from its inception, has tried to be a comprehensive form of psychotherapy that consciously and powerfully uses all three—cognitive, emotive, and behavioral—methods of personality change (Ellis, 1971, 1973, 1976a, 1977a, 1977c; Ellis & Grieger, 1977; Ellis & Knaus, 1977). It stresses, much more than other systems of therapy tend to do, a highly cognitive-teaching approach, without omitting the emotive and behavioral components. It does so not merely because it espouses a somewhat eclectic and multimodal approach to therapy but, more importantly, because its theory says that humans rarely think without simultaneously feeling and behaving and that any "true" (or "elegant") change in their disturbability seldom takes place without significant and lasting cognitive-emotive-behavioral improvement.

The Importance of Cognition in Therapy

As just stated, RET almost invariably utilizes a comprehensive thinking-feeling-acting form of psychological treatment. At the same time, it also stresses another point. Whereas a significant change in people's feelings or actions may often bring about limited philosophic change, a major change in a person's philosophy can help bring about highly important and lasting changes in both emotions and behaviors. This is because, according to RET and to cognitive psychology in general, humans are uniquely thinking, or symbolizing, animals. Unlike other members of the animal kingdom, they not only think in complex and even convoluted ways but have the unique ability to think about their thinking—and at times to think about thinking about their thinking. Consequently, RET employs a large number of cognitive methods, particularly that of disputing irrational beliefs, as will be explained below. RET should, therefore, be regarded as a highly depth-centered and philosophically oriented system of personality change (Ellis, 1968, 1970a, 1970b, 1974, 1977c, 1978a; Ellis & Grieger, 1977; Ellis & Harper, 1975; Raimy, 1975).

The A-B-C Theory of Irrational Thinking and Disturbance

As I said earlier, RET harks back to the Stoic view of emotional disturbance, particularly that of Epictetus. Shakespeare restated in *Hamlet* Epictetus' idea a little differently: "There's nothing either good or bad, but thinking makes it so."

In RET, we start with C, an emotional or behavioral Consequence (usually known as a neurotic symptom or disturbance). C is usually preceded by A, an Activating Experience or Event, such as a person's failing at some important task or getting rejected by another individual whose love he or she seeks. RET holds that, when A occurs and seemingly "causes" C, A does *not* directly cause C, although it indirectly contributes to it. It is B, the individual's Belief System *about* what is occurring at A, that more directly "creates" or "causes" C.

More specifically, RET hypothesizes that, whenever we get upset about just about anything at point A, we have *both* rational Beliefs (rB's) and irrational Beliefs (iB's) about A. Our rational Beliefs at B take the form of wishes, wants, and preferences—for example, "I prefer to succeed at this task and have others approve of me for succeeding. I decidedly don't like failing and having others disapprove of me for failing." These rational Beliefs (rB's) almost invariably lead to appropriate Consequences (aC's), such as sorrow, regret, or annoyance, when something obnoxious or unfortunate happens at A.

If we stayed rigorously with our rational Beliefs, RET contends, we wouldn't feel and act in a disturbed and self-defeating manner. These appropriate Consequences (aC's) would encourage us to either try to change the obnoxious or dislikable Activating Experiences that are occurring at A or else live sorrowfully (but without being upset) with them if they are truly unchangeable. Then we would tell ourselves at point B "Too bad! I cannot seem to succeed at this task, and people will continue to disapprove of me for failing at it. Well, it's not the end of the world. I'll just be as happy as I can be even though these unfortunate facts of life exist." The problem is that we have an innate as well as an acquired tendency to follow up our rational Beliefs (rB's) with irrational Beliefs (iB's), which almost invariably take the form of absolutistic demands, commands, and musts. Thus, when we fail and get disapproved by others at A, we irrationally tell ourselves "I *must* not fail like this, and I *shouldn't* be disapproved of by others! How *awful* that I did what I *must* not do—fail! I *can't stand* the poor results I'm getting by failing. I am a rotten person (R.P.) for behaving in this failing, disapprovable manner!"

To recapitulate, the A-B-C theory of RET states that the basic "cause" of disturbed emotional Consequences (at C) does not rest in the Activating Experiences that happen at A but in people's irrational Beliefs (iB's) with regard to these A's at point B. I outlined 10 or 12 basic irrational Beliefs (iB's) in my early writings on RET (Ellis, 1957a, 1957b, 1958, 1962). These iB's have been quoted and have inspired research papers by scores of clinicians and experimenters. They have also been used for many irrationality tests, such as those by Bessai (1975), Jones (1968), Kassinove (1977), and Shorkey and Whiteman (1977).

After thinking about this matter further, I reduced my original number of basic irrational Beliefs to three major *musts*, each of which includes several important subcategories (Ellis, 1976a; Ellis, 1977c; Ellis & Grieger, 1977; Ellis & Harper, 1975). These are: (1) "I *must* (or should or ought) perform well and/or be approved by significant others. It is *awful* (or *horrible* or *terrible*) if I don't! I *can't stand it*. I am a pretty *rotten person* when I fail in this respect!" (2) "You *must* treat me considerately and fairly. It is *horrible* if you don't! When you fail me, you are a *bad individual*, and I *can't bear* you and your crummy behavior!" (3) "Conditions *must* be the way I want them to be, and it is *terrible* when they are not! *I can't stand* living in such an awful world. It is an utterly abominable place!" If anyone subscribes to these three basic *musts* and many of their derivatives, various forms of emotional disturbance will almost inevitably follow.

Insight and RET

Although RET places great emphasis on cognition, it doesn't stress insight in the same way as psychoanalysis and some of the other psychodynamically oriented forms of therapy do. The reason is that RET doesn't assume that the kinds of insight emphasized by these forms of therapy will automatically or spontaneously lead to significant personality change. Instead, RET stresses three somewhat different kinds of insight that clients had better achieve.

Insight 1. Self-defeating or disturbed Consequences have clear-cut antecedent causes. Whereas psychoanalysis and conditioning theory state that these causes can be found mostly in past events, RET holds that they lie largely in the past and present innate reactivity of the individual who has these experiences. RET also holds that the immediate and most important "cause" of disturbed behavior lies in the person's *present* Belief System and in the Activating Experiences about which he or she has a certain Belief. More specifically, insight 1 sees self-defeating or disturbed Consequences as stemming mainly from the irrational Beliefs that people *bring to* the Activating Experiences occurring in their lives.

Insight 2. No matter how we originally become (or make ourselves) disturbed, we feel upset today because we are *still* reindoctrinating ourselves with the same kinds of irrational Beliefs that we originated in the past. Even if we learned some of these Beliefs from our parents and other early socializing agents, we *keep* repeating and retaining them ourselves. Therefore, our *self*-conditioning is much more important than our early conditioning on the part of others.

Insight 3. Even if we achieve clearly and powerfully insights 1 and 2 and thereby fully realize that we have created and keep carrying on our own disturbed feelings, these two insights will not automatically make us change our irrational Beliefs. Only if we constantly *work and practice,* in the present as well as in the future, to think, feel, and act *against* these iB's are we likely to surrender them and make ourselves significantly less disturbed. Without such awareness and practice, our self-therapy (as well as sessions with a professional therapist) will in all probability do us little good.

Although several other modern therapies—such as behavior therapy and reality therapy—seem to imply the need for insight 3, RET makes it quite explicit and keeps bringing it to the attention of its clients.

Humanistic Outlook

From its inception RET has taken the humanistic and existentialistic position that people create their own world by the phenomenological *view* they take of what happens to them. RET also accepts the humanistic-existentialistic philosophy that people had better define their own freedom, cultivate a good measure of individuality, live in dialogue with others, accept their personal experiencing as a highly important aspect of their lives, be aware of and present in the immediacy of the moment, and learn to accept their own human limitations and the fact that they will eventually die (Braaten, 1961; Combs & Snygg, 1960; Hartman, 1967; May, 1961, 1969).

In accordance with its humanistic outlook, RET puts particular emphasis, possibly more than any other major school of therapy, on what Standal (1959) and Rogers (1961) call unconditional positive regard and what RET practitioners call full, or unconditional, acceptance of oneself and others (Ellis, 1962, 1972b; Ellis & Grieger, 1977). As a consequence, RET takes the unusual stand that we'd better not rate ourselves, our essence, or our being but only our deeds, acts, and performances. According to the RET position, we can choose to do this limited kind of rating not in order to *prove* ourselves—that is, to strengthen our ego and self-esteem—but in order to *be* ourselves and *enjoy* ourselves.

Since RET has an active-directive as well as a phenomenological outlook (Ellis, 1978c), it endorses active methods of therapy similar to those employed by existentialists like Viktor Frankl (1966) rather than the more passive methods used by existentialists like Rollo May (1969).

Behavioral Outlook

Although RET is a cognitive-emotive-behavioral method of psychotherapy, it does not espouse the classical behaviorist position that people learn or are conditioned to be disturbed by early events or training and that the object of therapy is to have them relearn or be reconditioned so they can feel less disturbed. As already noted earlier, RET holds, instead, that people largely disturb or condition themselves to feel and act dysfunctionally and that it is their innate tendency to do so. There are, of course, many specific things we learn that help us disturb ourselves. As children, for example, we may learn that cockroaches are "horrible" or that airplanes are "very dangerous." But we learn most of these exaggerated and foolish ideas because we have an innate predisposition to hold such beliefs and because we can easily and with very little help from the environment invent these exaggerated, self-defeating notions ourselves.

Because RET holds that people are easily disturbable and that, even when they have persuaded themselves to give up irrational Beliefs, they easily fall back into self-defeating pathways, behavior modification or retraining experiences are an integral part of rational-emotive therapy. In fact, RET practitioners often use more operant conditioning and *in vivo* desensitization procedures than do many classical behavior therapists. Along with the usual behavior methods, however, RET just about invariably employs many cognitive and emotive approaches. Therefore, it constitutes a form of what Lazarus (1971a, 1976) calls "broad-spectrum" or "multimodal behavior therapy."

In its most elegant form, as I explain below, RET uses a considerable amount of cognitive restructuring or philosophic Disputing (at point D), after clients have been shown their irrational Beliefs (at point B). Therefore, behavior therapy that includes cognitive restructuring generally tends to employ some form of RET as its cognitive modality. But some behavior therapists wrongly believe that RET is synonymous with Disputing—that is, with arguing clients out of their irrationalities (see the articles by Mahoney and by Meichenbaum in Section 2 of this book). This is not true. Actually RET uses perhaps 10 or 20 major kinds of cognitive restructuring, with several varieties under each of these major headings. Such forms of restructuring include, for example, giving clients new self-statements, as well as the use of reattribution training, empirical disconfirmation of exaggerated ideas, positive thinking, thought stopping, hypnotic and nonhypnotic suggestion, rational-emotive imagery, and various other kinds of cognitive methods. In its general, or inelegant, form, RET is synonymous with cognitive-behavior therapy (CBT). In its more elegant form, it specializes in disputing, debating, and discriminating techniques of cognitive restructuring (Ellis, 1977a, 1977c, 1978c; Ellis & Grieger, 1977; Phadke, 1976).

Disturbance about Disturbance

RET has always emphasized the self-talking, or self-indoctrinating, aspect of human disturbance. This is not to say that humans cannot upset themselves by thinking in terms of images, felt meanings, mathematical formulations, or other kinds of nonverbal cognitions—for they certainly can! For the most part, however, they do tend to make themselves miserable or "emotionally disturbed" by talking to themselves in words, phrases, sentences, and paragraphs and, of course, in some kind of language that they have picked up in the culture in which they were reared.

Along with their innate tendency to talk to themselves, people are also self-observers. They *perceive* what they do, and, in the process, they observe their thoughts, feelings, and behaviors. Like other animals, they are conscious and perceptive; but, unlike other animals, they are also self-conscious and self-perceptive.

Because of their self-perception and self-consciousness, people can distinctly observe their own disturbances—their own disordered and self-defeating emotions and behaviors. If they feel anxious, for example, they usually *know* that they have this feeling. This awareness is often a good thing to have, because it permits people to do something to control their anxiety or to withdraw from the situations that they perceive as "anxiety provoking."

Unfortunately, however, many or most of us go much further than this. We take our primary symptom, anxiety, and make it into a secondary A, or new Activating Experience. We then look at this A, invent some irrational Beliefs about it—and then we're *really* upset. For the new iB's say something like "I *must* not feel anxious! And, since I do feel what I *must* not feel, (1) It's *awful*, (2) I *can't stand* it, and (3) I'm a *crummy person* for feeling the awful way that I do!" We then become anxious about feeling anxious (or depressed about feeling depressed or self-downing about feeling self-downing). In other words, we acquire the secondary symptom of anxiety about anxiety, which is in many ways worse and more pervasive than the primary symptom. Moreover, this secondary symptom may become so intense and constant that it seriously interferes with our getting back to our primary anxiety. Thus, it may keep us from seeing what we told ourselves to create the anxious state, from working at changing our irrational Beliefs about our original failure and rejection, and from making ourselves much less anxious (Ellis, 1971, 1973, 1977c; Ellis & Harper, 1975; Low, 1952; Weekes, 1969, 1972).

RET not only works with clients' original or primary symptoms, but it also, on theoretical grounds, looks for and often discovers their symptoms *about* these primary symptoms. Thus, it helps people uproot first their secondary disturbances and then their original ones. In this sense it is a more intense and "deeper" form of therapy than certain other forms of treatment that claim intensity and depth but really "deeply" consider a great many irrelevancies in a client's life.

Payoffs

People often manage to arrange some kind of payoff for their neurotic symptoms. Because they enjoy such a payoff, they make it quite difficult for themselves to face the disadvantages of their symptoms and to work at changing them (Berne, 1964; Ellis, 1962, 1977c). Psychodynamic therapists continually assume that these payoffs give people dramatic gains and joy. They may assume, for example, that, if John is fighting with his wife and refuses to have sex with her, the reason is that he hates his mother. Therefore, he enjoys his fights and his lack of sex with his wife because he unconsciously feels that he is thereby doing in his mother.

It is true that people often do get payoffs for acting in a self-defeating way and especially for not working at therapy to change their self-sabotaging behavior. Thus, John may be fighting with his wife because (1) he enjoys fighting; (2) he is able to put her down in the course of fighting and thereby cover up his own feelings of inadequacy; and (3) he really doesn't enjoy going to bed with his wife, so that fighting with her may give him an excuse to stay away from sex. Also, John may not work at the therapeutic process, assuming that he goes for help, because (1) if he gets over his hostility toward his wife, he will have to stay with her, which he really doesn't want to do; (2) he will have to work his butt off to change his easily manufactured feelings of hostility; and (3) after giving up his hostility, he will feel obliged to work on his self-downing, which will require even more effort on his part.

RET fully acknowledges that people often get neurotic gains from originating and maintaining their disturbed behavior; but it doesn't look for deep-seated, highly dramatic payoffs, as many psychodynamically oriented therapies do. Instead, it usually finds that the basic and often quite dramatic payoff is some kind of low frustration tolerance or the gaining of immediate ease. Thus, in John's case, at times he is likely to find it easier, or more immediately gratifying, to fight with his wife than to have a good relationship with her. That is, he may find it easier to fight with her and take the disadvantages that go with it than work on giving up his feelings of inadequacy. He may not want to go to the trouble of divorcing his wife and may want, instead, to manipulate her into divorcing him. He may avoid working on his feelings of hostility because he sees the task as too hard, even though it may bring real advantages. For these and similar reasons, John may arrange some payoffs and get neurotic gains from fighting with his wife and avoiding sex with her.

RET therapists look first for the easy-way-out, or low-frustration-tolerance, hypothesis when it appears that their clients may be arranging payoffs for themselves by remaining disturbed. Sometimes, of course, they do so for more dramatic ego-oriented reasons. But if one tests the easy-way-out theory, one frequently finds that it gives a better explanation for the creation and maintainance of emotional disturbance than do some of the more dramatic and "deeper" theories.

Difficulty with Basic Change

It has been found by many schools of therapy, from psychoanalysis to RET, that clients often resist changing even when they clearly see how they defeat themselves and what they could do to stop their self-defeating behavior. This phenomenon of resistance is variously explained by different schools— for example, in terms of people "not wanting to change," "spiting their parents by remaining the way they are," or "resenting the therapist and therefore not changing."

These are interesting theories, but I have found them usually invalid. It is true that a *few* clients resist changing for some of the reasons hypothesized by psychoanalytic and other "depth-centered" therapists. But since almost all people—clients and nonclients—who exhibit dysfunctional behavior have considerable difficulty changing the behavior and maintaining the change, these "special" reasons for their doing so seem far-fetched.

The RET theory is that most people have a natural tendency to resist basic personality change. No matter how much they want to behave differently and no matter how clearly they see how they can do so, they still have to force themselves *uncomfortably* and repeatedly to change the ineffectual act before they *comfortably* and *easily* do so. And since almost all humans have a natural affinity for comfort and are highly allergic to the pain they must go through to get a certain result, most of them just won't do what they'd better do in order to change—namely, work very hard and for a considerable period of time.

Another important consideration to which RET calls attention is that many of the harmful things that people do—such as smoking or overeating—are biologically enjoyable. Therefore, people get easily addicted to these things and have a rough time deciding to give them up and following up on their decision.

There is still another unfortunate aspect of dysfunctional habits: many of these habits are not only difficult to modify but easy to reestablish. For example, many individuals work hard to effectuate a rigorous program of exercise and finally achieve it after six months or a year. But then, come around a year after that, they have gradually fallen back into their old habits of rarely or never exercising. Regular exercise and many other good habits are hard to get into but easy to fall out of. Here, again, RET hypothesizes that people "naturally" tend to follow the path of least resistance. This means that it is easy for people, at least in the short run, to give up a hard-gained productive habit and fall back on an older defeating one.

Perhaps, as the psychodynamic therapies hypothesize, there are special reasons why once undisciplined individuals finally discipline themselves to do something onerous or to stop doing something unhealthy and why they then fall back on their old benighted pathways. Frankly, I have my doubts about these "special reasons," and I suspect that many analytic therapists often invent them. The far greater likelihood is that humans retrogress to foolish, undisciplined behavior mainly because that is their basic biological tendency— because it is very easy for most of them to take two steps forward and one step backward and, more often than we like to admit, to take one step forward and two steps backward!

Scepticism about the Special Origins of Dysfunctional Behavior

Almost all schools of psychotherapy stress the special or unique origins of dysfunctional behavior and assume that specific causative factors exist for such behavior. Furthermore, they presuppose that, if therapists and clients really understand these special causative factors (especially as they are revealed in the early events of the clients' lives), enormous therapeutic change will occur. Not so RET!

This is not to say that historical factors in emotional disturbance may not exist. They may, and they may even contribute to or exacerbate childhood and adult malfunctioning. But I am doubtful whether these factors truly "cause" the malfunctioning. And I am fairly convinced that most of us are born (and reared) with the irrational tendency to look for, to "discover," and to exaggerate the significance of "special" or "historical" reasons for our unhealthy personality traits. We also tend to speciously convince ourselves, when we "find" such reasons, that they indubitably exist and have vast importance. That is one of the root assumptions of psychoanalytic thinking and the reason why psychoanalysis survives in spite of its appalling record of inefficiency in helping people understand and solve their emotional problems.

In other words, I am hypothesizing that people innately *enjoy* looking for the historical "roots" of their disturbances; that they *like* "explaining" their present behavior by referring to their past acts, even though the connection between the two may be quite tenuous; and that they *naturally* confuse correlation with cause and effect. Therefore, if Mary tells me, as her therapist, that she hates men today and that she also hated her father in the past, both she and I will tend to falsely assume that her past experiences with her father *made* her loathe males today. We both will feel very satisfied with this "explanation," ignoring the fact that it is much more probable that both her early hatred of her father and her present loathing for other males spring from a common source. This source may be her immense low frustration tolerance. It may also be her unreasonable expectation that everyone whom she *wants* to like her and treat her well *must* do so and, if they don't do exactly that, they are *horrible people.*

I am also hypothesizing that, when Mary and I "determine" that her early hatred of her father indubitably "caused" her current hatred of men, we will fail to note that she hated only certain things about her father and that she by no means hates *all* males today—in fact, she devoutly loves a few of them. We will thereby falsify both her past and her present in order to come up with a better and "truer" fit for our hypothesis. We will do this because we are biased creatures who bring hypotheses to data and have no trouble making the two dovetail beautifully. What I am saying is that our own "natural" self-deceiving processes (which are largely innate rather than acquired) help us to devoutly believe that Mary once hated her father completely, that she now hates all men, and that the two "events" are causally connected.

To make matters worse, we do something else, which interferes even more with the processes of therapy and scientific thinking. Once I, as Mary's therapist, and she, as my client, "determine" that her father treated her poorly during her childhood, that his treatment of her *made* her hate him, and that this history of hatred *makes* her hate virtually all other men today, Mary's innate and acquired tendencies are such that, in all probability, she will *feel* delighted with this "explanation." In fact, she will feel so good about its "truth" that she will happily conclude that she now "knows" herself much more fully—when, actually, she misunderstands herself (and other humans with similar problems). And she (and I, as her therapist) will in all probability take her good feeling as indubitable "proof" of our hypothesis that her father's poor behavior toward her during her early childhood *made* her disturbed and still *makes* her upset today.

If I am correct about what I am saying here, people like Mary, as well as people like me, her therapist, are natural and biologically impelled crooked thinkers. We disturb ourselves because of our tendencies to make irrational conclusions about what happens in the world. We then, on the basis of our deep faith in these false conclusions, make up specious "evidence" to support these conclusions. Because we place this "evidence" in the Procrustean bed of our own hypothesizing, thus arriving at a nigh perfect fit, we feel great about this "marvelous" fit. Finally, we use our feeling as "proof" of the validity of our original hypotheses. By going through this kind of process, we bring our disturbed thinking to psychotherapy, and, in a sense, we make psychotherapy another kind of disturbance! For, when Mary (with my "therapeutic" help) comes to devoutly believe that her hatred of men today stems from her poor relationship with her father in the past, she ignores the real reason for her original *and* later hatreds—namely, her own insistence that people *must* act the way she wants them to act. Consequently, her new belief about the origin of her disturbance not only is largely false but leads her up the garden path. It leads her a million miles away from acknowledging how she really creates her own emotional problems and from seeing what she'd better do to eliminate her disturbance. After she has, with my "help," reached the epitome of "insight" into herself and her dysfunctional behavior, she is really more disturbed—or, at least, less capable of healthily changing herself—than ever. Her "marvelous" therapy has proven to be quite iatrogenic!

RET, then, along with classical behavior therapy, reality therapy, personal-construct therapy, and a few other kinds of treatment, holds that it is almost completely wasteful to look for and elaborate the "special" reasons why clients have current symptoms. Such "reasons," as noted above, are largely fictional. Even if they do exist, they are not easily ascertainable and would require considerable time and effort to dig up. And even when they are relevant, they have little to do with people's *overcoming* their disturbances.

Thus, a male client may know that he plays tennis anxiously and badly because his mother kept telling him that he could never play well. But having this knowledge will hardly help him give up his basic irrational Belief that he *must* play tennis well. His knowing in detail about the *origins* of his neurotic anxiety will not help him see exactly what he is *now* telling himself to recreate and maintain these attitudes and how he can presently *surrender* these irrational Beliefs. In fact, the more historical understanding he has of the origins of his disturbance, even if this understanding is accurate, the more he will probably sidetrack himself from clearly understanding and undoing—yes, undoing!—his anxiety.

RET tends to hold, in a pronounced but undogmatic way, that the "real" causes of human disturbance lie in the propensity of people to think crookedly, emote inappropriately, and act dysfunctionally—all of which are partly learned but largely innate. These causes also reside in people's specific tendencies to behave self-defeatingly, in accordance with their personal temperament and traits—tendencies that, again, stem largely from inherent dispositions. The "origins" of their disturbances, therefore, seem to stem mainly from the "special-ness" of their heredity rather than from that of their history. RET faces this reality instead of running away from it as so many other systems of psycho-therapy do. It assumes that, in spite of the strong innate tendencies of humans to act dysfunctionally much of the time, people can be helped to behave much more efficiently and less self-defeatingly by using RET principles and practices.

RATIONAL-EMOTIVE THERAPY GOALS

Many critics of RET wrongly accuse it of trying to get people to become less emotional—to become calm and serene, as Epictetus advocated and as Maultsby (1975) sometimes seems to encourage his clients and readers to be. Nothing could be further from the truth. RET assumes that emotion is basic to human living and that, if we were without strong feelings, we would probably not survive, or, at least, not live happily; therefore, in many ways RET tries to help people be more rather than less emotional. But, unlike virtually any other major school of therapy, RET clearly distinguishes inappropriate emotion from appropriate emotion. Consequently, it tries to encourage clients to have strong, sincere, and appropriate feelings and to surrender inappropriate or self-defeating feelings.

RET designates as appropriate feelings various kinds of desires, wishes, and preferences, as well as those feelings that occur naturally when human desires are blocked or frustrated. In RET's view, appropriate positive emotions include love, happiness, pleasure, and curiosity; appropriate negative emotions include sorrow, regret, annoyance, frustration, and displeasure.

Negative emotions like sorrow and regret are considered appropriate be-cause they usually help people change conditions that they see as objectionable, such as the condition of being rejected or failing to get a job. Sorrow and regret motivate us to get more of what we want and less of what we don't want in life.

Inappropriate emotions—like feelings of depression, anxiety, despair, inadequacy, and worthlessness—are deemed undesirable because they not only don't help us change obnoxious conditions but frequently help make them worse. Thus, if you first feel appropriately sorry about being rejected by some-one but then you become inappropriately depressed about this rejection, you will tend to pity yourself, moan, remain inert, and do nothing to get this person (or someone else) to accept you. And if you feel very angry about being treated unjustly by one of your friends, you may easily goad yourself to act so badly toward this friend that he or she will treat you even more unjustly.

The theory—as well as the practice—of RET holds that inappropriate emotions almost invariably seem to stem from (1) people's general tendency to think crookedly and from (2) their specific absolutistic demands and commands—from the dogmatic *shoulds* and *musts* into which they foolishly turn their desires and preferences. It is a basic assumption of RET that emotionally disturbed people have irrational ideas, inappropriate feelings, and dysfunctional behaviors and that these ideas, feelings, and behaviors directly flow from or are mainly "caused" by their absolutistic musts—by their *must*urbation. Without people's resorting to some kind of overgeneralized, magical thinking, practically none of what we call "emotional problems" would tend to occur.

If people want to stay alive and to enjoy themselves while alive and if they want to minimize the emotional disturbances that often seriously interfere with these major purposes, they need to seek several important goals. RET therapists try to help their clients achieve these goals, which are discussed below.

Self-Interest

Emotionally healthy people tend to be interested first in themselves and then in others. This doesn't mean that they don't become deeply involved in loving relationships with a few selected people. They wouldn't be emotionally healthy if they were *completely* absorbed in themselves. But they still put themselves first most of the time, since it is likely that others will do the same. And those people who spend their lives sacrificing themselves for others tend to get less than their share of happiness.

Social Interest

Humans almost invariably live in a social group. They have a biological tendency toward gregariousness and, therefore, rarely choose a completely lonely existence. Social interest is usually rational, in that humans would hardly survive if they had none of it, and they tend to be happier with than without it. If you want to live and enjoy yourself in the social group in which you choose to live, you had better act considerately and, to some degree, lovingly toward others. If you don't act morally and don't make efforts to protect the rights of others, it is highly likely that you will create the kind of a world in which you yourself do not, and in some real sense cannot, comfortably live.

Self-Direction

Emotionally healthy people tend to assume responsibility for their own lives and work at solving independently most of their own problems. While at times they may prefer the cooperation and help of others, they do not *need* or absolutistically *demand* this kind of support.

Tolerance

Mature and realistic individuals give other people the *right to be wrong*. Even if they dislike intensely the behavior of others, they don't condemn or damn them, as persons, for exhibiting such behavior.

Flexibility

Healthy people remain flexible in their ideas, are open to change, and take an unbigoted view of the variety of people around them. They don't make rigid, invariant rules either for themselves or for others.

Acceptance of Uncertainty

Emotionally mature men and women acknowledge and accept the fact that we live in a world of probability and chance, where absolute certainties do not, and probably never will, exist. They realize that it is not horrible— indeed, it is often fascinating and exciting—to live in this kind of probabilistic and uncertain world. They enjoy a good degree of order but don't whiningly demand or command it.

Commitment

Most people are healthier and happier when they are vitally absorbed in something outside of themselves—whether this something be people, things, or ideas. They preferably have at least one outstanding creative interest, as well as some major human involvement, which they consider so important that they may structure around it a good part of their everyday existence.

Scientific Thinking

Nondisturbed individuals tend to be more objective, rational, and scientific than disturbed ones. They feel deeply and act concertedly; but they also regulate their emotions and actions by reflecting on them and their consequences and by applying the rules of logic and of the scientific method to determine and evaluate these consequences.

Self-Acceptance

Healthy people are normally glad to be alive. They accept themselves just *because* they are alive and, as living creatures, have some capacity to enjoy themselves and to ward off needless pain. They don't measure their intrinsic worth by their extrinsic achievements or by what others think of them. If they are truly wise, they try to completely avoid rating themselves—their totality and their being. They attempt to enjoy rather than to prove themselves.

Risk Taking

Emotionally untroubled people realize that life involves a fair amount of risk taking. They ask themselves what they would really like to do, and then they try to do it, even though there is a good chance that they may fail at it. They tend to be adventurous, although not foolhardy. They are willing to try almost anything once, so they can see whether they like it or not. And they often look forward to some breaks in their life routines.

Nonutopianism

Undisturbed people accept the fact that utopias are impossible to achieve and that they will never get everything they want and completely avoid everything they don't want. They don't strive unrealistically for total joy or happiness or for total lack of anxiety, depression, self-downing, and hostility. They assume that they themselves, others, and the world itself will always be fallible and flawed. Even perfect mental health, they clearly see, is something of a chimera, although continual striving for a good measure of it is a viable option.

Striving for the goals that have just been described and supported by the theoretical formulations that were discussed earlier, the RET practitioner proceeds with the practice of therapy. Precisely how he or she proceeds will be outlined in detail in the following article.

REFERENCES

Adler, A. *Understanding human nature.* New York: Garden City Publishing Company, 1927. (Also, Greenwich, Conn.: Fawcett, 1974.)

Adler, A. *The science of living.* New York: Greenberg, 1929.

Adler, A. *Social interest: A challenge to mankind.* New York: Capricorn, 1964.

Bandura, A. *Principles of behavior modification.* New York: Holt, Rinehart & Winston, 1969.

Beck, A. T. *Depression.* New York: Hoeber-Harper, 1967.

Beck, A. T. *Cognitive therapy and the emotional disorders.* New York: International Universities Press, 1976.

Berne, E. *Transactional analysis in psychotherapy.* New York: Grove Press, 1961.

Berne, E. *Games people play.* New York: Grove Press, 1964.

Bessai, J. *A factorial assessment of irrational beliefs.* Master's thesis, Cleveland State University, August 1975.

Blazier, D. C. *Poor me, poor marriage.* New York: Vantage, 1975.

Braaten, L. J. The main theories of "existentialism" from the viewpoint of a psychotherapist. *Mental Hygiene,* 1961, *45,* 10–12.

Church, V. A. *Behavior law and remedies.* Dubuque, Iowa: Kendall/Hunt, 1975.

Combs, W., & Snygg, D. *Individual behavior.* New York: Harper, 1960.

Davison, G. C., & Neale, J. M. *Abnormal psychology.* New York: Wiley, 1975.

Diekstra, R. F. W., & Dassen, W. G. M. *Rationele therapie.* Amsterdam: Swets and Zeitlinger, 1976.

Ellis, A. *An introduction to the scientific principles of psychoanalysis.* Provincetown, Mass.: Journal Press, 1950.

Ellis, A. *How to live with a "neurotic."* New York: Crown Publishers, 1957. (Rev. ed., New York: Crown Publishers, 1975.) (a)

Ellis, A. Outcome of employing three techniques of psychotherapy. *Journal of Clinical Psychology*, 1957, *13*, 350–354. (b)

Ellis, A. Rational psychotherapy. *Journal of General Psychology*, 1958, *59*, 35–49.

Ellis, A. *Reason and emotion in psychotherapy.* New York: Lyle Stuart Inc., 1962. (Also, New York: Citadel, 1977.)

Ellis, A. *The art and science of love* (Rev. ed.). New York: Lyle Stuart, 1965. (Also, Bantam Books, 1965.) (a)

Ellis, A. *Sex without guilt* (Rev. ed.). New York: Lyle Stuart, 1965. (Also, New York: Grove Press, 1965. Hollywood, Calif.: Wilshire Books, 1970.) (b)

Ellis, A. What really causes therapeutic change. *Voices,* 1968, *4*(2), 90–97.

Ellis, A. The cognitive element in experiential and relationship psychotherapy. *Existential Psychiatry,* 1970, *28*, 35–52. (a)

Ellis, A. Rational-emotive therapy. In L. Hersher (Ed.), *Four psychotherapies.* New York: Appleton-Century-Crofts, 1970. (b)

Ellis, A. *Growth through reason.* Palo Alto: Science and Behavior Books, 1971. (Also, Hollywood, Calif.: Wilshire Books, 1971.)

Ellis, A. *The civilized couple's guide to extramarital adventure.* New York: Peter Wyden, 1972. (a)

Ellis, A. Psychotherapy and the value of a human being. In J. W. Davis (Ed.), *Value and valuation: Axiological studies in honor of Robert S. Hartman.* Knoxville: University of Tennessee Press, 1972. (Also, New York: Institute for Rational Living, 1972. (b)

Ellis, A. Psychotherapy without tears. In A. Burton (Ed.), *Twelve therapists.* San Francisco: Jossey-Bass, 1972. (c)

Ellis, A. *Humanistic psychotherapy: The rational-emotive approach.* New York: Julian Press, 1973. (Also, McGraw-Hill Paperbacks, 1973.)

Ellis, A. Rational-emotive therapy. In A. Burton (Ed.), *Operational theories of personality.* New York: Brunner/Mazel, 1974.

Ellis, A. Healthy and unhealthy aggression. *Humanitas,* 1976, *12*, 239–254. (a)

Ellis, A. *RET abolishes most of the human ego.* New York: Institute for Rational Living, 1976. (b)

Ellis, A. Certification for sex therapists. In W. Gemme (Ed.), *Progress in sexology.* New York: Plenum, 1977. (a)

Ellis, A. *A garland of rational songs.* Songbook and tape cassette recording. New York: Institute for Rational Living, 1977. (b)

Ellis, A. *How to live with—and without—anger.* New York: Reader's Digest Press, 1977. (c)

Ellis, A. Rational-emotive therapy: Research data that support the clinical and personality hypotheses of RET and other modes of cognitive-behavior therapy. *The Counseling Psychologist,* 1977, *7*(1), 2–42. (d)

Ellis, A. Religious belief in the United States today. *Humanist,* 1977, *37*(2), 38–41. (e)

Ellis, A. Why "scientific" professionals believe mystical nonsense. *Psychiatric Opinion,* 1977, *14*(2), 27–30. (f)

Ellis, A. *Workshop on "Cognitive behavior therapy."* Institute for Rational Living, New York City, January 16, 1977. (g)

Ellis, A. Family therapy: A phenomenological and active-directive approach. *Journal of Marriage and Family Counseling,* 1978, *4*(2), 43–50. (a)

Ellis, A. *The intelligent woman's guide to dating and mating.* New York: Lyle Stuart, 1978. (b)

Ellis, A. The rational-emotive approach to counseling. In H. M. Burks (Ed.), *Theories of counseling.* New York: McGraw-Hill, 1978. (c)

Ellis, A. Toward a new theory of personality. In R. J. Corsini (Ed.), *Readings in current personality theories.* Itasca, Ill.: Peacock, 1978. (d)

Ellis, A., & Grieger, R. *Handbook of rational-emotive therapy.* New York: Springer, 1977.

Ellis, A., & Harper, R. A. *Creative marriage.* New York: Lyle Stuart, 1961. (a)

Ellis, A., & Harper, R. A. *A guide to rational living.* Englewood Cliffs, N.J.: Prentice-Hall, 1961. (Also, Hollywood, Calif.: Wilshire Books, 1968.) (b)

Ellis, A., & Harper, R. A. *A new guide to rational living.* Englewood Cliffs, N.J.: Prentice-Hall, 1975. (Also, Hollywood, Calif.: Wilshire Books, 1975.)

Ellis, A., & Knaus, W. *Overcoming procrastination.* New York: Institute for Rational Living, 1977. (Also, New York: New American Library, 1979.)

Ellis, A., Wolfe, J. L., & Moseley, S. *How to prevent your child from becoming a neurotic adult.* New York: Crown, 1966. (Paperback edition, under the title *How to raise an emotionally healthy, happy child,* Hollywood, Calif.: Wilshire Books, 1972.)

Epictetus, *The works of Epictetus.* Boston: Little, Brown, 1899.

Eysenck, H. J. (Ed.). *Experiments in behavior therapy.* New York: Macmillan, 1964.

Ferenczi, S. *Further contributions to the theory and techniques of psychoanalysis.* New York: Basic Books, 1952. (Originally published, 1926.)

Frankl, V. E. *Man's search for meaning.* New York: Washington Square Press, 1966.

Franks, C. *Behavior therapy: appraisal and status.* New York: McGraw-Hill, 1969.

Garmezy, N. *Vulnerable and invulnerable children: Theory, research and intervention.* Washington: American Psychological Association, 1975.

Glasser, W. *Reality therapy.* New York: Harper, 1965.

Goldfried, M. R., & Davison, G. *Clinical behavior therapy.* New York: Holt, Rinehart & Winston, 1976.

Goldfried, M. R., & Merbaum, M. A perspective on self-control. In M. R. Goldfried & M. Merbaum (Eds.), *Behavior change through self control.* New York: Holt, Rinehart & Winston, 1973.

Goodman, D., & Maultsby, M. C., Jr. *Emotional well being through rational behavior training.* Springfield, Ill.: Charles C. Thomas, 1974.

Grossack, M. M. *You are not alone.* Boston: Marlborough, 1974.

Grossack, M. M. *Love and reason.* New York: New American Library, 1976.

Haley, J. *Strategies in psychotherapy.* New York: Grune & Stratton, 1963.

Haley, J. *Problem-solving therapy: New strategies for effective family therapy.* San Francisco: Jossey-Bass, 1976.

Hartman, R. W. *The measurement of value.* Carbondale, Ill.: Southern Illinois University Press, 1967.

Hauck, P. A. *Reason in pastoral counseling.* Philadelphia: Westminster, 1972.

Hauck, P. A. *Overcoming depression.* Philadelphia: Westminster, 1973.

Hauck, P. A. *Overcoming frustration and anger.* Philadelphia: Westminster, 1974.

Hauck, P. A. *Overcoming worry and fear.* Philadelphia: Westminster, 1975.

Horney, K. *Collected works.* New York: Norton, 1965.

Jones, R. G. *A factored measure of Ellis' irrational belief system, with personality and maladjustment correlates.* Doctoral dissertation, Texas Technological College, August 1968.

Kanfer, F. H., & Goldstein, A. P. (Eds.), *Helping people change.* New York: Pergamon, 1975.

Kassinove, H., Crisci, R., & Tiegerman, S. Developmental trends in rational thinking: Implications for rational-emotive, school mental health programs. *Journal of Community Psychology,* 1977, *5,* 266–274.

Kelly, G. *The psychology of personal constructs.* New York: Norton, 1955.

Kranzler, Gerald. *You can change how you feel: A rational-emotive approach.* Eugene, Or.: Author, 1974.

Lange, A. J., & Jakubowski, P. *Responsible assertive behavior.* Champaign, Ill.: Research Press, 1976.

Lazarus, A. A. *Behavior therapy and beyond.* New York: McGraw-Hill, 1971. (a)

Lazarus, A. A. New techniques for behavioral change. *Rational Living,* 1971, *6*(1), 2–7. (b)

Lazarus, A. A. *Multimodal therapy.* New York: Springer, 1976.

Lembo, J. M. *Help yourself.* Niles, Ill.: Argus Communications, 1974.

Lembo, J. M. *The counseling process: A rational behavioral approach.* New York: Libra, 1976.

Lembo, J. M. *How to cope with your fears and frustrations.* New York: Libra, 1977.

Little, B. L. *This will drive you sane.* Minneapolis, Minn.: CompCare Publications, 1977.

Low, A. A., *Mental health through will-training.* Boston: Christopher, 1952.

Mahoney, M. J. *Cognition and behavior modification.* Cambridge, Mass.: Ballinger, 1974.

Mahoney, M. J. A critical analysis of rational-emotive theory and therapy. *The Counseling Psychologist,* 1977, *7*(1), 44–46. (a)

Mahoney, M. J. Reflections on the cognitive learning trend in psychotherapy. *American Psychologist,* 1977, *32*, 5–14. (b)

Maslow, A. H. *Toward a psychology of being.* Princeton, N.J.: Van Nostrand, 1962.

Maultsby, M. D., Jr. The classroom as an emotional health center. *The Educational Magazine,* 1974, *31*(5), 8–11.

Maultsby, M. C., Jr. *Help yourself to happiness,* New York: Institute for Rational Living, 1975.

Maultsby, M. C., Jr., & Hendricks, A. *Five cartoon booklets illustrating basic rational-behavior therapy concepts.* Lexington: University of Kentucky, Rational Behavior Training Unit, 1974.

May, R. *Existential psychology.* New York: Random House, 1961.

May, R. *Love and will.* New York: Norton, 1969.

McMullen, R., & Casey, B. *Talk sense to yourself!* Lakewood, Col.: Jefferson County Mental Health Center, 1975.

Meichenbaum, D. *Cognitive behavior modification.* New York: Plenum, 1977. (a)

Meichenbaum, D. Dr. Ellis, please stand up. *The Counseling Psychologist,* 1977, *7*(1), 43–44. (b)

Morris, K. T., & Kanitz, J. M. *Rational-emotive therapy.* Boston: Houghton-Mifflin, 1975.

Murphy, R., & Simon, W. *An annotated bibliography of research on rational-emotive therapy and cognitive-behavior therapy.* New York: Institute for Rational Living, in press.

Perls, F. S. *Gestalt therapy verbatim.* Lafayette, Calif.: Real People Press, 1969.

Phadke, K. M. *Bull fighting: A royal road to mental health and happiness.* Unpublished manuscript, Bombay, 1976.

Piaget, J. *The language and thought of the child.* New York: Humanities Press, 1952.

Piaget, J. *The moral judgment of the child.* Glencoe, Ill.: Free Press, 1954.

Powell, J. *Fully human, fully alive.* Niles, Ill.: Argus, 1976.

Rachlin, H. Reinforcing and punishing thoughts: A rejoinder to Ellis and Mahoney. *Behavior Therapy,* 1977, *8*, 678–686.

Raimy, V. *Misunderstandings of the self: Cognitive psychotherapy and the misconception hypothesis.* San Francisco: Jossey-Bass, 1975.

Rimm, D. C., & Masters, J. C. *Behavior therapy.* New York: Academic Press, 1974.

Rogers, C. R. *On becoming a person.* Boston: Houghton-Mifflin, 1961.

Rogers, C. R. *Person centered psychology.* New York: Harper & Row, 1977.

Schutz, W. C. *Joy.* New York: Grove Press, 1967.

Shorkey, C., & Whiteman, V. L. Development of the rational behavior inventory. *Educational and Psychological Measurement,* 1977, *37*, 527–534.

Skinner, B. F. *Beyond freedom and dignity.* New York: Knopf, 1971.

Standal, S. W. *The need for regard: A contribution to the client-centered theory.* Unpublished doctoral dissertation, University of Chicago, 1959.

Thoresen, E. H. *Learning to think a rational approach.* Clearwater, Fla.: Institute for Rational Living, Florida Branch, 1975.

Tosi, D. J. *Youth, toward personal growth.* Columbus, Ohio: Merrill, 1974.

Watzlawick, P., Beaven, J. H., & Jackson, D. D. *Pragmatics of human communication.* New York: Norton, 1967.

Watzlawick, P., Weakland, J., & Fisch, R. *Change: Principles of problem formation and problem resolution.* New York: Norton, 1974.

Weekes, C. *Hope and help for your nerves.* New York: Hawthorne Books, 1969.

Weekes, C. *Peace from nervous suffering.* New York: Hawthorn Books, 1972.

Wolfe, J. L., & Brand, E. (Eds.) *Twenty years of rational therapy.* New York: Institute for Rational Living, 1977.

Young, H. *Rational counseling primer.* New York: Institute for Rational Living, 1974.

The Practice of
Rational-Emotive Therapy

ALBERT ELLIS
Institute for Rational-Emotive Therapy

The practice of RET is almost always a complex and comprehensive process. The reason is that RET therapists don't view their clients as individuals who have just a specific symptom or disturbed behavior that can be effectively isolated from the rest of their personalities and lives. Instead, they see their clients as individuals who usually have a combination of cognitive, emotive, and behavioral disturbances. Consequently, in order to help their clients, RET therapists employ many different kinds of rational, evocative-confrontational, and activity-oriented techniques to unravel some of the core problems. This means that RET makes use of a wide variety of psychological techniques and is never a monolithic and invariant treatment process. Some of the techniques that RET uses are those employed in regular behavior therapy, but its greatest similarity is with multimodal behavior therapy (Lazarus, 1971, 1976), with which general, or inelegant, RET is practically synonymous.

MAIN ASSUMPTIONS ABOUT COGNITION AND
EMOTIONAL DISTURBANCE

The core of RET, however, is its heavy cognitive emphasis. This emphasis follows directly from its main assumptions about cognition and emotional disturbance. A summary of these assumptions follows.

1. Human "thinking" and "emotion" do not constitute two disparate processes but significantly interrelate with each other. We tend to "cause" or "create" most of our feelings by our thinking, and we also "cause" some of our thinking by our emoting. Especially important from the point of view of psychotherapy and personality change is the fact that, if we experience disordered emotions (such as anxiety and depression), we can often significantly change such emotions by discovering and modifying the cognitions that underlie them. This kind of modification can be accomplished in many ways. One of

the most elegant of these consists of vigorously and persistently disputing, debating, and reconstructing our self-defeating cognitions that directly underlie our emotional hang-ups.

2. When people come to therapy with neurotic symptoms or Consequences (C) after they have gone through some Activating Experiences or Events (A), the RET practitioner assumes that A may importantly *contribute to* C but doesn't directly *cause* it. People's Beliefs (B) about A are the more direct "cause" of C. If this is true—as scores of research studies now seem to indicate (see my article on research data supporting RET's hypotheses in Section 2 of this book)—it would seem that effective therapy will concern itself mainly with B, people's Belief systems, rather than primarily with A or C. And this is what the RET therapist does: he or she tries to help clients discover and understand, as clearly as they are able, the detailed Beliefs with which they *make themselves*—yes, do not *become* but *make themselves*—disturbed.

3. RET therapists also assume that, when people feel or act in a disturbed manner at point C after experiencing some undesirable Activating Event at point A, their Beliefs (at point B) are of two major varieties: rational Beliefs (rB's) and irrational Beliefs (iB's). Since people have a large variety of "rational" and "irrational" Beliefs, RET zeroes in on the main ones only—those that have to do with emotional health and disturbance. The irrational Beliefs that are at the root of unhealthy and neurotic behaviors take the form of unrealistic or absolutistic expectations (or demands) about what is happening and about one's own and others' behaviors. The rational Beliefs that result in healthy behaviors take, instead, the form of realistic or relativistic desires, preferences, and wishes.

These same principles can be stated in terms of self-evaluation. We all have basic goals, purposes, and desires—particularly those of surviving and of being relatively happy with ourselves, with others, and with our surroundings. In order to fulfill these goals, we have the biological, as well as learned, tendency to ceaselessly evaluate our performances, those of others, and the surrounding conditions as "good" or "bad," "desirable" or "undesirable." Thus, we evaluate a caress as "good" and a toothache as "bad," because the former contributes to our happiness while the latter interferes with it.

I said that our tendency to evaluate, measure, or assess performances and events in the light of our goals of survival and happiness has a biological basis, because, if all of us suddenly stopped desiring and evaluating, human life would probably cease to exist. Therefore, we can call evaluation an intrinsically biological process. And, since men, women, and children do it in a rather different and far more complex way than other animals do it, evaluation is almost the essence of the human condition, as Frankl (1966) and many existentialist thinkers have claimed. Also, as Kelly (1955), Friedman (1975), and a good many other psychologists and philosophers have indicated, human evaluation is done in a uniquely creative, scientific, and predictive manner. Unlike other animals, humans act in a natural "rational" manner, in that they are self-conscious (they think about their thinking as well as merely think). They also have a pretty clear-cut notion that they have a future as well as a present and past life, and they use their thinking and evaluating abilities to plan for that future, thereby increasing their chances of surviving and being happy (Ellis, 1962, 1971, 1973, 1977c).

In RET terms, when people stick rigorously to desiring, wishing, and preferring, they remain rational; when they escalate their desires into absolutistic and often unrealizable demands or commands, they make themselves irrational. If they remain rational, they rarely, if ever, become what we call "emotionally disturbed." It is when they become irrational that they frequently make themselves "disturbed." Certain forms of disturbance—such as epilepsy, dyslexia, and some forms of psychosis—are basically neurological disorders that have little to do with desiring and commanding or with rationality and irrationality. But other forms of *emotional* disturbance, even though they have an important biological or neurological basis (as, of course, do *all* human processes), are very closely related to unrealistic expectations or demands.

The basic RET premise, then, is that, if humans had only or mostly desires and wishes and if they never or rarely evaluated their own, others', and the world's conditions in a commanding, absolutistic, and unrealistic way, they would have little or no "emotional" disturbance. They wouldn't be utterly happy or undisturbed, for they would still be heir to various "nonemotional" disorders. But they would be free of the vast majority of self-defeating thinking, feeling, and behavior that now frequently drive them to psychotherapy.

4. RET follows some of the teachings of Buddhism and the ancient Stoics, without, however, espousing many of the misleading overgeneralizations of these schools. RET assumes that, when people are emotionally disturbed and their disturbances can be tracked down to their crooked thinking, they can be helped to get rid of such disturbances. Helping them make a profound and deep-seated change in some of their values and encouraging them to replace absolutistic and overgeneralized demands with realistic wishes will make it possible for them to eliminate their disturbances and enable them to behave in a significantly less self-defeating manner in the future.

5. RET assumes that, when people view external situations, others' reactions, and their own behavior as out of their control and believe that they cannot cope "adequately" or "properly" with what is going on in their lives, they are likely to make themselves disturbed. When, instead, they see themselves as being in control of important aspects of their lives, they tend to be more relaxed and actually do more to help themselves live in accordance with their own basic goals.

6. People who feel emotionally disturbed tend to attribute motives, reasons, and causes to others and to outside events, thus distorting their own perceptions of reality. When these people come to see that they are making false attributions and assume responsibility for their own actions, they frequently feel and act better (that is, less self-defeatingly) in their relationships with others and in their responses to the environment.

These assumptions now have a large amount of research studies behind them and have been validated, at least partially, by controlled experimental studies (see my first article in Section 2 and the article by DiGiuseppe, Miller, and Trexler, also in Section 2). Other studies supporting the validity of RET's view of humans and of the possibility of bringing about personality changes keep appearing continually in the psychological literature (Murphy & Simon, in press; Ellis, 1980).

Other RET therapeutic hypotheses are validated by a great deal of supporting data in the form of clinical and case-study presentations (Ellis, 1980) but have not yet been sufficiently tested by controlled experiments. Here are some of them.

1. While it is highly desirable that we rate our deeds, feelings, and traits so we can see whether our behaviors and characteristics are helpful or self-defeating, it is undesirable that we rate our selves, our essences, our totality, and our personhoods. When we decide to live fully and enjoy ourselves, our goals are rational and sane. Rating and measuring are then helpful means of checking to see whether we are behaving in conformity to our goals. But as soon as we take what RET calls the "magical" or "illegitimate" jump from rating our traits and deeds to rating ourselves in our totality, we head toward psychological and emotional trouble. We become anxious or depressed and (ironically!) less able to change our goal-sabotaging characteristics.

2. Therapists had better give clients unconditional self-acceptance, carefully listen to their complaints, and see things from the clients' frames of reference. This kind of acceptance will help clients feel better, and so will warmth, support, encouragement, and approval by therapists. But *feeling better* is by no means equivalent to *getting better*, and in some ways the former interferes with the latter. Getting better means fully accepting ourselves under virtually *any* conditions, even when we do poorly at some tasks and even when others, including the therapist, don't particularly approve of us. Therapeutic support, therefore, may help "hook" clients on therapy and motivate them to work harder at it. But it also has potential drawbacks and limitations.

3. Intensive, depth-centered, or elegant psychotherapy doesn't consist of mere symptom removal; it also consists of helping clients achieve higher frustration tolerance about their symptoms. Thus, when a female client comes to therapy with a great fear of failure and rejection and damns herself whenever she fails and gets rejected, a RET-oriented therapist tries to help her overcome her anxiety and self-downing. But the therapist also investigates her ego anxiety and her discomfort-anxiety about her original anxiety and self-downing. She is probably telling herself "I *must* not feel anxious, because that makes me an inept, rotten individual!" thereby creating ego anxiety. And she is also quite likely to tell herself "I *must* not feel anxious and self-downing, because I *can't stand* the pain of feeling that way. That makes the world too horrible to live in!" thus creating discomfort-anxiety. Unless the therapist sees and works with both levels of this woman's symptoms—the primary level of the symptoms themselves and the secondary level of her condemning herself for and whining about the primary symptoms—elegant therapy is not likely to be accomplished. One of RET's goals is to help people dispute and eliminate the secondary symptoms of anxiety about their anxiety, depression about their depression, and guilt

about their hostility—as well as the primary feelings of anxiety, depression, and guilt in their own right.

4. Clients manifest their irrational Beliefs (iB's) in the form of unrealistic, antiempirical statements such as "If I fail this time, I will *never* be able to succeed in the future!" or "Since it is so horrible to die in a plane crash, there is a good chance that my plane will crash!" RET cognitive restructuring, or the Disputing of irrational Beliefs, includes debating and ripping up these kinds of antiempirical statements. But RET posits that behind such irrational Beliefs there almost invariably lie some basic *must*urbatory ideas and that these *musts* largely predetermine the antiempirical ideas. Thus, the full implicit philosophy behind the first irrational statement in this paragraph is "Since I *must* succeed every single time and I failed this time, I'll never be able to succeed in the future!" And the full philosophy behind the second irrational statement is "Because I *must* not die in the near future, it is horrible if I die in a plane crash; therefore there is a good chance that my plane will actually crash."

In other words, when people make outlandish antiempirical statements and believe devoutly in them, they generally have a tacit or implicit *must* that leads or encourages them to make such statements. Elegant therapy doesn't consist of merely combating such antiempirical observations but of getting at the fundamental *must*urbatory notions behind these observations and helping the clients to give them up. RET therapists, therefore, keep looking for the three basic *musts* that their clients hold—"I *must* do well!" "You *must* treat me beautifully!" and "The conditions I want *must* be easily available!"—and attempt to help their clients give up both the musts and the antiempirical statements that follow such musts.

5. Because people think largely in terms of language and can think much more precisely and clearly if they use the language properly, RET hypothesizes that semantic reeducation, which employs the principles of both general semantics and RET, can be an effective method of psychotherapy (Ellis, 1957a; Ellis & Harper, 1975; Moore, 1977).

6. RET, being a form of cognitive-emotive-behavioral therapy, employs activity homework assignments combined with a good deal of operant conditioning and self-management techniques. Skinner (1971) and other behaviorists usually favor reinforcement schedules rather than aversive conditioning or penalties for poor behavior. However, I have found that reinforcement works better for normally functioning children than for rather seriously disturbed adolescents and adults. I and other RET therapists, therefore, frequently use contingency management to help people change their dysfunctional behaviors, but we also use a good measure of self-enforced penalization. Thus, a male client who has trouble controlling his impulsive and compulsive sex behavior (such as compulsive exhibitionism) might be reinforced by allowing himself to eat favorite foods or engage in some sport after he has refrained from his compulsion for a certain period of time. He may also agree, however, to penalize himself by burning a 100-dollar bill (or a 1000-dollar bill, if necessary) every time he has given in to an exhibitory urge. RET holds that penalization, as

well as reinforcement, is often desirable to help D.C.'s (difficult customers!) change their self-defeating behaviors.

7. The RET therapist frequently disputes the poor logic and the specious data that clients marshal to support their irrational Beliefs. And he or she gives relevant information—such as sex information to individuals with problems of sexual inadequacy—that helps people undermine their own crooked thinking and change it into more rational Beliefs. But in elegant RET we also try to teach clients some of the main elements of logic and scientific thinking and show them how to apply this kind of thinking to their own personal problems (Ellis, 1962, 1977c; Edelstein, 1976; Fulmer, 1975; Guinagh, 1976; Phadke, 1977). It is hypothesized that the straighter and more scientific people's thinking is, the less disturbed they will become and remain.

COGNITIVE METHODS OF RET

The principles set forth in the preceding pages, as well as in the previous article, serve as a framework for actual RET clinical practice. In the course of this practice, RET practitioners virtually always use a number of cognitive, emotive, and behavioral techniques. Under each of these modalities, several specific methods may be employed with each client—but not, of course, the same methods. Some techniques, such as the Disputing of irrational Beliefs, tend to be used with virtually all RET clients. But other procedures, such as the paradoxical intention or the reduction of some of the client's beliefs to absurdity, are used only with selected individuals and when the therapist thinks that the client will benefit from them.

RET, then, is highly eclectic, in that it employs a multimodal approach and tailors several different therapeutic techniques, selected from a wide variety of sources, to individual clients (Lazarus, 1971, 1976). It is also very pragmatic. With most clients, the therapist starts off with the basic methods—methods that have worked well with a majority of people for the last quarter of a century. But, as soon as these methods appear to be getting poor or even mediocre results, the therapist switches to other procedures that he or she thinks may work better for that particular client.

All told, RET therapists tend to use perhaps 40 or 50 regular techniques, many of which will be outlined in this chapter. But they may also employ any number of other "irregular" methods—including somewhat idiosyncratic ones like body massage or psychodramatic abreaction—as long as these methods are used in a general RET philosophical framework and are not employed in a hit-or-miss manner because the therapist has some vague idea that they might work with certain clients.

RET, in other words, has a pronounced theoretical outlook; consequently, whatever techniques are employed are used in accordance with, and rarely against, this outlook. For example, since RET is based on the assumption that cognitive dogmatism, rigidity, and bigotry lead to *must*urbation and thence to emotional disturbance, it would rarely employ devout suggestion as a therapeutic technique, as some hypnotherapists or other therapists do. I said "rarely" because the RET practitioner might occasionally use even such an "irrational" procedure, if nothing else seemed to work with a client and it looked as if this procedure might be of some help. The rational-emotive therapist would tend to use this kind of method only temporarily, hoping that the client would later be amenable to the use of more scientific and "rational" procedures.

As I have noted several times before, the RET therapist generally incorporates into the therapeutic process a pronounced and forceful amount of cognitive methodology. Some RET practitioners are very heavily cognitive and didactic and use relatively few of the emotive and behavioral methods outlined later in this article. Few are on the other side of the fence and stress feelings and behaviors, with little emphasis on cognition. If they were doing this, it could be questioned whether they were really doing RET.

In regard to cognitive methodology, RET is in the forefront of the therapies (such as transactional analysis and psychoanalytically oriented therapy) that rely heavily on thinking, interpreting, explaining, and teaching. Although its special methodology, as explained in detail below, includes the Disputing of irrational Beliefs, this is only *one* cognitive RET procedure (Ellis, 1978a; Ellis & Abrahms, 1978). Theoretically, cognitive-oriented therapists have a dozen or more major procedures at their disposal. Each of these major procedures includes from 10 to 20 subcategories. Therefore, we can safely assume that there are between 100 and 200 forms of psychological treatment that can be labeled primarily "cognitive." And more are being invented almost every day! Some of the psychoeducational techniques that are most often used in RET and that fit better under the rubric of "cognition" than under that of "emotion" or "behavior" will now be outlined.

Disputing of Irrational Beliefs

The most elegant and probably the most common cognitive method of RET consists of the therapist's actively-directively Disputing the client's irrational Beliefs. If there is any fundamental rational-emotive method, this is probably it. So much so, in fact, that some commentators on RET wrongly assume that the Disputing or debating process (sometimes called "antiawfulizing" or "anti*must*urbation") *is* RET (Mahoney, 1977; Meichenbaum, 1977). It definitely is not! But if RET were totally devoid of this kind of Disputing, it would be almost unrecognizable.

As noted in the previous articles, Disputing usually starts with the therapist showing the client, in one way or another, the A-B-C's of RET. That is, the therapist shows the client that, after experiencing an Activating Event at point A, he or she experiences an emotional Consequence or disturbed symptom at point C not *because* of A but because of the set of Beliefs that he or she brings to A at point B. It is these Beliefs in general, and the irrational Beliefs (iB's) in particular, that more directly lead to or even "cause" the person's disordered emotional Consequences (C's). Once the therapist has demonstrated to the client that he or she is essentially causing his or her own disturbances by strongly and persistently maintaining certain irrational Beliefs, the next step is to teach the client how to Dispute these iB's at point D.

Let me illustrate this Disputing process by using a recent case in my practice. The client was a woman—whom we shall call Myra—who felt inadequate because of her inability to have any kind of orgasm and under any circumstances—in intercourse, in petting, or in masturbation. What she perceived as her sexual inadequacy filled her with shame. In other words, she had the primary symptom of sexual malfunctioning or inadequacy and the secondary symptom of shame (or guilt or feelings of self-downing) about having the primary symptom.

As is common (although not necessary) in RET, I first worked with Myra's secondary symptom—her shame about her sexual malfunctioning. I showed her that at point A (Activating Experience) she was failing to have orgasms and at point C (emotional Consequence) she felt ashamed of this failing. I explained that in all probability she was telling herself something important at B (her Belief system) to create this shame. What did she think she was telling herself at B?

She answered "I'm telling myself that it is very unpleasant never to have an orgasm, no matter what I do. This makes me different from other women. My husband doesn't like it. And that's pretty bad!"

"Good," I replied. She was zeroing in nicely on her rational Beliefs (rB's) about having no orgasms. Since her goals were to enjoy sex more by having orgasms and to be more pleasing to her husband and since her goals were not being fulfilled, it was rational and sensible for her to conclude "This is unpleasant. It's pretty bad that I and my husband are not getting what we want." However, I also pointed out, if she stayed with these rational Beliefs (rB's), she would hardly feel ashamed or self-downing. What *would* she feel, instead?

She thought for a moment and then realized that she would feel only sorry or disappointed. I agreed and congratulated her on her good thinking. For that is exactly what she would feel, sorrow and disappointment, and not shame, if she told herself *only* that not getting an orgasm was unpleasant and pretty bad. But since she *also* felt ashamed and self-downing, she was most probably telling herself something *more* than that. Now what did she believe, at point B, that made her feel ashamed? What was her iB—her irrational Belief?

She thought a while more, but had no good answer. "I think that all I tell myself is that it's pretty bad, that it's too bad that I never get an orgasm" she said. "Oh, no" I objected. As we had just agreed, that would lead only to sorrow and disappointment: "It's too bad that I never get orgasms; but that's the way it is—too bad." Why would such a self-message make her feel ashamed? It wouldn't, she admitted. Finally she said "I guess I'm also telling myself that I *should* get orgasms. Most other women do, and so should I. Yes, I think that's what I'm saying."

"Right!" I exclaimed. "You probably are saying something like that to yourself. And you are also saying something like 'Since I *should*, I really *must* get orgasms like other women do, and I don't get them; that's *awful*! I *can't stand* it! I must be something of a *turd* for being so inferior to most other women!' "

She smiled. "Well, not exactly in those words. But I guess you're right. I am saying that it's awful that I'm not like most women in that respect and that I am an inferior person. Yes, that seems to be what I'm telling myself."

"Fine" I said. Now we had her iB's (irrational Beliefs). And it was these, not her Activating Experiences at A or her rational Beliefs at B, that were really causing her feelings of shame and inadequacy. She agreed. She could see, after I pointed it out to her, that it was these iB's that were leading to her feelings of inferiority.

"But how can I change them?" she asked.

"Very simply" I answered. "By actively and vigorously Disputing them at point D." I explained that the way to do that was to ask herself several challenging questions, just as she would do in any mode of scientific inquiry. For her irrational Beliefs were not facts, they were merely *hypotheses*. And any unrealistic hypothesis can definitely be Disputed. The essence of the scientific method is exactly this: to set up a series of hypotheses, to see what results they lead to, and then to debate or challenge these hypotheses if the results seem to be poor.

More specifically, Myra could ask herself, at D, questions such as: Where is the evidence that I *should* get orgasms as other women do? Why, if I don't get orgasms, can't I *stand* the situation? Can I prove that it's *awful* if I never, even for the rest of my life, get a single climax? How does my sexual inadequacy make me an *inferior person*?"

Pressing Myra to ask herself these Disputing questions and to think out suitable answers led us to the following answers at point E—that is, new cognitive Effect of Disputing her irrational Beliefs:

1. "There is no evidence that I *should* get orgasms as other women do. It would be highly desirable if I did, and my husband and I would certainly feel better about it. But the fact that something is very desirable doesn't mean that I absolutely *have to* have it. There simply isn't any law that states that I must have what I want. And although I would be happi*er* if I could achieve orgasms, I still can be quite happy even if I never have an orgasm for the rest of my life."

2. "I obviously *can* stand my present lack of orgasm, and I can even stand it if I never get one. I have managed so far, all these years, and I clearly won't die because of it! If I tell myself, as I am doing, that I *can't* stand it, then I will just make myself *more* miserable. My intolerance for frustration will serve only to *increase* my feelings of frustration and irritability. So I'd better accept the fact that I don't *need* what I *want* and that I can very well *stand* what I don't *like*!"

3. "I can't think of any real proof that it's *awful* if, for the rest of my days, I fail to get a single climax. The thought that it's going to be so is unpleasant and distasteful. And my marriage may suffer from this problem—which is a really uncomfortable thought. But, as I read in *A New Guide to Rational*

Living, if I call something *awful* or *terrible*, I'm not merely saying that it is quite bad. I'm saying that it is *totally* bad, unbearable. Obviously, the fact that I can't achieve a climax isn't *that* bad, since it leaves me with many other pleasures, including sex pleasures, in my life. *Awful* also means that lack of orgasm is as bad as it possibly *could be,* when, of course, I could easily think of a good many worse things. *Awful* also implies that something is *more than* bad—something, so to speak, that is at least 101% bad. And, as *A New Guide* points out, nothing in the world can be *more than* 100% bad! *Awful,* in terms of failing to achieve orgasm, also really means that this lack of mine is worse than it *should* or *must* be. Presumably, what I think is that it *has to* be *less* bad than it is. But if it is as bad as it is, then it *must* be that bad! So the term *awful* or *terrible* really doesn't make any sense. If I keep using these senseless terms, I will only feel worse. And how will that *help* me achieve orgasm? It damned well won't!"

4. "My sexual inadequacy, especially if the situation doesn't change, no doubt makes me a person with an inferiority. But I can see now, especially after discussing it here in therapy, that it hardly makes me an inferior *person.* For my inferiority doesn't equal my total being. It is just a *part* of me, a single aspect. And even if this part will always remain inferior, so that I never achieve any true sex satisfaction with my husband or by myself, I'll still only be a person with an inferior trait. *I* won't be undesirable; only this *aspect* of me will be. Moreover, if *I* were really inferior, in the sense I think I am when I feel ashamed of myself for not having orgasms, I would be truly damnable—worthy of being put down by the universe and deprived of all possibility of pleasure, sexual or otherwise, for being thus damnable. Well, *am* I damnable and deserving only of pain or lack of pleasure? Of course not! No person, as far as I can see, is damnable for his or her weaknesses or deficiencies. Not even me!"

As Myra kept working at Disputing her irrational Beliefs and coming to the above conclusions over and over again, her feelings of shame about her deficiency began to fade. Within a few weeks of therapy she began to accept herself with her deficiency. At times she still had feelings of shame or unworthiness, especially when her husband seemed to make her feel inadequate for her lack of sexual responsiveness. But she was able to pull herself out of her self-recriminations and to feel sorry and disappointed but not self-downing or guilty.

Since E (the Effect of Disputing) is more useful if it results in some general conclusions that can be brought to any future situations similar to the present "disturbing" condition, I encouraged Myra to come up with such a general philosophy. She finally stated it in these terms: "I know that I will have various deficiencies all my life, because I am human and fallible. Even though some of these deficiencies are important and serious ones, they don't justify my putting *myself* down for them. Any deficiency I may have is certainly bad—even very bad at times. But *I* am never bad for having it!" I thought that this was an excellent summary statement of a new philosophy, of a new Effect that she could strive to maintain. It showed both of us that, if she kept to it, she could probably make herself much less ashamed and guilty about her deficiencies than she had before she came for therapy.

As soon as Myra came to the new Effects of Disputing outlined above and as soon as she felt less shame and guilt about her sexual dysfunction, we started to work on the sex problem itself. We agreed that at C (Consequence) she had complete lack of orgasm even when at A (Activating Experience) she wanted to have sex with her husband and started to go through the motions of having it. Although I held open the possibility that her lack of responsiveness could be more physical than mental, Myra seemed quite sure that there was something blocking her from getting fully aroused and orgasmic. The reason for such belief was that, on a few occasions, she thought that she might have had an orgasm during her sleep, even though she couldn't recall having ever had one during her waking life. Also, she felt that she often got so highly aroused and so close to orgasm, without actually achieving a climax, that she was certain that she could reach a climax and was merely blocked.

We assumed, therefore, that Myra had some Belief at B that blocked her from having the orgasms that she presumably was capable of achieving. So I asked her "When you are having sex with your husband (or with any other man you have had it with in the past) and you seem aroused but are not achieving orgasm, what are you telling yourself? What goes through your head as you seem to reach a sexual peak and then fall off?"

"I'm thinking of having an orgasm and trying to have it" she replied.

"But if you were *only* trying to have an orgasm—for example, focusing on highly sexual things—you might very well have it. I suspect that you're *also* focusing on something else. What?"

"Uh. Oh, yes: '*Will* I have it? Will it or won't it come off?' That's what I'm usually thinking about."

"Ah! 'And if it doesn't come off, if I don't have it—?' What? What are you saying to yourself about that?"

"Mmm. Oh, I can see what you're getting at! Of course! 'Wouldn't that be terrible! What a lousy sex partner I'd be!' Yes, that's it. And—uh—something more. Yes, something more. I can practically hear myself saying it, right now. 'All that effort for nothing! It's really no damned good that I should have to go to all this trouble, trying so hard to get an orgasm, and for nothing! How awful! How unfair! While so many other women have one so easily, with no effort at all!' "

Well, we had it—right there. Myra, unlike many other clients, was very good at looking into her own head and coming up with the Beliefs at point B that were most probably causing her to react badly at C, her disturbed Consequences. Her first set of irrational Beliefs, when we talked them over some more and put them together in detail, was "I *must* get sexually aroused fairly easily and come to orgasm, as most other women do. And if I don't, if I never get an orgasm, that's *awful.* I just *can't bear* it! And that proves I'm a pretty *rotten person!*" In other words, the same basic set of irrational Beliefs (iB's) that she had *after* failing to get an orgasm she really had *before* she tried to get one. Not only did she believe that it was horrible to *have* failed; she also believed that it was equally horrible *if* she failed in the future. Where putting herself down after she failed to reach an orgasm led her to feel shame and guilt, knowing before-hand that she *would* put herself down *if* she failed made her feel very anxious while having sex. And her anxiety was so distracting that it actually prevented her from having the orgasm she was so afraid of *not* having.

This, I explained to Myra (using the cognitive technique of information giving), was what often happens in sex failures. Getting aroused and orgasmic, especially in the case of a person who doesn't do so easily, requires steady and powerful focusing on sexy stimuli—on the physical sensations one is feeling at the moment and on the mental arousal one has when thinking about or imagin-ing present and future sex pleasure. But, instead of engaging in this kind of powerful focusing, Myra—as Masters and Johnson (1970) explain in their classic work on *Human Sexual Inadequacy*—kept spying on herself, thereby distracting herself from intense enjoyment. Hence, her sex activities never culminated in orgasm. The same kind of self-downing thinking that made her ashamed and depressed after failure also sabotaged her actually succeeding in the first place. And, as we agreed during our discussions, if she would give up insisting that she *must* have an orgasm, that it would be *terrible* if she didn't, and that she was a pretty *rotten individual* if she never achieved it, she would stop her self-spying and be able to focus much more intently on *enjoying* sex rather than *proving herself* sexually.

In addition to her self-flagellating propensity, with its consequent anxiety and sex blocking, Myra also had LFT—low frustration tolerance. When she had sex and was not fully aroused or orgasmic, her second set of irrational Beliefs was along these lines: "I *must* have sex enjoyment easily and quickly! Isn't it *terrible* that life doesn't give me the joy I'm entitled to! I *can't stand* such horrible frustration! The world is a pretty *rotten place* for treating me so un-fairly. Poor me, poor me!"

This set of irrational Beliefs, leading to abysmal low frustration or dis-comfort-anxiety (Ellis, 1978a) stopped Myra from accepting her sexual problem and from working harder to overcome it. I induced her to Dispute these iB's as follows:

Disputing: "Where is the evidence that I *must* have sex enjoyment easily and quickly?" *Answer:* "There is none! The only evidence I have in this regard is that I *do* have trouble coming to orgasm. I may even have this trouble for the rest of my life. But the fact that I have more difficulty in this respect than most other women hardly proves that I *must* not have this difficulty. Hell, if I have it, I have it—and that's that! Now, considering that I do have this problem, what am I going to do so I can overcome it?"

Disputing: "Why is it *terrible* when life doesn't give me the pleasure it *must* give me?" *Answer:* "It isn't! It's certainly frustrating, even obnoxious. But it's hardly *totally* obnoxious or *more than* obnoxious. And the more I see it as terrible, the more I add to its unpleasantness. So I'd better see it for what it really is—damned inconvenient, but no *more* than that! And it hardly stops me from having all sorts of other enjoyments, including sexual and loving enjoy-ments, in life—unless I *let* its 'terribleness' stop me!"

Disputing: "Where is it written that I *can't stand* this kind of sexual frustration?" *Answer:* "Nowhere! Or only in my silly head! I have stood it, of course, for a good many years now and have hardly died of lack of orgasm. And even if I never have an orgasm for the rest of my days, obviously I can stand it. Like it, no; but *stand* it, definitely yes! As long as I *think* I can!"

Disputing: "How does the world turn into a pretty *rotten place* for treating me in this unfair way?" *Answer:* "It does not! Of course, it has its hassles and injustices for everyone, including me. And even if I could prove that my situation, sexually and nonsexually, is *more* unfair than that of other women, how would this make the world and my life thoroughly rotten? It wouldn't! I'd better admit, moreover, that the world has given me certain advantages. I am bright, attractive, and well educated. Isn't it unfair, then, that I have these positive traits when many other women don't? Of course it is! Then why don't I whine about that? Besides, granting that the world and the conditions under which I live *may* be unfair to me, what is the point of my aggravating these conditions and thereby making them even more unfair? No point whatsoever! So, even if the world is not fair to me, at least *I* can be fair to myself and do the best *I* can to get all the enjoyment that is available to me in this presumably unfair world!"

As Myra, with my help, kept Disputing her irrational Beliefs, she still felt frustrated about not achieving orgasm. But she stopped annoying herself *about* this annoyance, so that her frustration became minimal. Moreover, as her self-downing decreased and her frustration tolerance increased, she became better prepared to work on her sexual problem. Thus we were able to proceed to other rational-emotive techniques to help her in that regard. This is why RET practitioners frequently zero in, as I did, almost immediately on their clients' serious problems, especially on their *must*urbation and "awfulizing." As soon as clients become preferring rather than demanding and wishing rather than needing, they are in a much better frame of mind to go on to the other cognitive, emotive, and behavioral aspects of treatment, which will enable them to go back to A and actually manage to change the Activating Experiences in the present and in the future. Once I helped Myra to understand her irrational Beliefs and to start giving them up—which occupied us for the first several weeks of therapy—she was able to go on to the other important aspects of RET.

Cognitive Homework

RET almost invariably includes many homework assignments, which are part of its behavioral processes. In Myra's case, the first homework took the form of cognitive assignments. She was asked to note and make a list of all the thoughts that came to her mind when she was having sex with her husband and was getting close to orgasm but failing to achieve it. She was also given the assignment of tracking down the absolutistic *shoulds* and *musts* in these internalized self-messages. Thus, when she noted that she was telling herself during intercourse "Look how long it's taking me to get fully aroused! I'll never be able to achieve orgasm! How *awful* that other women do it so easily, while I'm never able to achieve it!" she was asked to look for the underlying *must*urbation that, in an important sense, led to these thoughts. She soon was able to find it and expressed it as "I *must* get aroused as easily and quickly as other women do. *Therefore,* it is *awful* if I never do!" As she became adept at finding her underlying *shoulds* and *oughts,* she was able to practice Disputing them and giving them up.

A form of cognitive homework that is very frequently used in RET is the Self-Help Report Form published by the Institute for Rational-Emotive Therapy in New York City. I showed Myra this form during our first session and got her to fill it out regularly, at least once a week, for the several months that I saw her as a client. By filling out this form (which is reproduced on pp. 75–78), she was able to go over the basic A-B-C-D-E's of RET regularly and to learn how to do them properly and efficiently. Every time she came in with a filled-out form, I corrected it with her and showed her how she did go wrong. For example, at first she put under rational Beliefs (rB's) statements like "I have to enjoy myself sexually," when the correct statement would have been "I would like to enjoy myself sexually." Or she would fill out the form quite correctly, and end up with a new emotional Effect (eE) such as "I felt sorry rather than depressed." But when I questioned her as to whether she *really* felt sorry rather than depressed after she came to a cognitive Effect (cE)–"Not to experience an orgasm when I want one is not the worst thing in the world"–she would reply "No, I still felt depressed, but I knew that was wrong. So I put down the right answer on the form."

I would help her see, in such instances, that the thing to do was to put down the "wrong" answer on the form—namely, that she still felt depressed. For that would mean that she had *theoretically* arrived at the new cognitive Effect (cE) that not experiencing an orgasm was not the end of the world. But, *actually,* she still believed that it was. Noting this difference, she could then go back to cE and really work at believing it, instead of merely stating it and parroting it, as she was clearly doing.

Specific Method of Disputing Irrational Beliefs (DIBS)

One of RET's main formal cognitive methods is the specific technique of Disputing Irrational Beliefs (DIBS), which I have outlined in several of my books and which is published as a separate pamphlet by the Institute for Rational Living in New York City (Ellis, 1974, 1977c). This technique has the client take one major irrationality, particularly one absolutistic *must,* at a time and work on it systematically, with a prepared set of questions, to Dispute it. Every day, for at least ten minutes, the client goes over the same irrational Belief and thoroughly gives it up until, at the end of a month or so, he or she no longer really holds this belief or, at least, holds it with much less strength.

In the case of Myra, I had her use DIBS on several of her basic irrational Beliefs, particularly her idea that "I *must* be as effective and as sexually fulfilled

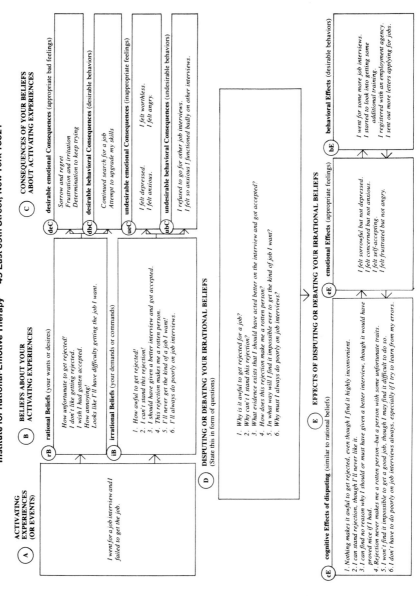

SAMPLE RATIONAL SELF HELP FORM

Institute for Rational-Emotive Therapy   45 East 65th Street, New York 10021

(A) **ACTIVATING EXPERIENCES (OR EVENTS)**

I went for a job interview and I failed to get the job.

(B) **BELIEFS ABOUT YOUR ACTIVATING EXPERIENCES**

(rB) rational Beliefs (your wants or desires)

How unfortunate to get rejected!
I don't like getting rejected.
I wish I had gotten accepted.
How annoying!
Looks like I'll have difficulty getting the job I want.

(iB) irrational Beliefs (your demands or commands)

1. How awful to get rejected!
2. I can't stand this rejection!
3. I should have given a better interview and got accepted.
4. This rejection makes me a rotten person.
5. I'll never get the kind of a job I want!
6. I'll always do poorly on job interviews.

(C) **CONSEQUENCES OF YOUR BELIEFS ABOUT ACTIVATING EXPERIENCES**

(deC) desirable emotional Consequences (appropriate bad feelings)

Sorrow and regret
Frustration and irritation
Determination to keep trying

(dbC) desirable behavioral Consequences (desirable behaviors)

Continued search for a job
Attempt to upgrade my skills

(ueC) undesirable emotional Consequences (inappropriate feelings)

I felt depressed.   I felt worthless.
I felt anxious.   I felt angry.

(ubC) undesirable behavioral Consequences (undesirable behaviors)

I refused to go for other job interviews.
I felt so anxious I functioned badly on other interviews.

(D) **DISPUTING OR DEBATING YOUR IRRATIONAL BELIEFS**
(State this in form of questions)

1. Why is it awful to get rejected for a job?
2. Why can't I stand this rejection?
3. What evidence exists that I should have acted better on the interview and got accepted?
4. How does this rejection make me a rotten person?
5. In what way will I find it impossible ever to get the kind of job I want?
6. Why must I always do poorly on job interviews?

(E) **EFFECTS OF DISPUTING OR DEBATING YOUR IRRATIONAL BELIEFS**

(cE) cognitive Effects of disputing (similar to rational beliefs)

1. Nothing makes it awful to get rejected, even though I find it highly inconvenient.
2. I can stand rejection, though I'll never like it.
3. I can find no reason why I should or must have given a better interview, though it would have proved nice if I had.
4. Rejection never makes me a rotten person—but a person with some unfortunate traits.
5. I won't find it impossible to get a good job, though I may find it difficult to do so.
6. I don't have to do poorly on job interviews always, especially if I try to learn from my errors.

(eE) emotional Effects (appropriate feelings)

I felt sorrowful but not depressed.
I felt concerned but not anxious.
I felt self-accepting
I felt frustrated but not angry.

(bE) behavioral Effects (desirable behaviors)

I went for some more job interviews.
I started to look into getting some additional training.
I registered with an employment agency.
I sent out more letters applying for jobs.

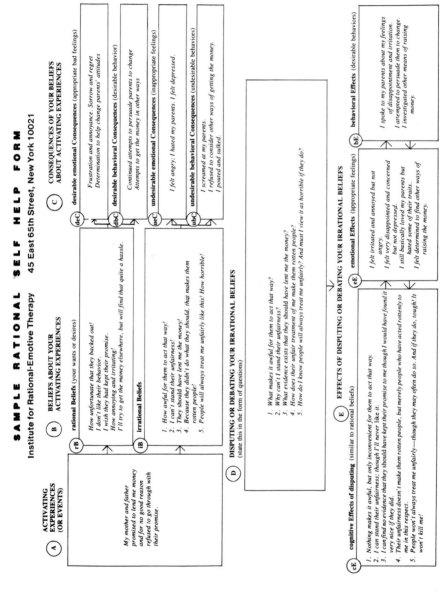

SAMPLE RATIONAL SELF HELP FORM

Institute for Rational-Emotive Therapy   45 East 65th Street, New York 10021

(A) **ACTIVATING EXPERIENCES (OR EVENTS)**

My mother and father promised to lend me money and for no good reason refused to go through with their promise.

(B) **BELIEFS ABOUT YOUR ACTIVATING EXPERIENCES**

(rB) **rational Beliefs** (your wants or desires)

How unfortunate that they backed out!
I don't like their behavior.
I wish they had kept their promise.
How annoying and irritating!
I'll try to get the money elsewhere, but will find that quite a hassle.

(iB) **irrational Beliefs**

1. How awful for them to act that way!
2. I can't stand their unfairness!
3. They should have lent me the money!
4. Because they didn't do what they should, that makes them rotten people!
5. People will always treat me unfairly like this! How horrible!

(C) **CONSEQUENCES OF YOUR BELIEFS ABOUT ACTIVATING EXPERIENCES**

(deC) **desirable emotional Consequences** (appropriate bad feelings)

Frustration and annoyance. Sorrow and regret
Determination to help change parents' attitudes

(dbC) **desirable behavioral Consequences** (desirable behavior)

Continued attempts to persuade parents to change
Attempts to get the money in other ways

(ueC) **undesirable emotional Consequences** (inappropriate feelings)

I felt angry: I hated my parents. I felt depressed.

(ubC) **undesirable behavioral Consequences** (undesirable behaviors)

I screamed at my parents.
I refused to consider other ways of getting the money.
I pouted and sulked.

(D) **DISPUTING OR DEBATING YOUR IRRATIONAL BELIEFS**
(state this in the form of questions)

1. What makes it awful for them to act that way?
2. Why can't I stand their unfairness?
3. What evidence exists that they should have lent me the money?
4. How does their unfair treatment of me make them rotten people?
5. How do I know people will always treat me unfairly? And must I view it as horrible if they do?

(E) **EFFECTS OF DISPUTING OR DEBATING YOUR IRRATIONAL BELIEFS**

(cE) **cognitive Effects of disputing** (similar to rational beliefs)

1. Nothing makes it awful, but only inconvenient for them to act that way.
2. I can stand their unfairness; though I'll never like it.
3. I can find no evidence that they should have kept their promise to me though I would have found it very nice if they did.
4. Their unfairness doesn't make them rotten people, but merely people who have acted rottenly to me in this respect.
5. People won't always treat me unfairly—though they may often do so. And if they do, tough! It won't kill me!

(eE) **emotional Effects** (appropriate feelings)

I felt irritated and annoyed but not angry.
I felt very disappointed and concerned but not depressed.
I still basically loved my parents but hated some of their traits.
I felt determined to find other ways of raising the money.

(bE) **behavioral Effects** (desirable behaviors)

I spoke to my parents about my feelings of disappointment and irritation.
I attempted to persuade them to change.
I investigated other means of raising money.

RATIONAL SELF HELP FORM

Institute for Rational-Emotive Therapy 45 East 65th Street, New York 10021

INSTRUCTIONS: Please fill out the **ueC** section (undesirable emotional Consequences) and the **ubC** section (undesirable behavioral Consequences) **first.** Then fill out all the A-B-C-D-E's. PLEASE PRINT LEGIBLY. BE BRIEF!

(A) **ACTIVATING EXPERIENCES (OR EVENTS)**

(B) **BELIEFS ABOUT YOUR ACTIVATING EXPERIENCES**

(rB) rational Beliefs (your wants or desires)

(iB) irrational Beliefs (your demands or commands)

(C) **CONSEQUENCES OF YOUR BELIEFS ABOUT ACTIVATING EXPERIENCES**

(deC) desirable emotional Consequences (appropriate bad feelings)

(dbC) desirable behavioral Consequences (desirable behaviors)

(ueC) undesirable emotional Consequences (inappropriate feelings)

(ubC) undesirable behavioral Consequences (undesirable behaviors)

(D) **DISPUTING OR DEBATING YOUR IRRATIONAL BELIEFS**
(State this in the form of questions)

(E) **EFFECTS OF DISPUTING OR DEBATING YOUR IRRATIONAL BELIEFS**

(cE) cognitive Effects of disputing (similar to rational beliefs)

(eE) emotional Effects (appropriate feelings)

(bE) behavioral Effects (desirable behaviors)

1. FOLLOW-UP. What new GOALS would I now like to work on? ....
    ....
    ....
    ....

What specific ACTIONS would I now like to take?...
    ....
    ....

2. How soon after feeling or noting your undesirable emotional CONSEQUENCES (ueC's) or your undesirable behavorial CONSEQUENCES (ubC's) of your irrational BELIEFS (iB's) did you look for these iB's and DISPUTE them?................
    ....
    ....

How vigorously did you dispute them? ....
    ....

If you didn't dispute them, why did you not do so?...
    ....

3. Specific HOMEWORK ASSIGNMENT(S) given you by your therapist, your group or yourself: ....
    ....
    ....

4. What did you actually do to carry out the assignment(s)? ....
    ....

5. How many times have you actually worked at your homework assignments during the past week?..........................
    ....

6. How many times have you actually worked at DISPUTING your irrational BELIEFS during the past week?...............
    ....

7. Things you would now like to discuss with your therapist or group ....
    ....
    ....

as most other women are." On one occasion, for example, she filled out a DIBS sheet on this *must*urbatory idea along the following lines:

Question 1: What irrational Beliefs do I want to Dispute and surrender?
Answer: I must be as effective and sexually fulfilled as most other women are.
Question 2: Can I rationally support this belief?
Answer: No, I don't think I can support it.
Question 3: What evidence exists of the truth of this belief?
Answers:

a. No evidence exists, for I don't control the universe. The fact that I would like to be as effective and as sexually fulfilled as most other women doesn't mean that I *have* to be.
b. If I really *had to be* as sexually fulfilled as other women are, then I *would* be. But since often I am not, it is clear that I don't *have to* be.
c. When I say that I *must* be as sexually adept as other women, what I am really saying is that there have to be conditions that will make me that sexy. But the conditions that *do* exist in my life right now for biological, psychological, or other reasons do *not* make me that sexually adept. Under the *present* conditions, therefore, I really *must* be the way I am—which is proof that there is, at the same time, no reason why I *must* simultaneously be the opposite of what I am!"
d. The statement "I must be as effective and sexually fulfilled as most other women are" really means that I must not have some serious deficiencies. And if this is really one of them, then it is!
e. By my belief that I must be as good sexually as most other women are, I really mean that, because I *want* to be, I *must* be. But that is an utter non sequitur! No matter how much I want something, there is no reason why I *must* get my want fulfilled. What grandiosity on my part to *think* that I must!

Question 4: What evidence exists of the falseness of my belief that I must be as orgasmic as other women are?
Answer: The belief clearly has some false elements in it, because, if I did *have to* achieve orgasm as well as other women do, I would simply achieve it. The fact that I never have achieved it yet and that I may never do so for the rest of my life is pretty good proof that I don't *have to* achieve it.
Question 5: What are the worst possible things that could actually happen to me if I never achieved the orgasm that I think I must achieve?
Answers:

a. I would lose pleasure—which I certainly can afford to lose, since I haven't had it all these years and yet I am still alive and kicking.
b. I could possibly lose my husband, who might leave me because of his displeasure in my not achieving any degree of climax. It's most unlikely that he would leave me for this reason, since he really doesn't seem to care that much whether or not I come to climax. But I could possibly lose him. Even then, I wouldn't lose *myself*—just him. And there are probably other satisfactory males in the world who would accept me with my orgasmic deficiency.

c. I would continue to be frustrated by coming so close to orgasm and never quite reaching it. Well, that would be highly annoying, particularly if it continued forever. But I could live and still be a happy person even under these annoying conditions.

d. It is possible that all the men I would really like during my life would take issue with my orgasmic deficiency and leave me after a while because of it. If this occurred, the worst that would happen is that I would be without a steady partner. Well, even *that* wouldn't be the end of the world—though I would damn well not like it!

e. My husband and other possible men in my life might not leave me for not being orgasmic, but they could keep hassling and criticizing me for this failing. All right, so they might! If so, I could teach myself not to take them too seriously or at least not down myself because of their criticism. Then I would find their hassles and criticism annoying, but only annoying and not devastating.

Question 5: What good things could happen or could I make happen if I never achieved the heights of orgasm that I think I must achieve?

Answers:

a. I could relax and let myself enjoy the kind of sex I am having, even though I never reached a climax through it.

b. I could focus on enjoying my husband's pleasure in sex and in achieving orgasm and get closer to him just because I focused on this in spite of my own disappointing performance.

c. I could give up on achieving the acme of sex fulfillment and see what other kinds of pleasure I could have in life.

d. I could devote myself more to love than to sex and find satisfactions there that I might never be able to achieve in the sex arena.

e. I could use this continuing frustration as a challenge to show myself that I can still accept myself, work at not resenting my husband and other women who do have more sex pleasure, and raise my level of frustration tolerance so that I would accept this real loss without whining about it and acting as if nothing else were of any value in life.

By using the special technique of Disputing Irrational Beliefs (DIBS), Myra finally gave up the idea that she *had* to have as much sex pleasure as most other women seem to have. Once she had done that, she was in a much better position to actually work at obtaining more sexual satisfaction and trying to achieve a climax.

Imaging Methods

I used several imaging methods with Myra, especially rational-emotive imagery (REI), which is outlined later in this article. Masters and Johnson (1970) are not in favor of fantasy methods in sex therapy, because they believe that any kind of thinking is likely to get worriers into trouble. However, I have found for a great number of years that, if people with fast ejaculation train themselves to have less sexy thoughts and if people with slow ejaculation or with orgasmic difficulties train themselves to have more sexy thoughts, both can often improve their performances.

In Myra's case, I determined that she thought mostly of worrisome, anti-sexual things when she was having sex with her husband and had quite rarely highly exciting, sexy thoughts or fantasies. Therefore I encouraged her to use the kinds of fantasies outlined by Comfort (1972), Friday (1973), Ellis (1976b), Garrity (1969), Livingstone (1975), and other advocates of sexual imagery. I asked her what really aroused her sexually when she spontaneously got highly excited or when she deliberately tried to masturbate. She replied that she got much more aroused by thinking of herself dominating men than she did by any other kind of thought or imagery. So I had her practice fantasies in the course of which she had men do her bidding and particularly do what she would like them to do to turn her on—such as sucking her breasts for a long period of time, using their mouths and tongues on her genitals, and giving in immediately to any wish that she happened to have.

At first, she said that she could do this kind of sexual imagery only briefly, since she had great difficulty focusing on it and maintaining it in her mind. But by getting her to do it first for a minute or two each day and then gradually lengthening the amount of time, she was finally able to focus on it quite in-tently and to continue to do so for ten or more minutes at a time. This imagery resulted in her getting "really hot," as she put it. By doing it by herself and by using firm digital massage while masturbating her clitoral area while she was focusing on the imagery, she was finally able to get an occasional orgasm—the first ones she had ever achieved in her life. Later, as she continued to practice this kind of intense, prolonged imagery during masturbation, she was able to bring herself to climax fairly regularly. Still later, she was able to do so with her husband, while he manipulated her clitoral region in a firm manner similar to the way in which she did it herself. Finally, with the same kind of imagery, she occasionally was able to achieve orgasm, especially just before and during her menstrual periods, during actual penile-vaginal intercourse. At no time, however, was she able to achieve orgasm without accompanying intense imagery. So it appeared that in her particular case only a combination of fantasy and firm clitoral manipulation would regularly bring her to climax.

Bibliotherapy

One of the main cognitive techniques used in RET is bibliotherapy. Clients are encouraged to read the basic RET self-help books, especially *A Guide to Successful Marriage* (Ellis & Harper, 1971; originally published, under the title *Creative Marriage,* 1961), *How to Live with—and without—Anger* (Ellis, 1977c), *Humanistic Psychotherapy: The Rational-Emotive Approach* (Ellis, 1973), and *A New Guide to Rational Living* (Ellis & Harper, 1975). Myra read these books, as well as the package of pamphlets that we give to all our clients at the Institute for Rational-Emotive Therapy. In addition, because she had specific sex prob-lems, she was urged to read *The Sensuous Person* (Ellis, 1972b), *Sex and the Liberated Man* (Ellis, 1976b), and *The Art and Science of Love* (Ellis, 1965). She found almost all this material helpful and thought that she made some of her best therapeutic advances as a result of reading it.

Using RET with Others

Another of RET's favorite cognitive techniques is that of showing clients how to employ rational-emotive therapy with others, thus helping them use it more effectively with themselves. As John Dewey (1922/1930) pointed out many years ago, we learn by doing and by teaching others. Therefore, I showed Myra how to use the principles of RET with some of her friends and associates, particularly with her husband. For he, too, when she first came to therapy, had distinct feelings of sexual inadequacy, particularly in regard to his not being able to bring her to orgasm. So I showed her how to help him with his own problems. She was to make him see that his Activating Experience at point A (that is, his inability to bring her to orgasm) did not cause his emotional Consequence at point C (that is, his feelings of shame about this lack of ability). Instead, he kept having irrational Beliefs (iB's) at point B that led him to feel inadequate about what was happening at A.

Myra became quite a good rational-emotive therapist with her husband. Through her talks with me (in which I supervised her therapy with him) and by getting him to read *A New Guide to Rational Living* (Ellis & Harper, 1975), she helped him to feel self-accepting despite his sex "failures" with her. As her husband began to improve considerably in this respect, she could see that RET actually worked and started to use it even more vigorously on herself. Her actively Disputing his irrational Beliefs, some of which were exactly the same as her own, also helped her with her personal Disputing. As she noted, with some surprise, during one of our sessions, "Even though he succeeds marvelously at his work as a dentist and wins the love of practically all his patients, I now see that he has the same deep-seated feelings of inadequacy as I have. How amazing! I always thought I downed myself about sex because I really haven't succeeded too well in anything else. But now I see that he, who has done so beautifully at work, at sports, and at almost everything he has attempted, also puts himself down about not giving me an orgasm. How silly! It really has helped me a great deal to understand this and to show him exactly what he is doing to castigate himself and how he need not do this."

Employing New Self-Statements

Although the elegant form of RET usually involves active Disputing of irrational Beliefs and the use of logico-empirical analysis, in its less elegant form RET also uses the teaching of new and more rational self-statements to replace the old, irrational ones. Thus, after working on discovering a good many of her *shoulds* and *musts* (as noted above), Myra was encouraged to replace them with nonabsolutistic preferences and wishes. For several weeks she carried around 3x5 cards with her on which she had written such statements as "I don't *have* to achieve orgasm but still definitely would *like* to do so," "I don't *need* what I *want*," and "I'd better give up all my *shoulds.*" She would look at these cards several times each day and think about their messages until they began to sink into her head.

EMOTIVE TECHNIQUES OF RET

With Myra, as well as with virtually all my clients, I employed a number of emotive-evocative methods. These are some of the methods I employed with her.

Unconditional Acceptance

I think I can safely say that at almost all times, in the course of our several months of once-a-week individual- and once-a-week group-therapy sessions, I fully accepted Myra with all her emotional and other disabilities. Not that this was, at times, easy! For Myra at first whined and wailed considerably about her lack of orgasm and her general incompetence. Nothing I said to try to show her that she also had a good many competencies would convince her that she was anything but completely worthless. No matter what evidence I marshaled to show her that she had done beautifully in school, had a good many friends, and was quite talented as a sculptor, she insisted that she *really* was an utter slob and that I and others were taken in by her superficial charm. She kept insisting that nothing would do her any good, including the therapy sessions with me, and that everything was hopeless.

Nonetheless, I accepted her with her negativism and showed her in several ways that I could accept *her* in spite of *it*. Even when she kept calling our office trying to get through to me on the phone, when I had specifically told her that she was to do so only in case of a real emergency, I was able to point out her poor behavior but to refrain from putting her down for it. Not that I wasn't tempted, on several occasions, to really tell her off. But, with the use of RET, I kept reminding myself that *she* was not a louse even though her behavior was quite lousy. And I actually got myself to believe this and to convey my belief to her!

Role Playing

Role playing, as originally outlined by Moreno (1934) and later employed by Perls (1969), is frequently used as an emotive method in RET but not necessarily in the abreactive form that other schools of therapy use it. In Myra's case, I used role playing, in individual as well as group sessions, to show her how she could ask her husband to engage in the kinds of sex practices she wanted. Thus, in the individual sessions, I sometimes played her husband and got her to ask me what she wanted me to do sexually. In the group sessions, I got other members of the group to act as her husband and to show a certain degree of stubbornness and little understanding as she asked them to do some of the things that she wanted him to do. She was to persist, against this kind of odds, in asking (but not demanding!) what she wanted.

Another of Myra's problems was her inability to be assertive with her mother-in-law and to refuse to comply with some of her requests. So we had Myra, during group sessions, role-play some scenes with a female member of the group acting as her mother-in-law. These scenes related to Myra refusing at times to visit with her mother-in-law, not engaging in long phone conversations with her, and doing things she normally found difficult to be firm about.

At other times I or other male members of the group would deliberately criticize Myra, as she said her husband tended to do. We would encourage her to overreact at first, in a hurt manner, to this kind of criticism, then to see what she was telling herself, and finally to change her self-downing irrational Beliefs, so that she could then react to his criticism without feeling hurt.

Modeling

The relationship between client and therapist is an element of the RET therapeutic process, as it is in virtually all forms of therapy. By seeing the therapist steadily, clients do relate to him or her, both in actual sessions and in their own heads, and are affected by this relating process. In my interaction with Myra, I liked her to a certain degree and probably showed this liking to her; but I didn't see her as my particular cup of tea, so I didn't feel or act very warmly toward her. But in the course of our relationship, I did show her—by being direct, forthright, outspoken, and unafraid of criticism (by her and by the members of a therapeutic group of which she became a member)—that I could fairly consistently follow some of the main principles of RET myself and that I was willing to be myself and take the consequences of my actions. A similar approach was taken by a few members of her therapeutic group, especially those who had been in it a while and were using RET principles to good effect. These group members were able to show Myra, by fully accepting her (even when she acted very stupidly) and by being open and authentic in the group, that it is quite possible for people to be themselves and to not put themselves down for so being.

As Myra's case shows, a good deal of the relationship aspect of RET is emotive modeling. This is probably true of all therapy but is especially true of RET practice. RET practitioners are able to be themselves and act as they really want to act for the very reason that they are working to give up their dire *needs* (but not their desires) for others' approval. In Myra's case, I and some other members of her therapy group did some fairly good emotive modeling for her. I think that, if Myra became able to be herself more, with her husband as well as with other intimate associates in her life, it was in part because we were able to be ourselves with her.

Passionate Self-Statements

As I indicated in my discussion on cognitive methods of RET, I helped Myra to change some of her negative statements about herself, others, and the world to more positive and more constructive statements. But I also encouraged her, on several occasions, to voice these new statements to herself vigorously and powerfully—or emotively. As I have noted for a good many years now, what we call "emotions" or "feelings" largely consist of, or are at least derived from, quite vehement and dramatic self-verbalizations. If I say to myself "I like to be with Josephine. It's really very nice talking with her or going to bed with her," I tend to feel warm, friendly, and cooperative toward Josephine. But if I say to myself "It's fabulously great to be with Josephine! I get more out of talking with her and going to bed with her than I could ever possibly get with any other woman in the world!" I emphasize and dramatize my beliefs about Josephine. Thus, I can make myself fall violently in love with her and even consider quite seriously a life-long relationship.

In Myra's case, when I first saw her for therapy she was powerfully holding on to her self-damning and discomfort-anxiety attitudes. So I gave her the homework assignments of frequently telling herself, in a highly vigorous and repetitive manner, things like: "I *don't* have to get an orgasm. I definitely *can* be a satisfied and happily married woman even if I never do!" "I damned well *can* stand the loss of sexual pleasure. I'll never like it, but I can very definitely *lump* it!" "Granted that it's hard for me to work at enjoying sex more, while many other women enjoy it easily. So it's hard! It's going to be much harder if I *don't* work at it!" By making these kinds of passionate and strong statements to herself very often and by forcing herself to make them to others (to me, to the other group members, and to her husband), Myra came to really believe in them. And, as she became more and more convinced of their truth, she believed less and less in the nutty, irrational Beliefs (iB's) with which she came to therapy.

Rational-Emotive Imagery

I have been using rational-emotive imagery (REI) with my clients ever since I learned it from Maxie C. Maultsby's (1971) original formulations. Maultsby normally uses it in conjunction with rational self-analysis, with Disputing of irrational Beliefs, and with techniques to help people replace their negative self-statements with positive ones. I use it, however, somewhat differently (Maultsby & Ellis, 1974). To illustrate my technique, here is a typical example of rational-emotive imagery as I once employed it with Myra.

"Close your eyes" I told her during one of our early individual sessions. "Imagine that you are having sex with your husband, that you are really quite horny, and that you would like very much to finish it off by having an orgasm. But, no matter how hard you try, no matter what you do and what you think about in your head to help yourself come to orgasm, nothing works. You get highly aroused, and you get almost to the top; but you keep fizzling out. And, after trying for half an hour or so, thoroughly exhausting yourself in the process, your husband indicates that he's had enough and shows a good deal of disappointment in your not being able to come to climax. You're highly frustrated and exhausted. He's rather critical and comments that he thinks that you'll probably never come to orgasm and that that's really pretty bad. Now—can you really imagine this kind of scene happening? Intensely imagine and fantasize it until you see it very clearly."

Myra at first resisted imagining this scene, since she obviously knew that it would cause her a great deal of pain. But I encouraged her to persist, and she soon said that she could see the scene clearly.

"All right" I said. "Now that you're imagining, and very vividly, this scene in which you want to get an orgasm, you're really horny, but you just can't in any way reach a climax no matter how hard you try, how do you honestly feel in your gut? Picture your failing to get what you want. See it very intensely. And picture your husband's being very disappointed in you. Now —how do you honestly feel?"

"Very ashamed" Myra replied. "Ashamed and—yes—depressed."

"All right. Get in touch with your shame and depression. Let yourself really feel these feelings. Get right with them. Really experience them. Are you fully in touch with them? Are you truly feeling them?"

"Yes" said Myra wincing. And she looked really ashamed and depressed.

"Fine! Now keep the same intense image in your head: you are still trying to get an orgasm and are failing miserably, and your husband is still keenly disappointed in you. Keep that exact same image. Don't change it. And let yourself, as you now focus on that same picture in your head, feel *only* disappointed, *only* sorrowful about your sex failure and your husband's disappointment. No shame, no depression now! Only keen disappointment and sorrow. But no shame! No depression! Now, let's see you do that."

At first Myra said that she couldn't change her feelings. She kept feeling ashamed and depressed and thought that she couldn't change to disappointment and sorrow alone, without shame and depression.

"Don't give up" I said. "You can change them. We can all change our feelings if we work at it. Now make yourself feel disappointed and sorrowful but *not* ashamed and depressed. You can do it!"

Myra obviously tried hard to change her feelings, and soon she was able to do so. Virtually all people, I find, can make themselves feel almost any way they want to feel—at least for a few seconds or a few minutes. I have tried REI on literally hundreds of clients, often during public demonstrations. And only about 2% say that they are unable to change their inappropriate feelings (such as despair, depression, anxiety, hostility, and feelings of worthlessness) to appropriate feelings (such as sorrow, regret, disappointment, and annoyance). And even these few, when I give them the homework assignment of continuing to work on changing their feelings while imagining something "disastrous" happening to them, can later do so. Anyway, Myra was soon able to feel only disappointed and sorrowful.

"All right, fine!" I said. "*How* did you change your feelings? What did you do to change them?"

She thought for a moment. "I changed them by saying to myself, 'OK, so I failed. And he is very disappointed in me for failing. That's just what I don't want. But it won't kill me. If I *never* succeed in having an orgasm, it still won't kill me. It's bad, yes. I really don't like it. But I can take it. The world won't come to an end!'"

"Fine!" I said. "That's a good method. As you see, you changed one of your basic views, one of your fundamental cognitions. That's what I invariably find: when people change their feelings, as you just did, they do so by changing some of their main ideas, their chief irrational Beliefs. So you just did this and did it quite well. What I want you to do now is work for at least five or ten minutes a day on the same thing you just did. Do it every single day for the next month or so. Use rational-emotive imagery to first imagine one of the worst things that could happen to you sexually. Imagine your failing to reach an orgasm and your husband being very disappointed in you. Let yourself intensely see this in your mind's eye. And let yourself feel, as you just did, ashamed and depressed.

"Then change your feelings—again, as you just did—by changing one of your major cognitions into a new, sensible idea. For example, 'I really don't like what is happening. But I can take it. The world won't come to an end!' Do what you just did, every day for at least five or ten minutes. And use the kind of thinking you just did—and other thoughts that will keep occurring to you as you keep doing this daily. Use whatever thoughts work to help you change your inappropriate emotions of shame and depression to the appropriate emotions of disappointment and sorrow. And keep doing this, every single day—including Saturdays and Sundays!—until you easily and automatically begin to feel disappointed and regretful, instead of ashamed and depressed, whenever you think of this 'gruesome' image. Do you understand what you are to do for your homework assignment with rational-emotive imagery?"

"Yes, I think so. I'm to imagine the worst about my sex failure, let myself feel horrified about it, and then change my feelings to disappointment and regret. Change them just as I did now—or in some other ways that will occur to me, as you said they would."

"Right! Do just that. And you'll see, as you do it, that you will start *practicing* the new, appropriate feelings of concern and sorrow but not of shame and depression. For, right now, you are doing exactly the opposite. Whenever you think about failing sexually or you actually fail, you are practicing thinking the wrong thoughts and feeling the inappropriate feelings of shame and depression. For the next 30 days or so, you are to use REI to practice imagining the worst, and you are to practice thinking sensible and rational thoughts and feeling appropriate feelings. Then, a month or so from now, you will have had this suitable practice, and, whenever thoughts of failing sexually come to your mind, you will tend spontaneously and automatically to feel sorry and regretful rather than ashamed and depressed. Do you see?"

"Yes. I think I see. It won't be easy, but I think I can do it."

"No, it won't be easy, because you now easily and 'naturally' do the opposite; that is, you practice making yourself needlessly upset. So it will be hard, at first, for you to practice imagining the worst and *not* upsetting yourself. But you did it just now, here, and you can do it any time you want, by yourself. Do you think, however, that you actually *will* do it—do this rational-emotive imagery, for five or ten minutes every day, until you make yourself feel first inappropriately depressed and ashamed and then appropriately sorry and disappointed? Will you persist at it, every day, even though it is hard and you want to avoid doing it?"

"I think I will. I really want to get over my shame and depression at failing sexually. So I think I will."

"Fine! But, if you start avoiding doing the REI, you can use operant conditioning or self-management principles to encourage yourself to do it. Do you know how to use them?"

"Vaguely."

"All right. To use self-management principles, all you do is reward yourself every day that you do the rational-emotive imagery for at least five to ten minutes and change your feelings while doing it. You may also penalize yourself every day that you fail to do it. For example, what do you like to do that you tend to do every day of the week? Can you think of some activity that you really like?"

"Uh. Something I do almost every day?"

"Yes, something you really enjoy and therefore keep doing almost every day."

"Well—listening to music, I guess."

"You listen to music just about every day?"

"Yes, unless there's really no time for it. But I try to listen to the radio or my record collection for an hour or more every day."

"Good. If, starting tomorrow, you do five to ten minutes of rational-emotive imagery and you do it early in the day, you can let yourself listen to music *later*. But, remember, no music until you do the REI! Make listening to the music contingent on doing the rational-emotive imagery. Understand?"

"Yes. No music till I finish five or ten minutes of REI."

"Right. And what do you hate to do—something you usually avoid doing because you dislike it so much?"

"Hate to do?"

"Yes, really hate and go out of your way to avoid."

"Mmm. I can't think of anything I hate that much."

"I'm sure you can! How about cleaning the toilet? Or talking for a while with someone you find very boring?"

"Oh, yes. You reminded me! Talking to my mother-in-law. I really hate that! We always have the same boring conversation about her health problems over and over again."

"OK. Let's use that. If tomorrow evening arrives and you still haven't done your five to ten minutes of REI, you then force yourself to call your mother-in-law, right then and there if it's not too late, or at the latest the very next day. And you speak to her and listen to her health problems for at least a half hour."

"A half hour!?"

"Yes, a half hour. But, remember: if you do the REI, you don't have to speak with her at all. Only if you *don't* do it! That way, your penalty of talking with her will encourage you to do your REI."

"It certainly will! Oh, I'll do the REI all right—at least, under those conditions!"

"Fine. So, if you do the REI regularly every day, you don't have to give up any listening to music and you don't have to speak with your mother-in-law. But if you don't do it, use the reinforcement and use the penalty. You'll see how they'll help you do it!"

"I'm sure they will!"

Actually, Myra did the rational-emotive imagery every day for the next month without having to deprive herself of any music or even once call her mother-in-law. But other people who are not as disciplined do require the contingent reinforcements and penalties to help them do their homework assignments steadily.

Within two weeks of starting to do REI regularly, Myra reported to me and to her therapy group that she could easily think of herself failing sexually and imagine her husband being keenly disappointed in her, without feeling ashamed or self-downing. Almost always now, and quite automatically, she felt just sorry and disappointed. She thought that REI was one of the best RET techniques that she had employed to work on her shame and depression about her sex failures.

Shame-Attacking Exercises

I realized, a number of years ago, that shame is the essence of many people's disturbances. These people are "afraid" to do many things, such as speak in public or take examinations, because they think that they *must* succeed and that it would be utterly "shameful" if they didn't and because they would then view themselves as rotten individuals. They also know that if they did, say, speak in public or take an examination with their present "fearful" or "shameful" feelings, they would suffer extreme discomfort. They want, at all costs, to avoid this discomfort and the subsequent additional feelings of "shame" that they would experience (because, presumably, everyone else is fairly comfortable, under similar conditions). So they treat these "shameful" experiences like the plague. Consequently, they never become familiar with them and view them with escalating discomfort. The result is that they have a "gruesome" time just contemplating these experiences—or, rather, nonexperiences.

I invented, at first for my rational marathon encounter groups and later for my regular therapy groups and individual clients, shame-attacking exercises. In the course of these exercises, the clients are assigned to do, usually in the form of homework, some "shameful," "humiliating," or "ridiculous" things and to make a real attempt to do them without feeling ashamed and to even regard them as adventures. Thus, they may wear "loud" clothing in public, yell out the stops on buses and trains, refuse to tip a waiter who has given them poor service, or ask someone for something that they normally would feel ashamed to ask for.

In Myra's case, we agreed that her first assignment would be to walk a banana down the street on a red leash on a bright sunny afternoon when many people were out strolling. Needless to say, she hesitated a great deal before carrying out her assignment. But, when she finally forced herself to do it, she was amazed at how practically all the people she met while walking the banana went out of their way to ignore her, looked the other way, and pretended that nothing unusual was going on. This was a good learning experience for Myra, because it showed her that others were just as ashamed of "unusual" things as she was. It also showed her that, once she got used to walking the banana down the street, she could actually enjoy and laugh at the experience.

She then was able to give herself the assignment of going into a sex shop and conspicuously asking about the different kinds of vibrators they sold. Finally, after getting used to the other shame-attacking exercises and desensitizing some of her anxieties by doing them, she was able to have several down-to-earth talks with her husband, to tell him some of the things she liked and didn't like sexually, and to arrange with him for a pattern of sex that included much more oral-genital relations and less penile-vaginal copulation.

Other Loosening-Up Exercises

Many emotive-evocative exercises are used in RET, especially in therapy and encounter groups. The aim of these exercises is to bring out material that ordinarily might not be disclosed in regular therapy sessions and to arrange for an *in vivo* desensitization process with several of the client's peers. In Myra's case, she was a member of one of my therapy groups for six months, and, in the course of this experience, she participated in a ten-hour marathon, which is part of the group process at the Institute for Rational-Emotive Therapy in New York. During her group activities, she did several risk-taking things (for example, sing one of her own songs to the group), disclosed some incidents in her life that she had never publicly voiced before (such as getting caught once for stealing at Woolworth's), forced herself to say ten good things about herself to the other group members, engaged in some mild physical contacts that at first seemed fearsome to her, and went through a number of other self-revealing and exciting exercises that helped bring out some of the things that she bothered herself about.

She got so much out of these experiences that she also arranged to participate in one of the 14-hour rational-encounter marathons held by the Institute. She participated with 15 other people, all of whom were complete strangers to her. The night she returned home from this marathon, she found that she was able to communicate with her husband on a much more open and honest level than she had ever been able to do before. This, combined with her other individual- and group-therapy experiences, helped her to form a much deeper and authentic relationship with him.

BEHAVIORAL TECHNIQUES OF RET

When I began to do RET in early 1955, I realized that verbal therapy alone can be exceptionally useful in helping people see exactly what they are doing to disturb themselves and how they can stop indoctrinating themselves with irrational Beliefs (iB's) that lead to neurotic Consequences (C's). But I also realized that some form of active homework assignments is almost always necessary before the person actually changes his or her thinking, emoting, and behaving. I probably saw this because, although behavior therapy at that time was almost unknown, I had read some of the early experiments of John B. Watson and his co-workers, which showed that *in vivo* desensitization can work very well with children and adults. I was also aware of the work of other pioneers in the field, such as Dunlap (1946), Herzberg (1945), and Salter (1949), who had actively sent clients out to do what they were afraid of doing in order to break their dysfunctional habits in practice as well as in theory.

The most important thing, however, was the fact that I entered the field of psychotherapy with a specialization in marriage and family counseling and in sex therapy. In my field, I found that it was virtually always necessary to supplement the therapy sessions with specific instructions to the clients with regard to what they were supposed to do with themselves and others in between sessions (Ellis, 1954). Largely as a result of my experience with using active-directive methods of therapy in the course of my marriage and family counseling and sex therapy, I almost completely abandoned my psychoanalytic training and practice and began to develop RET.

Following my own lead with the techniques I had originated for my clients with marital and sex problems, I incorporated behavioral assignments into RET. Also, as I had done in my earlier practice, I used largely *in vivo* behavioral methods rather than the imaginal desensitization techniques that many other behavioral therapists, such as Cautela (1966) and Wolpe (1958, 1973), tend to favor. This doesn't mean that RET *has to* include *in vivo* homework assignments, since its behavioral components can be carried out in many different ways. But a full course of RET treatment with a person presenting fairly serious problems would rarely be effectuated without the inclusion of at least some *in vivo* retraining procedures.

In Myra's case, as indicated above, she was given several assignments that included going out in public or relating with her husband in shame-attacking and self-disclosing ways, as well as the cognitive assignments of filling out the Self-Help Report Form. She was also given the imaging assignments mentioned earlier. And, in spite of the fact that when she became anxious and depressed about her poor sexual performance with her husband she tended to avoid sex with him and to plead various excuses (such as tiredness and headaches), she agreed to carry out the assignment of having intercourse with him at least twice a week. When, at one point during the therapy, she balked at visiting her mother-in-law with her husband, even though he asked her to do so only a few times a year, she then agreed to accompany her husband. Not only that—she agreed to talk with her mother-in-law for half an hour, instead of avoiding her as she usually did, in order to prove to herself that she could stand being with her and that it wasn't the most awful thing in the world to talk to her for a while. After she proved this to herself, she was able to sanely avoid having much contact with her mother-in-law, with whom she really had little in common, instead of avoiding her in a terrified and irrational fashion.

Operant Conditioning and Self-Management

RET often makes use of operant conditioning—Skinner's (1971) approach of having people reward themselves on a contingency basis only after they have performed certain onerous or disciplined tasks. As Premack (1965) has indicated, almost any relatively easy or enjoyable behavior can be used to reinforce a relatively hard or less enjoyable act that the individual wants to perform but has difficulty doing. Consequently, we frequently help our RET clients by showing them how they can use operant conditioning to do something they view as too difficult or fearsome—for example, writing a term paper, going for a job interview, or making a social overture to someone. All they have to do is allow themselves rewarding things—such as eating, reading, or listening to music —*after* they have done the "too difficult" or "fearsome" thing. And, as noted above, we also advise them, if they have trouble using reinforcements or rewards to help discipline themselves, to employ swift and distinctly painful penalties if they don't engage in those disciplines.

For example, Myra had a very good appetite but didn't gain weight easily, so she was able to use food as a reinforcer when she wanted to force herself to have sex with her husband, to do shame-attacking exercises, or to work at overcoming the horror of being with her mother-in-law. As a penalty for not disciplining herself in the desired manner, she would eat obnoxious foods or force herself to call her mother-in-law and to have a half-hour boring telephone conversation with her. She found—as do many of my clients—that, once she set these kinds of penalties for herself and was determined to use them if she avoided certain unpleasant tasks, she almost always did the tasks and tended to have little trouble doing them.

Relaxation Methods

Relaxation methods usually take the form of physically relaxing one's muscles, as in Jacobsen's (1942) progressive-relaxation method. Since these techniques involve activity, they are usually classified as behavioral methods of therapy. Actually, they consist mainly of cognitive distraction. When we feel anxious about something, we make a point of focusing on muscular relaxation, on our breathing, on the sensations we are feeling in our bodies (Schultz & Luthe, 1959), or on yoga exercises. We concentrate so strongly on what we are doing and on the physical results we are getting that we become unable to focus, at the same time, on how badly things are going for us and how awful it is that they are going so badly.

In other words, relaxation methods involve powerful cognition as well as physical activity. They are healthfully distracting when we want to temporarily stop worrying and concentrate, instead, on some other aspect of life. Various types of mental distraction—like meditation, thought stopping, and positive thinking—are also highly distracting and often interrupt our worrisome obsessiveness. These methods, therefore, are very compatible with RET and are often recommended to rational-emotive clients. Personally, however, when I show my clients how to relax or how to use other distracting methods, I let them know that these methods are normally only palliatives. They do away with anxiety and low frustration tolerance temporarily—wash them out of the mind, so to speak, for the nonce. But, since these methods are not philosophic or Disputing ways of undermining irrational Beliefs, the Beliefs will almost always return later to plague the disturbed individual. So I recommend to my clients that they by all means use relaxation methods but that they not delude themselves that these methods will elegantly solve their problems.

In Myra's case, she already had been practicing yoga for several years before she came to therapy, and she continued to use it, at times, for relaxation purposes. We discussed how she benefited from it, and she agreed that it gave her only temporary relief from her anxiety and self-damning. She would use it to relax herself after she had not achieved an orgasm and was putting herself down for it. But the self-damning, of course, later returned! After she began to use RET Disputing to give up her self-flagellation, she found the yoga no longer necessary but still highly relaxing when she was in a very stressful situation.

Skill Training

RET includes, as many therapies do today, a considerable amount of skill training. Such training is practically never done by itself but on the foundation of anti*must*urbational and antiawfulizing methodology. If people are merely taught skills—such as assertion training or sex-skills training—they can easily put them in the *wrong* philosophic network and convince themselves that they are worthwhile individuals *because* they perform these skills well.

This is what Myra tended to do at the beginning of therapy. I showed her, as I often do in RET-oriented sex therapy, that sex does *not* equal intercourse and that, even if she never had an orgasm during penile-vaginal copulation, it didn't very much matter, because she could still probably get an orgasm in various other ways (Ellis, 1954, 1965, 1976b, 1978b; Hite, 1976; Kinsey, Pomeroy, Martin, & Gebhard, 1953). I also explained to her that sex relations with her husband didn't always have to start in a climate of high arousal and desire on the part of both of them. If they decided to have sex when one of them was not particularly aroused but the other was, the unaroused partner might later become excited and wind up by having unusually good sex (Ellis, 1972b, 1976b). I also explained that from time to time it might be helpful if she had intercourse by assuming the surmounting position herself instead of letting her mate get on top of her, as they almost always did. In that manner, she would have greater freedom to rub her clitoral region against his pubic bone and might come closer to orgasm in the process.

Myra accepted these instructions and quickly began to put them to use, sometimes with excellent results. As noted earlier, she also started to practice intense sexual imagery while having sex with her husband. This kind of skill training led to greater heights of pleasure for both of them and, ultimately, to her own orgasm through masturbation and, occasionally, intercourse. The sex skills that she learned in therapy seemed to help her considerably and may well have been a prerequisite to her finally achieving orgasmic satisfaction. But, typically, at first she felt so pleased with herself for enjoying sex more and for reaching climax that she reported to a group therapy session, immediately after she had an unusually good time in bed with her husband, "I really made it that time! Now I can see that I'm just as good as any woman. Maybe I'm not the greatest sexpot in the world, but at least I'm perfectly normal sexually. So I can stop beating myself over the head about that!"

I and a few members of the group showed her, however, that some of her conclusions were false and dangerous. Perhaps she had proved, by using the sex skills she had learned in therapy, that she was perfectly normal sexually and that she could enjoy herself in bed as much as any normal woman could. But that didn't mean that she was a good person *because* of her newly discovered sexual ability. If this were so, she would presumably fall back into a state of "badness" and of renewed self-flagellation if she happened to lose her newly acquired sex skills. With the help of the group, Myra came to see this very important point and said she was glad that she was now able to make the distinction implied in it. "You're right!" she said to the group. "I am determined to accept myself, as a woman and as a person, even if I fail to make it sexually in the future. I don't want to see myself as 'good' because I function well in bed. I want to be able to accept myself unconditionally, whether or not my sex ability rises or falls."

In any event, RET does include a good amount of skill training in those instances in which the client lacks some social, assertion, marital, sexual, vocational, or other skill that he or she would like to have. Skill training helps the person to stop downing himself or herself for the deficiency and often helps the person work on A in the A-B-C's of RET so that he or she gains the desired skill. As usual, it is a behavioral technique within a highly cognitive framework.

TECHNIQUES AND APPROACHES AVOIDED OR MINIMIZED IN RET

As stated in various ways so far, RET is a comprehensive system of psychotherapy that uses a large variety of cognitive, emotive, and behavioral methods. But it doesn't do so merely because these methods often seem to work or because they are effective in helping certain clients rid themselves of unpleasant symptoms. Most of the time RET uses a variety of techniques on theoretical grounds—because RET is interested in people's surrendering their basic irrational Beliefs (iB's) and arriving at some radically new, much more rational and realistic, philosophy of life. Therefore, although RET is in some ways quite eclectic and multimodal, it also rests on a distinct theory of human behavior and of personality change. RET assumes that, if this theory is followed, the employment of different kinds of therapeutic techniques becomes highly efficient. The trouble with pure eclecticism and even with systematically applied multimodal procedures is that they may work in the long run but they may also be quite wasteful in terms of the therapist's time and the clients' time and money. In other words, they are often useful but uneconomic, while RET attempts to be both useful and economic.

Because RET is theoretically based and because it strives for effective therapy that will help the greatest number of individuals in the deepest possible way with a minimum of expenditure of time and energy on their and their therapists' part, RET usually avoids or minimizes several therapeutic techniques that are very popular with various other schools of therapy. Some of these techniques and approaches follow.

Lengthy Descriptions of Activating Experiences

Many clients like to engage in lengthy and detailed descriptions of their Activating Experiences. One reason is that often they enjoy doing so and wrongly believe that it will help them overcome their Consequences or symptoms. Another reason is that they have read about the presumably good results that have been achieved in therapy by encouraging people to spew out for months (or even for years!) the minute details of their lives. RET practitioners are not that interested in the details of what happened and in where and when it happened. Essentially, they are not too interested in past history. As a matter of fact, RET regards long-winded histories as irrelevant and sidetracking, for it sees this kind of narrative as having little or nothing to do with the client's present disturbances. Therefore, RET therapists encourage their clients to narrate their Activating Experiences in a relatively brief and nonobsessive manner.

Overemphasis on the Client's Emotional Consequences or Feelings

The RET practitioner usually starts the first therapy session by determining the client's disturbance or emotional Consequence (C), such as feelings of anxiety, depression, despair, hostility, or worthlessness. If the client is experiencing obnoxious or frustrating events and feels only displeased, sorry, regretful, or annoyed, RET assumes that there is really no serious emotional problem, that the client is reacting appropriately to the obnoxious conditions, and that psychotherapy is not actually indicated.

The therapist, therefore, makes some effort to determine what C is and to see whether it is a truly inappropriate feeling. Clients are not, however, encouraged to revel in their feelings or to describe them at great length—mainly to acknowledge what they feel and to describe their feelings succinctly. If the therapist believes that a client is denying or playing down his or her feelings, various dramatic-evocative techniques may be employed to bring such feelings to the surface and to have them acknowledged. But clients who greatly enjoy reveling in their feelings and describing them ad nauseam are stopped in their tracks and carefully and decidedly brought back to B—the Beliefs with which they are largely creating these feelings and by which they continue to maintain them. Where many other schools of therapy emphasize C and encourage an almost endless obsession with it, RET briefly starts with C but then puts a much greater emphasis on B, the Beliefs that underlie C.

Abreaction and Catharsis

Abreaction and catharsis are used to some degree in RET, since clients are often encouraged to disclose their "real" feelings and to fully acknowledge that they have them. But where some other schools of therapy—such as Reichian, primal, experiential, and Gestalt therapy—put a heavy emphasis on abreaction and catharsis, particularly on the releasing of feelings of hostility by clients, RET largely abjures this kind of emphasis. This is because a large amount of research by Bandura (1973), Berkowitz (1970), Geen, Stonner, and Hope (1975), and other investigators of hostility has shown that abreaction and catharsis are more likely to exacerbate than to reduce hostile feelings and, therefore, to do more harm than good.

These research results seem to back the RET thesis that, when people express their anger, either verbally or nonverbally and either directly or indirectly, they tend to reindoctrinate themselves with anger-creating ideas. An example is the irrational Belief (iB) that others *must* not act in the unkind or unfair ways in which they indubitably act and that they are *rotten bastards* for doing so. RET, therefore, tries to help clients to understand the philosophic sources of their anger and other self-defeating feelings and to eliminate these sources rather than concentrate on expressing, suppressing, or repressing the feelings. Instead of overfocusing on C, RET helps clients to get back to B and to surrender the iB's by which they create their dysfunctional C's.

Psychodynamic Interpretations and Techniques

RET minimizes or avoids altogether most of the main psychoanalytic and psychodynamic interpretations and techniques. These include free association, dream analysis, establishment of an intense transference relationship between therapist and client, explanation of the client's present symptoms in terms of past experiences, and disclosure and analysis of the so-called Oedipus complex. It views free association and dream analysis as largely wasteful procedures and replaces them with incisive probing and questioning about what is going on at A (present Activating Experiences), what clients are telling themselves about A at B (their Belief systems), and what disturbed feelings and behaviors they are getting at C (emotional and behavioral Consequences of their iB's).

RET attempts to give clients a considerable amount of empathy and understanding but generally avoids the kind of therapeutic warmth that helps make these clients more dependent than they are when they start therapy. It considers most explanations of present symptoms in terms of past "traumatic" events quite specious, misleading, and useless. It sees the so-called Oedipus complex as a minor, and usually rare, result of clients' dire need for approval and perfection. When males, for example, have an Oedipus complex, it is not because they lust after their mothers but because they have the irrational Belief (iB) that they *must* not have such incestuous feelings and *must* not be disapproved by others for having them. Instead of wasting time analyzing clients' so-called Oedipus complex, RET continually brings up, logically analyzes, and helps them surrender their dire love needs and their insistences that they *have to* follow some of the sex regulations of their culture.

Encounter-Movement Excesses

As noted previously, RET often uses a number of encounter exercises or emotive-evocative techniques for helping people open up and disclose their underlying feelings. But it places these exercises solidly within a philosophic or problem-solving context and does not make an excessive use of them just because clients and therapists alike are often fascinated by them and enjoy doing them. Thus, RET specializes in shame-attacking and risk-taking procedures in the course of individual- and group-therapy sessions and as homework assignments. The RET therapist does not merely give these assignments in their own right but includes a rational discussion of the assignments that helps clients see what they are doing and also encourages them to tell themselves to make such procedures "shameful" and "risky." It also shows clients how they can think, emote, and behave differently to undo their "shameful" or "embarrassing" feelings.

SUMMARY

In looking over the cognitive, emotive, and behavioral methods that are commonly employed in RET, as well as some of the popular therapeutic procedures that RET minimizes or avoids, we can see that rational-emotive therapists tend to emphasize a fairly rapid-fire, active-directive, persuasive-philosophic approach to psychological treatment. They continually challenge clients to validate their observations and ideas and show them how to do this kind of challenging or Disputing themselves. RET therapists logically parse some of the fundamental irrational Beliefs (iB's) that clients hold and demonstrate how and why these do not lead to desirable emotional and behavioral results. They also reduce some irrational Beliefs to absurdity, often in a highly humorous way. They teach clients how to think scientifically, so that they can subsequently incisively observe, logically parse, and effectively annihilate new self-defeating ideas and behaviors that they may experience in the future.

RET acknowledges that there are many kinds of psychological treatment and a number of techniques under each treatment modality. But an efficient system—such as RET strives to be—aims to save time and effort on the part of both therapists and client; to help clients zero in on their major problems and start working to ameliorate them in a reasonably short period of time; to be effective with a large number of different kinds of clients; to offer an "elegant" or "deep" solution that deals with basic difficulties and encourages clients to continue the therapeutic process by themselves long after the sessions with the therapist have ended; and to produce relatively long-lasting results.

On most of these counts some amount of clinical and experimental evidence now exists that RET works as well as or better than other commonly used therapeutic procedures (DiGiuseppe, Miller, & Trexler, 1977; Ellis & Grieger, 1977; Ellis & Harper, 1975; Lembo, 1976; Morris & Kanitz, 1975; Murphy & Simon, in press). If RET does turn out to be an unusually effective means of therapy, this will probably be because of the depth and hardheadedness of its philosophic position. I am referring to the fact that it zeroes in on and combats absolutistic, dogmatic, and superstitious thinking more intensively than do other systems of therapy. Also, it is designed to be realistic and unindulgent, and it strives, incisively and determinedly, to get to the core of and to vigorously and actively undermine the childish demandingness that seems to be the main element of serious emotional disturbance.

REFERENCES

Bandura, A. *Aggression: A social learning analysis.* Englewood Cliffs, N.J.: Prentice-Hall, 1973.

Berkowitz, L. Experimental investigations of hostility catharsis. *Journal of Consulting and Clinical Psychology,* 1970, *35,* 1–7.

Cautela, J. R. Treatment of compulsive behavior by covert sensitization. *Psychological Record,* 1966, *16,* 33–41.

Comfort, A. *The joy of sex.* New York: Crown, 1972.

Dewey, J. *Human nature and conduct.* New York: Modern Library, 1930. (Originally published, 1922.)

DiGiuseppe, R. A., Miller, J., & Trexler, D. A review of rational-emotive psychotherapy outcome studies. *The Counseling Psychologist.* 1977, 7(1), 64–72.

Dunlap, K. *Personal adjustment.* New York: McGraw-Hill, 1946.

Edelstein, M. The ABC's of rational-emotive therapy: Pitfalls in going from D to E. *Rational Living,* 1976, *11*(1), 28–30.

Ellis, A. *The American sexual tragedy.* New York: Twayne, 1954. (Revised edition: New York, Lyle Stuart & Grove Press, 1962.)

Ellis, A. *How to live a "neurotic."* New York: Crown, 1957. (a)

Ellis, A. Outcome of employing three techniques of psychotherapy. *Journal of Clinical Psychology,* 1957, *13,* 350–354. (b)

Ellis, A. *Reason and emotion in psychotherapy.* New York: Lyle Stuart, 1962. (Also, New York: Citadel, 1977.)

Ellis, A. *The art and science of love* (revised ed.). New York: Lyle Stuart and Bantam Books, 1965.

Ellis, A. *Growth through reason.* Palo Alto: Science and Behavior Books, 1971. (Also, Hollywood, Calif.: Wilshire Books, 1971.)

Ellis, A. *Executive leadership: A rational approach.* Secaucus, N.J.: Citadel Press, 1972. (a)
Ellis, A. *The sensuous person: Critique and corrections.* New York: Lyle Stuart and New American Library, 1972. (b)
Ellis, A. *Humanistic psychotherapy: The rational-emotive approach.* New York: Julian Press and McGraw-Hill Paperbacks, 1973.
Ellis, A. Experience and rationality: The making of a rational-emotive therapist. *Psychotherapy: Theory, Research and Practice,* 1974, *11,* 194–198.
Ellis, A. Healthy and unhealthy aggression. *Humanitas,* 1976, *12,* 239–254. (a)
Ellis, A. *Sex and the liberated man.* New York: Lyle Stuart, 1976. (b)
Ellis, A. Certification for sex therapists. In W. Gemme (Ed.), *Progress in sexology.* New York: Plenum, 1977. (a)
Ellis, A. *A garland of rational songs.* Songbook and tape cassette recording. New York: Institute for Rational Living, 1977. (b)
Ellis, A. *How to live with—and without—anger.* New York: Reader's Digest Press, 1977. (c)
Ellis, A. *Discomfort anxiety: A new cognitive-behavioral construct* (cassette recording). New York: BMA Audio Cassettes, 1978. (a)
Ellis, A. Rational-emotive therapy. In R. J. Corsini (Ed.), *Current psychotherapies* (2nd ed.). Itasca, Ill.: Peacock, 1978. (b)
Ellis, A., & Abrahms, E. *Brief psychotherapy in medical and health practice.* New York: Springer, 1978.
Ellis, A. *A comprehensive bibliography of articles and books on rational-emotive therapy and cognitive-behavior therapy.* New York: Institute for Rational Living, 1980.
Ellis, A., & Grieger, R. *Handbook of rational-emotive therapy.* New York: Springer, 1977.
Ellis, A., & Gullo, J. *Murder and assassination.* New York: Lyle Stuart, 1972.
Ellis, A., & Harper, R. A. *Creative marriage.* New York: Lyle Stuart, 1961. (Paperback edition, under the title *A guide to successful marriage.* Hollywood, Calif.: Wilshire Books, 1971.)
Ellis, A., & Harper, R. A. *A new guide to rational living.* Englewood Cliffs, N.J.: Prentice-Hall, 1975. (Also, Hollywood, Calif.: Wilshire Books, 1975.)
Frankl, V. E. *Man's search for meaning.* New York: Washington Square Press, 1966.
Friday, N. *My secret garden.* New York: Trident Press, 1973.
Friedman, M. *Rational behavior.* Columbia: University of South Carolina Press, 1975.
Fulmer, G. Equality, toleration and truth. *Rational Living,* 1975, *10*(1), 38–40.
Garrity, T. ("J"). *The sensuous woman.* New York: Lyle Stuart, 1969.
Geen, R. G., Stonner, D., & Hope, G. L. The facilitation of aggression: Evidence against the catharsis hypothesis. *Journal of Personality and Social Psychology,* 1975, *31,* 721–726.
Guinagh, B. Disputing clients' logical fallacies. *Rational Living,* 1976, *11*(2), 15–18.
Herzberg, A. *Active psychotherapy.* New York: Grune & Stratton, 1945.
Hite, S. *The Hite report.* New York: Macmillan, 1976.
Jacobsen, E. *You must relax.* New York: McGraw-Hill, 1942.
Kelly, G. *The psychology of personal constructs.* New York: Norton, 1955.
Kinsey, A. C., Pomeroy, W. B., Martin, C. M., & Gebhard, P. H. *Sexual behavior in the human female.* Philadelphia: Saunders, 1953.
Lazarus, A. A. *Behavior therapy and beyond.* New York: McGraw-Hill, 1971.
Lazarus, A. A. *Multimodal therapy.* New York: Springer, 1976.
Lembo, J. *The counseling process: A cognitive-behavioral approach.* New York: Libra, 1976.
Livingstone, C. (J. Aphrodite), *To turn you on.* New York: Simon & Schuster, 1975.
Mahoney, M. J. A critical analysis of rational-emotive theory and therapy. *The Counseling Psychologist,* 1977, 7(1), 44–46.
Masters, W. H., & Johnson, V. E. *Human sexual inadequacy.* Boston: Little, Brown, 1970.
Maultsby, M. C., Jr. *Handbook for rational self-counseling.* Madison, Wis.: Association for Rational Thinking, 1971.
Maultsby, M. C., Jr., & Ellis, A. *Technique for using rational-emotive imagery.* New York: Institute for Rational Living, 1974.

Meichenbaum, D. Dr. Ellis, please stand up. *The Counseling Psychologist,* 1977, 7(1), 43–44.

Moore, R. H. *Alienation in college students: A rational and semantic analysis.* Doctoral dissertation, Walden University, April 1977.

Moreno, J. L. *Who shall survive?* Washington, D.C.: Nervous and Mental Diseases Publishing Company, 1934.

Morris, K. T., & Kanitz, J. M. *Rational-emotive therapy.* Boston: Houghton-Mifflin, 1975.

Murphy, R., & Simon, W. *An annotated bibliography of research on rational-emotive therapy and cognitive-behavior therapy.* New York: Institute for Rational Living, in press.

Perls, F. S. *Gestalt therapy verbatim.* Lafayette, Calif.: Real People Press, 1969.

Phadke, K. M. *Bull fighting: A royal road to health and happiness.* Unpublished manuscript, Bombay, 1976.

Premack, D. Reinforcement theory. In D. Levine (Ed.), *Nebraska Symposium on Motivation.* Lincoln: University of Nebraska Press, 1965.

Salter, A. *Conditioned reflex therapy.* New York: Creative Age, 1949.

Schultz, J. H., & Luthe, W. *Autogenic training.* New York: Grune & Stratton, 1959.

Skinner, B. F. *Beyond freedom and dignity.* New York: Knopf, 1971.

Wolpe, J. *Psychotherapy by reciprocal inhibition.* Stanford, Calif.: Stanford University Press, 1958.

Wolpe, J. *The practice of behavior therapy.* New York: Pergamon Press, 1973.

RATIONAL-EMOTIVE THERAPY: RESEARCH AND CONCEPTUAL SUPPORT

2

Rational-Emotive Therapy: Research Data That Support the Clinical and Personality Hypotheses of RET and Other Modes of Cognitive-Behavior Therapy

ALBERT ELLIS

Institute for Rational-Emotive Therapy

ABSTRACT

This article examines 32 important clinical and personality hypotheses of rational-emotive therapy (RET) and other modes of cognitive-behavior therapy and lists a large number of research studies that provide empirical confirmation of these hypotheses. It concludes that (1) a vast amount of research data exists, most of which tends to confirm the major clinical and personality hypotheses of RET; (2) these data keep increasing by leaps and bounds; (3) RET hypotheses nicely lend themselves to experimental investigation and therefore encourage a considerable amount of research; (4) researchers have not yet tested some of

The author wishes to thank Linda Eckstein for her help in organizing and collating the material in this article.

the major RET formulations and could do so with profit to the fields of psychotherapy and personality theory.

No theory of psychotherapy stands up well without a good body of experimental evidence to support it; and although rational-emotive therapy (RET),
like many other theories of personality change, sounds fine, hangs together with
a good deal of logical consistency, and seems (on the basis of clinical and anecdotal evidence) to get favorable results, it does not merit much faith as a "good"
theory unless it has more rigorously obtained research evidence behind it. Fortunately, it has. For its main propositions seem stated in such a clear-cut, testable manner that an unusually large number of studies have appeared since I
systematically formulated them in the late 1950s and early 1960s (Ellis, 1958,
1962). And well over 90% of these studies have offered statistically confirming
evidence favoring RET hypotheses.

Outcome studies of rational-emotive therapy appear elsewhere, along with
experimental studies of many tests of irrationality derived from RET (see Di-
Giuseppe, Miller, & Trexler, 1977). I shall therefore omit these data and merely
note that they seem impressive. Researchers have tested RET procedures against
other therapies and against control groups in about 75 instances and have found
almost uniformly favorable results. Another 25 or so studies of rationality scales
derived from RET have also appeared; and, again, virtually all of them have
shown that the dozen basic irrational ideas that I first formulated in 1957 (Ellis,
1957b, 1958) significantly differentiate various kinds of emotionally disturbed
groups from control groups. So RET's clinical record, as measured by controlled
experiments, appears unusually good. As Smith and Glass (1977) have shown in
a review of hundreds of psychotherapy research experiments, RET proved second
only to systematic desensitization in this respect, with eight other leading types
of psychotherapy following behind these two. A notable record—especially considering that RET entered the field relatively late and that the populations in
the RET studies had more complicated and more typical emotional disorders
than the target symptoms of the SD studies—which often included atypical
"neurotic" reactions, such as fear of snakes.

I shall review a good many major clinical and personality hypotheses of
RET and the research studies that appear to support these hypotheses. In almost every instance, I found that well over 90% of the published studies supported the RET theory, while less than 10% gave equivocal or negative results.
Some of these negative findings stemmed from faulty methodology; others
pose questions for future research. Because I located so many confirmatory
researches and have only limited space in this review, I shall largely omit the
nonconfirmatory studies. I shall also concentrate on recent researches and cite
older ones mainly when they include pioneering or classic researches. Otherwise,
the present paper would go on endlessly.

The great bulk of the studies cited in this paper include experimental and
control groups, with a statistical analysis of obtained differences in the performances of these groups. A few do not comprise studies in their own right but

give important reviews of many other experimental studies. And a few consist of clinical studies of a number of individuals, with statistical differentiation of groups or subgroups but with no actual control group.

I shall try to state below, as clearly as I can, most of the major RET hypotheses; and I shall then cite the confirmatory studies under each hypothesis. Many other systems of psychotherapy, in addition to RET, also would tend to go along with many of these hypotheses—especially cognitive systems, such as those of Adler (1927, 1929), Berne (1961, 1964), Dubois (1907), Herzberg (1945), Kanfer (Kanfer & Phillips, 1970; Kanfer & Goldstein, 1975), Kelly (1955), Low (1952), Phillips (1956), Rotter (1954), Stekel (1950), and Thorne (1950, 1961). The modern systems of cognitive-behavior therapy, most of which employ RET or significantly overlap with it, would also tend to endorse most of these hypotheses (Beck, 1976; Goldfried & Davison, 1976; A. A. Lazarus, 1971, 1976; Mahoney, 1974; Meichenbaum, 1977). The present article therefore represents a review of the research literature that supports cognitive-behavior therapy in general as well as RET in particular. But it more particularly derives its hypotheses from RET theory and practice; and I have written it to show that this particular system of psychotherapy has immense—indeed, almost awesome—research backing. This does not mean that only RET hypotheses have empirical confirmation. Non-RET theories may have it too. But I only consider hypotheses specifically posited by RET (and sometimes endorsed by other therapeutic systems as well) in the present article.

A final introductory word. Although many of the studies cited originated with clinicians who specifically wanted to test RET or cognitive-behavior theories, most of them did not. They come from the psychological laboratories of literally hundreds of experimental, social, developmental, and other psychologists who have no particular stake in validating or disputing RET, who do not practice psychotherapy, and who often seem completely unaware of rational-emotive theory and who cite no references to it in their bibliographies. Though I have my own biases, of course, the fact that so many non-RET-oriented researchers have published data supporting many of the most important RET theories impressively substantiates the hypotheses I shall now proceed to list.

THE ABC THEORY OF RET

Hypothesis No. 1: Thinking Creates Emotion

Human thinking and emotion do not constitute two disparate or different processes but significantly overlap. Cognition represents a mediating operation between stimuli and responses. What we call emotions and behaviors do not stem merely from people's reactions to their environment but also from their thoughts, beliefs, and attitudes about that environment. In terms of the RET theory of emotion and personality, A (an Activating Event or Activating Experience) does not exclusively cause C (an emotional Consequence) in the gut.

B (people's Beliefs about A) more importantly and more directly contribute to (or "cause") C (Ellis, 1957a, 1957b, 1958, 1962).

This hypothesis seems central to the whole field of RET and cognitive-behavior therapy and has an enormous amount of research that solidly supports it. Pioneer researchers and theoreticians in the area include Bandura (1969, 1974), S. L. Bem (1967), Davitz (1969), Irwin (1971), Kagan (1972), Kelly (1955, 1969), Bannister (1971), Bannister and Mair (1968), Bannister and Fransella (1973), Kendler (1971), Kilty (1969), Langner (1966), A. A. Lazarus (1971, 1974, 1976), R. S. Lazarus (1966), R. S. Lazarus and Averill (1975), R. S. Lazarus, Averill, and Opton (1970), H. London and Nisbett (1974), Luria (1961), Luria and Yudovich (1959), Mandler (1975), Meichenbaum (1971, 1975c, 1977), Mischel (1968, 1976), Neisser (1966), Pavlov (1941), Rokeach (1960, 1968, 1973), Schachter (1965, 1966, 1971), Schachter and Singer (1962) and Zimbardo (1969). Almost innumerable studies and reviews of research have appeared that support the view that, in general, human emotion and behavior include cognitive mediation and for the most part have important cognitive origins. I list scores of these below under more specific headings. You may find additional general confirmation of this central RET theory in Bergin (1970), Bergin and Strupp (1970), Deci (1975), Guernette (1972), Jacobs and Sachs (1971), K. J. Kaplan (1972), Lewis, Wolman, and King (1971), Loveless and Brody (1974), Luce and Pepper (1971), Norman (1975), Poetter (1970), Rollins (1975), Russell and Brandsma (1974), Si (1973), Spivack and Shure (1974), Theisen (1973), Wardell and Royce (1975), Weimer and Palermo (1974), and Weiner (1974).

Hypothesis No. 2: Semantic Processes and Self-Statements

People invariably talk to themselves (and others), and the kinds of things they say to themselves, as well as the form in which they say these things, significantly affect their emotions and behavior and sometimes lead them to feel emotionally disturbed. Effective psychotherapy partly consists of helping them talk to themselves more precisely, empirically, rationally, and unabsolutistically.

Pioneers in the field of psychotherapy and allied disciplines who have espoused this hypothesis and worked to develop techniques of semantitherapy include Beier (1966), Blois (1963), Bois (1966, 1972), Bourland (1968, 1969), Chemodurow (1971), Ellis (1957a, 1958, 1962, 1971a, 1973c, 1977), Ellis and Harper (1975), Kelly (1955), Korzybski (1933), Mahoney (1974), Meichenbaum (1971, 1975c, 1977), Mosher (1966), Osgood (1971), Phillips (1956), and Velten (1968).

Studies that confirm the importance of semantic processes in human emotion and in psychotherapeutic change include those by Alperson (1975), Beilin, Lust, Sack, and Natt (1975), Boudewyns, Tanna, and Fleischman (1975), Davitz (1969), Early (1968), Hays and Waddell (1976), Kaplan (1970), Levinson, Davidson, Wolff, and Citron (1973), McGuigan (1970), O'Donnell and Brown (1973), Osgood (1971), Payne (1971), Perlman (1972), Rimm and Litvak

(1969), Rychlak (1973), Schill, Evans, Monroe, and Ramanaiah (1976), Staats (1975), Staats, Gross, Guay, and Carlson (1973), and Walton (1971).

Hypothesis No. 3: Mood States and Cognition

People's mood states significantly depend upon what they believe or tell themselves. When they tell themselves and believe in optimistic, hopeful, cheerful ideas, they tend to feel happy, elated, joyous, or serene; and when they tell themselves and believe in pessimistic, cynical, hopeless ideas and to make predictions about an unenjoyable future, they tend to feel sad, morose, miserable, and depressed. Effective therapy often includes helping clients to have optimistic and cheerful ideas and to surrender their unduly pessimistic views of the present and future.

This hypothesis about mood states represents an important subheading under the general idea of cognitions significantly contributing to emotions; and it also relates to the subjects of expectancy, positive thinking, and learned helplessness, discussed later in this article. As a hypothesis in its own right it mainly stems from the theorizing of the cognitive-behavior therapists and philosophers listed in the previous sections of this article and from my own particular theories of rational-emotive therapy (Ellis, 1957a, 1958, 1962, 1971a, 1973c, 1973d, 1973e, 1977; Ellis and Harper, 1975).

The pioneering study that presents data confirming this hypothesis consisted of Velten's (1968) investigation of one group of female college students who concentrated upon 60 self-referent statements intended to produce elation, a second group who concentrated on 60 statements intended to produce depressing moods, and a third group who concentrated on statements intended as neither self-referent nor pertaining to mood. Significant differences appeared in the moods of all three groups and "post-experimental questionnaire data strongly supported the conclusion that elation and depression treatments had indeed respectively induced elation and depression."

Velten's pioneering study has had several replications in various forms, just about all of which have confirmed his original findings. These include studies by Aderman (1972), Blue (1975), Coleman (1975), and Hale and Strickland (1976).

Hypothesis No. 4: Awareness, Insight, and Self-Monitoring

Humans have the ability not only to think (and generalize) but to think about their thinking and to think about thinking about their thinking. They almost invariably observe and cognize about their behavior, and by such observation and cognition they significantly affect or change this behavior. Whenever they feel emotionally disturbed (e.g., anxious, depressed, or hostile), they tend to perceive and think about their disturbance and thereby either make themselves more disturbed (e.g., anxious about their anxiety or depressed about their feelings of depression) or make themselves less disturbed. Awareness, insight, understanding, and self-monitoring, therefore, comprise cognitive processes that significantly affect behavior and behavior change. Psychotherapists have as one of their main functions the helping of their clients to increase their awareness of precisely what they do to disturb themselves and to use this awareness to change their dysfunctional behavior.

In various ways, important elements of this hypothesis exist in virtually all the major systems of psychotherapy—including those advocated by Adler (1927, 1929), Berne (1961, 1964), Ellis (1957b, 1958, 1962, 1973d), Freud (1965), Kelly (1955), Jung (1954), and Perls (1969). Even the presumably abreactive, nonverbal, or physically oriented systems of psychotherapy importantly use, whether consciously or unconsciously, highly cognitive awareness-related elements (Ellis, 1970, 1973c, 1974a, 1974b, 1974c; Raimy, 1975).

Clinical presentations showing that awareness or insight helps humans change their dysfunctional behavior abound in the professional literature, including the references cited in the previous paragraph. Controlled experimental studies indicating that when subjects get specifically aware of their cognitions (and other aspects of their behavior) they make greater changes or retain these changes in their emotions and behaviors more than when they have little or no specific awareness have appeared with increased frequency in recent years. Other studies show that various kinds of performances and emotions lead to significantly improved results when coding, cognitive rehearsal, and various other kinds of mental practice occur. Researches demonstrating the efficacy of awareness and cognitive rehearsal include those by Bandura and Jeffery (1973), Batson (1975), Cradler and Goodwin (1971), P. H. Friedman (1972), Geen, Rakosky, and Pigg (1972), J. G. Jones (1965), Muehleman (1972), O'Donnell and Brown (1973), Rokeach (1971), Schumsky (1972), Thorpe, Amatu, Blakey, and Burns (1975), Vargas and Adesso (1976), Vandell, Davis, and Clugston (1943), A. C. Wagner (1973), Wexler (1974a, 1974b), and Wortman (1975).

A somewhat related set of studies stems from the work on cognitive dissonance by Festinger (1957) and Heider (1946). This theory holds that humans have great trouble holding two dissonant ideas and that they have an innate and pronounced tendency to make adjustments when they do and to "resolve" this dissonance in some semisatisfactory manner. Literally scores of researches have attested at least to the partial validity of this hypothesis and have found that cognitive processes that reduce dissonance serve as a highly important factor in personality integration and disorder. Festinger (1957, 1962) has summarized some of the main literature, and some other relevant studies include those by Innes (1972), N. A. Rosen and Wyer (1972), and Zanna and Cooper (1974).

Another large series of studies of the effects of self-monitoring on psychotherapeutic and other behavioral change has also appeared in the behavior-therapy literature during the last decade. These studies almost uniformly tend to show that when people monitor their own behavior—e.g., simply record the number of cigarettes they consume or the amount of calories they eat every day—they frequently change their dysfunctional habits without employing any other kinds of reinforcements or penalties. The self-monitoring process and the other cognitions which go with it seem to provide them with sufficient intrinsic reinforcements or penalties. Similarly, studies have shown that self-monitoring frequently brings better therapeutic results than monitoring by outside observers and that self-monitoring methods, when added to other cognitive-behavioral techniques, increase the efficacy of these other techniques. Experimenters who have presented evidence in these connections include S. M. Johnson and White (1971), Kanfer (1970a, 1970b), Kazdin (1974), Mahoney, Moore, Wade, and Moura (1973), Mahoney, Moura, and Wade (1973), Pribram and McGuinness (1975), and Richards, McReynolds, Holt, and Sexton (1976).

Hypothesis No. 5: Imaging and Fantasy

People not only think about what happens to them in words, phrases, and sentences but do so in nonverbal ways, including images, fantasies, dreams, and other kinds of pictorial representations. Such images contain the same kind of cognitive mediating messages as do verbal self-statements, and these cognitions contribute significantly to their emotions and behaviors, to their emotional disturbances, and to their helping themselves change their emotions, behaviors, and disturbances.

Psychoanalytic writers have specially pioneered in proposing that images and fantasies have enormous influence over the emotions and behavior of most people (Freud, 1965). Many nonpsychoanalytic therapists, such as Assagioli (1965), have also emphasized fantasy in their work with clients. But as Singer (1972, 1974) points out in a most impressive review of the imagery literature, both the more orthodox behavior therapists—such as Cautela (1966a) and Wolpe (1958)—and the cognitive-behavior therapists—such as Bandura (1969), Beck (1970), B. M. Brown (1967), A. A. Lazarus (1971, 1976), and Stampfl and Levis (1967)—also make extensive use of imaginative methods. As Singer properly notes, "When the behaviorists flock over into so extensive a reliance on private 'internal' processes we know the cognitive revolution is really on its way."

Specific studies which validate the important connection between subjects' imaging and emotive and behavioral changes include those by Barrett (1970), Barlow and Agras (1973), Berecz (1972), Chappell and Stevenson (1936), Grossberg and Wilson (1968), Haney and Euse (1976), Levinson, Davidson, Wolff, and Citron (1973), McConaghy (1967), Laws and Pawlowski (1974), Rychlak (1973), Spanos, Horton, and Chaves (1975), and Wenger, Averill, and Smith (1968). Singer (1974) includes scores of other interesting and relevant studies.

Although Joseph Wolpe (1958) has done his best to minimize cognitive factors in behavior therapy and to talk about deconditioning or desensitizing procedures as if they utilized almost pure instrumental or Pavlovian conditioning and although B. F. Skinner (1953, 1971) has steadfastly refused to look in the "black box" of cognition that seems to lie behind operant conditioning, we can ironically observe that the most popular and most effective of all the conventional behavior-therapy techniques used in psychotherapy consists of Wolpe's systematic desensitization method. In this method, clients imagine disturbance-provoking stimuli (such as their approaching a snake or delivering a public speech). Imagination, of course, constitutes a highly cognitive process. Clients then focus (another cognitive method!) on relaxing their muscles and feeling unanxious, until they gradually desensitize themselves to the images they fear. Finally, they seem to conclude—yes, *cognitively* conclude—that they need not fear snakes or public speaking.

Almost innumerable controlled studies of systematic desensitization have appeared which show the efficacy of this imaging method. Instead of listing them here, let me list some comprehensive reviews of the literature which includes them: Bandura (1969), Eysenck (1960, 1964), Franks (1969), P. London (1969), Paul (1966), Rachman (1968), Ullman and Krasner (1965), Wolpe (1958, 1973), Wolpe and Lazarus (1966), Yates (1976).

Building on the work of Wolpe and of Homme (1965), Cautela (1966a, 1966b, 1967, 1971, 1973) created a form of behavior therapy, called covert desensitization, in the course of which clients imagine maladaptive behavior they want to control (such as smoking or overeating) and then imagine in detail a noxious or aversive scene, such as feeling sick and vomiting. Similarly, in covert reinforcement, clients can strengthen their desirable behaviors by imagining reinforcing images and rewarding themselves in their heads rather than *in vivo*. Although, like all behavioral and imaginative methods, covert desensitization and reinforcement have their limitations, many studies show their effectiveness, including those by Asher and Donner (1968), Barlow, Leitenberg, Agras, and Wincze (1969), Bellack, Glanz, and Simon (1976), Binder (1975), Cautela, Walsh, and Wish (1971), Diament and Wilson (1975), Hekmat and Vanian (1971), Horan, Baker, Hoffman, and Shute (1975), Hurley (1976), Janda and Rimm (1972), Marshall, Boutilier, and Minnes (1974), Mahoney (1969), Mullen (1968), Viernstein (1968), Segal and Sims (1972), and Wisocki (1973).

Hypothesis No. 6: Interrelation of Cognition, Emotion, and Behavior

Human cognition, emotion, and behavior do not constitute separate entities but all significantly interrelate and importantly affect one another. Cognition significantly contributes to emotion and to action, emotion to cognition and to action, and action to cognition and to emotion. When people change one of these three modalities of behaving, they concomitantly tend to change the other two. Effective therapy consists of the therapist's consciously trying to help clients ameliorate their emotional disturbances and behavioral dysfunctioning by teaching them a variety of cognitive, emotive, and behavioral techniques of personality change.

Although virtually all systems of psychotherapy seem to implicitly or unconsciously subscribe to this hypothesis, few of the well-known systems explicitly do so, and RET represents a notable exception in this respect (Ellis,

1958, 1962, 1968, 1971a, 1973c, 1977; Ellis & Harper, 1975). Some of the main therapists who have forcefully espoused an interactional, cognitive-affective-behavioral system of psychotherapy include Goldfried and Davison (1976), A. A. Lazarus (1971, 1976), Meyer (1948, 1958), and Pion (1976).

Some experimenters who have shown that when subjects experience distinct changes in their behavior they also experience significant changes in their cognitions and emotions include S. S. Becker, Horowitz, and Campbell (1973), Bell (1972), Briggs and Weinberg (1973), Bull (1960), Byrne, Fisher, Lamberth, and Mitchell (1974), Caulfield and Martin (1976), Cooper and Goethals (1974), Detweiler and Zanna (1976), Diamond and Shapiro (1973), Dua (1970), Fisher and Winkler (1975), Grzesiak and Locke (1975), Kopel and Arkowitz (1974), A. Jacobs, Jacobs, Cavior, and Burke (1974), Krisher, Darley, and Darley (1973), Laird (1974), Leitenberg, Agras, Butz, and Wincze (1971), Levey and Martin (1975), Maranon (1924), Perez (1973), Ryan, Krall, and Hodges (1976), Schachter and Singer (1962), and Strong and Gray (1972).

Experimenters and reviewers who have confirmed the idea that changes in cognitions tend to produce significant changes in emotion and behavior include Acock and deFleur (1972), Arnheim (1969), Arnold (1960), Bandura (1974), Batson (1975), H. A. Brown (1973), Dienstbier, Hillman, Lehnhoff, Hillman, and Valkenaar (1975), Hickey (1976), Kiesler (1971), Klix (1971), Longstreth (1971), Lott and Murray (1975), Marshall, Strawbridge, and Keltner (1972), McReynolds, Barnes, Brooks, and Rehagen (1973), Raimy (1975), Spielberger and Gorsuch (1966), Start (1960), Wexler (1974a, 1974b), and Yulis, Brahm, Charnes, Jacard, Picota, and Rutman (1975).

Studies that present evidence that changing human emotions significantly affects subjects' cognitions and behaviors include those by Cook, Pallak, and Sogin (1976), Coons and McEachern (1967), Dutta, Kanungo, and Friebergs (1972), Giesen and Hendrick (1974), Hale and Strickland (1976), Horowitz (1973), Horowitz and Becker, (1971a, 1971b, 1971c), Horowitz, Becker, and Moskowitz (1971), Levey and Martin (1975), Landfield (1971), Strickland, Hale, and Anderson (1975), and Wine (1971).

Hypothesis No. 7: Biofeedback and Control of Physiological Processes

When people perceive their own thinking, emotive, and physiological processes, they think about (and often awfulize about) these processes; and they thereby significantly affect their subsequent behavior, both in healthy (self-helping) and unhealthy (self-defeating) ways. By perceiving, focusing on, and cognizing about their physiological reactions, they can sometimes change these reactions dramatically, either consciously or unconsciously—e.g., increase or decrease their pulse rates, their galvanic skin reactions, their experiences of pain, and many central or autonomic nervous-system functions which they usually do not voluntarily control. Their ability to do so apparently depends to a large degree on their cognitions; and this fact provides clear-cut evidence of the significant influence of cognition on emotive and behavioral functions.

Pioneering studies and theoretical formulations in regard to biofeedback processes have emerged from the work of E. Green (1973), Kamiya (1968), N. Miller (1969), Olds (1960), and many other researchers. Their work has sparked other studies by a large number of investigators, just about all of which indicates that biofeedback, perceptual feedback, and other forms of cognitive-physical processes help subjects change their thinking, emoting, and behaving. Relevant studies and reviews in this area include those by Borkovec (1973a, 1973b), Friar and Beatty (1976), Herman and Prewett (1975), M. Jacobs, Jacobs, Feldman, and Cavior (1973), Laird (1974), Lang, Sproufe, and Hastings (1967), Melnick (1973), Mulholland (1973), Powers (1973), Rokeach (1975), Rutner (1973), Schwartz (1973), Riddick and Meyer (1973), Roberts, Kewman, and Macdonald (1973), Sirota, Schwartz, and Shapiro (1974), E. J. Thomas (1973), and S. Trotter (1973).

A special series of studies indicates that people have much more ability than they generally recognize to control and regulate their feelings of physical pain—including studies by Bobey and Davidson (1970), Chaves and Barber (1974), Crue (1975), Holmes and Frost (1976), Nisbett and Schachter (1966), and Spanos, Horton, and Chaves (1975).

A vast number of studies indicate that cognitive processes can significantly influence many different kinds of other physiological reactions, including respiratory rate, electrodermal and vasomotor activity, cardiac activity, sexual arousal, and other physical responses. Research papers and reviews in this area include those by Adamson, Romano, Burdick, Corman, and Chebib (1972), Allison (1970), Altman (1973), Baer and Fuhrer (1970), Black (1970), Burdick (1972), Carlson, Travers, and Schwab (1969), S. W. Cook and Harris (1937), Graham (1972), Grossberg and Wilson (1968), Haney and Euse (1976), Henson and Rubin (1971), B. T. Jordan and Kempler (1970), C. S. Jordan and Simprelle (1972), R. S. Lazarus (1966, 1975), Loftis and Ross (1974a, 1974b), Mathews (1971), McCarron and Appel (1971), May (1974), Mowrer (1938), Post (1973), Proctor and Malloy (1971), Rakover and Levita (1973), Ray and Walker (1973), Rule and Hewitt (1971), P. L. Russell and Brandsma (1974), Shean, Faia, and Schmaltz (1974), Vantress and Williams (1972), Warson and Huey (1969), Wenger, Averill, and Smith (1968), and Wooley (1972).

Hypothesis No. 8: Innate Influences on Emotions and Behavior

Humans appear to have very strong innate as well as acquired tendencies to think, emote, and behave in certain ways, although virtually none of their behavior stems solely from instinct and just about all of it has powerful environmental and learning factors that contribute to its "causation." Particularly in the field of disturbed emotions, both innate biological tendencies and acquired learning help create and sustain what we call emotional disturbance. Therapists would better, therefore, face these facts and sometimes communicate them to clients in order to help these clients see (1) the complex reasons for their disturbance, (2) how hard they will probably have to work to make themselves less disturbed, and (3) how easily they can fall back to dysfunctional behavior that they have previously ameliorated.

Almost all leading psychotherapists tend to emphasize, and probably to overemphasize, the importance of early childhood training or conditioning in the creation of human disturbance, and very few of them importantly stress genetic or constitutional factors, even though their basic theories implicitly, and often very strongly, subsume such factors. Although Freud (1965) and Adler (1927, 1929) had some strong biological leanings, most of their followers have ignored these leanings and almost exclusively stressed the role of environmental forces in disturbance. Body-oriented therapies, such as those stemming from the theories of Reich (1949), clearly involve biological underpinnings. But virtually all the practitioners of these theories, including Reich himself, so intensively stress the importance of environmental teaching and training in overcoming tendencies to disturbance that they unequivocally state or imply that such tendencies also derive from almost purely environmental influences. They tend to neglect, almost entirely, the fairly obvious point that, even when a physical or emotional disorder, such as a muscular weakness, dyslexia, or childhood autism, has distinct biological determinants, we can often help those afflicted with such a disorder by specific education, conditioning, and retraining.

RET seems to comprise one of the few major psychotherapies that frankly and unapologetically stresses the powerful organic and biological factors that exist in human disturbance (Ellis, 1962, 1971a, 1973c, 1974a, 1974b, 1976a; Maultsby, 1975). I have for many years collected data on the biological basis of human disturbance that support RET hypotheses in this connection; and, if I ever get around to publishing this material, it may well take several thick volumes. Let me cite here just a few of the important studies and reviews that tend to prove, though not of course with absolute certainty, that emotional disturbance springs from profound and complex biological as well as sociological influences; that early childhood learning definitely contributes to psychological disorder but has a significantly greater effect on innately vulnerable than nonvulnerable children; that certain serious psychological ailments, such as manic-depressive psychosis and schizophrenia almost surely have a powerful biological (as well as environmental) basis; and that social and therapeutic conditioning can greatly help disturbed individuals even when they clearly appear to have innately predisposed handicaps.

A small sample of relevant research studies and reviews in this area includes those by Ainsworth (1969), Altman (1972), Bender (1953, 1963, 1968), Bowers (1971), Browning (1971), Brainerd (1970), Cameron, Titus, Kostin, and Kostin (1973), Casler (1974), Chess, Thomas, and Birch (1965), Churchill (1969), Confino (1973), Freedman (1974), Etzioni (1968), Freedman and Keller (1963), Garmezy (1975), R. Jellinek (1973), Kalish (1970), Kallmann (1960), Kety (1967), Kraines (1966), Lovaas and Schriebman (1971), Mahler (1968), Mandell, Segal, Kuszenski, and Knapp (1972), Marks (1970), McWhinnie (1967), Meehl (1962), Novak and van der Veen (1968), Oltman and Friedman (1965, 1966), Osborn (1968), Rimland (1964), D. Rosenthal (1962, 1970, 1973), D. Rosenthal and Kety (1968), C. Russell and Russell (1957), Schmeck (1972), E. Schopler and Loftin (1969), Seligman (1971), Slater and Cowie (1971), A. Thomas,

Chess, and Birch (1968, 1970), Van den Berg (1972), Wender (1969), Willner and Struve (1970), and Wolpe (1970).

Hypothesis No. 9: Expectancy Influences

When people expect that something will happen or expect that others will act or respond in a certain way, they act significantly differently than when they have other kinds of expectancies. Their cognitive expectancy importantly influences both their degree of emotional disturbance and the ways in which they react to therapy and to their therapists; and in RET and related cognitive behavior procedures therapists can use clients' expectancies to help them overcome their disturbances.

This expectancy hypothesis has received pioneering statements and confirmations by therapists like Jerome Frank (1961, 1968), Meichenbaum (Meichenbaum & Smart, 1971), Mowrer (1938), D. Rosenthal and Frank (1956), R. Rosenthal (1966, 1973), and many other psychologists and therapists. They have shown that clients' and therapists' expectations significantly affect the outcome of psychotherapy; that students who receive direct expectancy statements improve significantly relative to control groups; that subjects' expectations seem more powerful than their experiences in establishing conditioned galvanic skin responses; that a very powerful placebo effect exists in psychotherapy; that all kinds of psychological experimenter expectancies seriously affect the outcomes of behavioral researches; and that demand or conformism expectancies induce clients and others to emote and behave in special ways.

Literally scores of researchers have done controlled experiments showing that different kinds of expectancy influence people to make emotional and behavioral changes. Confirmatory studies in this area include those by Austin and Walster (1974), Borkovec (1972, 1973a, 1973b), Babad (1973), Breznitz (1967), Brickman and Hendricks (1975), Brickman, Linsenmeier, and McCareins (1976), S. W. Cook and Harris (1937), G. C. Davison, Tsujimoto, and Glaros (1973), Deane (1966), DuCette and Wolk (1973), Dweck (1975), Eagly and Acksen (1971), Garfield, Gershon, Sletten, Sundland, and Ballou (1967), Grings (1973), J. E. Johnson (1973), Lang, Goeckner, Adesso, and Marlett (1975), Legant and Mettee (1973), Lick and Bootzin (1975), Loeb, Beck, Diggory, and Tuthill (1967), Lott and Murray (1975), Marcia, Rubin, and Efran (1969), McMahan (1973), Meichenbaum, Bowers, and Ross (1969), Nowicki and Walker (1974), Persely and Leventhal (1972), Pope, Siegman, Cheek, and Blass (1972), Rappaport (1972), G. M. Rosen (1975, 1976), Rubovits and Maehr (1973), Schaefer, Tregerthan, and Colgan (1976), M. Snyder, Schulz, and Jones (1974), Tori and Worell (1973), G. T. Wilson and Thomas (1973), M. N. Wilson and Rappaport (1974), Wyer (1973), and Ziemelis (1974).

In addition to these studies, another group of studies exists, including some of those listed in the last two paragraphs, which specifically show that, when experimenters give placebos to psychotherapy clients or other subjects and deliberately lead them to believe that these placebos have a therapeutic effect, the clients or subjects actually experience pronounced emotional and behavioral changes. Validations of the efficacy of placebos include experiments by E. M. Jellinek (1946), Paul (1966), D. Rosenthal and Frank (1956), Wolf (1950), Wolf and Pinsky (1954), and Steinmark and Borkovec (1974).

Another related area of cognitive expectation consists of the field of conformism or demand expectancy. Asch (1952) and his associates discovered that humans, including intelligent college students, when asked to make anti-empirical choices (such as declare that they see a 2½-inch stick as shorter than a 2-inch stick) will very frequently make such a choice if they think that people around them have also made this antiempirical decision. They have such a dire love need or conformism need—in RET terms—that they actually make themselves falsely view reality (or at least falsely report on their views of it) in order to please others.

Following up on Asch's work, many investigators have reported that subjects significantly change their thoughts, feelings, and behaviors when they expect that others want them to do so. They give in to what they conceive of as the "demands" of these others and go out of their way, often against their own best interests, to fill these "demands." In the field of psychotherapy, in particular, clients frequently give responses to therapists and actually change their behaviors as much, or more, in accordance with what they think their therapists want them to do as in accordance with their own basic wishes. Many experiments have provided evidence of this expectancy demand characteristic of subjects and of clients, including those by Berquist and Klemm (1973), Borkovec and Glasgow (1973), McReynolds and Tori (1972), Milgrim (1974), Page (1972), and Pliner and Cappell (1974).

Hypothesis No. 10: Locus of Control

When people view situations, others' reactions, and their own behavior as within their own control, they act differently than when they view these situations and behaviors as stemming from external sources or as outside their own control. They can therefore improve their dysfunctional emoting and behaving if a therapist helps them see how they *use* external sources to react to and see how they to a large degree can take control of their own thoughts, feelings, and actions and thereby minimize their disturbances.

In the field of psychology, this hypothesis stems from the pioneering work of many experimentalists, particularly Witkin (1954), who developed tests showing how some people have field dependency and let themselves feel influenced by environmental conditions around them, while others seem "field-independent" and let themselves feel less influenced, in a passive-dependent manner, by their environment. Going even beyond Witkin's work, Rotter (1954, 1964, 1966, 1971, 1975) and his associates have done, for more than 20 years, an immense amount of work on the problem of locus of control. As Lefcourt (1976) indicates in a comprehensive review of the literature inspired by Witkin, Rotter, and other researchers on locus of control, "Whether people, or other species for that matter, believe that they are actors and can determine their own fates within limits will be seen to be of critical importance to the way in which they cope with stress and engage in challenges."

Lefcourt (1966, 1976) lists over 200 studies concerned with locus of control, virtually all of which show that people do think, emote, and act differently when they believe that they control important aspects of their lives than when they see these aspects beyond their own control. Typical studies that he lists, and others that he does not, include those by Brisset and Nowicki (1973), Calhoun, Cheney, and Dawes (1974), Chaikin and Karley (1973), Ehri and Muzio (1974), Felton and Biggs (1972), Gilbert (1976), L. M. Harris (1976), Houston (1972), H. Levenson (1973), Nowicki, Bonner, and Feather (1972), Nowicki and Walker (1974), Phares (1971), Pines (1973), Riemer (1975), Roth and Bootzin (1974), M. Snyder, Schulz, and Jones (1974), Sogin and Pallak (1976), Williams and Stack (1972), Wolman, Lewis, and King (1971), and Worchel and Andreoli (1974).

Hypothesis No. 11: Attribution Errors

Humans attribute motives, reasons, and causes to other people and to external events and internal physical states; and they significantly influence their own emotions and behavior by these attributions, even when they base them on quite false or misleading perceptions and conceptions. A good deal of their emotional disturbance stems from misattributions; and we may often help them overcome such disturbance by helping them to understand and change their cognitive misattributions.

Many social and experimental psychologists, such as D. J. Bem (1965, 1966, 1967), Kelley (1968), and Schachter and Singer (1962), have pioneered in formulating attribution theory; and their formulations have led to a vast number of studies, almost all of which confirm this theory. Classic experiments by G. C. Davison, Tsujimoto, and Glaros (1973) and G. C. Davison and Valins (1969) showed how subjects who attributed their physiological changes to themselves rather than to a drug made significantly greater therapeutic gains than those who falsely made drug attributions. A study by Geer, Davison, and Gatchel (1971) indicated that subjects who believed they had control over their reaction time had fewer spontaneous skin conductance responses and smaller SCR's to shock than subjects who didn't feel they had control. Nisbett and Schachter (1966) showed that subjects will behave more emotionally if they identify an emotional stimulus as the source of their arousal or pain than if they do not identify the stimulus as the source. Schachter and Singer (1962) found that "given a state of physiological arousal for which an individual has no immediate explanation, he will label this state and describe his feelings in terms of the cognitions available to him." Valins (1966, 1967) found that, when a subject thinks his heart rate has changed in response to a photo of a nude female, he will consider her more attractive and desire a copy of her photo more than another photo to which he falsely thinks his heart rate has not changed. Valins and Ray (1967) led subjects to believe that snake stimuli did not affect them internally and found that these subjects, in comparison to suitable controls, later manifested more approach behavior when confronted with a live snake.

Similar experiments that show that subjects significantly emoted or acted differently from control subjects when they falsely believed certain "facts" about external conditions or about their own reactions almost uniformly support the attribution hypothesis. These include studies by Batson (1975), Blechman and Dannemiller (1976), Cantor, Zillmann, and Bryant (1975), Borkovec (1973a), Colson (1974), Cook, Pallak, and Sogin (1976), Detweiler and Zanna (1976), Elliott and Denney (1975), Geen, Rakosky, and Pigg (1972), Giesen and Hendrick (1974), V. A. Harris and Katkin (1975), Holmes and Frost (1976), Hirschman (1975), Kleinke (1975), Koenig (1973), Kravetz (1974), Krebs (1975), Krisher, Darley, and Darley (1973), Lick (1975), Loftis and Ross (1974a, 1974b), Riddick and Meyer (1973), Rodin (1976), Ross, Lepper, and Hubbard (1975), Sullivan (1969), Whalen and Henker (1976), and Wooley (1972).

A special series of attribution studies involves the effects of people's attributing certain phenomena or effects to their own behavior, control, or self-rating or their attributing the same phenomena to other sources. These studies overlap with the locus-of-control studies which I considered earlier in this article and, to some extent, also overlap with self-rating studies, also considered. Of the many investigations done in this area, almost all show more significant behavioral and emotional changes when people see themselves in certain ways and attribute events and feelings to themselves than when they attribute the same events and feelings to external conditions or to nonself causes. Reported studies in this area which confirm RET hypotheses include those by Bandler, Madaras, and Bem (1968), Bugenthal, Whalen, and Henker (1975), Corah and Boffa (1970), S. L. Bem (1970), Dienstbier, Hillman, Lehnhoff, Hillman, and Valkenaar (1975), R. L. Miller, Brickman, and Bolen (1975), E. Jones, Kanouse, Kelley, Nisbett, Valins, and Weiner (1972), Kopel and Arkowitz (1975), and Pennebaker and Sanders (1976).

Increasing attention gets paid these days to techniques of helping people change their false and misleading attributions when these lead to dysfunctional results, but few studies showing empirical validation of such techniques exist at present. Confirmatory evidence in this area appears in studies and reviews by Dweck (1975), Rimm and Masters (1974), and Wein, Nelson, and Odom (1975).

COGNITIVE MEDIATION OF EMOTIONAL DISTURBANCE

Hypothesis No. 12: Irrational Thinking

Humans have strong innate and acquired tendencies to set up basic values (especially the values of survival and happiness) and to think and act both rationally (abetting the achievement of their basic values) or irrationally (sabotaging the achievement of such values). Virtually all humans frequently have several important irrational ideas, or absolutistic and antiempirical modes of thinking, that interfere with their healthy thoughts, emotions, and behaviors;

and when they change these ideas their dysfunctional behavior also tends to significantly change. In efficient therapy, the therapist attempts to show clients their irrational thinking and to help them (in cognitive, emotive, and behavioral ways) to surrender or change these self-defeating philosophies or beliefs.

Many pioneering psychotherapists have promulgated or endorsed this hypothesis—including Adler (1927, 1929), Dubois (1907), Ellis (1962), Kelly (1955), Low (1952), Phillips (1956), and Wolberg (1967). Freud specifically endorsed it in his original formulations (Breuer & Freud, 1895/1957) by calling emotional disturbance *ideogenic*. Although he and most psychoanalysts later focused more on transference methods and other emotive aspects of therapy, they have at least implicitly always tried to show clients their unrealistic and irrational thinking and to help them give it up.

An impressive amount of data now exists that demonstrates that the specific kinds of irrational thoughts posited by RET (Ellis, 1957a, 1957b, 1958, 1962, 1971a, 1973c; Ellis & Harper, 1975) exist in different populations and have significant correlations with emotional disturbance. Since DiGiuseppe, Miller, and Trexler summarize this evidence in their article in this section of the book, I shall omit it here.

Scores of related studies also exist that experimentally show that various kinds of disturbed or malfunctioning populations employ significantly more disordered or irrational thinking than do less severely disturbed groups. Let me list a few of these studies, most of them recent and a few of them pioneering or classic. These indicate that disturbed or peculiar individuals tend to have various kinds of cognitive difficulties and to think irrationally or disorderedly in many different ways, including: (1) abstraction difficulties (Braff & Beck, 1974; Wright, 1973); (2) analytic thinking problems (Ehri & Muzio, 1974); closedness (Heilbrun, 1973); conceptual organization difficulty (Depue & Fowles, 1974); decentering (Suchotliff, 1970); disattending to strong aspects of meaning (Chapman, Chapman, & Daut, 1976); gullibility (Dmitruk, Collins, & Clinger, 1973); idiosyncratic construct systems (Widom, 1976); hopelessness (Cassidy, Flanagan, & Spellman, 1957; Seligman, 1975); incapacity for formal operations (Kilburg & Siegel, 1973); injustice collecting (Collins, 1974); intrusive thoughts (Horowitz, Becker, & Malone, 1973); logical deviation (DeWolfe & McDonald, 1972); magical thinking (Collins, 1974); mnemonic disorganization (Larsen & Fromholt, 1976); overgeneralization (Mourer, 1973); overinclusive thinking (Harrow, Himmelhoch, Tucker, Hersh, & Quinlan, 1972; Craig, 1973; Davis & Blaney, 1976); and role-taking deficiencies (Davis & Blaney, 1976).

In a special review of the nature and ubiquity of human irrationality I list literally scores of basic and important irrational beliefs and behaviors of humans and show how they commonly exist in virtually all people at all times in all climes (Ellis, 1976a). In this article I cite some of the researchers who have presented large amounts of evidence for the hypothesis that all humans often tend to act irrationally and that they probably have a pronounced biological, as well as cultural, tendency to do so—including researchers such as Frankel (1973), Frazer (1959), Hoffer (1951), Korzybski (1933), Kurtz (1973), Lévi-

Strauss (1970), Pitkin (1932), Rachleff (1973), and Sperry (1975). I could extend this list almost endlessly.

Psychologists have presented evidence showing the ubiquity of many forms of irrational thinking, particularly authoritarianism, bigotry, and prejudice. They have shown how prejudiced cognitions significantly affect many different kinds of emotional and behavioral reactions; how such irrational prejudices often correlate with emotional disturbances; and how the diminishing or extirpation of these prejudices may have important therapeutic results. Confirmatory researches in these regards include studies by Alexander and Sagatun (1973), Becker (1960), Becker, Spielberger, and Parker (1963), Davies (1970), Dunlap, Gaertner, and Mangelsdorff (1973), Dutton and Lake (1973), Fox (1969), Geller and Berzins (1976), Genther, Shuntich, and Bunting (1975), McCrame and Kimberly (1973), Langer and Abelson (1974), Kemp (1961), Landy and Sigall (1974), Lincoln and Levinger (1972), Long (1976a, 1976b, 1976c), Marquis (1973), Ray and Walker (1973), S. Rosen, Johnson, Johnson, and Tesser (1973), Ross, Lepper, and Hubbard (1975), Rubovits and Maehr (1973), Silverman and Cochrane (1972), S. Schwartz (1973), Stephan, Lucker, and Aronson (1976), Tesser and Conlee (1975), West and Schultz (1976), Wyer (1976), and Ziemelis (1974).

Hypothesis No. 13: Self-Rating

People have very strong innate and acquired tendencies not only to rate their acts, behaviors, performances, and traits as "good" or "bad" but to rate their *selves,* their *essences,* their *totalities* in the same manner; and their self-ratings profoundly influence their emotions and behaviors and constitute one of the main sources of their emotional disturbances. Effective psychotherapy importantly consists of helping individuals who down themselves to have high self-acceptance and to rate themselves unconditionally as good or, preferably, to continue to rate their acts and traits, in accordance with the enjoyable or unenjoyable results they produce, but to refuse to rate their *selves* or *essences* at all.

The first part of this hypothesis—that people who rate themselves usually or frequently end up with low self-esteem and would better learn to rate themselves unconditionally as good—seems implicit in the work of Freud (1965) and his followers but has more explicit formulations in the writings of Adler (1927, 1929), Berne (1964), Branden (1969), Fromm (1941, 1947), Horney (1965), Lecky (1945), Jung (1954), and C. R. Rogers (1961, 1971). The second part of this hypothesis—that people had better learn to refuse to rate their selves or essences at all, while they still continue to rate their traits—gets vaguely hinted at in some writings, particularly Zen Buddhist literature (Suzuki, 1956; Suzuki, Fromm, & DeMartino, 1963). Only rational-emotive writings appear to state it with great clarity and precision (Ellis, 1957a, 1971a, 1973c, 1977; Ellis & Grieger, 1977; Ellis & Harper, 1975; Ellis & Knaus, 1977; Lembo, 1976; Morris & Kanitz, 1975; Young, 1974).

Considerable experimental evidence exists that shows that humans do rate themselves and that they enormously affect their emotions and behaviors by the kind of self-ratings they choose. Verifying studies include those by Beck (1967), Beck and Hurvich (1959), Beck and Stein (1967), D. J. Bem (1967), Brainerd (1969), Cunningham and Berberian (1976), Grossack, Armstrong, and Lussiev (1966), Kaczkowski and Owen (1972), H. B. Kaplan and Pokorny (1969), Forrest and Hokanson (1975), Glasgow and Arkowitz (1975), Kingsbury, Stevens, and Murray (1975), LaPuc and Harmatz (1970), Maracek and Mettee (1972), Meichenbaum and Smart (1971), Mischel, Ebbesen, and Zeiss (1976), Nosanchuk and Lightstone (1974), Regan, Gosselink, Hubsch, and Ulsh (1975), Rychlak, Carlsen, and Dunning (1974), Sheehan and Marsh (1974), Shortell and Biller (1970), Shrauger and Terbovic (1976), Steber (1974), Vidman (1972), Walster, Walster, Piliavin, and Schmidt (1973), and Wine (1971).

Virtually no studies exist investigating the validity of the RET hypothesis that unconditional self-acceptance or self-regard would better consist of no rating of oneself or essence, with the exception of a partially confirming study by T. W. Miller (1976). More studies of this specific RET hypothesis would seem called for.

Hypothesis No. 14: Defensiveness

When people perceive their behavior as "bad," "wrong," "incompetent," or "shameful," they frequently refuse to acknowledge to themselves and/or to others that they have thought or acted "badly," and they use various kinds of cognitive defenses to obscure or deny their "wrong" acts. To this end, they rationalize, project, repress, compensate, use reaction formation, and employ other modes of defense mechanisms. Their main motive for utilizing such cognitive defenses stems from their self-rating and self-damning (which I examine elsewhere in this article). A highly effective technique of undoing these defenses and of helping people change their dysfunctional behavior of defending themselves from perceiving consists of enabling them to give up their self-condemnation and to stop their awfulizing about frustrations and inconveniences they encounter.

Freud (1965) and his followers (A. Freud, 1948/1975; Fenichel, 1945) formulated the theory of cognitive defensiveness and, to my way of thinking, thereby made perhaps the most useful contribution of psychoanalysis to effective psychotherapy. Many experimental studies presenting evidence for defense mechanisms and their significant effects on human emotion and behavior have appeared. I shall make no attempt to list them here but shall merely refer to some summary reviews of the literature—such as those by Blum (1966), Ellenberger (1970), Ellis (1950), Jurjevich (1974), and Sears (1943). A few recent studies showing evidence for defensiveness include those by Love, Sloan, and Schmidt (1976), Muehleman (1973), Pagano (1973), and Regan, Gosselink, Hubsch, and Ulsh (1975).

I have as yet found no studies which specifically test the RET hypothesis that cognitive defensiveness will become minimized or disappear when people change their irrational ideas about self-rating and self-damning. This would appear a fruitful field for future study.

Hypothesis No. 15: Low Frustration Tolerance

People have an innate and acquired tendency to have low frustration tolerance (LFT)—to do things that seem easier in the short run even though they often bring poor results in the future; to go for immediate gratification and stimulation seeking that offer highly specious rewards; and to procrastinate and avoid behaviors and disciplines that would bring them greater ultimate rewards. While their hedonistic views and ways help them survive and achieve greater happiness in some respects, their powerful tendencies toward short-range rather than long-range hedonism frequently prove self-defeating. Emotional disturbance largely consists of or involves distinct low frustration tolerance. Whenever people make themselves anxious, depressed, hating, or undisciplined and even when they note their symptoms and determine to work to ameliorate them, they usually sabotage their therapeutic efforts to some extent, or they make temporary gains and fall back to previously disturbed ways, partly or largely as a result of their seeking immediate ease or comfort and of giving in to their LFT. Effective therapy often consists of enabling clients to achieve higher frustration tolerance or a philosophic outlook that acknowledges that gain rarely exists without pain, that they would better work at changing themselves, and that the human condition ordinarily and usually requires, for maximum happiness and freedom, a considerable amount of life-long discipline, including an active determination to change obnoxious stimuli when possible but also to accept them when they prove unchangeable.

Although many therapists—including Adler (1927, 1929) and Freud (1965)—have pointed out that humans had better resort to delayed gratification in order to act sanely, few psychotherapies have stressed this point to any considerable degree. RET (Ellis, 1957a, 1962, 1971a, 1974c; Ellis & Harper, 1975; Ellis & Knaus, 1977) and reality therapy (Glasser, 1965) have perhaps pioneered in this respect.

Many psychological studies, especially in recent years, have presented evidence that low frustration tolerance looms importantly in human disturbance. Ainslie (1974) and Mischel and Mischel (1975) have presented comprehensive reviews of the large amount of research data that has accumulated to support the hypothesis that LFT mightily contributes to emotional disturbance and behavioral malfunctioning and that this disturbance ameliorates when experimenters or therapists help people to gain higher frustration tolerance. Some specific relevant studies in this area include those by Hildebrandt, Feldman, and Ditrichs (1973), Leon and Chamberlain (1973), D. T. Miller and Karniol (1976), Mischel and Baker (1975), Mischel and Ebbesen (1970), Mischel, Ebbesen, and Raskoff Zeiss (1972), Mischel and Gilligan (1964), Mischel and Moore (1973), Mowrer and Ulmann (1945), Patterson and Mischel (1976), Shaffer and Hendrick (1974), and Whitehill, DeMeyer-Gapin, and Scott (1976).

Hypothesis No. 16: Anticipation of Threat

People not only react to real threat and display fear or anxiety when such danger exists but also anticipate or imagine conditions of threat and often react with as much disturbance to such anticipation or imagination as they do to actual conditions of threat. Anticipation of threat therefore constitutes an important cognitive mediating process in emotional disturbance, and therapists had better deal with it or head it off in effective psychotherapy.

A good many researchers have investigated the idea that various kinds of anticipation of threat or stress lead to emotional disturbance and that certain other kinds of anticipation minimize or alleviate disturbance. Thus, Fritz and Marks (1954) found that a one-minute tornado warning proved more disruptive of effective behavior than none at all or than a much longer warning period and that people who have a long time to make anticipatory preparation may feel significantly more disturbance than those who have a shorter waiting period. Additional confirmation of this and related hypotheses appear in studies by Folkins (1970), Grings (1973), Krupat (1974), Jordan and Kempler (1970), R. S. Lazarus (1966), Nomikos, Opton, Averill, and Lazarus (1968), Jordan and Simprelle (1972), Rakover and Levita (1973), Szpiler and Epstein (1976), and Suls and Miller (1976).

RATIONAL-EMOTIVE THERAPY TECHNIQUES

Hypothesis No. 17: Active-Directive Therapy

Because people have very powerful innate and acquired tendencies to disturb themselves emotionally and to act dysfunctionally, because they think, feel, and behave in self-defeating ways from early childhood onward, because they adhere strongly to their self-sabotaging thoughts and feelings, and because they easily fall back into them once they have temporarily changed, they will tend to receive more effective help from a highly active-directive than from a more passive and unintrusive psychotherapeutic approach.

Outstanding theoreticians and researchers endorsing the active-directive position in psychotherapy have included Adler (1927, 1929), Alexander and French (1946), Ellis (1957b, 1958, 1962, 1972a, 1972b, 1974b), Ferenczi (1926/1952), Garner (1970), Greenwald (1967), Haley (1961, 1963), Herzberg (1945), Hill (1955), Homme (1969), Goldfried and Davison (1976), Goldfried and Merbaum (1973), Janov (1970), Jurjevich (1973), Kelly (1955), Lange and Jakubowski (1976), Matarazzo (1962), Perls (1969), O'Connell (1966), Piaget (1970), Regardie (1952), Reich (1949), J. N. Rosen (1953), Salzman (1963), Salter (1949), Thorne (1950), Wolberg (1967), and Wolpe (1958; Wolpe and Lazarus, 1966).

More concrete studies and reviews presenting evidence favoring the effectiveness of active-directive forms of therapy over more passive forms have recently appeared in many books and journals, including writings by Blumberg

(1972), Coons (1972), Curran, Gilbert, and Little (1976), Doster (1972), Harari (1971), Kanfer and Karas (1959), Mendel (1970), Mitchell and Namenkek (1972), O'Connell, Baker, Hanson, and Ermalinski (1973), Packwood (1974), Padfield (1976), Schiavo, Alexander, Barton, and Parsons (1976), Vernallis, Holson, Shipper, and Butler (1972), Warren and Rice (1972), and Winship and Kelley (1976).

Hypothesis No. 18: Disputing and Persuasion

Because people frequently hold irrational, logically inconsistent, antiempirical, and absolutistic ideas, because these ideas tend to bring them needless self-defeating results, and because they do not accord with reality, a therapist or other helper or teacher can show them how their irrational beliefs do not hold up as true and demonstrate that their continuing to believe irrationalities will almost inevitably bring them gratuitous pain. Such a therapist or helper can often persuade them to change or surrender their irrational beliefs and the dysfunctional behaviors to which they contribute. Effective psychotherapy importantly includes the therapist's actively and directively disputing, challenging, and questioning clients' irrational philosophies and persuading them to adopt less self-defeating beliefs.

Although many therapists, as indicated previously in this article, have acknowledged the profound influence of irrational thinking on the creation and maintenance of emotional disturbance, surprisingly few have unequivocally advocated active-directive methods of disputing these beliefs. To some extent, however, Adler (1927, 1929), Dreikurs (1974), Dubois (1907), Ellis (1957a, 1958, 1962, 1971a, 1973c, 1973e, 1974b, 1974c, 1975b, 1975c, 1976e; Ellis and Gullo, 1972; Ellis and Grieger, 1977), Frankl (1966), Jurjevich (1973, 1974), Phillips (1956), and Raimy (1975) have taken a distinctively persuasive therapeutic stance.

A large number of studies showing the importance and effectiveness of persuasion appear in the experimental and social-psychology literature. Rather than try to cite them, I shall refer to the reviews of the literature included by Abelson (1959/1975), Hovland and Janis (1959), and Rosnow and Robinson (1967). Some of the more recent relevant studies showing the effect of persuasion on personality change include those by D. J. Bem (1965, 1966), Beutler, Jobe, and Elkins (1974), Miller, Brickman, and Bolen (1975), Packwood and Parker (1973), Reed and Janis (1974), Steele and Ostrom (1974), and Truax, Fine, Moravec, and Millis (1968).

A special RET hypothesis, which I formulated a number of years ago, states that, when therapists or others try to persuade people to give up their irrational ideas and to adopt less self-defeating notions, not only do these people get helped but, consciously or unconsciously, the therapists tend to help themselves give up their own irrationalities and improve their own functioning. This hypothesis receives some confirmation in studies by Bard (1973) and Perlman (1972).

Hypothesis No. 19: Homework

Because people habituate themselves to thinking, emoting, and acting in certain dysfunctional ways and consciously or unconsciously overpractice these behaviors over a period of time until they turn into their "second nature" and resist change with great difficulty, they almost always require considerable active practice to undo these self-defeating habits and to keep them from recurring. Effective psychotherapy therefore includes a considerable amount of active-directive homework assignments, especially in the form of *in vivo* practice that interrupts or contradicts dysfunctional behavior. It often includes forced, repetitive, and massed cognitive, emotive, and behavioral *in vivo* and imaginative homework.

Therapists have unofficially used active-directive homework assignments probably since the beginning of man and woman. Modern therapists who have particularly pioneered in advocating such assignments include Ellis (1954, 1957a, 1962, 1971b, 1973a, 1973e, 1974c, 1976d, 1976e) Ellis and Harper (1975) Ellis and Grieger (1977), Herzberg (1945), Masters and Johnson (1970), Maultsby (1971, 1975), Maultsby and Ellis (1974), Salter (1949), Shelton and Ackerman (1974), and Wolpe (1958).

Many researchers have confirmed the value of active-directive homework procedures in psychotherapy, including Azrin and Powers (1975), Bandura, Jeffery, and Gajdos (1975), Barlow, Leitenberg, Agras, and Wincze (1969), Christensen and Arkowitz (1974), Everaerd, Rijken, and Emmelkamp (1973), Clore and Jeffrey (1972), Crowe, Marks, Agras, and Leitenberg (1972), Dua (1972), Christensen, Arkowitz, and Anderson (1975), Eberle, Rehm, and McBurney (1975), Gelder, Bancroft, Gath, Johnston, Mathews, and Shaw (1973), Hoehn-Saric, Frank, and Gurland (1968), Leitenberg, Agras, Butz, and Wincze (1971), Leitenberg and Wincze (1970), K. R. Mitchell, and Mitchell (1971), Rosenberg (1960), Sherman, Mulac, and McCann (1974), and Boulougouric and Bassiakos (1973).

A more specific RET hypothesis, ever since I created this system of psychotherapy early in 1955, states that *in vivo* homework assignments will usually tend to help emotionally disturbed people more than will various other kinds of active-directive therapy methods, such as systematic desensitization, which tend to remain more imaginative and theoretical than does contact desensitization. Thus, if clients who have a fear of approaching members of the other sex merely practice systematic desensitization during therapy sessions or when by themselves, as against actually going out and forcing themselves to encounter a number of members of the other sex, they will tend, says this RET hypothesis, to experience lesser reduction of their fears. Similarly, RET hypothesizes that clients who practice only rational-emotive imagery (Maultsby, 1971; Maultsby & Ellis, 1974) will overcome their disturbances to a lesser degree than those who practice *in vivo* homework in connection with these disturbances.

Evidence favoring the view that *in vivo* or contact homework assignments work more effectively than other kinds of assignments or other therapeutic procedures appears in research studies by Cooke (1966), G. C. Davison (1965),

Dua (1970), D'Zurilla, Wilson, and Nelson (1973), Emmelkamp and Wessels (1975), Garfield, Darwin, Singer, and McBrearty (1967), Gentry (1970), Hodgson, Rachman, and Marks (1972), Kirsch, Wolpin, and Knutson (1975), Leitenberg and Callahan (1973), Leitenberg, Agras, Edwards, Thomson, and Wincze (1970), Litvak (1969a, 1969b), Marks, Viswanathan, Lipsedge, and Gardner (1972), Marks (1971), Murphy and Bootzin (1973), Rimm and Medeiros (1970), Ritter (1968), J. Schopler and Compere (1971), Schroeder and Rich (1976), Sherman (1972), Watson, Gaind, and Marks (1972), Stadter (1973), G. T. Wilson and Davison (1971), and Zajonc (1968).

Hypothesis No. 20: Insult and Intent

People tend to feel more disturbed and change their behavior more drastically when they think that others have tried to denigrate or insult them than when they see these others as acting badly but not insultingly. Their perceptions of others' intentions to harm or down them also tend to affect them more than their perceptions of the actual harm these others cause them. Efficient therapy therefore often consists of helping clients not to take others' insults too seriously and of helping them noncondemningly accept others who act against them even when these others intentionally do so.

Few of the major schools of therapy emphasize this point very clearly or specifically, although it is a cornerstone of RET (Ellis, 1957a, 1962, 1971a, 1974c, 1977; Ellis & Harper, 1975). For I and other RET practitioners continually show our clients that insults really do not hurt them unless they take such insults too seriously and that, even when others do intentionally harm or down them, these others have a right to act wrongly (because of their human fallibility) and that refusing to give them this right will cause more disturbance than the harm they try to cause.

Evidence that people distinctly upset themselves or make significant changes in their behavior when they feel insulted appears in scores of studies of attribution, expectancy, rating, and the instigation of anger, many of which I list in other sections of this article. Other studies of a confirming nature include those by Lang, Goeckner, Adesso, and Marlett (1975), Rule and Hewitt (1971), and Steele (1975).

Studies showing that subjects' perception of the "good" or "bad" intentions of others, even when these perceptions had no empirical foundation, significantly affected their attitudes and behaviors toward themselves and toward these others include experiments by Ellsworth and Langer (1976), Greenwell and Dengerink (1973), Harris and Huang (1974), Heller, Pallak, and Picek (1973), Lincoln and Levinger (1972), Legant and Mettee (1973), and Salili, Mach, and Billmore (1976).

Hypothesis No. 21: Abreaction of Dysfunctional Emotions

Abreaction or catharsis of dysfunctional emotions, and particularly of various forms of anger (including hostility, resentment, rage, and physical aggression), may have palliative effects on relieving these emotions, but they often prove iatrogenic in that they tend to reinforce the philosophies or beliefs that people employ to create these feelings. Thus, the philosophy behind anger almost invariably includes the rational belief "I don't like your behavior, and I wish you would stop it!" and the irrational belief, or absolutistic command, "Because I don't like your behavior, you must stop it! And you rate as a rotten person if you don't!" Expression or abreaction of anger reinforces people's irrational belief and thereby helps them *feel* better instead of *get* better. By giving up the irrational command that others treat them fairly or that the world must provide what they want, humans lose rather than suppress or repress anger; and they thereby improve their emotional health and render themselves less prone to future anger.

This RET view of people's creating their own angry reactions and having a great deal of ability to expunge their anger and minimize their feeling it, even when unjustly provoked, originated largely with philosophers rather than psychologists—including such thinkers as Epictetus (1899), Marcus Aurelius (1900), Melden (1969), Spinoza (1901), Shibles (1974), and Wittgenstein (1958). Some psychologists, however, have at least partly espoused it—including Charny (1968), deRivera (1970), Ellis (1957a, 1962, 1971a, 1973c, 1975a, 1976b, 1977; Ellis & Gullo, 1972; Ellis & Harper, 1975), Hauck (1974), Knaus (1974), Lange and Jakubowski (1976), Lembo (1976), Low (1952), Maultsby (1975), Novaco (1975), Peters (1970), and Tosi (1974).

Various experimenters have investigated the theory that anger partly or largely originates in human cognitions and have come up with data supporting this theory—including Bandura and Walters (1963), Berkowitz and Alioto (1973), Berkowitz, Lepinski, and Angulo (1969), W. Block (1976), K. L. Block (1975), Frodi (1974), Geen and Stonner (1973), Konecni (1975), Lang, Goeckner, Adesso, and Marlett (1975), Legant and Mettee (1973), Lehman (1972), Novaco (1975), Pastore (1950, 1952), and Pisano and Taylor (1971). I may parenthetically note, incidentally, that just as anger seems to have its cognitive origins, so also does love. Various modern investigators—such as Bleda (1974), Duck and Spencer (1972), Landy and Sigall (1974), and Walster, Walster, Piliavin, and Schmidt (1973)—have come up with experimental evidence backing this hypothesis.

More to the point, the RET theory that abreaction has only limited therapeutic effects and that it often leads to increase in hostility and punitiveness has received confirmation in literally scores of recent experiments—as Berkowitz (1970b) has shown in a brilliant review of the literature. Some of the many important studies in this respect include those by Auerswald (1974), Bandura and Walters (1963), Bandura and Wittenberg (1971), Baron (1974), Berkowitz (1964, 1966, 1970b), Berkowitz and Alioto (1973), Berkowitz, Green, and Macaulay (1962), Berkowitz, Lepinski, and Angulo (1969), Berkowitz and Rawlings (1963), Drabman and Thomas (1974), Feshbach (1971), Frodi (1974), Geen and Stonner (1973), Geen, Stonner, and Hope (1975), Hokanson (1970), Konecni (1975), Leyens, Camino, Parke, and Berkowitz (1975), Liebert and Baron (1972), Nelson, Gelfand, and Hartmann (1969), Straus (1974), and M. K. Wagner (1968).

Not too much attention has yet turned to the experimental study of relieving or removing feelings of anger by cognitive methods. But some confirmation of the basic RET hypotheses in this connection appears in studies by K. L. Block (1975), Barton (1972), Kaufmann and Feshbach (1963), Novaco (1975), and Pisano and Taylor (1971).

Hypothesis No. 22: Choice of Behavioral Change

Although pure free will does not seem to exist, and although human behavior at least in part gets determined by biological and environmental factors or "causes" over which an individual has relatively little control, so that a high degree of probability exists that people will do one thing and not do another, they also have a large degree of choice or will and can, with considerable amounts of work, partly determine how they feel and act. Because of their ability in this respect, they can come to therapy and choose to work (or not to work) at helping themselves, and they can thereby choose significantly to change some of their most "natural" and long-practiced disturbances. As they remove their emotional blocks, they can also choose to actualize their potential for greater enjoyment and personality growth.

This hypothesis, or aspects of it, underlies virtually all forms of psychotherapy; but various therapists and educators have particularly emphasized it—including Adler (1927, 1929), Assagioli (1965), Dewey (1922/1930), Ellis (1962, 1973c; Ellis & Harper, 1975), M. Friedman (1975), Perls (1969), and C. R. Rogers (1961, 1971). Although some degree of free choice remains central to the entire field of psychotherapy (and of liberal education), few experiments have specifically tested this theory. Some which have validated the hypothesis that humans can to some degree choose how they think, emote, and behave include the following. A review of the research literature on attitudes led Ajzen and Fishbein (1973) to conclude that "the most immediately relevant predictor of a specific action is the person's behavioral intention. Although problems can arise with regard to the intention-behavior relationship, empirical research has shown that high correlations between these two variables can be obtained."

Cappell and Pliner (1973) found that subjects do have volitional control over marijuana intoxication and can make themselves come down from such intoxication if they wish to do so. Ellsworth and Langer (1976) showed that a stare does not have to get perceived as a threatening signal nor does it automatically elicit flight. Subjects have the ability to interpret it in such a manner as to approach strangers in a friendly, helpful way. Davidson and Steiner (1971) found that subjects can interpret reinforcements and penalties in different ways and that therefore "behavior therapy may be assumed to evoke complex cognitive and evaluative processes which are not comfortably handled by the Skinnerian model. To a greater degree than rats or even chimpanzees, humans appear to impose meaning upon social situations." Zimbardo (1973) discovered that, when people agree to play the role of prisoner to another, they frequently choose to unduly restrict themselves. He concluded that in self-chosen situations, such as marriage, many of us "choose to remain prisoners because being passive and dependent frees us from the need to act and be responsible for our actions. The prison of fear constructed in the delusions of the paranoid is no less confining or less real than the cell that every shy person erects to limit his own freedom in anxious anticipation of being ridiculed and rejected by his guards—often guards of his own making."

The studies tend to show, in other words, that people to a large extent choose their emotional disturbances—and therefore can distinctly choose to surrender them (Greenwald, 1976). Which tends to confirm one of the main RET hypotheses!

Hypothesis No. 23: Self-Control

When people perceive their behavior as less than desirable or when they feel emotionally disturbed, they have considerable ability to determine to change and to follow various kinds of self-control or self-management procedures to bring about such change. They often modify their emotions and behavior more by self-control principles than when controlled or directed by others. Self-control has very strong cognitive (as well as behavioral) elements, and effective therapy often consists of helping clients to use a considerable amount of cognitive-related self-management.

I have cited some amount of research studies favoring this hypothesis previously in this article—especially under the headings of self-perception, biofeedback, imaging, homework, and self-monitoring. In spite of this evidence, most major psychotherapies have neglected self-management principles in the past, and only a few, such as behavior therapy (Wolpe, 1958, 1973; Wolpe & Lazarus, 1966), rational-emotive therapy (Ellis, 1962, 1969, 1971a, 1973a, 1973c, 1974a; Ellis & Harper, 1975), and reality therapy (Glasser, 1965), have very clearly espoused encouraging clients to use systematic self-control.

Pioneers in the theory and practice of self-control have included many cognitive-behavior therapists, including Cautela (1969), Goldfried and Merbaum (1973), Goldfried and Davison (1976), Kanfer (1970a, 1970b), Meichenbaum (1975a, 1975b, 1975c; Meichenbaum & Cameron, 1973); Mischel and Mischel (1975), Stuart (1969), and Watson and Tharp (1977).

Almost innumerable studies have appeared demonstrating that cognitive-behavioral self-control methods work; that they frequently have advantages over externally directed behavior change; and that self-control procedures, even when highly "behavioral," have clear-cut and important cognitive elements. These include studies by Baker, Cohen, and Saunders (1973), Batterson and Mischel (1976), Blackwood (1970), G. C. Davison (1968), Drummond (1974), Felixbond and O'Leary (1973), Goldfried (1971), Gottman and McFall (1972), M. B. Harris (1969), M. B. Harris and Bruner (1971), M. B. Harris and Rothberg (1972), Knapp (1976), Levinson, Shapiro, Schwartz, and Tursky (1971), Mann (1972), Marston (1972), McReynolds and Church (1973), Rose, Glasgow, and Barrera (1976), Sherman and Plummer (1973), Sobell and Sobell (1973), and Spiegler, Cooley, Marshall, Prince, Puckett, and Skenazy (1976).

Hypothesis No. 24: Coping with Distress and Threat

People's ability to cope with distress and threat seems significantly affected by their conceptions of how well they think they can cope. Teaching them skills or strategies of coping may help them cope—not so much because they can thus deal with people and things better but because they *conclude* that they can and thereby increase their *confidence* in their ability to do so. Having greater confidence, they usually cope better—or cope worse but think they do better. Even when they learn poor strategies—such as that of whining and screaming about the hassles that beset them or such as the tactic of aggressively instead of assertively dealing with others—they may feel much better because they view such "coping" behavior as "good" and "effective." Teaching coping skills and helping clients to strongly believe that they can cope with conditions of distress and threat constitute effective methods of psychotherapy or behavior change.

Pioneering studies of and theorizing about coping behavior and people's attitudes toward their ability to cope stem from the work of Richard S. Lazarus and his associates (R. S. Lazarus, 1966; R. S. Lazarus & Alpert, 1964). Following up on Lazarus' work, and especially investigating the attitude of learned helplessness and its relationship to feelings of depression, Martin Seligman and his associates (Seligman, 1975) have provided a large body of significant research and have sparked many other relevant studies.

Researches that tend to confirm the importance of an individual's perceptions and attitudes about his or her coping ability appear in a comprehensive review of the literature by Averill (1973). Some specific confirmatory findings relating to the RET hypothesis about coping appear in publications by Averill, Opton, and Lazarus (1969), G. C. Davison (1967), D. Glass, Singer, and Friedman (1969), D. Glass and Singer (1972), Goldfried and Trier (1974), Houston (1975), Kazdin (1973), Neufeld (1976), Sanchez-Craig (1976), and Speisman, Lazarus, Nordkoff, and Davison (1964).

Learned helplessness studies, according to Seligman's (1975) conclusions and interpretations, generally show that, when children, adolescents, and adults feel consistently thwarted in the fulfillment of some important desire, they frequently conclude (rightly or wrongly) that they have no hope of ever achieving such fulfillment, and they tend to severely depress themselves because of their cognitions about their frustrated and "impossible" state. Specific confirmation of this hypothesis appears in studies by Gatchel, Paulus, and Maples (1975), Gatchel and Proctor (1976), Dweck and Reppucci (1973), D. Glass, Singer, and Friedman (1969), Hiroto and Seligman (1975), Klein, Fencil, and Seligman (1976), and Seligman (1973). Studies which show that learned helplessness can also get reversed, so that cognitions of hopelessness change along with feelings of depression, include those published by Klein and Seligman (1976), Schmickley (1976), and Seligman (1975).

Hypothesis No. 25: Diversion or Distraction

People tend to focus mainly on one thing at a time, so that, if they want to stop concentrating on one set of disturbing thoughts (such as awfulizing about failure, rejection, or frustration), they can significantly change their emotions and behaviors, at least temporarily, by concentrating on other non-disturbing cognitions or occurrences (e.g., on pleasure, meditation, fantasies, relaxation, or physical sensations). A great deal of psychotherapy consequently consists of cognitive diversion or distraction; and this form of treatment can often lead to good therapeutic results.

Although virtually all forms of psychotherapy, in one way or another, utilize important elements of cognitive diversion, not many authorities seem to have specifically acknowledged this point. The few pioneering formulators in this area include Benson (1975), Ellis (1962, 1971a, 1973c, 1977; Ellis & Grieger, 1977). At the same time, by consciously advocating the techniques of noncoital concentration, the sensate focus, and the use of concrete imaging, many leading sex therapists seem to acknowledge the importance of diverting or distracting cognitions. Pioneers in this regard include Ellis (1954, 1975b, 1976d), Hartman and Fithian (1972), H. S. Kaplan (1974), Masters and Johnson (1970), and Semans (1956).

Some studies that present evidence that when people distract themselves in various ways from various kinds of disturbed thoughts, feelings, and actions they significantly change their behaviors include those of Geer and Fuhr (1976), Lewinsohn and Graf (1973), Linden (1973), Little and Jackson (1974), N. Miller, Baron, and Baron (1973), Patterson and Mischel (1976), Sergio, Brahm, Charnes, Jacard, Picota, and Rutman (1975), Trotter (1973), Wallace (1970), and Mischel, Ebbesen, and Raskoff Zeiss (1972).

Wolpe (1958; Wolpe & Lazarus, 1966) has recommended thought-stopping procedures as a therapeutic technique for allaying anxiety, and a study by Rimm, Saunders, and Westel (1975) has confirmed the efficacy of this diversionary method. Mischel and Moore (1973) also investigated the hypothesis that children's ability to wait for a delayed reward significantly depends on whether they focus on rewards abstractly, and thereby remind themselves of the advantages of delay, or whether they focus concretely on the arousing quality of the rewards and thereby make themselves feel more frustrated and undermine their self-control. They found that these different kinds of focusing or concentrating did indeed significantly affect the children's frustration tolerance. These and similar studies tend to validate the RET hypothesis that focusing on one kind of thinking or diverting oneself with another kind of thinking importantly influences human behavior.

Hypothesis No. 26: Education and Information

People largely teach or condition themselves, as well as accept the teachings of others, to make themselves emote and behave in various ways; and their self-conditioning and acceptance of the teachings of others significantly contribute to their emotional disturbances. Effective psychotherapy importantly consists of education and reeducation—of providing clients, in a variety of ways, with salient information and instruction that will help them understand what they have done to disturb themselves and what they can do to make themselves less disturbed.

Although just about all psychotherapies appear educational and information giving, perhaps the majority of leading theorists and practitioners minimize or ignore this aspect and emphasize—not to mention overemphasize!—various other aspects, such as the relationship between client and therapist, the ventilation of feelings by the client, and the uncovering of unconscious motivations and blockings—ignoring the fact that even these aspects of therapy include highly educative and informational elements! Some therapeutically oriented writers, however, have frankly and unashamedly endorsed the role of education in personality change—including Adler (1927, 1929), G. Brown (1971), Dinkmeyer (1973), Dreikurs (1974), Educational Research Council of America (1971a, 1971b), Ellis (1962, 1973a, 1973b, 1977), Knaus (1974), and Raimy (1975).

Although rational-emotive education has arrived lately on the scene of emotional education, and although the first publications in the area have recent origins (Ellis, 1971b, 1972a, 1973b; D. A. Brown, 1974a, 1974b; Knaus, 1974), quite a few research studies have already appeared that back up the RET view that rational-emotive methods, taught to children or adults in classroom settings, usually by regular teachers, can help people significantly to overcome their tendencies to emotional disturbance. Such studies include presentations by Bokor (1971), Brody (1974), P. Cooke (1974), deVoge (1974), DiGiuseppe (1975), Gustav (1968), Katz (1974), Knaus and Bokor (1975), Kujoth (1976), Lafferty (1962), Sharma (1970), Sydel (1972), Taylor (1975), and Zingle (1965).

Related studies showing that other forms of education or instruction can help individuals significantly to change their emotions and behavior include those by Doster (1972), Dua (1971), Eisler, Hersen, and Agras (1973), Dell (1973), Heitler (1973), Hoxter (1967), Green and Marlatt (1972), Meichenbaum, Turk, and Rogers (1972), Sarason and Ganzer (1973), Palkes, Stewart, and Kahana (1968), R. W. Rogers and Deckner (1975), Schleifer and Douglas (1973), Schumsky (1972), and Taffel, O'Leary, and Armel (1974).

Another series of controlled studies tests the hypothesis that the giving of specific information will help various kinds of subjects significantly change their feelings and behaviors. Confirmatory evidence in this connection appears in published papers by Crawford and Haaland (1972), A. M. Davison and Denney (1976), Diamond (1972), M. F. Kaplan and Anderson (1973), Nisbett and Borgida (1975), Shapiro, Litman, and Hendry (1973), Singerman, Borkovec, and Baron (1976), and Wyer (1973).

Still another group of studies brings out evidence that certain kinds of self-instruction will help change the dysfunctional behavior of groups of subjects. This group includes studies by Bornstein and Quevillon (1976), Hartig and Kanfer (1973), Robin, Armel, and O'Leary (1975), Smith (1975), and Thorpe (1975).

A number of researchers have investigated the effects of using special kinds of information giving to help promote personality change—including the use of bibliotherapy, programmed texts, and audiovisual materials. Studies in this area which show positive results include those by Atkinson (1974), Allen (1973), Bastien and Jacobs (1974), Fielding, Erickson, and Bettin (1971), Hagen (1974), Hagen, Foreyt, and Durham (1976), Hunt and Azrin (1973), LaFleur and Johnson (1972), McClellan and Stieper (1973).

Hypothesis No. 27: Suggestion and Hypnotic Suggestion

Humans have a strong tendency to think, emote, and behave in accordance with the strong suggestions of others, even when these suggestions lead to poor individual or social results. They take such suggestions and make them into powerful autosuggestions, on the basis of which they significantly affect their own behavior. Their strong tendencies to act gullibly contribute to much of their emotional disturbance. By the same token, they can frequently ameliorate this disturbance by acting on autosuggestion, on the suggestion of others, or on hypnotic suggestion. Almost all psychotherapy contains mighty elements of suggestion, and an effective form of therapy consciously uses it to some extent. However, efficient or elegant therapy at the same time tries to help clients to achieve less suggestibility and to make themselves more influenceable by their own empirically and experimentally based thinking and less influenceable by the absolutistic suggestion of others.

Bernheim (1886/1947) may have first clearly stated the hypothesis that suggestion and autosuggestion, rather than mesmerism, animal magnetism, or some other mysterious force, make hypnosis a powerful therapeutic tool. Freud (1965), who used a good deal of hypnosis in his early experiments with clients, also finally realized that it had few special qualities in its own right and that it largely consisted of suggestion. Modern therapists and researchers who have clearly seen that suggestion has powerful effects on both disturbance and the amelioration of disturbance and that much of the behavioral and therapeutic effects achieved by hypnosis stem from the suggestive elements that almost always constitute a large part of the hypnotic state, include Barber (1961, 1966, 1969), Blum and his associates (Blum, Geiwitz & Stewart, 1967; Blum and Porter, 1974; Blum and Wohl, 1971), Coué (1923), Ellis (1962, 1974c, 1977), Hart (1956), Levitt and his associates (Levitt, Den Breeijen, & Persky, 1960; Levitt, Persky, & Brady, 1964), and Peale (1948, 1952).

A great many experimental studies and reviews have appeared which show that different kinds of suggestion contribute to people's experiencing profound behavioral changes—some of which I have listed previously in this article under the headings of attribution and expectancy. Various other confirmatory studies have appeared, including those by Berzins and Ross (1972), Borkovec (1973b), Foreyt and Hagen (1973), Hampson, Rosenthal, and Frank (1954), Morrison and Walters (1972), C. R. Snyder and Larson (1972), Meath, Feldberg, Rosenthal, and Frank (1954), Nowlis and Nowlis (1956), Shaw and Margulis (1974), Sloane, Cristol, Pepernik, and Staples (1970), Sparks (1962), and Wolf (1950).

A large number of studies have also appeared that clearly demonstrate the effectiveness of hypnotic suggestion on behavior change, including those by Baunitz, Unesthal, and Berglund (1975), Bowers (1973), Barber and Calverley (1965, 1966), Barber, Walker, and Hahn (1973), Dalal and Barber (1969), Diamond, Gregory, Lenney, Steadman, and Talone (1974), Gibbons, Kilbourne, Saunders, and Castles (1970), Gordon (1967), Greene and Reyher (1972), Hilgard, MacDonald, Marshall, and Morgan (1974), Lauer (1968), Roberts, Kewman, and Macdonald (1973), Roper (1967), Sheehan and Bowman (1973), Sparks (1962), Weinstein, Abrams, and Gibbons (1970), and Zimbardo, Marshall, and Marlash (1971).

The specific hypothesis of Coué (1923), Peale (1948, 1952), and others that positive thinking, or autosuggestively convincing oneself that one can do certain tasks well, often produces good results has occasionally been tested and confirmed—as in studies by Kanfer, Karoly, and Newman (1975) and Suinn and Richardson (1971). The specific hypothesis of RET that positive thinking works but that it remains a less elegant and less effective form of therapy than helping people to scientifically attack and invalidate their negative thinking (Ellis, 1962; Ellis & Harper, 1975) does not seem to have led to any validating studies yet.

Hypothesis No. 28: Modeling and Imitation

People have innate and acquired tendencies to imitate or model themselves after others and to significantly change their thoughts, emotions, and actions in accordance with those they perceive in their models. They frequently acquire or ameliorate their emotional disturbances by conscious or unconscious modeling. Imitating and modeling almost always involve powerful cognitive mediating processes; and when people explicitly perceive how they can use modeling they can more easily and intensively help themselves than when they have little or no awareness of using imitation. Effective therapy often includes the therapist's consciously using modeling procedures and sometimes helping clients gain specific awareness of how they can employ imitation to help themselves overcome their disturbances.

Bandura (1968, 1969) and his associates have pioneered in the theory and practice of modeling for behavior change. Other psychotherapists—such as Ellis (1962, 1971a, 1974c, 1977) and Rogers (1961, 1971)—have also indicated that what often seems "relationship" or "reinforcement" in therapy really to a large degree consists of modeling. Thus, the existentialist, client-centered, or RET therapist reveals himself or herself to clients, shows a minimum of upsetness and a maximum amount of openness, and thereby models "good" or "healthy" behavior—which clients can then consciously or unconsciously adopt in part and thereby help themselves change.

Many experimenters have presented evidence that modeling helps instigate significant behavior change, that it involves distinct cognitive mediating processes, and that modeling with specific informational and awareness elements often proves more helpful than modeling without such elements. Some of the main studies in this connection include those by Braun (1972), Denney (1975), Denney and Sullivan (1976), Fiedler and Windheuser (1974), Goodwin and Mahoney (1975), M. B. Harris (1970), Hall and Hinkle (1972), Jabichuk and Smeriglio (1975), Kauffman, LaFleur, and Hallahan (1975), LaFleur and Johnson (1972), Leitenberg and Wincze (1970), Marburg, Mouston, and Holmes (1976), Meichenbaum, Turk, and Rogers (1972), O'Connor (1972), Moore and Sipprelle (1971), Olson (1971), Rathus (1973), Prentice (1972), Rachman (1972), Rachman, Hodgson, and Marks (1971), and Sarason (1973).

Hypothesis No. 29: Problem Solving

People tend to use problem solving and related cognitive methods in dealing with and overcoming their emotional disturbances and their behavioral dysfunctioning. Those deficient in problem-solving abilities and skills tend to wind up more disturbed and malfunctioning than those with greater skills in this area. Showing clients how to increase their problem-solving skills constitutes one effective cognitive form of psychotherapy.

Problem-solving methods of therapy have had pioneering applications in the theories and practices of Ellis (1962, 1971a, 1974c, 1977) and others (Ellis & Harper, 1975; D'Zurilla & Goldfried, 1971; Goldfried & Davison, 1976; Goldfried & Goldfried, 1975; Goldfried & Merbaum, 1973; Spivack & Shure, 1974). Gagné (1959), though not a therapist, has also pioneered in theorizing about the efficacy of problem-solving methods.

Confirmatory studies have shown that people with problem-solving deficiencies do tend to behave in a more disturbed fashion than those without such deficiencies and that the teaching of problem-solving methods to clients can serve as a highly effective therapeutic technique. Relevant studies include those by D'Zurilla and Goldfried (1971), Levenson and Neuringer (1971), Platt, Spivack, Altman, and Altman (1974), Mendonca and Siess (1976), and Vincent, Weiss, and Birchler (1975).

Hypothesis No 30: Role-Playing and Behavioral Rehearsal

When people adopt a role and role-play an important event or hypothetical event, they frequently influence themselves to experience thoughts, feelings, and behaviors that significantly differ from those they would otherwise experience. They can often disturb themselves and also help ameliorate their disturbances by role-playing experiences. Like modeling and imitation, role-playing includes distinct cognitive elements and these elements help people change their dysfunctional feelings and actions. Role-playing that includes a clear-cut cognitive analysis of the feelings invoked during role enactment and that includes cognitive restructuring of the attitudes revealed by the role-playing experiences will prove more therapeutically effective than role-playing without this kind of cognitive analysis or cognitive restructuring.

J. L. Moreno (1934, 1947) has outstandingly pioneered in role-playing theory and research, as have some of his followers, such as Corsini, Shaw, and Blake (1961), Corsini (1966), Greenberg (1974), and Yablonsky (1965). In the field of psychotherapy, Kelly (1955) has enthusiastically favored role-playing as a therapeutic technique, and many behavior therapists have used it under the name of behavioral rehearsal (A. A. Lazarus, 1971, 1976).

Research backing the thesis that role-playing has specific cognitive-behavioral components and that, when it goes with rational or cognitive restructuring, it has distinct therapeutic benefits appears in studies by O'Connell (1972), O'Connell, Baker, Hanson, and Ermalinski (1973, 1974), O'Connell and Hanson (1971), Schopler and Compere (1971), and Zimbardo and Ebbesen (1970).

Hypothesis No. 31: Skill Training

When people receive effective training in certain skills—e.g., in assertion, in socializing, in sex technique, or in values clarification—they frequently significantly change their thinking, emoting, and behaving and sometimes make themselves considerably less emotionally disturbed. These changes arise not merely from their increased skills but also from their perceptions of their abilities and their self-ratings about their newly acquired competencies. Effective therapy often includes some amount of skill training and the helping of clients to perceive their abilities and capacities differently as they acquire new skillls. It also includes helping them to accept themselves unconditionally in spite of their remaining lack of skills. Just as skill training enables clients to change their perceptions of their abilities, so does helping them to perceive themselves differently enable them to acquire better skills.

The older and conventional psychotherapies usually tend to neglect skill training, although they may unacknowledgedly do some amount of it. RET, however, has emphasized skill training from its earliest days (Ellis, 1962, 1969, 1971a, 1972a, 1973c; Ellis & Harper, 1975), and behavior therapy has particularly pioneered in skill training (Goldfried & Davison, 1976; Lange & Jakubowski, 1976; A. A. Lazarus, 1971, 1976; LoPiccolo, 1971; LoPiccolo & Miller, 1975; Masters & Johnson, 1970; Rimm & Masters, 1974; Salter, 1949; Wolpe, 1958; Wolpe & Lazarus, 1966).

Of the many studies that have appeared that demonstrate the therapeutic effectiveness of skill training and the existence of an important cognitive element in skill training, let me list a few: Argyle, Bryant, and Trower (1974), P. Byrne (1973), Christensen (1974), Curran and Gilbert (1975), Glass, Gottman, and Shmurak (1976), Glasgow and Arkowitz (1975), Hodgson and Urban (1975), Rehm, Fuchs, Roth, Kornblith, and Roman (1975), Schwartz and Gottman (1974), Usher (1974), and Yulis (1976).

Hypothesis No. 32: Differences between RET and
Other Types of Therapy

Although RET uses many techniques that partially overlap with those used in other systems of therapy, significant differences exist between the practice of RET and that of several other major therapies.

I conceive RET as particularly overlapping with cognitive-behavior therapy and as one of the major cognitive-behavior techniques (Ellis, 1969). Several other authorities also see it as an integral part of the cognitive-behavior therapy movement (Beck, 1976; Goldfried and Davison, 1976; A. A. Lazarus, 1971, 1976; Mahoney, 1974; Meichenbaum, 1974a, 1974b, 1974c, 1977; Rimm & Masters, 1974). At the same time, RET differs in many respects from most other major systems of psychotherapy—including Gestalt therapy, experiential therapy (Ellis, 1976c, 1976e, 1977), client-centered therapy, and psychoanalysis.

Research data showing some significant differences between the practice of RET and the practice of other forms of therapy have appeared in studies by Raskin (1965, 1966), Woodard, Burck, & Sweeney (1975), Zimmer & Cowles (1972), Zimmer & Pepyne (1971), and Zimmer, Wightman, and McArthur (1970). Significant differences in the practice as well as the outcome of RET, when compared to other types of therapy, also exist in many of the clinical outcome studies reported by DiGiuseppe, Miller, and Trexler (1977).

DISCUSSION

This article states many of the important clinical and theoretical hypotheses of rational-emotive therapy (RET) in particular and of cognitive-behavior therapy in general and lists a great number of research studies that provide empirical confirmation of these hypotheses. It concentrates mainly on recent researches and largely ignores a good deal of additional evidence that one can find in the studies of the clinical outcomes of RET procedures when used in controlled experiments and in the studies of irrational ideas, since DiGiuseppe, Miller, and Trexler cover some of this evidence (see their article in this section of the book). It also omits a huge amount of corroborative clinical and anecdotal data included in literally hundreds of articles and books that Ellis (1980) has listed in a comprehensive bibliography of rational-emotive therapy and cognitive-behavior therapy; and it omits some corroborative material included in the bibliographies of M. J. Mahoney (1974), Meichenbaum (1974c, 1976), and Zingle and Mallet (1976).

I think I can safely conclude, on the basis of the studies cited in this article, that (1) a vast amount of research data exists most of which tends to confirm the major clinical and theoretical hypotheses of RET; (2) these data keep increasing by leaps and bounds; (3) RET hypotheses nicely lend themselves to experimental investigation and have therefore encouraged an enormous amount of research, especially considering that RET formulations have arrived so recently on the scene; (4) researchers have not yet tested some of the important RET formulations and could do so with much profit to the field of psychotherapy and personality theory. RET, like classical behavior therapy, stems from empirical clinical observations and tries to rigorously confirm its theories by using the scientific method. Moreover, it employs criteria of rationality and effective living that stress scientific investigation, scepticism, empiricism, and antiabsolutism (Bartley, 1962, 1968; Ellis, 1971a, 1973c, 1973e, 1977, 1978; Mahoney, 1976). It seems amazing that some critics, such as Arbuckle (1975), would see it as authoritarian and that other critics, such as Wolpe (Ellis & Wolpe, 1974) would see it as lacking empirical confirmation. I hope that the present review helps to dispel such misperceptions and doubts.

REFERENCES

Abelson, H. I. *Persuasion.* New York: Springer, 1959. (Rev. ed.: New York: Springer, 1975.)

Acock, A. C., & deFleur, M. L. A configurational approach to continency in the attitude behavior relationship. *American Sociological Review,* 1972, *36,* 714–726.

Adamson, J., Romano, K., Burdick, J., Corman, C., & Chebib, F. Physiological responses to sexual and unpleasant film stimuli. *Journal of Psychosomatic Research,* 1972, *16,* 153–162.

Aderman, D. Elation, depression, and helping behavior. *Journal of Personality and Social Psychology,* 1972, *24,* 91–101.

Adler, A. *Understanding human nature.* New York: Garden City Publishing Company, 1927.

Adler, A. *The science of living.* New York: Greenberg, 1929.

Ainslie, G. Specious reward: A behavioral theory of impulsiveness and impulse control. *Psychological Bulletin,* 1974, *82,* 463–496.

Ainsworth, M. D. S. Object relations, dependency, and attachment: A theoretical review of the infant-mother relationship. *Child Development,* 1969, *16,* 969–1025.

Ajzen, I., & Fishbein, M. Attitudinal and normative variables as predictors of specific behaviors. *Journal of Personality and Social Psychology,* 1973, *27,* 41–57.

Alexander, C. N., Jr., & Sagatun, I. An attributional analysis of experimental norms. *Sociometry,* 1973, *36,* 127–142.

Alexander, F., & French, T. M. *Psychoanalytic therapy.* New York: Ronald, 1946.

Allen, G. J. Treatment of test anxiety by group-administered and self-administered relaxation and study counseling. *Behavior Therapy,* 1973, *4,* 349–360.

Allison, J. Lancet. *Hospital Times,* May 1, 1970, 1.

Alperson, B. L. In search of Buber's ghosts: A calculus for interpersonal phenomenology. *Behavioral Science,* 1975, *20,* 79–90.

Altman, L. K. Some manic-depressive cases are found to be inherited through genetic defect. *New York Times,* August 16, 1972, *1,* 20.

Altman, L. K. Heart research has key to sudden fatal attacks. *New York Times,* November 26, 1973, *1,* 52.

Arbuckle, D. S. Ellis on Ellis. *Counselor Education and Supervision,* 1975, *15,* 70–71.

Argyle, M., Bryant, B., & Trower, P. Social skills training and psychotherapy: A comparative study. *Psychological Medicine,* 1974, *4,* 435–443.

Arnheim, R. *Visual thinking.* London: Faber & Faber, 1969. (Also, Berkeley: University of California Press, 1969.)

Arnold, M. *Emotions and personality* (2 volumes). New York: Columbia University Press, 1960.

Asch, S. E. *Social psychology.* New York: Prentice-Hall, 1952.

Asher, B., & Donner, L. Covert sensitization with alcoholics: A controlled replication. *Behaviour Research and Therapy,* 1968, *6,* 7–12.

Assagioli, R. *Psychosynthesis.* New York: Viking, 1965.

Atkinson, D. R. Lay psychology books as an aid to counseling. *Personnel and Guidance Journal,* 1974, *53,* 123–126.

Auerswald, M. C. Differential reinforcing power of restatement and interpretation on client production of affect. *Journal of Counseling Psychology,* 1974, *21,* 9–14.

Austin, W., & Walster, E. Reactions to confirmations and disconfirmations of expectancies of equity and inequity. *Journal of Personality and Social Psychology,* 1974, *30,* 208–216.

Averill, J. R. Personal control over aversive stimuli and its relationship to stress. *Psychological Bulletin,* 1973, *80,* 286–303.

Averill, J. R., Opton, E. J., Jr., & Lazarus, R. S. Cross-cultural studies of psychophysiological responses during stress and emotion. *International Journal of Psychology,* 1969, *4,* 83–102.

Azrin, N. H., & Powers, M. A. Eliminating classroom disturbances of emotionally disturbed children by positive practice procedures. *Behavior Therapy,* 1975, *6,* 525–534.

Babad, E. Y. Effects of informational input on the "social deprivation-satiation effect." *Journal of Personality and Social Psychology,* 1973, *27,* 1–5.

Baer, P. E., & Fuhrer, M. J. Cognitive processes in the differential trace conditioning of electroderma and vasomotor activity. *Journal of Experimental Psychology,* 1970, *84,* 176–178.

Baker, B. L., Cohen, D. C., & Saunders, J. T. Self-directed desensitization for acrophobia. *Behaviour Research and Therapy,* 1973, *11,* 79–89.

Bandler, R. J., Madaras, G. R., & Bem, D. J. Self observation as a course of pain perception. *Journal of Personality and Social Psychology,* 1968, *9,* 205–209.

Bandura, A. Modeling approaches to the modification of phobic disorders. In R. Porter (Ed.), *The role of learning in psychotherapy.* London: Churchill, 1968, 201–217.

Bandura, A. *Principles of behavior modification.* New York: Holt, Rinehart & Winston, 1969.

Bandura, A. *Psychological modeling: Conflicting theories.* Chicago: Aldine-Atherton, 1971.

Bandura, A. Behavior theory and the models of man. *American Psychologist,* 1974, *29,* 859–869.

Bandura, A., & Jeffery, R. W. Role of symbolic coding and rehearsal processes in observational learning. *Journal of Personality and Social Psychology,* 1973, *26,* 122–130.

Bandura, A., Jeffery, R. W., & Gajdos, E. Generalizing change through participant modeling with self-directed mastery. *Behaviour Research and Therapy,* 1975, *13,* 141–152.

Bandura, A., & Walters, R. H. *Aggression.* Chicago: National Society for the Study of Education, 1963.

Bandura, A., & Wittenberg, C. The impact of visual media on personality. In J. Segal (Ed.), *The mental health of the child.* Washington: National Institute of Mental Health, 1971, 247–266.

Bannister, D. (Ed.). *Perspectives in personal construct theory.* New York: Academic Press, 1971.

Bannister, D., & Fransella, F. *Inquiring man.* Baltimore: Penguin, 1973.

Bannister, D., & Mair, J. M. M. *The evaluation of personal constructs.* New York: Academic Press, 1968.

Barber, T. X. Physiological effects of "hypnosis." *Psychological Bulletin,* 1961, *58,* 390–419.

Barber, T. X. The effects of "hypnosis" and motivational suggestions on strength and endurance: A critical review of research studies. *British Journal of Social and Clinical Psychology,* 1966, *5,* 42–50.

Barber, T. X. *Hypnosis: A scientific approach.* Cincinnati: Van Nostrand Reinhold, 1969.

Barber, T. X., & Calverley, D. S. Empirical evidence for a theory of "hypnotic" behavior: The suggestibility-enhancing effects of motivational suggestions, relaxation-sleep suggestions and suggestions that the subject will be effectively "hypnotized." *Journal of Personality,* 1965, *33,* 256–270.

Barber, T. X., & Calverley, D. S. Toward a theory of "hypnotic" behavior: Experimental analysis of suggested amnesia. *Journal of Abnormal Psychology,* 1966, *71,* 95–107.

Barber, T. X., Walker, P. C., & Hahn, K. Effects of hypnotic induction and suggestions on nocturnal dreaming and thinking. *Journal of Abnormal Psychology,* 1973, *82,* 414–427.

Bard, J. A. Rational proselytizing. *Rational Living,* 1973, *8,* 24–26.

Barlow, D. H., & Agras, W. S. Fading to increase heterosexual responsiveness in homosexuals. *Journal of Applied Behavior Analysis,* 1973, *6,* 355–366.

Barlow, D. H., Leitenberg, H., & Agras, W. S. *Preliminary report of the experimental control of sexual deviation by manipulation of the noxious scene in sensitization.* Paper read at the meeting of the Eastern Psychological Association, Washington, D.C., 1968.

Barlow, D., Leitenberg, H., Agras, W. S., & Wincze, J. The transfer gap in systematic desensitization: An analogue study. *Behaviour Research and Therapy,* 1969, *7,* 191–196.

Baron, R. A. Reducing the influence of an aggressive model: The restraining effects of peer censure. *Journal of Experimental and Social Psychology,* 1972, *8,* 266–275.

Baron, R. A. Sexual arousal and physical aggression. *Bulletin of the Psychonomic Society,* 1974, *3,* 337–339.

Barrett, C. L. Runaway imagery in systematic desensitization therapy and implosive therapy. *Psychotherapy: Theory, Research and Practice,* 1970, *7,* 233–236.

Bartley, W. W. *The retreat to commitment.* New York: Knopf, 1962.

Bartley, W. W. Theories of demarcation between science and metaphysics. In I. Laktos & A. Musgrave (Eds.), *Problems in the philosophy of science.* Amsterdam: North Holland Publishing Company, 1968, 40–64.

Barton, R. A. Reducing the influence of an aggressive model. *Journal of Experimental and Social Psychology,* 1972, *8,* 266–275.

Bastien, S., & Jacobs, A. An experimental study of the effectiveness of written communication as a form of psychotherapy. *Journal of Consulting and Clinical Psychology,* 1974, *42,* 151.

Batson, C. D. Attribution as a mediator of bias in helping. *Journal of Personality and Social Psychology,* 1975, *32,* 455–466.

Batterson, C., & Mischel, W. Effects of temptation inhibiting and task facilitating plans on self control. *Journal of Personality and Social Psychology,* 1976, *33,* 209–217.

Baunitz, S. C. B., Unesthal, L. E., & Berglund, B. K. A posthypnotically released emotion as a modifier of behavior. *International Journal of Clinical and Experimental Hypnosis,* 1975, *33,* 120–129.

Beck, A. T. *Depression.* New York: Hoeber-Harper, 1967.

Beck, A. T. Role of fantasies in psychotherapy and psychopathology. *Journal of Nervous and Mental Disease,* 1970, *150,* 3–17.

Beck, A. T. Cognitive themes of dreams held key to basic thought processes. *Roche report: Frontiers of psychiatry,* January 1971, 1-2.

Beck, A. T. *Cognitive therapy and the emotional disorders.* New York: International Universities Press, 1976.

Beck, A. T., & Hurvich, M. S. Psychological correlates of depression. I. Frequency of "masochistic" dream content in a private practice sample. *Psychosomatic Medicine,* 1959, *21,* 50–55.

Beck, A. T., & Stein, D. The self concept in depression. Unpublished study, reported in A. T. Beck, *Depression.* New York: Hoeber-Harper, 1967.

Becker, J. Achievement-related characteristics of manic-depressives. *Journal of Abnormal Social Psychology,* 1960, *60,* 334–339.

Becker, J., Spielberger, C. D., & Parker, J. B. Value achievement and authoritarian attitudes in psychiatric patients. *Journal of Clinical Psychology,* 1963, *19,* 57–61.

Becker, S. S., Horowitz, M. J., & Campbell, L. Cognitive responses to stress: Effects of changes in demand and sex. *Journal of Abnormal Psychology,* 1973, *87,* 519–522.

Beier, E. G. *The silent language of psychotherapy: Social reinforcement of unconscious processes.* Chicago: Aldine, 1966.

Beilin, H., Lust, B., Sack, L. G., & Natt, H. M. *Studies in the cognitive basis of language development.* New York: Academic Press, 1975.

Bell, B. D. Critical reflections on a cognitive-physiological theory of emotion. *Kansas Journal of Sociology,* 1972, *8,* 49–59.

Bellack, A. S., Glanz, L. W., & Simon, R. Self-reinforcement style and covert imagery in the treatment of obesity. *Journal of Consulting and Clinical Psychology,* 1976, *44,* 490–491.

Bem, D. J. An experimental analysis of self-persuasion. *Journal of Experimental Social Psychology,* 1965, *1,* 199–218.

Bem, D. J. Inducing belief in false confessions. *Journal of Personality and Social Psychology,* 1966, *3,* 707–710.

Bem, D. J. Self-perception: An alternative interpretation of cognitive dissonance phenomena. *Psychological Review,* 1967, *74,* 183–200.

Bem, S. L. Verbal self-control: The establishment of effective self-instruction. *Journal of Experimental Psychology,* 1967, *74,* 485–491.

Bem, S. L. *Beliefs, attitudes, and human affairs.* Monterey, Calif.: Brooks/Cole, 1970.

Bender, L. Childhood schizophrenia. *Psychiatric Quarterly,* 1953, *27,* 663–681.

Bender, L. Mental illness in childhood and heredity. *Eugenics Quarterly,* 1963, *10,* 1–11.

Bender, L. Childhood schizophrenia: A review. *International Journal of Psychiatry,* 1968, *5,* 211–220.

Bender, L., & Hitchman, I. L. A longitudinal study of 90 schizophrenic women. *Journal of Nervous and Mental Disease,* 1956, *124,* 337–345.

Benson, H. *The relaxation response.* New York: Morrow, 1975.

Berecz, J. Modification of smoking behavior. *Journal of Consulting and Clinical Psychology,* 1972, *38,* 244–250.

Bergin, A. E. Cognitive therapy and behavior therapy: Foci for a multidimensional approach to treatment. *Behavior Therapy,* 1970, *1,* 205–212.

Bergin, A. E., & Strupp, H. H. New directions in psychotherapy research. *Journal of Abnormal Psychology,* 1970, *75,* 1–10.

Berkowitz, L. The effects of observed violence. *Scientific American,* 1964, *5,* 130–139.

Berkowitz, L. On not being able to aggress. *Journal of Social and Clinical Psychology,* 1966, *5,* 130–139.

Berkowitz, L. Aggressive humor as a stimulus to aggressive responses. *Journal of Personality and Social Psychology,* 1970, *16,* 710–717. (a)

Berkowitz, L. Experimental investigations of hostility catharsis. *Journal of Consulting and Clinical Psychology,* 1970, *35,* 1–7. (b)

Berkowitz, L., & Alioto, J. T. The meaning of an observed event as a determinant of its aggressive consequences. *Journal of Personality and Social Psychology,* 1973, *28,* 206–217.

Berkowitz, L., Green, J. A., & Macaulay, J. R. Hostility catharsis as the reduction of emotional tension. *Psychiatry,* 1962, *25,* 23–31.

Berkowitz, L., Lepinski, J. P., & Angulo, E. J. Awareness of own anger level and subsequent aggression. *Journal of Personality and Social Psychology,* 1969, *11,* 293–300.

Berkowitz, L., & Rawlings, E. Effects of film violence on inhibitions against subsequent aggression. *Journal of Abnormal and Social Psychology,* 1963, *66,* 405–412.

Berne, E. *Transactional analysis in psychotherapy.* New York: Grove Press, 1961.

Berne, E. *Games people play.* New York: Grove Press, 1964.

Bernheim, H. *Suggestive therapeutics: A treatise on the nature and uses of hypnosis.* New York: London Book Company, 1947. (Originally published, 1886.)

Berquist, W. H., & Klemm, H. D., Acquisition of verbal concepts as a function of explicit and implicit experimental demands and repression-sensitization. *Journal of General Psychology,* 1973, *89,* 67–80.

Berzins, J. E., & Ross, W. F. Experimental assessment of the responsiveness of addict patients to the "influence" of professionals versus other addicts. *Journal of Abnormal Psychology*, 1972, *80*, 141-148.

Beutler, L. E., Jobe, A. R., & Elkins, D. Outcomes in group psychotherapy: Using persuasion theory. *Journal of Consulting and Clinical Psychology*, 1974, *42*, 547-553.

Binder, C. V. A note on covert processes and the natural environment. *Behavior Therapy*, 1975, *6*, 568.

Black, P. (Ed.). *Physiological correlates of emotion.* New York: Academic Press, 1970.

Blackwood, R. The operant conditioning of verbally mediated self control in the classroom. *Journal of School Psychology*, 1970, *8*, 257-258.

Blechman, E. A., & Dannemiller, E. A. Effects of performance of perceived control over noxious noise. *Journal of Consulting and Clinical Psychology*, 1976, *44*, 601-607.

Bleda, P. R. Toward a clarification of the role of cognitive and affective processes in the similarity-attraction relationship. *Journal of Personality and Social Psychology*, 1974, *29*, 368-373.

Block, K. L. *A cognitive approach to the reaction of aggression.* Doctoral dissertation, University of Georgia, 1975.

Block, W. *Defending the undefendable.* New York: Fleet Press, 1976.

Blois, R. S. Dr. Ellis: A comparison of rational therapy and the structural differential. *Symbols,* October-November 1963, *2*, (4), 3-4.

Blue, R. *The effects of self induced mood states on behavior and physiological arousal.* M.A. thesis, Georgia State University, 1975.

Blum, G. S. *Psychodynamics: The science of unconscious mental forces.* Belmont, Calif.: Wadsworth, 1966.

Blum, G. S., Geiwitz, J. P., & Stewart, C. G. Cognitive arousal: The evolution of a model. *Journal of Personality and Social Psychology*, 1967, *5*, 138-151.

Blum, G. S., & Porter, M. L. Effects of the restriction of conscious awareness in a reaction time task. *International Journal of Clinical and Experimental Hypnosis*, 1974, *22*, 335-345.

Blum, G. S., & Wohl, B. M. An experimental analysis of the nature and operation of anxiety. *Journal of Abnormal Psychology*, 1971, *78*, 1-8.

Blumberg, R. W. Therapist leadership and client dogmatism in a therapy analogue. *Psychotherapy: Theory, Research and Practice*, 1972, *9*, 132-134.

Bobey, M. J., & Davidson, P. O. Psychological factors affecting pain tolerance. *Journal of Psychosomatic Research*, 1970, *14*, 371-376.

Bois, S. J. *The art of awareness: A textbook on general semantics.* Dubuque, Iowa: Brown, 1966.

Bois, S. J. The Power of words. *ETC.,* 1972, *29*, 299-304.

Bokor, S. *A study to determine the effects of a self-concept enhancement program in increasing self-concept in black, disadvantaged sixth-grade boys.* M.A. thesis, Queens College, 1971.

Borkovec, T. D. Effects of expectancy on the outcome of systematic desensitization. *Behavior Therapy*, 1972, *2*, 37-38.

Borkovec, T. D. The effects of instructional suggestion and physiological cues on analogue fear. *Behavior Therapy*, 1973, *4*, 185-192. (a)

Borkovec, T. D. The role of expectancy and physiological feedback in fear research: A review with special reference to subject characteristics. *Behavior Therapy*, 1973, *4*, 491-505. (b)

Borkovec, T. D., & Glasgow, R. E. Boundary conditions of false heart-rate feedback effects on avoidance behavior: A resolution of discrepant results. *Behaviour Research and Therapy*, 1973, *11*, 171-177.

Bornstein, P. H., & Quevillon, R. P. The effects of self-instructional package on overactive preschool boys. *Journal of Applied Behavior Analysis*, 1976, *9*, 179-188.

Boudewyns, P. A., Tanna, V., & Fleischman, D. Language repertoires and personality constructs: Their significance for behavior therapy. *Behavior Therapy,* 1975, *6,* 707–709.

Boulougouric, J. D., & Bassiakos, L. Case histories and shorter communications. *Behaviour Research and Therapy,* 1973, *11,* 227–231.

Bourland, D. D., Jr. The semantics of a non-Aristotelian language. *General Semantics Bulletin,* 1968, No. 35, 60–63.

Bourland, D. D., Jr. The un-isnesss of is. *Time,* May 23, 1969, 69.

Bowers, K. S. Sex and susceptibility as moderator variables in the relationship of creativity and hypnotic susceptibility. *Journal of Abnormal Psychology,* 1971, *78,* 93–100.

Bowers, K. S. Hypnosis, attribution and demand characteristics. *International Journal of Clinical and Experimental Hypnosis,* 1973, *21,* 226–238.

Braff, D. L., & Beck, A. T. Thinking disorder in depression. *Archives of General Psychiatry,* 1974, *31,* 456–459.

Brainerd, C. J. Perceived experiential correlates of apperceptively measured self-evaluations and affects in the late adolescent female. *Developmental Psychology,* 1969, *1,* 1-2.

Brainerd, C. J. Personal worth and perception of one's parents. *Rational Living,* 1970, *4,* 17–19.

Branden, N. *The psychology of self-esteem.* Los Angeles: Nash, 1969.

Braun, S. H. Effects of schedules of direct or vicarious reinforcement and modeling cues on behavior in extinction. *Journal of Personality and Social Psychology,* 1972, *22,* 356–365.

Breuer, J., & Freud, S. *Studies on hysteria.* New York: Basic Books, 1957. (Originally published, 1895.)

Breznitz, S. Incubation of threat: Duration of anticipation and false alarm as determinants of the fear reaction to an unavoidable frightening event. *Journal of Experimental Research in Personality,* 1967, *2,* 173–179.

Brickman, P., & Hendricks, M. Expectancy for gradual or sudden improvement and reaction to success and failure. *Journal of Personality and Social Psychology,* 1975, *32,* 893–900.

Brickman, P., Linsenmeier, A. W., & McCareins, A. G. Performance enhancement by relevant success and irrelevant failure. *Journal of Personality and Social Psychology,* 1976, *33,* 149–160.

Briggs, C. H., & Weinberg, R. A. Effects of reinforcement in training children's conceptual tempos. *Journal of Educational Psychology,* 1973, *65,* 383–394.

Brissett, M., & Nowicki, S., Jr. Internal versus external control of reinforcement and reaction to frustration. *Journal of Personality and Social Psychology,* 1973, *25,* 35–44.

Brody, M. B. *The effect of rational emotive affective education on anxiety, self-esteem and frustration tolerance.* Doctoral dissertation, Temple University, 1974.

Brown, B. M. *The use of induced imagery in psychotherapy.* Unpublished manuscript, 1967.

Brown, D. A. The fourth "R": A psychologist takes RBT to school. *Perspectives,* 1974, *1,* 4-6. (a)

Brown, D. A. Rational success. *A.R.T. in Daily Living,* 1974, *3,* 7. (b)

Brown, G. *Human teaching for human learning.* New York: Viking, 1971.

Brown, H. A. Role of expectancy manipulation in systematic desensitization. *Journal of Consulting and Clinical Psychology,* 1973, *41,* 405–411.

Browning, R. M. Treatment effects of a total behavior modification program with five autistic children. *Behaviour Research and Therapy,* 1971, *9,* 319–327.

Bugenthal, D., Whalen, C., & Henker, B. *Causal attributions of hyperactive children and motivational assumptions of two behavior change approaches: Evidence for an interactionist position.* Unpublished manuscript, University of California at Santa Barbara, 1975.

Bull, N. An introduction to attitude psychology. *Journal of Clinical and Experimental Psychopathology,* 1960, *27,* 147–156.

Burdick, J. A. Cardiac activity and attitude. *Journal of Personality and Social Psychology,* 1972, *22,* 80–86.

Byrne, D., Fisher, J. D., Lamberth, J., & Mitchell, H. Evaluations of erotica: Facts of feelings. *Journal of Personality and Social Psychology,* 1974, *29,* 111–116.

Byrne, P. *Stage and sex differences in moral and ego development prior and consequent of independence training.* Unpublished doctoral dissertation, University of Toronto, 1973.

Calhoun, L. G., Cheney, T., & Dawes, A. S. Locus of control, self reported depression and perceived causes of depression. *Journal of Consulting and Clinical Psychology,* 1974, *42,* 736.

Cameron, P., Titus, D. G., Kostin, J., & Kostin, M. The life satisfaction of nonnormal persons. *Journal of Consulting and Clinical Psychology,* 1973, *41,* 207–214.

Cantor, J. R., Zillmann, D., & Bryant, J. Enhancement of experienced sexual arousal in response to erotic stimuli through misattribution of unrelated residual excitation. *Journal of Personality and Social Psychology,* 1975, *32,* 69–75.

Cappell, H. D., & Pliner, P. L. Volitional control of marijuana intoxication: A study of the ability to come down on command. *Journal of Abnormal Psychology,* 1973, *82,* 428–434.

Carlson, W. A. & Travers, M. W., & Schwab, E. A., Jr. *A laboratory approach to the cognitive control of anxiety.* Paper presented at the American Personnel & Guidance Association meeting, Las Vegas, March 31, 1969.

Casler, L. *Is marriage necessary?* New York: Human Sciences Press, 1974.

Cassidy, W. L., Flanagan, N. B., & Spellman, M. Clinical observations in manic-depressive disease: A quantitative study of 100 manic-depressive patients and 50 medically sick controls. *Journal of the American Psychoanalytic Association,* 1957, *164,* 1535–1546.

Caulfield, J. B., & Martin, R. B. Establishment of praise as a reinforcer in chronic schizophrenics. *Journal of Consulting and Clinical Psychology,* 1976, *44,* 61–67.

Cautela, J. R. A behavior therapy approach to pervasive anxiety. *Behaviour Research and Therapy,* 1966, *4,* 99–111. (a)

Cautela, J. R. Treatment of compulsive behavior by covert sensitization. *Psychological Record,* 1966, *16,* 33–41. (b)

Cautela, J. R. Covert sensitization. *Psychological Reports,* 1967, *20,* 459–468.

Cautela, J. R. Behavior therapy and self-control: Techniques and implications. In C. M. Franks (Ed.), *Behavior therapy: Appraisal and status.* New York: McGraw-Hill, 1969, 323–340.

Cautela, J. R. Covert extinction. *Behavior Therapy,* 1971, *2,* 192–200.

Cautela, J. R. Covert processes and behavior modification. *Journal of Nervous and Mental Disease,* 1973, *157,* 27–35.

Cautela, J. R., Walsh, K., & Wish, P. The use of covert reinforcement in the modification of attitudes toward the mentally retarded. *Journal of Psychology,* 1971, *77,* 257–260.

Chaikin, A. L., & Karley, J. M. Victim or perpetrator? Defensive attribution of responsibility and the need for order and justice. *Journal of Personality and Social Psychology,* 1973, *25,* 268–275.

Chapman, L. J., Chapman, J. P., & Daut, R. L. Schizophrenic inability to disattend from strong aspects of meaning. *Journal of Abnormal Psychology,* 1976, *85,* 35–40.

Chappell, M., & Stevenson, T. Group psychological training in some organic conditions. *Mental Hygiene,* 1936, *20,* 588–597.

Charny, I. W. The psychotherapist as teacher of an ethic of nonviolence. *Voices,* 1968, *3*(4), 57–66.

Chaves, J. F., & Barber, T. X. Cognitive strategies, experimenter modeling and expectation in the attenuation of pain. *Journal of Abnormal Psychology,* 1974, *83,* 336–363.

Chemodurow, T. Introduction to transactional-semantic psychotherapy. *American Journal of Psychotherapy,* 1971, *25,* 619–634.

Chess, S., Thomas, T., & Birch, H. G. *Your child is a person.* New York: Viking, 1965.

Christensen, A., & Arkowitz, H. Preliminary report on practice dating and feedback as treatment for college dating problems. *Journal of Counseling Psychology,* 1974, *21,* 92–95.

Christensen, A., Arkowitz, H., & Anderson, J. Practice dating as treatment for college dating inhibitions. *Behaviour Research and Therapy,* 1975, *13,* 321–331.

Christensen, C. *Development and field testing of an interpersonal coping skills program.* Toronto: Ontario Institute for Studies in Education, 1974.

Churchill, D. W. Psychotic children and behavior modification. *American Journal of Psychiatry,* 1969, *125,* 585–590.

Clore, G., & Jeffrey, K. M. Emotional role playing, attitude change and attraction toward a disabled person. *Journal of Personality and Social Psychology,* 1972, *23,* 105–111.

Coleman, R. E. Manipulation of self-esteem as a determinant of mood of elated and depressed women. *Journal of Abnormal Psychology,* 1975, *84,* 693–700.

Collins, B. E. Four components of the Rotter international-external scale belief in a difficult world, a just world, a predictable world and a politically responsive world. *Journal of Personality and Social Psychology,* 1974, *29,* 381–391.

Colson, C. E. The evaluation of pornography: Effects of attitude and perceived physiological reaction. *Archives of Sexual Behavior,* 1974, *3,* 307–323.

Confino, B. A conversation with Jerome Kagan. *Saturday Review,* April 1973, 41–43.

Cook, D. A., Pallak, M. S., & Sogin, S. R. The effect of consensus on attitude change and attribution of causality. *Personality and Social Psychology Bulletin,* 1976, *2,* 248–251.

Cook, S. W., & Harris, R. E. The verbal conditioning of the galvanic skin reflex. *Journal of Experimental Psychology,* 1937, *21,* 201–210.

Cooke, G. The efficacy of 2 desensitization procedures: An analogue study. *Behaviour Research and Therapy,* 1966, *4,* 17–24.

Cooke, P. *An investigation of the effectiveness of rational-emotive therapy and its training sessions in Rochester.* Rochester, N.Y.: Author, 1974.

Coons, W. H. Psychotherapy and verbal conditioning in behavior modification. *The Canadian Psychologist,* 1972, *13,* 1–5.

Coons, W. H., & McEachern, D. I. Verbal conditioning, acceptance of self and acceptance of others. *Psychological Reports,* 1967, *20,* 715–722.

Cooper, J., & Goethals, G. R. Unforeseen events and the elimination of cognitive dissonance. *Journal of Personality and Social Psychology,* 1974, *29,* 441–445.

Corah, N. L., & Boffa, J. Perceived control, self-observation and response to aversive stimulation. *Journal of Personality and Social Psychology,* 1970, *16,* 1–14.

Corsini, R. J. *Role playing in psychotherapy: A manual.* Chicago: Aldine, 1966.

Corsini, R. J., Shaw, M. E., & Blake, R. R. *Roleplaying in business and industry.* New York: Free Press, 1961.

Coué, E. *My method.* New York: Doubleday, Page 1923.

Cradler, J. D., & Goodwin, D. L. Conditioning of verbal behavior as a function of age, social class, and type of reinforcement. *Journal of Educational Psychology,* 1971, *62,* 279–284.

Craig, R. J. Interpersonal competition, overinclusive thinking, and schizophrenia. *Journal of Consulting and Clinical Psychology,* 1973, *40,* 9–14.

Crawford, J. L., & Haaland, G. A. Predecisional information seeking and subsequent conformity in the social influence process. *Journal of Personality and Social Psychology,* 1972, *23,* 112–119.

Crowe, M. J., Marks, I. M., Agras, W. S., & Leitenberg, H. Time-limited desensitization, implosion and shaping for phobic patients: A crossover study. *Behaviour Research and Therapy,* 1972, *10,* 319–328.

Crue, B. (Ed.). *Pain: Research and treatment.* New York: Academic Press, 1975.

Cunningham, T., & Berberian, V. Sex differences in the relationship of self concept to locus of control in children. *Personality and Social Psychology Bulletin,* 1976, *2,* 277–281.

Curran, J. P., & Gilbert, F. S. A test of the relative effectiveness of a systematic desensitization program and an interpersonal skills training program with date-anxious subjects. *Behavior Therapy,* 1975, *6,* 510–521.

Curran, J. P., Gilbert, F. S., & Little, L. M. A comparison between behavioral replication training and sensitivity training approaches to heterosexual dating anxiety. *Journal of Counseling Psychology, 1976, 23,* 190–196.

Dalal, B. S., & Barber, T. Yoga, "yogic feats," and hypnosis in the light of empirical research. *American Journal of Clinical Hypnosis, 1969, 11,* 155–166.

Davidson, A. R., & Steiner, I. D. Reinforcement schedules and attributed freedom. *Journal of Personality and Social Psychology, 1971, 19,* 357–366.

Davies, R. L. *Relationship of irrational ideas to emotional disturbance.* M. Ed. thesis, University of Alberta, 1970.

Davis, K. M., & Blaney, P. H. Overinclusion and self-dieting in schizophrenia. *Journal of Abnormal Psychology, 1976, 85,* 51–60.

Davison, A. M., & Denney, D. R. Covert sensitization and information in the reduction of nailbiting. *Behavior Therapy, 1976, 7,* 512–518.

Davison, G. C. Relative contributions of differential relaxation and graded exposure to in vivo desensitization of a neurotic fear. *Proceedings of the 73rd Annual Convention of the American Psychological Association,* 1965, 209–210.

Davison, G. C. Anxiety under total curarization: Implications for the role of muscular relaxation in the desensitization of neurotic fears. *Journal of Nervous and Mental Disease,* 1967, *143,* 443–448.

Davison, G. C. The elimination of a sadistic fantasy by a client-controlled conditioning technique: A case study. *Journal of Abnormal Psychology,* 1968, *73,* 84–90.

Davison, G. C., Tsujimoto, R. N., & Glaros, A. Attribution and the maintenance of behavior change in falling asleep. *Journal of Abnormal Psychology,* 1973, *82,* 124–133.

Davison, G. C., & Valins, S. Maintenance of self-attributed and drug-attributed behavior change. *Journal of Personality and Social Psychology,* 1969, *11,* 25–33.

Davitz, J. R. *The language of emotion.* New York: Academic Press, 1969.

Deane, G. E. Human heart rate responses during experimentally induced anxiety: Effects of instructions on acquisition. *Journal of Experimental Psychology,* 1966, *67,* 193–195.

Deci, E. L. *Intrinsic motivation.* New York: Plenum, 1975.

Dell, D. M. Counselor power base, influence attempt, and behavior change in counseling. *Journal of Counseling Psychology,* 1973, *20,* 399–495.

Denney, D. R. The effects of exemplary and cognitive models and self rehearsal on children interrogative strategies. *Journal of Experimental Child Psychology,* 1975, *19,* 476–488.

Denney, D. R., & Sullivan, B. J. Desensitization and modeling treatments of spider fear using two types of scenes. *Journal of Consulting and Clinical Psychology,* 1976, *44,* 573–579.

Depue, R. A., & Fowles, D. C. Conceptual ability, response interference, and arousal in withdrawn and active schizophrenics. *Journal of Consulting and Clinical Psychology,* 1974, *47,* 509–518.

DeRivera, J. *Description of project on aggression.* New York: Department of Psychology, New York University, 1970.

Detweiler, R. A., & Zanna, M. P. Physiological mediation of attitudinal responses. *Journal of Personality and Social Psychology,* 1976, *33,* 107–116.

DeVoge, C. A behavioral approach to RET with children. *Rational Living,* 1974, *9*(1), 23–26.

Dewey, J. *Human Nature and conduct.* New York: Modern Library, 1930. (Originally published, 1922.)

DeWolfe, A. S., & McDonald, R. K. Sex differences and institutionalization in the word associations of schizophrenics. *Journal of Consulting and Clinical Psychology,* 1972, *39,* 215–221.

Diament, C., & Wilson, G. T. An experimental investigation of the effects of covert sensitization in an analogue eating situation. *Behavior Therapy,* 1975, *6,* 499–509.

Diamond, M. J. The use of observationally presented information to modify hypnotic susceptibility. *Journal of Abnormal Psychology,* 1972, *79,* 174–180.

Diamond, M. J., Gregory, J., Lenney, E., Steadman, C., & Talone, J. H. An alternative approach to personality correlates of hypnotizability: Hypnosis-specific mediational attitudes. *International Journal of Clinical and Experimental Hypnosis,* 1974, *32,* 346–353.

Diamond, M. J., & Shapiro, J. L. Changes in locus of control as a function of encounter group experiences. *Journal of Abnormal Psychology,* 1973, *82,* 514–518.

Dienstbier, R. A., Hillman, D., Lehnhoff, J., Hillman, J., & Valkenaar, M. C. An emotion attribution approach to moral behavior: Interfacing cognitive and avoidance theories of moral development. *Psychological Review,* 1975, *82,* 299–315.

DiGiuseppe, R. *A developmental study of the efficacy of rational-emotive education.* Doctoral dissertation, Hofstra University, 1975.

DiGiuseppe, R., Miller, N., & Trexler, L. A review of rational-emotive therapy outcome studies. *The Counseling Psychologist,* 1977, *7*(1), 64–72.

Dinkmeyer, D. *Developing understanding of self and others.* Circle Pines, Minn.: American Guidance Services, 1973.

Dmitruk, V. M., Collins, R. W., & Clinger, D. L. The "Barnum effect" and acceptance of negative personal evaluation. *Journal of Consulting and Clinical Psychology,* 1973, *41,* 192–194.

Doster, J. A. Effects of instuctions, modeling and role rehearsal on interview verbal behavior. *Journal of Consulting and Clinical Psychology,* 1972, *39,* 202–209.

Drabman, R. S., & Thomas, M. H. Does media violence increase children's toleration of real-life aggression? *Developmental Psychology,* 1974, *10,* 418–421.

Dreikurs, R. *Psychodynamics, psychotherapy and counseling* (Rev. ed.). Chicago: Alfred Adler Institute, 1974.

Drummond, D. *Self instructional training: An approach to disruptive classroom behavior.* Unpublished doctoral dissertation, University of Oregon, 1974.

Dua, P. S. Comparison of the effects of behaviorally oriented action and psychotherapy re-education on introversion-extraversion, emotionality, and internal-external control. *Journal of Counseling Psychology,* 1970, *17,* 567–572.

Dua, P. S. Effects of laboratory training on anxiety. *Journal of Counseling Psychology,* 1971, *19,* 171–172.

Dua, P. S. Group desensitization of a phobia with three massing procedures. *Journal of Counseling Psychology,* 1972, *10,* 125–129.

Dubois, P. *The psychic treatment of nervous disorders.* New York: Funk & Wagnalls, 1907.

DuCette, J., & Wolk, S. Cognitive and motivational correlates of generalized expectancies for control. *Journal of Personality and Social Psychology,* 1973, *26,* 420–426.

Duck, S. W., & Spencer, C. Personal constructs and friendship formation. *Journal of Personality and Social Psychology,* 1972, *23,* 40–45.

Dunlap, S. M., Gaertner, S. L., & Mangelsdorff, A. D. Personality and attitudes: A re-emphasis upon the cognitive component. *Journal of Psychology,* 1973, *85,* 249–255.

Dutta, S., Kanungo, R. N., & Friebergs, V. Retention of affective material: Effects of intensity of affect on retrieval. *Journal of Personality and Social Psychology,* 1972, *23,* 64–80.

Dutton, D. G., & Lake, R. A. Threat of own prejudice and reverse discrimination in interracial situations. *Journal of Personality and Social Psychology,* 1973, *28,* 94–100.

Dweck, C. S. The role of expectations and attributions in the alleviation of learned helplessness. *Journal of Personality and Social Psychology,* 1975, *31,* 674–685.

Dweck, C. S., & Reppucci, N. D. Learned helplessness and reinforcement responsibility in children. *Journal of Personality and Social Psychology,* 1973, *25,* 109–116.

D'Zurilla, T. J., & Goldfried, M. R. Problem solving and behavior modification. *Journal of Abnormal Psychology,* 1971, *78,* 107–126.

D'Zurilla, T. J., Wilson, G. T., & Nelson, R. A preliminary study of the effectiveness of graduated prolonged exposure in the treatment of irrational fear. *Behavior Therapy,* 1973, *4,* 672–685.

Eagly, A. H., & Acksen, B. A. The effect of expecting to be evaluated on change toward favorable and unfavorable information about oneself. *Sociometry*, 1971, *34*, 411–422.

Early, C. J. Attitude learning in children. *Journal of Educational Psychology*, 1968, *59*, 176–180.

Eberle, T. M., Rehm, L. P., & McBurney, D. H. Fear decrement to anxiety to anxiety hierarchy items: Effects of stimulus intensity. *Behaviour Research and Therapy*, 1975, *13*, 255–261.

Educational Research Council of America. *Dealing with aggressive behavior (teacher's manual and student book for junior high school). Dealing with causes of behavior (teacher's manuals and student books for grades 4-5).* Cleveland: Educational Research Council of America, 1971. (a)

Educational Research Council of America. *Drugs, alcohol, tobacco, and human behavior (teacher's manuals and student books for elementary, junior, and senior high schools).* Cleveland: Educational Research Council of America, 1971. (b)

Ehri, L. C., & Muzio, I. M. Cognitive style and reasoning about speed. *Journal of Educational Psychology*, 1974, *66*, 569–571.

Eisler, R. M., Hersen, M., & Agras, W. S. Effects of videotape and instructional feedback on nonverbal marital interaction: An analog study. *Behavior Therapy*, 1973, *4*, 551–558.

Ellenberger, H. F. *The discovery of the unconscious.* New York: Basic Books, 1970.

Elliott, C. H., & Denney, D. R. Weight control through covert sensitization and false feedback. *Journal of Consulting and Clinical Psychology*, 1975, *43*, 842–850.

Ellis, A. *An introduction to the scientific principles of psychoanalysis.* Provincetown, Mass.: Journal Press, 1950.

Ellis, A. *The American sexual tragedy.* New York: Twayne, 1954. (Rev. ed.: New York: Lyle Stuart & Grove Press, 1962.)

Ellis, A. *How to live with a "neurotic" at home and at work.* New York: Crown, 1957. (Rev. ed., 1975.) (a)

Ellis, A. Outcome of employing three techniques of psychotherapy. *Journal of Clinical Psychology*, 1957, *13*, 334–350. (b)

Ellis, A. Rational psychotherapy. *Journal of General Psychology*, 1958, *59*, 35–49.

Ellis, A. *Reason and emotion in psychotherapy.* New York: Lyle Stuart, 1962.

Ellis, A. What *really* causes therapeutic change. *Voices*, 1968, *4*(2), 90–97.

Ellis, A. A cognitive approach to behavior therapy. *International Journal of Psychiatry*, 1969, *8*, 896–900.

Ellis, A. The cognitive element in experiential and relationship psychotherapy. *Existential Psychiatry*, 1970, *28*, 35–52.

Ellis, A. *Growth through reason.* Palo Alto, Calif.: Science and Behavior Books, 1971. (Also, Hollywood, Calif.: Wilshire Books, 1971.) (a)

Ellis, A. *Rational-emotive therapy and its application to emotional education.* New York: Institute for Rational Living, 1971. (b)

Ellis, A. Emotional education in the classroom: The living school. *Journal of Clinical Child Psychology*, 1972, *1*(3), 19–22. (a)

Ellis, A. Psychotherapy and the value of a human being. In J. W. Davis (Ed.), *Value and valuation: Axiological studies in honor of Robert S. Hartman.* Knoxville: University of Tennessee Press, 1972, 117–139. (Reprinted: New York: Institute for Rational Living, 1972.) (b)

Ellis, A. Are cognitive behavior therapy and rational therapy synonymous? *Rational Living*, 1973, *8*(2), 8–11. (a)

Ellis, A. Emotional education at the living school. In M. M. Ohlsen (Ed.), *Counseling children in groups.* New York: Holt, Rinehart & Winston, 1973, 79–93. (b)

Ellis, A. *Humanistic psychotherapy: The rational-emotive approach.* New York: Julian Press and McGraw-Hill Paperbacks, 1973. (c)

Ellis, A. My philosophy of psychotherapy. *Journal of Contemporary Psychotherapy*, 1973,

6, 13–18. (d)

Ellis, A. Rational-emotive therapy. In R. Corsini (Ed.), *Current psychotherapies.* Itasca, Ill.: Peacock, 1973, 167–206. (e)

Ellis, A. Cognitive aspects of abreactive therapy. *Voices,* 1974, *10*(1), 48–56. (a)

Ellis, A. Experience and rationality: The making of a rational-emotive therapist. *Psychotherapy: Theory, Research and Practice,* 1974, *11*, 194–198. (b)

Ellis, A. Rational-emotive therapy. In A. Burton (Ed.), *Operational theories of personality.* New York: Brunner-Mazel, 1974, 308–344. (c)

Ellis, A. On the disvalue of mature anger. *Rational Living,* 1975, *19*(1), 24–27. (a)

Ellis, A. The rational-emotive approach to sex therapy. *The Counseling Psychologist,* 1975, *5*, 14–21. (b)

Ellis, A. *Techniques for disputing irrational beliefs (DIBS).* New York: Institute for Rational Living, 1975. (c)

Ellis, A. The biological basis of human irrationality. *Journal of Individual Psychology,* 1976. (a)

Ellis, A. Healthy and unhealthy aggression. *Humanitas,* 1976, *12*, 239–254. (b)

Ellis, A. *RET abolishes most of the human ego.* New York: Institute for Rational Living, 1976. (c)

Ellis, A. *Sex and the liberated man.* New York: Lyle Stuart, 1976. (d)

Ellis, A. The what and how of psychotherapy: The rational-emotive view. *Journal of Contemporary Psychotherapy,* 1976, *8*(1), 20–28. (e)

Ellis, A. *How to live with—and without—anger.* New York: Reader's Digest Press, 1977.

Ellis, A. Toward a new theory of personality. In R. J. Corsini, *A sourcebook of personality theory.* Itasca, Ill.: Peacock, 1978.

Ellis, A., & Simon, W. *An annotated bibliography of research on rational-emotive therapy and cognitive-behavior therapy.* New York: Institute for Rational Living, 1980.

Ellis, A., & Grieger, R. *Handbook of rational-emotive therapy.* New York: Springer, 1977.

Ellis, A., & Gullo, J. *Murder and assassination.* New York: Lyle Stuart, 1972.

Ellis, A., & Harper, R. A. *A new guide to rational living.* Englewood Cliffs, N.J.: Prentice-Hall, 1975. (Also, Hollywood, Calif.: Wilshire Books, 1975.)

Ellis, A., & Knaus, W. *Overcoming procrastination.* New York: Institute for Rational Living, 1977.

Ellis, A., & Wolpe, J. The forum: Rational-emotive revisited. *Professional Psychology,* 1974, *5*, 111–112.

Ellsworth, P. C., & Langer, E. J. Staring and approach: An interpretation of the stare as a nonspecific activator. *Journal of Personality and Social Psychology,* 1976, *33*, 117–122.

Emmelkamp, P. M. G., & Wessels, H. Flooding in imagination versus flooding in vivo: A comparison with agoraphobics. *Behaviour Research and Therapy,* 1975, *13*, 7–15.

Epictetus. *The works of Epictetus.* Boston: Little, Brown, 1899.

Etzioni, A. Basic human needs, alienation and inauthenticity. *American Sociological Review,* 1968, *33*, 870–885.

Everaerd, W. T. A. M., Rijken, H. M., & Emmelkamp, P. M. G. A comparison of "flooding" and "successive approximation" in the treatment of agoraphobia. *Behaviour Research and Therapy,* 1973, *11*, 105–117.

Eysenck, H. J. *Behavior therapy and the neuroses.* New York: Macmillan, 1960.

Eysenck, H. J. (Ed.). *Experiments in behavior therapy.* New York: Macmillan, 1964.

Felixbond, J. J., & O'Leary, K. D. Effects of reinforcement on children's academic behavior as a functioning of self-determined and externally imposed contingencies. *Journal of Applied Behavior Analysis,* 1973, *6*, 241–250.

Felton, G. S., & Biggs, B. E. Teaching internalization behavior to collegiate low achievers in group psychotherapy. *Psychotherapy: Theory, Research and Practice,* 1972, *9*, 281–283.

Fenichel, O. *Psychoanalytic theory of neurosis.* New York: Norton, 1945.

Ferenczi, S. *Further contributions to the theory and techniques of psychoanalysis.* New York: Basic Books, 1952. (Originally published, 1926.)

Feshbach, S. The function of aggression and the regulation of aggressive drive. *Psychological Review,* 1964, *71,* 257–272.

Feshbach, S. Dynamics and morality of violence and aggression. *American Psychologist,* 1971, *26,* 281–292.

Festinger, L. *A theory of cognitive dissonance.* Evanston, Ill.: Row, Peterson, 1957.

Festinger, L. Cognitive dissonance. *Scientific American,* 1962, *207,* 93–102.

Fiedler, P., & Windheuser, H. Modification of creative behavior through modeling processes. *Zeitschrift für Entwicklungspsychologie und Pedagogische Psychologie,* 1974, *6,* 262–280.

Fielding, L. T., Erickson, E., & Bettin, B. Modification of staff behavior: A brief note. *Behavior Therapy,* 1971, *2,* 550–553.

Fisher, E. B., & Winkler, R. C. Self control over intrusive experiences. *Journal of Consulting and Clinical Psychology,* 1975, *43,* 911–916.

Folkins, C. H. Temporal factors and the cognitive mediators of stress reaction. *Journal of Personality and Social Psychology,* 1970, *14,* 173–184.

Foreyt, J. P., & Hagen, R. L. Covert sensitization: Conditioning or suggestion? *Journal of Abnormal Psychology,* 1973, *82,* 17–23.

Forrest, M. S., & Hokanson, J. E. Depression and autonomic arousal reduction accompanying self-punitive behavior. *Journal of Abnormal Psychology,* 1975, *84,* 346–357.

Fox, E. E. *A life orientation scale: Correlates of biophilia and necrophilia.* Doctoral dissertation, University of Alberta, 1969.

Frank, J. D. *Persuasion and healing: A comparative study of psychotherapy.* Baltimore: Johns Hopkins University Press, 1961.

Frank, J. D. The influence of patients' and therapists' expectations on the outcome of psychotherapy. *British Journal of Medical Psychology,* 1968, *41,* 349–356.

Frankel, C. The nature and sources of irrationalism. *Science,* 1973, *180,* 922–931.

Frankl, V. E. *Man's search for meaning.* Washington Square Press, 1966.

Franks, C. *Behavior therapy: Appraisal and status.* New York: McGraw-Hill, 1969.

Frazer, J. G. *The new golden bough.* New York: Criterion Books, 1959.

Freedman, D. G. Boy with immune deficiency challenges theories in three years of his life in plastic bubble. *New York Times,* October 7, 1974, 41.

Freedman, D. G., & Keller, B. Inheritance of behavior in infants. *Science,* 1963, *140,* 196–198.

Freud, A. *The ego and the mechanisms of defense.* New York: International Universities Press, 1975. (Originally published, 1948.)

Freud, S. *Standard edition of the complete psychological works of Sigmund Freud.* London: Hogarth, 1965.

Friar, L., & Beatty, J. Migraine: Management by trained control of vasoconstriction. *Journal of Consulting and Clinical Psychology,* 1976, *44,* 46–53.

Friedman, A. S., Cowitz, B., Cohen, H. W., & Granick, S. Syndromes and themes of psychotic depression: A factor analysis. *Archives of General Psychiatry,* 1963, *9,* 504–509.

Friedman, M. *Rational behavior.* Columbia: University of South Carolina Press, 1975.

Friedman, P. H. The effects of modeling, role-playing and participation on behavior change. *Progress in Experimental Personality Research,* 1972, *6,* 41–81.

Fritz, C. E., & Marks, E. S. The NORC studies of human behavior in disaster. *Journal of Social Issues,* 1954, *10,* 26–41.

Frodi, A. On the elicitation and control of aggressive behavior. *Goteborg Psychological Reports,* 1974, *4,* 1–16.

Fromm, E. *Escape from freedom.* New York: Rinehart, 1941.

Fromm, E. *Man for himself.* New York: Rinehart, 1947.

Gagné, R. M. Problem solving and thinking. *Annual Review of Psychology,* 1959, *10,* 147–172.

Garfield, S. L., Gershon, S., Sletten, I., Sundland, D. M., & Ballou, S. Chemically induced anxiety. *International Journal of Neuropsychiatry,* 1967, *3,* 426–433.

Garfield, Z. H., Darwin, P. L., Singer, B. A., & McBrearty, J. F. Effect of "in vivo" training on experimental desensitization of a phobia. *Psychological Reports,* 1967, *20,* 515-519.

Garmezy, N. *Vulnerable and invulnerable children: Theory, research and intervention.* Washington: American Psychological Association, 1975.

Garner, H. H. *Psychotherapy: Confrontation problem-solving technique.* St. Louis, Mo.: Warren H. Green, 1970.

Gatchel, R. J., Paulus, P. B., & Maples, C. W. Learned helplessness and self reported affect. *Journal of Abnormal Psychology,* 1975, *84,* 732-734.

Gatchel, R. J., & Proctor, J. D. Physiological correlates of learned helplessness in man. *Journal of Abnormal Psychology,* 1976, *85,* 27-34.

Geen, R. G., Rakosky, J. J., & Pigg, R. Awareness of arousal and its relation to aggression. *British Journal of Social Psychology,* 1972, *11,* 115-221.

Geen, R. G., & Stonner, D. Context effects on observed violence. *Journal of Personality and Social Psychology,* 1973, *25,* 145-150.

Geen, R. G., Stonner, D., & Hope, G. L. The facilitation of aggression: Evidence against the catharsis hypotheses. *Journal of Personality and Social Psychology,* 1975, *31,* 721-726.

Geen, R., Stonner, D., & Kelley, D. R. Aggression anxiety and cognitive appraisal of aggression threat stimuli. *Journal of Personality and Social Psychology,* 1974, *29,* 196-200.

Geer, J. H., Davison, G. C., & Gatchel, R. J. Reduction of stress in humans through non-veridical perceived control of aversive stimulation. *Journal of Personality and Social Psychology,* 1971, *16,* 731-735.

Geer, J. H., & Fuhr, R. Cognitive factors in sexual arousal: The role of distraction. *Journal of Consulting and Clinical Psychology,* 1976, *44,* 238-243.

Gelder, M. G., Bancroft, J. H., Gath, D. H., Johnston, D. W., Mathews, A. M., & Shaw, P. M. Specific and non-specific factors in behavior therapy. *British Journal of Psychiatry,* 1973, *123,* 445-462.

Geller, J. D., & Berzins, J. I. A-B distinction in a sample of prominent psychotherapists. *Journal of Consulting and Clinical Psychology,* 1976, *44,* 77-82.

Genther, R., Shuntich, R., & Bunting, K. Racial prejudice, belief similarity and human aggression. *Journal of Psychology,* 1975, *91,* 229-234.

Gentry, W. D. In vivo desensitization of an obsessive cancer fear. *Journal of Behavior Therapy and Experimental Psychiatry,* 1970, *1,* 315-318.

Gibbons, D., Kilbourne, L., Saunders, A., & Castles, C. The cognitive control of behavior: A comparison of systematic desensitization and hypnotically induced "directed experience" techniques. *American Journal of Clinical Hypnosis,* 1970, *23,* 141-145.

Giesen, M., & Hendrick, C. Effects of false positive and negative arousal feedback on persuasion. *Journal of Personality and Social Psychology,* 1974, *30,* 449-457.

Gilbert, L. A. Situational factors and the relationship between locus of control and psychological adjustment. *Journal of Counseling Psychology,* 1976, *23,* 302-309.

Glasgow, R. E., & Arkowitz, H. The behavioral assessment of male and female social competence in dyadic heterosexual interactions. *Behavior Therapy,* 1975, *6,* 488-498.

Glass, C. R., Gottman, J. M., & Shmurak, S. H. Response-acquisition and cognitive self-statement modification approaches to dating-skills training. *Journal of Counseling Psychology,* 1976.

Glass, D., Singer, J. E., & Friedman, L. N. Psychic cost of adaptation to an environment stress. *Journal of Personality and Social Psychology,* 1969, *12,* 200-210.

Glass, D., & Singer, J. E. *Stress and adaptation.* New York: Academic Press, 1972.

Glasser, W. *Reality therapy.* New York: Harper, 1965.

Gliedman, L. H., Nash, E. H., Imber, S. D., Stone, A. R., & Frank, J. D. Reduction of symptoms by pharmacologically inert substances and by short-term psychotherapy. *Archives of Neurology and Psychiatry,* 1958, *79,* 345-351.

Goldfried, M. R. Systematic desensitization as training in self-control. *Journal of Consulting and Clinical Psychology,* 1971, *37,* 228–234.

Goldfried, M. R., & Davison, G. *Clinical behavior therapy.* New York: Holt, Rinehart & Winston, 1976.

Goldfried, M. R., & Goldfried, A. Cognitive change methods. In F. H. Kanfer & A. P. Goldstein (Eds.), *Helping people change.* New York: Pergamon, 1975, 89–116.

Goldfried, M. R., & Merbaum, M. A perspective on self-control. In M. R. Goldfried & M. Merbaum (Eds.), *Behavior change through self-control.* New York: Holt, Rinehart & Winston, 1973.

Goldfried, M. R. & Trier, C. S. Effectiveness of relaxation as an active coping skill. *Journal of Abnormal Psychology,* 1974, *83,* 348–355.

Goodwin, S. E., & Mahoney, M. J. Modification of aggression through modeling: An experimental probe. *Journal of Behavior Therapy and Experimental Psychiatry,* 1975, *6,*(3), 200–202.

Gordon, J. E. (Ed.). *Handbook of clinical and experimental hypnosis.* New York: Macmillan, 1967.

Gottman, J. M., & McFall, R. M. Self-monitoring effects in a program for potential high school dropouts: A time series analysis. *Journal of Consulting and Clinical Psychology,* 1972, *39,* 273–281.

Graham, D. T. Psychosomatic medicine. In N. S. Greenfield & R. A. Sternbach (Eds.), *Handbook of psychophysiology.* New York: Holt, Rinehart & Winston, 1972.

Green, A. H., & Marlatt, G. A. Effects of instructions and modeling upon affective and descriptive verbalization. *Journal of Abnormal Psychology,* 1972, *80,* 189–196.

Green, E. New consciousness: Biofeedback for mind-body self regulation: Healing and creativity. *Cooperator,* 1973, *5,* 8–9.

Greenberg, I. A. *Psychodrama: Theory and therapy.* New York: Behavioral Publications, 1974.

Greene, R. J., & Reyher, J. Pain tolerance in hypnotic analgesic and imagination states. *Journal of Abnormal Psychology,* 1972, *79,* 29–38.

Greenwald, H. (Ed.). *Active psychotherapies.* New York: Atherton, 1967.

Greenwald, H. *Direct decision therapy.* San Diego: Edits, 1976.

Greenwell, J., & Dengerink, H. A. The role of perceived versus actual attack in human physical aggression. *Journal of Personality and Social Psychology,* 1973, *26,* 66–71.

Grings, W. W. Cognitive factors in electrodermal conditioning. *Psychological Bulletin,* 1973, *79,* 200–210.

Grossack, M. M., Armstrong, T., & Lussiev, G. Correlates of self-actualization. *Journal of Humanistic Psychology,* 1966, *6,* 87.

Grossberg, J. M., & Wilson, H. K. Physiological changes accompanying the visualization of fearful and neutral situations. *Journal of Personality and Social Psychology,* 1968, *10,* 124–133.

Grzesiak, R. C., & Locke, B. J. Cognitive and behavioral correlates to overt behavior change within a token economy. *Journal of Consulting and Clinical Psychology,* 1975, *43,* 272.

Guernette, J. *Emotion and cognition: An inquiry into recent and current research within the context of the theoretical basis of rational-emotive psychotherapy.* Unpublished manuscript, College Station, Texas, 1972.

Gustav, A. Success is——: Locating composite sanity. *Rational Living,* 1968, *3,* 1–6.

Hagen, R. L. Group therapy versus bibliotherapy in weight reduction. *Behavior Therapy,* 1974, *5,* 222–234.

Hagen, R. L., Foreyt, J. P., & Durham, T. W. The dropout problem: Reducing attrition in obesity research. *Behavior Therapy,* 1976, *7,* 463–476.

Hale, W., & Strickland, B. Induction of mood states and their effects on cognitive and social behaviors. *Journal of Consulting and Clinical Psychology,* 1976, *44,* 155.

Haley, J. Control in psychotherapy with schizophrenics. *Archives of General Psychiatry,* 1961, *5,* 340–353.

Haley, J. *Strategies in psychotherapy.* New York: Grune & Stratton, 1963.

Hall, R. A., & Hinkle, J. E. Case histories and shorter communications. *Behaviour Research and Therapy,* 1972, *10,* 407–410.

Hampson, J. L., Rosenthal, D., & Frank, J. D. A comparative study of the effects of mephenesin and placebo on the symptomatology of a mixed group of psychiatric outpatients. *Bulletin of Johns Hopkins Hospital,* 1954, *95,* 170–177.

Haney, J. N., & Euse, F. J. Skin conductance and heart rate responses to neutral, positive and negative imagery: Implications for covert behavior therapy procedures. *Behavior Therapy,* 1976, *7,* 494–503.

Harari, H. Interpersonal models in psychotherapy and counseling: A social-psychological analysis of a clinical problem. *Journal of Abnormal Psychology,* 1971, *78,* 127–133.

Harris, L. M. Cognitive variables and behavior modification of obesity. *Behavior Therapy,* 1976, *7,* 563–564.

Harris, M. B. Self-directed program for weight control: A pilot study. *Journal of Abnormal Psychology,* 1969, *74,* 263–270.

Harris, M. B. Reciprocity and generosity: Some determinants of sharing in children. *Child Development,* 1970, *41,* 313–328.

Harris, M. B., & Bruner, C. G. A comparison of a self-control and a contract procedure for weight control. *Behaviour Research and Therapy,* 1971, *9,* 347–354.

Harris, M. B., & Huang, L. C. Aggression and the attribution process. *Journal of Social Psychology,* 1974, *92,* 209–216.

Harris, M. B., & Rothberg, C. A self-control approach to reducing smoking. *Psychological Reports,* 1972, *31,* 165–166.

Harris, V. A., & Katkin, E. S. Primary and secondary emotional behavior: An analysis of the role of autonomic feedback on affect, arousal and attribution. *Psychological Bulletin,* 1975, *82,* 904–916.

Harrow, M., Himmelhoch, J., Tucker, G., Hersh, J., & Quinlan, D. Overinclusive thinking in acute schizophrenic patients. *Journal of Abnormal Psychology,* 1972, *79,* 161–168.

Hart, H. *Autoconditioning.* Englewood Cliffs, N. J.: Prentice-Hall, 1956.

Hartig, M., & Kanfer, F. H. The role of verbal self-instructions in children's resistance to temptation. *Journal of Personality and Social Psychology,* 1973, *25,* 259–267.

Hartman, W. E., & Fithian, M. A. *Treatment of sexual dysfunction.* Long Beach, Calif.: Center for Marital and Sexual Studies, 1972.

Hauck, P. A. *Overcoming frustration and anger.* Philadelphia: Westminister Press, 1974.

Hays, V., & Waddell, K. J. A self-reinforcing procedure for thought stopping. *Behavior Therapy,* 1976, *7,* 559.

Heider, F. Attitudes and cognitive organization. *Journal of Psychology,* 1946, *21,* 108–112.

Heilbrun, A. B. Adaptation to aversive maternal control and perception of simultaneously presented evaluative cues: A further test of a developmental model of paranoid behavior. *Journal of Consulting and Clinical Psychology,* 1973, *41,* 301–307.

Heitler, J. B. Preparation of lower-class patients for expressive group psychotherapy. *Journal of Consulting and Clinical Psychology,* 1973, *41,* 251–260.

Hekmat, H., & Vanian, D. Behavior modification through covert semantic desensitization. *Journal of Consulting and Clinical Psychology,* 1971, *36,* 248–251.

Heller, J. F., Pallak, M. S., & Picek, J. M. The interactive effects of intent and threat on boomerang attitude change. *Journal of Personality and Social Psychology,* 1973, *26,* 273–279.

Henson, D. E., & Rubin, H. B. Voluntary control of eroticism. *Journal of Applied Behavior Analysis,* 1971, *4,* 37–44.

Herman, S. H., & Prewett, M. An experimental analysis of feedback to increase sexual arousal in a case of homo and heterosexual impotence: A preliminary report. *Journal of Behavior Therapy and Experimental Psychology,* 1975, *5,* 1–4.

Herzberg, A. *Active psychotherapy.* New York: Grune & Stratton, 1945.

Hickey, K. S. Internal-external locus of control and environmental cohesiveness. *Personality and Social Psychology Bulletin,* 1976, *2,* 282–285.

Hildebrandt, D. E., Feldman, S. E., & Ditrichs, R. A. Rules, models, and self-reinforcement in children. *Journal of Personality and Social Psychology,* 1973, *25,* 1–5.

Hilgard, E. R., MacDonald, H., Marshall, G., & Morgan, A. H. Anticipation of pain and of pain control under hypnosis: Heart rate and blood pressure responses in the blood pressure test. *Journal of Abnormal Psychology,* 1974, *38,* 561–568.

Hill, L. B. *Psychotherapeutic intervention in schizophrenia.* Chicago: University of Chicago Press, 1955.

Hinkle, J. E. Case histories and shorter communications. *Behaviour Research and Therapy,* 1972, *10,* 407–410.

Hiroto, D. S., & Seligman, M. E. P. Generality of learned helplessness in man. *Journal of Personality and Social Psychology,* 1975, *31,* 311–327.

Hirschman, R. Cross-modal effects of anticipatory bogus heart rate feedback in a negative emotional context. *Journal of Personality and Social Psychology,* 1975, *31,* 13–19.

Hodgson, J., & Urban, H. *A comparison of interpersonal training programs in the treatment of depressive states.* Unpublished manuscript, 1975.

Hodgson, R., Rachman, S., & Marks, I. M. The treatment of chronic obsessive-compulsive neurosis: Follow-up and further findings. *Behaviour Research and Therapy,* 1972, *10,* 181–189.

Hoehn-Saric, R., Frank, J. D., & Gurland, B. J. Focused attitude change in neurotic patients. *Journal of Nervous and Mental Disease,* 1968, *147,* 124–133.

Hoffer, E. *The true believer.* New York: Harper, 1951.

Hokanson, J. E. Physiological evaluation of the catharsis hypotheses. In E. Megaree & J. E. Hokanson (Eds.), *The dynamics of aggression.* New York: Harper & Row, 1970, 74–96.

Holmes, D. S., & Frost, R. O. Effect of false autonomic feedback on self-reported anxiety, pain perception and pulse rate. *Behavior Therapy,* 1976, *7,* 330–334.

Homme, L. E. Perspectives in psychology: XXIV. Control of coverants, the operants of the mind. *Psychological Record,* 1965, *15,* 501–511.

Homme, L. E. *Coverant control therapy: A special case of contingency management.* Paper read at the 1966 convention of the Rocky Mountain Psychological Association, Albuquerque, May 1966.

Homme, L. E. *How to use contingency contracting in the classroom.* Champaign, Ill.: Research Press, 1969.

Horan, J. J., Baker, S. B., Hoffman, A. M., & Shute, R. E. Weight loss through variations in the coverant control paradigm. *Journal of Consulting and Clinical Psychology,* 1975, *43,* 68–72.

Horney, K. *Collected works.* New York: Norton, 1965.

Horowitz, M. J. Cognitive response to erotic and stressful films. *Archives of General Psychiatry,* 1973, *29,* 81–84.

Horowitz, M. J., & Becker, S. S. Cognitive responses to stress and experimental demand. *Journal of Abnormal Psychology,* 1971, *78,* 86–92. (a)

Horowitz, M. J., & Becker, S. S. Cognitive response to stressful stimuli. *Archives of General Psychiatry,* 1971, *25,* 419–428. (b)

Horowitz, M. J., & Becker, S. S. The compulsion to repeat trauma. *Journal of Nervous and Mental Disease,* 1971, *153,* 32–40. (c)

Horowitz, M. J., Becker, S. S., & Malone, P. Stress: Different effects on patients and non-patients. *Journal of Abnormal Psychology,* 1973, *82,* 547–551.

Horowitz, M. J., Becker, S. S., & Moskowitz, M. I. Intrusive and repetitive thought after stress: A replication study. *Psychological Reports,* 1971, *29,* 763–767.

Houston, B. K. Control over stress. *Journal of Personality and Social Psychology,* 1972, *21,* 249–255.

Houston, B. K. *Dispositional anxiety and the effectiveness of cognitive coping strategies in stressful laboratory and classroom situations.* Paper presented at Conference on Dimensions of Anxiety and Stress, Oslo, 1975.

Hovland, C. I., & Janis, I. L. *Personality and persuasibility.* New Haven, Conn.: Yale University Press, 1959.

Hoxter, A. L. *Irrational beliefs and self-concept in two kinds of behavior.* Doctoral dissertation, University of Alberta, 1967.

Hunt, G. M., & Azrin, N. H. A community-reinforcement approach to alcoholism. *Behaviour Research and Therapy,* 1973, *11,* 91–104.

Hurley, A. D. Covert reinforcement: The contribution of the reinforcing stimulus to treatment outcome. *Behavior Therapy,* 1976, *7,* 374–378.

Innes, J. M. Dissonance reduction in the therapist and its relevance to aversion therapy. *Behavior Therapy,* 1972, *3,* 441–443.

Irwin, F. W. *Intentional behavior and motivation: A cognitive theory.* New York: Lippincott, 1971.

Jabichuk, A., & Smeriglio, U. *The influence of symbolic modeling on the social behavior of preschool children with low levels of social responsiveness.* Unpublished manuscript, University of Western Ontario, 1975.

Jacobs, A., Jacobs, M., Cavior, N., & Burke, J. Anonymous feedback: Credibility and desirability of structured emotional and behavioral feedback delivered in groups. *Journal of Counseling Psychology,* 1974, *21,* 106–111.

Jacobs, A., & Sachs, L. B. (Eds.). *The psychology of private events: Perspective on covert response systems.* New York: Academic Press, 1971.

Jacobs, M., Jacobs, A., Feldman, G., & Cavior, N. Feedback and the "credibility gap": Delivery of positive and negative and emotional and behavioral feedback in groups. *Journal of Consulting and Clinical Psychology,* 1973, *41,* 215–223.

Janda, L. H., & Rimm, D. C. Covert sensitization in the treatment of obesity. *Journal of Abnormal Psychology,* 1972, *80,* 37–42.

Janov, A. *The primal scream.* New York: Delta Books, 1970.

Jellinek, E. M. Clinical tests on comparative effectiveness of analgesic drugs. *Biometrics Bulletin,* 1946, *2,* 87.

Jellinek, R. Mythology as a science. *New York Times,* May 12, 1973, 31.

Johnson, J. E. Effects of accurate expectations about sensations on the sensory and distress components of pain. *Journal of Personality and Social Psychology,* 1973, *27,* 261–275.

Johnson, S. M., & White, G. Self observation as an agent of behavioral change. *Behavior Therapy,* 1971, *2,* 488–497.

Jones, E., Kanouse, D., Kelley, H., Nisbett, R., Valins, S., & Weiner, B. *Attribution: Perceiving the causes of behavior.* Morristown, N.J.: General Learning Press, 1972.

Jones, J. G. Motor learning without demonstration of physical practice, under two conditions of mental practice. *Research Quarterly,* 1965, *36,* 220–276.

Jordan, B. T., & Kempler, B. Hysterical personality: An experimental investigation of sex-role conflict. *Journal of Abnormal Psychology,* 1970, *75,* 172–176.

Jordan, C. S., & Simprelle, C. N. Physiological correlates of induced anxiety with normal subjects. *Psychotherapy: Theory, Research and Practice,* 1972, *9*(1), 20–23.

Jung, C. G. *The practice of psychotherapy.* New York: Pantheon, 1954.

Jurjevich, R. M. *Direct psychotherapy: 28 American originals.* Miami: University of Miami Press, 1973.

Jurjevich, R. M. *The hoax of Freudism.* Philadelphia: Dorrance, 1974.

Kaczkowski, H., & Owen, K. Anxiety and anger in adolescent girls. *Psychological Reports,* 1972, *31,* 281–282.

Kagan, J. Motives and development. *Journal of Personality and Social Psychology,* 1972, *22,* 51–56.

Kalish, R. A. I am, therefore I think. *Professional Psychology,* 1970, *1,* 392–394.

Kallmann, F. V. Review of psychiatric progress 1959: Heredity and genius. *American Journal of Psychiatry,* 1960, *116,* 577–581.

Kamiya, J. Conscious control of brain waves. *Psychology Today*, 1968, *1*(11), 57–61.

Kanfer, F. H. *The maintenance of behavior by self-generated stimuli and reinforcement.* Paper presented at the Conference on Perspectives in the Psychology of Private Events. Morgantown, W. Va., April 1970. (a)

Kanfer, F. H. *Self-regulation: Research, issues and speculations.* In C. Neuringer & J. L. Michael (Eds.), *Behavior modification in clinical psychology.* New York: Appleton-Century-Crofts, 1970, 178–220. (b)

Kanfer, F. H., & Goldstein, A. P. (Eds.). *Helping people change.* New York: Pergamon, 1975.

Kanfer, F. H., & Karas, S. Prior experimenter-subjects interaction and verbal conditioning. *Psychological Reports*, 1959, *5*, 343–353.

Kanfer, F. H., Karoly, P., & Newman, A. Reduction of children's fear of the dark by competence-related and situational threat-related verbal cues. *Journal of Consulting and Clinical Psychology*, 1975, *43*, 251–258.

Kanfer, F. H., & Phillips, S. Self-control in behavior modification. In F. H. Kanfer & S. Phillips (Eds.), *Learning foundations of behavior therapy.* New York: Wiley, 1970, 433–460.

Kaplan, H. B. Self-derogation and adjustment to recent life experiences. *Archives of General Psychiatry*, 1970, *72*, 324–331.

Kaplan, H. B., & Pokorny, A. D. Self-derogation and psychosocial adjustment. *Journal of Nervous and Mental Disease*, 1969, *149*, 421–434.

Kaplan, H. S. *The new sex therapy.* New York: Brunner-Mazel, 1974.

Kaplan, K. J. From attitude formation to attitude change: Acceptance and impact as cognitive mediators. *Sociometry*, 1972, *35*, 448–467.

Kaplan, M. F., & Anderson, N. H. Information integration theory and reinforcement theory as approaches to interpersonal attraction. *Journal of Personality and Social Psychology*, 1973, *28*, 301–312.

Katz, S. The effect of emotional education on locus of control and self-concept. Doctoral dissertation, Hofstra University, 1974.

Kauffman, J. M., LaFleur, N. K., & Hallahan, D. P. Imitation as a consequence for children's behavior: Two experimental case studies. *Behavior Therapy*, 1975, *6*, 535–542.

Kaufmann, H., & Feshbach, S. The influence of antiaggressive communication upon response to provocation. *American Psychologist*, 1963, *18*, 387–388.

Kazdin, A. E. Covert modeling and the reduction of avoidance behavior. *Journal of Abnormal Psychology*, 1973, *81*, 87–95.

Kazdin, A. E. Reactive self monitoring: The effects of response desirability, goal setting, and feedback. *Journal of Consulting and Clinical Psychology*, 1974, *42*, 704–716.

Kelley, H. H. Interpersonal accommodation. *American Psychologist*, 1968, *23*, 399–410.

Kelly, G. *The psychology of personal constructs.* New York: Norton, 1955.

Kelly, G. *Clinical psychology and personality: Selected papers of George Kelly.* New York: Wiley, 1969.

Kemp, C. C. Influence of dogmatism on counseling. *Personnel and Guidance Journal*, 1961, *39*, 662–665.

Kendler, H. H. Environmental and cognitive control of behavior. *American Psychologist*, 1971, *26*, 962–973.

Kety, S. S. Current biochemical approaches to schizophrenia. *New England Journal of Medicine*, 1967, *276*, 325–331.

Kiesler, C. A. *The psychology of commitment: Experiments linking behavior to belief.* New York: Academic Press, 1971.

Kilburg, R. R., & Siegel, A. W. Formal operations in reactive and process schizophrenics. *Journal of Consulting and Clinical Psychology*, 1973, *40*, 371–376.

Kilty, K. M. On the relationship between affect and cognition. *Psychological Reports*, 1969, *25*, 215–219.

Kingsbury, S. J., Stevens, D. P., Murray, E. J. Evaluation apprehension in verbal conditioning: Test of four subject effects models. *Journal of Personality and Social Psychology*, 1975, *32*, 271–277.

Kirsch, I., Wolpin, M., & Knutson, J. L. A comparison of in vivo methods for rapid reduction of "stage fright" in the college classroom: A field experiment. *Behavior Therapy*, 1975, *6*, 165–171.

Klein, D. C., Fencil, M. E., & Seligman, M. E. P. Learned helplessness, depression and the attribution of failure. *Journal of Personality and Social Psychology*, 1976, *33*, 506–516.

Klein, D. C., & Seligman, M. E. P. Reversal of performance deficits and perceptual deficits in learned helplessness and depression. *Journal of Abnormal Psychology*, 1976, *83*, 11–26.

Kleinke, C. L. Effects of false feedback about response lengths on subjects' perception of an interview. *Journal of Social Psychology*, 1975, *95*, 99–104.

Klix, F. *Information und Verhalten*. Berlin: VEB Deutscher Verlag der Wissenschaften, 1971.

Knapp, T. J. The Premack principle in human experimental and applied settings. *Behaviour Research and Therapy*, 1976, *14*, 133–147.

Knaus, W. J. *Rational-emotive education: A manual for elementary school teachers*. New York: Institute for Rational Living, 1974.

Knaus, W. J., & Bokor, S. The effect of rational-emotive education lessons on anxiety and self-concept in 6th grade students. *Rational Living*, 1975, *10*(2), 7–10.

Koenig, K. False emotional feedback and the modification of anxiety. *Behavior Therapy*, 1973, *4*, 193–202.

Konecni, V. J. The mediation of aggressive behavior: Arousal level versus anger and cognitive labeling. *Journal of Personality and Social Psychology*, 1975, *32*, 706–712.

Kopel, S. A., & Arkowitz, H. S. Role-playing as a source of self observation and behavior change. *Journal of Personality and Social Psychology*, 1974, *29*, 677–686.

Kopel, S. A., & Arkowitz, H. The role of attribution and self-perception in behavior change: Implications for behavior therapy. *Genetic Psychology Monographs*, 1975, *92*, 175–212.

Korzybski, A. *Science and sanity*. Lancaster, Pa.: Lancaster Press, 1933.

Kraines, S. H. Manic depressive syndrome: A physiologic disease. *Diseases of the Nervous System*, 1966, *27*, 1–19.

Kravetz, D. F. Heart rate as a minimal cue for the occurrence of vicarious classical conditioning. *Journal of Personality and Social Psychology*, 1974, *29*, 125–131.

Krebs, D. Empathy and altruism. *Journal of Personality and Social Psychology*, 1975, *32*, 1134–1146.

Krisher, H. P. III, Darley, S. A., & Darley, J. M. Fear provoking recommendations intentions to take preventive actions, and actual preventive actions. *Journal of Personality and Social Psychology*, 1973, *26*, 301–308.

Krupat, E. Context as a determinant of perceived threat: The role of prior experience. *Journal of Personality and Social Psychology*, 1974, *29*, 731–736.

Kujoth, R. K. *The differential effects of teaching rational idea concepts versus teaching insight concepts on community college students in a course in human relations*. Doctoral dissertation, Marquette University, 1976.

Kurtz, P. Gullibility and nincompoopery. *Religious Humanism*, Spring 1973, 1–6.

Lafferty, J. C. Values that defeat learning. *Proceedings of the 8th Inter-Institutional Seminar in Child Development*. Dearborn, Mich.: Edison Institute, 1962.

LaFleur, N. K., & Johnson, R. G. Separate effects of social modeling and reinforcement in counseling adolescents. *Journal of Counseling Psychology*, 1972, *19*, 292–295.

Laird, J. D. Self-attribution of emotion: The effects of expressive behavior on the quality of emotional experience. *Journal of Personality and Social Psychology*, 1974, *20*, 475–486.

Landfield, A. W. *Personal construct systems in psychotherapy*. Chicago, Ill.: Rand McNally, 1971.

Landy, D., & Sigall, H. Beauty is talent: Task evaluation as a function of the performer's physical attractiveness. *Journal of Personality and Social Psychology*, 1974, *29*, 299–304.

Lang, A., Goeckner, D., Adesso, V., & Marlett, G. A. Effects of alcohol on aggression in male social drinkers. *Journal of Abnormal Psychology,* 1975, *84,* 508–518.

Lang, P. J., Sproufe, L. A., & Hastings, V. E. Effects of feedback and instructional set on the control of cardiac-rate variability. *Journal of Experimental Psychology,* 1967, *75,* 425–431.

Lange, A., & Jakubowski, P. *Responsible assertive behavior.* Champaign, Ill.: Research Press, 1976.

Langer, E. J., & Abelson, R. P. A patient by any other name . . . Clinical group difference in labeling bias. *Journal of Consulting and Clinical Psychology,* 1974, *42,* 4–9.

Langner, S. K. *Mind: An essay on human feeling.* Baltimore: Johns Hopkins University Press, 1966.

LaPuc, P., & Harmatz, M. Verbal conditioning and therapeutic change. *Journal of Consulting and Clinical Psychology,* 1970, *35,* 70–78.

Larsen, S. F., & Fromholt, P. Mnemonic organization and free recall in schizophrenia. *Journal of Abnormal Psychology,* 1976, *85,* 61–65.

Lauer, J. W. Hypnosis in the relief of pain. *Medical Clinics of North America,* 1968, *52,* 217–224.

Laws, D. R., & Pawlowski, A. V. An automated fading procedure to alter sexual responsiveness in pedophiles. *Journal of Homosexuality,* 1974, *1,* 149–163.

Lazarus, A. A. *Behavior therapy and beyond.* New York, McGraw-Hill, 1971.

Lazarus, A. A. Desensitization and cognitive restructuring. *Psychotherapy: Theory, Research and Practice,* 1974, *11,* 98–102.

Lazarus, A. A. *Multimodal therapy.* New York: Springer, 1976.

Lazarus, R. S. *Psychological stress and the coping process.* New York: McGraw-Hill, 1966.

Lazarus, R. S. A cognitively oriented psychologist looks at biofeedback. *American Psychologist,* 1975, *31,* 555–563.

Lazarus, R. S., & Alpert, E. Short-circuiting of threat by experimenting altering cognitive appraisal. *Journal of Abnormal and Social Psychology,* 1964, *69,* 195–205.

Lazarus, R. S., & Averill, J. R. Emotion and cognition: With special reference to anxiety. In C. K. D. Spielberger (Ed.), *Anxiety: Current trends in theory and research* (Vol. 2). New York: Academic Press, 1975.

Lazarus, R. S., Averill, J. R., & Opton, E. M., Jr. Towards a cognitive theory of emotion. In M. B. Arnold (Ed.), *Third International Symposium on Feelings and Emotion.* New York: Academic Press, 1970.

Lecky, P. *Self-consistency.* New York: Island Press, 1945.

Lefcourt, H. M. Internal versus external control of reinforcement: A review. *Psychological Bulletin,* 1966, *65,* 206–220.

Lefcourt, H. M. *Locus of control: Current trends in theory and research.* Hillsdale, N.J.: Erlbaum, 1976.

Legant, P., & Mettee, D. R. Turning the other cheek versus getting even: Vengeance, equity, and attraction. *Journal of Personality and Social Psychology,* 1973, *25,* 243–253.

Lehman, P. Cognitive factors in anger and aggression. *Rational Living,* 1972, *7*(1), 40–43.

Leitenberg, H., Agras, S., Butz, R., & Wincze, J. Relationship between heart rate and behavioral change during the treatment of phobias. *Journal of Abnormal Psychology,* 1971, *78,* 59–68.

Leitenberg, H., Agras, S., Edwards, J. A., Thomson, L. E., & Wincze, J. P. Practice as a psychotherapeutic variable: An experimental analysis within single cases. *Journal of Psychiatric Research,* 1970, *7,* 215–225.

Leitenberg, H., & Callahan, E. J. Reinforced practice and reduction of different kinds of fears in adults and children. *Behaviour Research and Therapy,* 1973, *11,* 19–30.

Leitenberg, H., & Wincze, J. P. An experimental analysis of the effectiveness of "shaping" in reducing maladaptive avoidance behavior: An analogue study. *Behaviour Research and Therapy,* 1970, *8,* 165–173.

Lembo, J. *The counseling process: A rational behavioral approach.* New York: Libra, 1976.

Leon, G. R., & Chamberlain, K. Comparison of daily eating habits and emotional states of overweight persons successful or unsuccessful in maintaining a weight loss. *Journal of Consulting and Clinical Psychology,* 1973, *41,* 108–115.

Levenson, H. Multidimensional locus of control in psychiatric patients. *Journal of Consulting and Clinical Psychology,* 1973, *41,* 397–404.

Levenson, M., & Neuringer, C. Problem-solving behavior in suicidal adolescents. *Journal of Consulting and Clinical Psychology,* 1971, *37,* 433–436.

Levey, A. B., & Martin, I. Classical conditioning of human evaluative responses. *Behaviour Research and Therapy,* 1975, *13,* 221–226.

Levinson, B. L., Shapiro, D., Schwartz, G. E., & Tursky, B. Smoking elimination by gradual reduction. *Behavior Therapy,* 1971, *2,* 477–487.

Levinson, J. R., Davidson, R. E., Wolff, P., & Citron, M. A comparison of induced imagery and sentence strategies in children's paired-associate learning. *Journal of Educational Psychology,* 1973, *64,* 306–309.

Lévi-Strauss, C. *The savage mind.* Chicago: University of Chicago Press, 1970.

Levitt, E. E., Den Breeijen, A., & Persky, H. The induction of clinical anxiety by means of a standardized hypnotic technique. *American Journal of Clinical Hypnosis,* 1960, *2,* 206–214.

Levitt, E. E., Persky, H., & Brady, P. *Hypnotic induction of anxiety: A psychoendocrine investigation.* Springfield, Ill.: Charles C Thomas, 1964.

Lewinsohn, P. M., & Graf, M. Pleasant activities and depression. *Journal of Consulting and Clinical Psychology,* 1973, *41,* 261–268.

Lewis, W. C., Wolman, R. N., & King, M. The development of the language of emotions. *American Journal of Psychiatry,* 1971, *127,* 1491–1497.

Leyens, J. P., Camino, L., Parke, R. D., & Berkowitz, L. Effects of movie violence on aggression as a function of group dominance and cohesion. *Journal of Personality and Social Psychology,* 1975, *32,* 346–360.

Lick, J. Expectancy, false galvanic skin response feedback and systematic desensitization in the modification of phobic behavior. *Journal of Consulting and Clinical Psychology,* 1975, *43,* 557–567.

Lick, J., & Bootzin, R. Expectancy factors in the treatment of fear: Methodological and theoretical issues. *Psychological Bulletin,* 1975, *82,* 917–931.

Liebert, R. M., & Baron, R. A. Some immediate effects of televised violence on children's behavior. *Developmental Psychology,* 1972, *6,* 275–281.

Lincoln, A., & Levinger, G. Observers' evaluations of the victim and the attacker in an aggressive incident. *Journal of Personality and Social Psychology,* 1972, *22,* 202–210.

Linden, W. Practicing of meditation by school children and their levels of field dependence-independence, test anxiety and reading achievement. *Journal of Consulting and Clinical Psychology,* 1973, *41,* 139–143.

Little, S., & Jackson, B. The treatment of test anxiety through attentional and relaxation training. *Psychotherapy: Theory, Research and Practice,* 1974, *2,* 175–178.

Litvak, S. B. Attitude change by stimulus exposure. *Psychological Reports,* 1969, *25,* 391–396. (a)

Litvak, S. B. A comparison of two brief group behavior therapy techniques on the reduction of avoidance behavior. *Psychological Records,* 1969, *19,* 329–334. (b)

Loeb, A., Beck, A. T., Diggory, J. C., & Tuthill, R. Expectancy level of aspiration, performance and self evaluation in depression. *Proceedings of the Annual Convention of the American Psychological Association,* 1967, *2,* 193–194.

Loftis, J., & Ross, L. Effects of misattribution of arousal upon the acquisition and extinction of a conditioned emotional response. *Journal of Personality and Social Psychology,* 1974, *30,* 673–682. (a)

Loftis, J., & Ross, L. Retrospective misattribution of a conditioned emotional response. *Journal of Personality and Social Psychology,* 1974, *30,* 683–687. (b)

London, H., & Nisbett, R. E. (Eds.). *Thought and feeling: Cognitive alteration of feeling states.* Chicago: Aldine, 1974.

London, P. *Behavior control.* New York: Harper & Row, 1969.
Long, S. *Cognitive perceptual factors in the political alienation process: A test of six models.* Unpublished manuscript, New Haven, Conn., 1976. (a)
Long, S. *Irrational ideation and political reality: A theory of political alienation.* Unpublished manuscript, New Haven, Conn., 1976. (b)
Long, S. *Irrationality and systematic rejection: Insights from Ellis' rational behavior theory.* Unpublished manuscript, New Haven, Conn., 1976. (c)
Longstreth, L. E. A cognitive interpretation of secondary reinforcement. *Nebraska Symposium on Motivation,* 1971, *19,* 33–80.
LoPiccolo, J. Case study: Systematic desensitization of homosexuality. *Behavior Therapy,* 1971, *2,* 394–399.
LoPiccolo, J., & Miller, V. H. A program for enhancing the sexual relationship of normal couples. *The Counseling Psychologist,* 1975, *5,* 9–13.
Lott, D. R., & Murray, E. J. The effect of expectancy manipulation on outcome in systematic desensitization. *Psychotherapy: Theory, Research and Practice,* 1975, *12,* 1–7.
Lovaas, O. I., & Schriebman, L. Stimulus overselectivity of autistic children in a two stimulus situation. *Behaviour Research and Therapy,* 1971, *9,* 305–310.
Love, R. E., Sloan, L. R., & Schmidt, M. J. Viewing pornography and sex guilt: The priggish, the prudent and the profligate. *Journal of Consulting and Clinical Psychology,* 1976, *44,* 624–629.
Loveless, E. J., & Brody, H. M. The cognitive base of psychotherapy. *Psychotherapy: Theory, Research and Practice,* 1974, *11,* 81–89.
Low, A. A. *Mental health through will-training.* Boston: Christopher, 1952.
Luce, G., & Pepper, E. Mind over body, mind over mind. *New York Times Magazine,* September 12, 1971, 34–35, 132–139.
Luria, A. R. *The role of speech in the regulation of normal and abnormal behavior.* Oxford: Pergamon Press, 1961.
Luria, A. R., & Yudovich, F. *Speech and the development of mental processes in the child.* London: Staples Press, 1959.
Mahler, M. S. *On human symbiosis and the vicissitudes of individuation. Vol. 1: Infantile psychosis.* New York: International Universities Press, 1968.
Mahoney, M. J. Toward an experimental analysis of coverant and emotional arousal. *Journal of Abnormal Psychology,* 1969, *74,* 181–187.
Mahoney, M. J. *Cognition and behavior modification.* Cambridge, Mass.: Ballinger, 1974.
Mahoney, M. J. *Philosophy of science: A survey of recent developments.* Unpublished manuscript, University Park, Penn., 1976.
Mahoney, M. J., Moore, B. S., Wade, T. C., & Moura, N. G. Effects of continuous and intermittent self-monitoring on academic behavior. *Journal of Consulting and Clinical Psychology,* 1973, *41,* 65–69.
Mahoney, M. J., Moura, N. G., & Wade, T. C. Relative efficacy of self-reward, self-punishment and self-monitoring techniques for weight loss. *Journal of Consulting and Clinical Psychology,* 1973, *40,* 404–407.
Mandell, A. J., Segal, D. S., Kuszenski, R., & Knapp, S. The search for the schizococcus. *Psychology Today,* October 1972, 68–72.
Mandler, G. *Mind and emotion.* New York: Wiley, 1975.
Mann, R. A. The behavior therapeutic use of contingency contracting to control an adult behavior problem: Weight control. *Journal of Applied Behavior Analysis,* 1972, *5,* 99–109.
Manno, B., & Marston, A. R. Weight reduction as a function of negative covert reinforcement (sensitization) versus positive covert reinforcement. *Behaviour Research and Therapy,* 1972, *10,* 201–207.
Marecek, J., & Mettee, D. R. Avoidance of success as a function of self-esteem, level of esteem certainty, and responsibility for success. *Journal of Personality and Social Psychology,* 1972, *22,* 98–107.
Maranon, G. Contribution à l'étude de l'action émotive de l'adrenaline. *Revue Française*

d'Endocrinologie, 1924, *2*, 301–325.

Marburg, C. G., Mouston, B. K., & Holmes, D. S. Influence of multiple models on the behavior of institutionalized retarded children: Increased generalization to other models and other behaviors. *Journal of Consulting and Clinical Psychology*, 1976, *44*, 514–519.

Marcia, J. E., Rubin, B. M., & Efran, J. S. Systematic desensitization: Expectancy change or counter-conditioning? *Journal of Abnormal Psychology*, 1969, *74*, 832–887.

Marcus Aurelius, *The thoughts of the emperor Marcus Aurelius Antoninus*. Boston: Little, Brown, 1900.

Marks, I. M. The origins of phobic states. *American Journal of Psychotherapy*, 1970, *24*, 652–676.

Marks, I. M. *Recent advances in the treatment of phobic obsessive-compulsive and sexual disorders*. Paper presented at the second annual Conference on Behavior Modification, Los Angeles, October 9, 1971.

Marks, I. M., Viswanathan, R., Lipsedge, M. S., & Gardner, R. Enhanced relief of phobias by flooding during waning diazepam effect. *British Journal of Psychiatry*, 1972, *121*, 493–505.

Marquis, P. C. Experimenter-subject interaction as a function of authoritarianism and response set. *Journal of Personality and Social Psychology*, 1973, *25*, 289–296.

Marshall, W. L., Boutilier, J., & Minnes, P. The modification of phobic behavior by covert reinforcement. *Behavior Therapy*, 1974, *5*, 469–480.

Marshall, W. L., Strawbridge, H., & Keltner, A. The role of mental relaxation in experimental desensitization. *Behaviour Research and Therapy*, 1972, *10*, 355–366.

Marston, A. R. Toward the use of self-control in behavior modification. *Journal of Consulting and Clinical Psychology*, 1972, *39*, 429.

Masters, W. H., & Johnson, V. E. *Human sexual inadequacy*. Boston: Little, Brown, 1970.

Matarazzo, J. D. Frequency and duration characteristics of speech and silence behavior during interviews. *Journal of Clinical Psychology*, 1962, *18*, 416–426.

Mathews, A. M. Psychophysiological approaches to the investigation of desensitization and related procedures. *Psychological Bulletin*, 1971, *76*, 83–93.

Maultsby, M. C., Jr. Systematic written homework in psychotherapy. *Psychotherapy*, 1971, *8*, 195–198.

Maultsby, M. C., Jr. *Help yourself to happiness*. New York: Institute for Rational Living, 1975.

Maultsby, M. C., Jr., & Ellis, A. *Technique for using rational-emotive imagery*. New York: Institute for Rational Living, 1974.

May, J. R. *Physiological activity to internally and externally phobic thoughts*. Doctoral dissertation, Temple University, 1974.

McCarron, L. T., & Appel, V. H. Categories of therapist verbalizations and patient-therapist autonomic response. *Journal of Consulting and Clinical Psychology*, 1971, *37*, 123–134.

McClellan, T. A., & Stieper, D. R. A structured approach to group marriage counseling. *Rational Living*, 1973, *8*(2), 12–18.

McConaghy, N. Penile volume change to moving pictures of male and female nudes in heterosexual and homosexual males. *Behaviour Research and Therapy*, 1967, *5*, 43–48.

McCrame, E. W., & Kimberly, J. Rank inconsistency, conflicting expectations and injustice. *Sociometry*, 1973, *36*, 152–176.

McGuigan, F. N. Covert oral behavior during the silent performance of language tasks. *Psychological Bulletin*, 1970, *74*, 309–326.

McMahan, I. D. Relationships between causal attributions and expectancy of success. *Journal of Personality and Social Psychology*, 1973, *28*, 108–114.

McReynolds, W. T., Barnes, A. R., Brooks, S., & Rehagen, N. J. The role of attention-placebo influences in the efficacy of systematic desensitization. *Journal of Consulting and Clinical Psychology*, 1973, *41*, 86–92.

McReynolds, W. T., & Church, A. Self-control, study skills development and counseling approaches to the improvement of study behavior. *Behaviour Research and Therapy,* 1973, *11,* 233–235.

McReynolds, W. T., & Tori, C. A further assessment of attention-placebo effects and demand characteristics in studies of systematic desensitization. *Journal of Consulting and Clinical Psychology,* 1972, *38,* 261–264.

McWhinnie, A. M. *Adopted children—how they grow up: A study of their adjustment as adults.* New York: Humanities Press, 1967.

Meath, J. A., Feldberg, T. M., Rosenthal, D., & Frank, J. D. *A comparative study of reserpine and placebo in the treatment of psychiatric outpatients.* Unpublished manuscript, 1954.

Meehl, P. Schizotaxia, schizotype, and schizophrenia. *American Psychologist,* 1962, *17,* 827–838.

Meichenbaum, D. *Cognitive factors in behavior modification: Modifying what clients say to themselves.* Research Report No. 25. Waterloo: University of Waterloo, 1971.

Meichenbaum, D. *Cognitive-behavior modification newsletter No. 1.* Waterloo: University of Waterloo, 1974. (a)

Meichenbaum, D. *Self-instruction and the therapeutic modification of self statements or cognitive type behavior therapy.* Paper presented at the 8th annual convention of the Association for Advancement of Behavior Therapy, Chicago, November, 1974. (b)

Meichenbaum, D. *Therapist manual for cognitive behavior modification.* Waterloo: University of Waterloo, 1974. (c)

Meichenbaum, D. Enhancing creativity by modifying what subjects say to themselves. *American Educational Research Journal,* 1975, *12,* 129–145. (a)

Meichenbaum, D. Theoretical and treatment implications of developmental research of verbal control of behavior. *Canadian Psychological Review,* 1975, *16,* 18–28. (b)

Meichenbaum, D. Toward a cognitive theory of self control. In G. Schwartz & D. Shapiro (Eds.), *Consciousness and self-regulation: Advances in research.* New York: Plenum, 1975. (c)

Meichenbaum, D. *Cognitive-behavior modification newsletter No. 2.* Waterloo: University of Waterloo, 1976.

Meichenbaum, D. *Cognitive behavior modification.* New York: Plenum, 1977.

Meichenbaum, D., Bowers, K. S., & Ross, R. R. A behavioral analysis of teacher expectancy effect. *Journal of Personality and Social Psychology,* 1969, *13,* 306–316.

Meichenbaum, D., & Cameron, R. *An examination of cognitive and contingency variables in anxiety relief procedures.* Unpublished manuscript, University of Waterloo, 1973.

Meichenbaum, D., & Cameron, R. The clinical potential of modifying what clients say to themselves. *Psychotherapy: Theory, Research and Practice,* 1974, *11,* 115–124.

Meichenbaum, D., & Smart, I. Use of direct expectancy to modify academic performance and attitudes of college students. *Journal of Counseling Psychology,* 1971, *18,* 531–535.

Meichenbaum, D., Turk, L., & Rogers, J. M. Implications of research on disadvantaged children and cognitive-training programs for educational television: Ways of improving "Sesame Street." *Journal of Special Education,* 1972, *6,* 27–50.

Melden, A. The conceptual dimension of emotion. In T. Mischel (Ed.), *Human action.* New York: Academic Press, 1969.

Melnick, J. A comparison of replication techniques in the modification of minimal dating behavior. *Journal of Abnormal Psychology,* 1973, *81,* 51–59.

Mendel, W. M. Authority: Its nature and use in the therapeutic relationship. *Hospital and Community Psychiatry,* November 1970, 35–38.

Mendonca, J. D., & Siess, T. F. Counseling for indecisiveness: Problem solving and anxiety management training. *Journal of Counseling Psychology,* 1976, *23,* 339–347.

Meyer, A. *The commonsense psychiatry of Dr. Adolf Meyer* (A. Lieb, Ed.). New York: McGraw-Hill, 1948.

Meyer, A. *Psychobiology: A science of man.* Springfield, Ill.: Charles C Thomas, 1958.

Milgrim, S. *Obedience to authority.* New York: Harper & Row, 1974.

Miller, D. T., & Karniol, R. The role of rewards in externally and self-imposed delay of gratification. *Journal of Personality and Social Psychology,* 1976, *33,* 594–600.

Miller, N. Learning of visceral and glandular responses. *Science,* 1969, *163,* 34–35.

Miller, N., Baron, R. S., & Baron, P. H. The relation between distraction and persuasion. *Psychological Bulletin,* 1973, *80,* 310–323.

Miller, R. L., Brickman, P., & Bolen, D. Attribution versus persuasion as a means for modifying behavior. *Journal of Personality and Social Psychology,* 1975, *31,* 430–441.

Miller, T. W. *An exploratory investigation comparing self-esteem with self-acceptance in reducing social evaluative anxiety.* Doctoral dissertation, Syracuse University, 1976.

Mischel, W. *Personality and assessment.* New York: Wiley, 1968.

Mischel, W. Facilitating self-control. *Proceedings of the 17th International Congress of Applied Psychology,* 1971, 55–57.

Mischel, W. The self as the person: A cognitive social learning view. In A. Wandersman (Ed.), *Behavioristic and humanistic approaches to personality change.* New York: Pergamon Press, 1976.

Mischel, W., & Baker, N. Cognitive appraisals and transformations in delay behavior. *Journal of Personality and Social Psychology,* 1975, *31,* 254–261.

Mischel, W., & Ebbesen, E. B. Attention in delay of gratification. *Journal of Personality and Social Psychology,* 1970, *16,* 329–337.

Mischel, W., Ebbesen, E. B., & Raskoff Zeiss, A. M. Cognitive and attentional mechanisms in delay of gratification. *Journal of Personality and Social Psychology,* 1972, *21,* 204–218.

Mischel, W., Ebbesen, E. B., & Raskoff Zeiss, A. M. Determinants of selective memory about the self. *Journal of Consulting and Clinical Psychology,* 1976, *44,* 92–103.

Mischel, W., & Gilligan, C. Delay of gratification motivation for the prohibited gratification and response to temptation. *Journal of Abnormal and Social Psychology,* 1964, *69,* 411–417.

Mischel, W., & Mischel, H. A cognitive social learning approach to morality and self regulation. In T. Lickana (Ed.), *Morality: A handbook of moral behavior.* New York: Holt, Rinehart & Winston, 1975.

Mischel, W., & Moore, B. Effects of attention to symbolically presented reward on self-control. *Journal of Personality and Social Psychology,* 1973, *28,* 172–179.

Mitchell, K. M., & Namenkek, T. M. Effects of therapist confrontation on subsequent client and therapist behavior during the first therapy interview. *Journal of Counseling Psychology,* 1972, *19,* 196–201.

Mitchell, K. R., & Mitchell, D. M. Migraine: An exploratory treatment application of programmed behavior therapy techniques. *Journal of Psychosomatic Research,* 1971, *15,* 137–157.

Moore, C. H., & Sipprelle, C. M. Vicarious verbal conditioning in a quasi-group therapy situation. *Behavior Therapy,* 1971, *2,* 40–45.

Moreno, J. L. *Who shall survive?* Washington: Nervous and Mental Diseases Publishing Company, 1934.

Moreno, J. L. *Theater of spontaneity.* Beacon, N.Y.: Beacon House, 1947.

Morris. K. T., & Kanitz, J. M. *Rational-emotive therapy.* Boston: Houghton-Mifflin, 1975.

Morrison, B. J., & Walters, S. B. The placebo effect: 1. Situational anxiety and model behavior. *Journal of Psychonomic Science,* 1972, *27,* 80–82.

Mosher, D. I. Are neurotics victims of their emotions? *ETC.,* 1966, *23,* 225–234.

Mourer, S. A. A prediction of patterns of schizophrenic error resulting from semantic generalization. *Journal of Abnormal Psychology,* 1973, *81,* 250–254.

Mowrer, O. H. Preparatory set (expectancy): A determinant in motivation and learning. *Psychological Review,* 1938, *45,* 62–91.

Mowrer, O. H., & Ulmann, A. D. Time as a determinant in integrative learning. *Psychological Review,* 1945, *52,* 61–90.

Muehleman, J. T. The effects of cognitive rehearsal and cognitive reappraisal on fearful behavior. *Dissertation Abstracts International,* 1972, *32,* 5452.

Muehleman, J. T. *The effect of negative expectancy on choice and approach towards aversive tasks.* Paper presented at the Southeastern Psychological Association meeting, New Orleans, 1973.

Muirden, G. Teachers are human too! *Associate News,* June 7, 1976, *10,* 16–17.

Mulholland, T. B. It's time to try hardware in the classroom. *Psychology Today,* 1973, *7*(6), 103–104.

Mullen, F. G. *The effect of covert sensitization on smoking behavior.* Unpublished study, Queens College, Charlottesville, N.C., 1968.

Murphy, C. M., & Bootzin, R. R. Active and passive participation in the contact desensitization of snake fear in children. *Behavior Therapy,* 1973, *4,* 203–211.

Neisser, U. *Cognitive psychology.* New York: Appleton-Century-Croft, 1966.

Nelson, J. D., Gelfand, D. M., & Hartmann, D. P. Children's aggression following competition. *Child Development,* 1969, *40,* 1085–1097.

Neufeld, R. W. J. Evidence of stress as a function of experimentally altered appraisal of stimulus aversiveness and coping adequacy. *Journal of Personality and Social Psychology,* 1976, *33,* 632–646.

Nisbett, R. E., & Borgida, E. Attribution and the psychology of prediction. *Journal of Personality and Social Psychology,* 1975, *32,* 932–943.

Nisbett, R. E., & Schachter, S. Cognitive manipulation of pain. *Journal of Experimental Social Psychology,* 1966, *2,* 227–236.

Noble, G. Effects of different forms of filmed aggression on children's constructive and destructive play. *Journal of Personality and Social Psychology,* 1973, *26,* 54–59.

Nomikos, M. S., Opton, E. M., Jr., Averill, J. R., & Lazarus, R. S. Surprise versus suspense in the production of stress reaction. *Journal of Personality and Social Psychology,* 1968, *2,* 204–208.

Norman, R. Affective cognitive consistency, attitudes, conformity, and behavior. *Journal of Personality and Social Psychology,* 1975, *32,* 85–91.

Nosanchuk, T. A., & Lightstone, J. Canned laughter and public and private conformity. *Journal of Personality and Social Psychology,* 1974, *29,* 153–156.

Novaco, R. *A treatment program for the management of anger through cognitive and relaxation controls.* Unpublished doctoral dissertation, Indiana University, Bloomington, 1974.

Novaco, R. *Anger control: The development and evaluation of an experimental treatment.* Lexington, Mass.: Lexington Books, 1975.

Novak, A. L., & van der Veen, F. Not the family but "how he sees it" called crucial factor in disturbed child. *Mental Health Scope,* 1968, *2,* 1–3.

Nowicki, S., Jr., Bonner, J., & Feather, B. Effects of locus of control and differential analogue interview procedures on the perceived therapeutic relationship. *Journal of Consulting and Clinical Psychology,* 1972, *38,* 434–438.

Nowicki, S., & Walker, C. The role of generalized and specific expectancies in determining academic achievement. *Journal of Social Psychology,* 1974, *94,* 275–280.

Nowlis, V., & Nowlis, H. H. The description and analysis of mood. *Annals of New York Academy of Sciences,* 1956, *65,* 345–355.

O'Connell, W. E. Psychotherapy for everyman: A look at action therapy. *Journal of Existential Psychology,* 1966, *7,* 85–91.

O'Connell, W. E. Adlerian action therapy technique. *Journal of Individual Psychology,* 1972, *28,* 184–191.

O'Connell, W. E., Baker, R. R., Hanson, P. G., & Ermalinski, R. Action therapy: An intervention for increasing involvement in human interaction training. *Group Psychotherapy and Psychodrama,* 1973, *26,* 92–96.

O'Connell, W. E., Baker, R. R., Hanson, P. G., & Ermalinski, R. Types of "negative nonsense." *International Journal of Social Psychiatry,* 1974, *20,* 122–127.

O'Connell, W. E., & Hanson, P. G. Patient's cognitive changes in human relations training. *Journal of Individual Psychology,* 1970, *26,* 57–63.

O'Connell, W. E., & Hanson, P. G. The negative nonsense of the passive patient. *Rational Living,* 1971, *6*(1), 24-27.

O'Connor, R. D. Relative efficacy of modeling, shaping and the combined procedures for modification of social withdrawal. *Journal of Abnormal Psychology,* 1972, *79,* 327-334.

O'Donnell, J. M., & Brown, M. J. K. The classical conditioning of attitudes: A comparative study of ages 8-18. *Journal of Personality and Social Psychology,* 1973, *26,* 379-385.

Olds, J. Positive emotional systems studies by techniques of self-stimulation. *Psychiatric Research Reports,* 1960, *12,* 238-258.

Olson, P. Effects of modeling and reinforcement on adult chronic schizophrenics. *Journal of Consulting and Clinical Psychology,* 1971, *36,* 126-132.

Oltman, J. E., & Friedman, S. Report on parental deprivation in psychiatric disorders. *Archives of General Psychiatry,* 1965, *12,* 46-55.

Oltman, J. E., & Friedman, S. Report on parental deprivation in psychiatric disorders: II. In affective illness. *Diseases of the Nervous System,* 1966, *27,* 239-244.

Osborn, F. *The future of human heredity.* New York: Weybright & Talley, 1968.

Osgood, C. E. Exploration in semantic space: A personal diary. *Journal of Social Issues,* 1971, *27,* 5-64.

Packwood, W. T. Loudness as a variable in persuasion. *Journal of Counseling Psychology,* 1974, *21,* 1-2.

Packwood, W. T., & Parker, C. A. A method for rating counselor social reinforcement and persuasion. *Journal of Counseling Psychology,* 1973, *20,* 38-43.

Padfield, M. The comparative effects of two counseling approaches on the intensity of depression among rural women of low socioeconomic status. *Journal of Counseling Psychology,* 1976, *23,* 209-214.

Pagano, D. F. Information-processing differences in repressors and sensitizers. *Journal of Personality and Social Psychology,* 1973, *26,* 105-109.

Page, M. M. Demand characteristics and the verbal operant conditioning experiment. *Journal of Personality and Social Psychology,* 1972, *23,* 372-378.

Palkes, H., Stewart, M., & Kahana, B. Porteus maze performance of hyperactive boys after training in self-directed verbal commands. *Child Development,* 1968, *39,* 817-826.

Parrino, J. Effect of pretherapy information on learning in psychotherapy. *Journal of Abnormal Psychology,* 1971, *77,* 17-24.

Pastore, N. A neglected factor in the frustration-aggression hypothesis: A comment. *Journal of Psychology,* 1950, *29,* 271-279.

Pastore, N. The role of arbitrariness in the frustration-aggression hypothesis. *Journal of Abnormal Social Psychology,* 1952, *47,* 728-731.

Patterson, C., & Mischel, W. Effects of temptation inhibiting and task facilitating plans on self control. *Journal of Personality and Social Psychology,* 1976, *33,* 209-217.

Paul, G. L. *Insight versus desensitization in psychotherapy: An experiment in anxiety reduction.* Stanford, Calif.: Stanford University Press, 1966.

Pavlov, I. P. *Conditioned reflexes and psychiatry.* New York: International Publishers, 1941.

Payne, B. Uncovering destructive self-criticism: A teaching technique. *Rational Living,* 1971, *6*(2), 26-30.

Peale, N. V. *A guide to confident living.* New York: Prentice-Hall, 1948.

Peale, N. V. *The power of positive thinking.* Englewood Cliffs, N.J.: Prentice-Hall, 1952. (Also, Greenwich, Conn.: Fawcett Publications, 1962.)

Pennebaker, J. W., & Sanders, D. Y. American graffiti: Effects of authority and reactance arousal. *Personality and Social Psychology Bulletin,* 1976, *2,* 264-267.

Perez, R. C. The effects of experimentally induced failure, self-esteem, and sex on cognitive differentiation. *Journal of Abnormal Psychology,* 1973, *81,* 74-79.

Perlman, G. Change in self and ideal self-concept congruence of beginning psychotherapists. *Journal of Clinical Psychology,* 1972, *28,* 404-408.

Perls, F. S. *Gestalt therapy verbatim.* Lafayette, Calif.: Real People Press, 1969.
Persely, G., & Leventhal, D. B. The effects of therapeutically oriented instructions and the pairing of anxiety imagery and relaxation in systematic desensitization. *Behavior Therapy,* 1972, *3,* 417–424.
Peters, H. The education of the emotions. In M. Arnold (Ed.), *Feelings and emotions.* New York: Academic Press, 1970, 187–203.
Phares, E. J. Internal-external control and the reduction of reinforcement value after failure. *Journal of Consulting and Clinical Psychology,* 1971, *37,* 386–390.
Phillips, E. L. *Psychotherapy.* Englewood Cliffs, N.J.: Prentice-Hall, 1956.
Piaget, J. *Science of education and the psychology of the child.* New York: Orion Press, 1970.
Pines, H. A. An attributional analysis of locus of control orientation and source of informational dependence. *Journal of Personality and Social Psychology,* 1973, *26,* 262–272.
Pion, R. *Cognitive affective behavior therapy.* Unpublished paper, Honolulu, 1976.
Pisano, R., & Taylor, S. P. Reduction of physical aggression: The effects of four strategies. *Journal of Personality and Social Psychology,* 1971, *19,* 237–242.
Pitkin, W. B. *A short introduction to the history of human stupidity.* New York: Simon & Schuster, 1932.
Platt, J. J., Spivack, G., Altman, N., & Altman, D. Adolescent problem-solving thinking. *Journal of Consulting and Clinical Psychology,* 1974, *42,* 787–793.
Pliner, P., & Cappell, H. Modification of affective consequences of alcohol: A comparison of social and solitary drinking. *Journal of Abnormal Psychology,* 1974, *83,* 418–423.
Poetter, R. *Theoretical justifications for and some causes of therapeutic change in rational-emotive psychotherapy.* Columbus: Ohio University Dept. of Psychology, 1970.
Pope, B., Siegman, A. W., Cheek, J., & Blass, T. Some effects of discrepant role expectations on interviewee verbal behavior in the initial interview. *Journal of Consulting and Clinical Psychology,* 1972, *39,* 501–507.
Post, R. E. Report on project on simulated behavior states. *Health, Education and Welfare News,* July 30, 1973, 1–2.
Powers, W. T. Feedback: Beyond behaviorism. *Science,* 1973, *185,* 351–356.
Prentice, N. M. The influence of live and symbolic modeling on promoting moral judgment of adolescent delinquents. *Journal of Abnormal Psychology,* 1972, *80,* 157–161.
Pribram, K. H., & McGuinness, D. Arousal, activation, and effort in the control of attention. *Psychological Review,* 1975, *82,* 116–149.
Proctor, S., & Malloy, T. E. Cognitive control of conditioned emotional responses: An extension of behavior therapy to include the experimental psychology of cognition. *Behavior Therapy,* 1971, *2,* 294–306.
Rachleff, O. S. *The occult conceit.* New York: Bell Publishing, 1973.
Rachleff, O. S. *The secrets of superstitions: How they help, how they hurt.* Garden City, N.Y.: Doubleday, 1976.
Rachman, S. *Phobias: Their nature and control.* Springfield, Ill.: Charles C Thomas, 1968.
Rachman, S. Clinical applications of observational learning. *Behavior Therapy,* 1972, *3,* 379–397.
Rachman, S., Hodgson, R., & Marks, J. M. The treatment of chronic obsessive-compulsive neurosis. *Behaviour Research and Therapy,* 1971, *9,* 237–247.
Raimy, V. *Misunderstandings of the self: Cognitive psychotherapy and the misconception hypothesis.* San Francisco: Jossey-Bass, 1975.
Rakover, S. S., & Levita, S. Heart rate acceleration as a function of anticipation time for task performance and reward. *Journal of Personality and Social Psychology,* 1973, *28,* 39–43.
Rappaport, H. Modification of avoidance behavior: Expectancy, automatic reactivity, and verbal report. *Journal of Consulting and Clinical Psychology,* 1972, *39,* 404–414.
Raskin, N. J. The psychotherapy research project of the American Academy of Psychotherapists. *Proceedings of the 73rd Annual Convention of the American Psycho-*

logical Association, 1965, 253–254.

Raskin, N. J. *Diversity, congruence and confidence.* Paper presented at the American Psychological Association convention, New York, Sept. 3, 1966.

Rathus, S. A. Instigation of assertive behavior through videotape-mediated assertive models and directed practice. *Behaviour Research and Therapy*, 1973, *11*, 57–65.

Ray, R. E., & Walker, E. C. Biographical self-report correlates of female guilt response to visual erotic stimuli. *Journal of Consulting and Clinical Psychology*, 1973, *41*, 93–96.

Reed, H., & Janis, I. I. Effects of a new type of psychological treatment on smokers' resistance to warnings about health hazards. *Journal of Consulting and Clinical Psychology*, 1974, *42*, 748.

Regan, J. W., Gosselink, H., Hubsch, J., & Ulsh, E. Do people have inflated views of their own ability? *Journal of Personality and Social Psychology*, 1975, *31*, 295–301.

Regardie, F. Active psychotherapy. *Complex*, 1952, *7*, 3–14.

Rehm, L., Fuchs, C., Roth, D., Kornblith, S., & Roman, J. *Self-control and social skills training in the modification of depression.* Unpublished manuscript, 1975.

Reich, W. *Character analysis.* New York: Orgone Institute Press, 1949.

Richards, C. S., McReynolds, W. T., Holt, S., & Sexton, T. Effects of information feedback and self-administered consequences on self-monitoring study behavior. *Journal of Counseling Psychology*, 1976, *23*, 316–321.

Riddick, C., & Meyer, R. G. The efficacy of automated relaxation training with response contingent feedback. *Behavior Therapy*, 1973, *4*, 331–337.

Riemer, B. S. Influence of causal beliefs on affect and expectancy. *Journal of Personality and Social Psychology*, 1975, *31*, 1163–1167.

Rimland, B. *Infantile autism.* New York: Appleton-Century-Crofts, 1964.

Rimm, D. C. *Thought stopping and covert assertion.* Unpublished manuscript, Carbondale, Southern Illinois University, 1973.

Rimm, D. C., & Litvak, S. B. Self-verbalization and emotional arousal. *Journal of Abnormal Psychology*, 1969, *74*, 181–187.

Rimm, D. C., & Masters, J. C. *Behavior therapy.* New York: Academic Press, 1974.

Rimm, D. C., & Medeiros, D. C. The role of muscle relaxation in participant modeling. *Behaviour Research and Therapy*, 1970, *8*, 127–132.

Rimm, D. C., Saunders, W. D., & Westel, W. Thought stopping and covert assertion in the treatment of snake phobics. *Journal of Consulting and Clinical Psychology*, 1975, *43*, 92–93.

Ritter, B. The group desensitization of children's snake phobias using vicarious and contact desensitization procedures. *Behaviour Research and Therapy*, 1968, *6*, 1–6.

Roberts, A. H., Kewman, D. G., & Macdonald, H. Voluntary control of skin temperature: Unilateral changes using hypnosis and feedback. *Journal of Abnormal Psychology*, 1973, *82*, 163–168.

Robin, A. L., Armel, S., & O'Leary, K. D. The effects of self instruction on writing deficiencies. *Behavior Therapy*, 1975, *6*, 178–187.

Rodin, J. Menstruation, reattribution and competence. *Journal of Personality and Social Psychology*, 1976, *33*, 345–353.

Rogers, C. R. *On becoming a person.* Boston: Houghton-Mifflin, 1961.

Rogers, C. R. *Carl Rogers on encounter groups.* New York: Harper & Row, 1971.

Rogers, R. W., & Deckner, C. W. Effects of fear appeals and physiological arousal upon emotion, attitudes and cigarette smoking. *Journal of Personality and Social Psychology*, 1975, *32*, 222–230.

Rokeach, M. *The open and closed mind.* New York: Basic Books, 1960.

Rokeach, M. *Beliefs, attitudes, and values.* San Francisco: Jossey-Bass, 1968.

Rokeach, M. Persuasion that persists. *Psychology Today*, 1971, *5*(4), 68–71, 92.

Rokeach, M. *The nature of human values.* New York: Free Press, 1973.

Rokeach, M. Long term value change initiated by computer feedback. *Journal of Personality and Social Psychology*, 1975, *32*, 467–476.

Rokeach, M., & Kliejunas, P. Behavior as a function of attitude toward object and attitude toward situation. *Journal of Personality and Social Psychology*, 1972, *22*, 194–201.

Rollins, N. A Soviet study of consciousness and unconsciousness. *Journal of Individual Psychology*, 1975, *30*, 230–238.

Roper, P. The effects of hypnotherapy on homosexuality. *The Canadian Medical Association Journal*, 1967, *96*, 319–327.

Rose, G. M., Glasgow, R. E., & Barrera, M. A controlled study to assess the clinical efficacy of totally self administered systematic desensitization. *Journal of Consulting and Clinical Psychology*, 1976, *44*, 208–217.

Rosen, G. M. Subjects' initial therapeutic expectancies towards systematic desensitization as a function of varied instructional sets. *Behavior Therapy*, 1975, *6*, 230–237.

Rosen, G. M. Subjects' initial therapeutic expectancies and subjects' awareness of therapeutic goals in systematic desensitization: A review. *Behavior Therapy*, 1976, *7*, 14–27.

Rosen, J. N. *Direct analysis*. New York: Grune & Stratton, 1953.

Rosen, N. A., & Wyer, R. S. Some further evidence for the "Socratic effect" using a subjective probability model of cognitive organization. *Journal of Personality and Social Psychology*, 1972, *24*, 420–424.

Rosen, S., Johnson, R. D., Johnson, M. J., & Tesser, A. Interactive effects of news valence and attraction on communicator behavior. *Journal of Personality and Social Psychology*, 1973, *28*, 298–300.

Rosenberg, M. J. Cognitive reorganization in response to the hypnotic reversal of attitudinal affect. *Journal of Personality*, 1960, *28*, 39–63.

Rosenthal, D. Familial concordance by sex with respect to schizophrenia. *Psychological Bulletin*, 1962, *59*, 401–421.

Rosenthal, D. *Genetic theory and abnormal behavior*. New York: McGraw-Hill, 1970.

Rosenthal, D. Inherited criminality supported by Rosenthal. *APA Monitor*, 1973, *4*, 6–7.

Rosenthal, D., & Frank, J. D. Psychotherapy and the placebo effect. *Psychological Bulletin*, 1956, *33*, 294–302.

Rosenthal, D., & Kety, S. S. (Eds.). *The transmission of schizophrenia*. Elmsford, N.Y.: Pergamon, 1968.

Rosenthal, R. *Experimenter effects in behavioral research*. New York: Appleton-Century-Crofts, 1966.

Rosenthal, R. The Pygmalion effect lives. *Psychology Today*, 1973, *7*(4), 56–64.

Rosnow, R. L., & Robinson, E. J. *Experiments in persuasion*. New York: Academic Press, 1967.

Ross, L., Lepper, M. R., & Hubbard, M. Perseverance in self-perception and social perception: Biased attributional processes in the debriefing paradigm. *Journal of Personality and Social Psychology*, 1975, *37*, 880–892.

Roth, S., & Bootzin, R. R. Effects of experimentally induced expectancies of external control: An investigation of learned helplessness. *Journal of Personality and Social Psychology*, 1974, *29*, 253–264.

Rotter, J. B. *Social learning and clinical psychology*. Englewood Cliffs, N.J.: Prentice-Hall, 1954.

Rotter, J. B. *Clinical psychology*. Englewood Cliffs, N.J.: Prentice-Hall, 1964.

Rotter, J. B. Generalized expectancies for internal versus external control of reinforcement. *Psychological Monographs*, 1966, *80* (1, Whole No. 609).

Rotter, J. B. External and internal control. *Psychology Today*, 1971, *5*(1), 37–39, 58–59.

Rotter, J. B. Some problems and misconceptions related to the construct of internal versus external control of reinforcement. *Journal of Consulting and Clinical Psychology*, 1975, *48*, 56–67.

Rubovits, P. C., & Maehr, M. L. Pygmalion black and white. *Journal of Personality and Social Psychology*, 1973, *25*, 210–218.

Rule, B. G., & Hewitt, L. S. Effects of thwarting on cardiac response and physical aggression. *Journal of Personality and Social Psychology*, 1971, *19*, 181–187.

Russell, C., & Russell, W. M. S. An approach to human ethology. *Behavior Science*, 1957, *2*, 169–200.

Russell, P. L., & Brandsma, J. M. A theoretical and empirical integration of the rational and emotive and classical conditioning theories. *Journal of Consulting and Clinical Psychology*, 1974, *42*, 389–397.

Rutner, I. T. The effects of feedback and instructions on phobic behavior. *Behavior Therapy*, 1973, *4*, 338–348.

Ryan, V. L., Krall, C. A., & Hodges, W. F. *Journal of Consulting and Clinical Psychology*, 1976, *44*, 638–645.

Rychlak, J. F. Time orientation in the positive and negative free phantasies of mildly abnormal high school males. *Journal of Consulting and Clinical Psychology*, 1973, *41*, 175–180.

Rychlak, J. F., Carlsen, N. L., & Dunning, L. F. Personal adjustment and the free recall of materials with affectively positive or negative meaningfulness. *Journal of Abnormal Psychology*, 1974, *83*, 480–487.

Salili, F., Mach, M., & Billmore, G. Achievement and morality: A cross-cultural analysis of causal attribution and evaluation. *Journal of Personality and Social Psychology*, 1976, *33*, 327–337.

Salter, A. *Conditioned-reflex therapy*. New York: Creative Age, 1949.

Saltmarsh, R. E. Development of empathic interview skills through programmed instruction. *Journal of Counseling Psychology*, 1973, *20*, 375–377.

Salzman, L. Psychotherapy as intervention. *American Journal of Psychoanalysis*, 1963, *22*(1), 1–5.

Sanchez-Craig, B. M. Cognitive and behavioral coping strategies in the reappraisal of stressful social situations. *Journal of Counseling Psychology*, 1976, *23*, 7–12.

Sarason, I. G. Test anxiety and cognitive modeling. *Journal of Personality and Social Psychology*, 1973, *28*, 58–61.

Sarason, I. G., & Ganzer, V. J. Modeling and group discussion in the rehabilitation of juvenile delinquents. *Journal of Counseling Psychology*, 1973, *20*, 442–449.

Schachter, S. A cognitive physiological view of emotion. In O. Klineberg & R. Christie (Eds.), *Perspectives in social psychology*, New York: Holt, Rinehart, & Winston, 1965, 75–103.

Schachter, S. The interaction of cognitive and physiological determinants of emotional state. In C. Spielberger (Ed.), *Anxiety and behavior*. New York: Academic Press, 1966.

Schachter, S. *Emotion, obesity and crime*. New York: Academic Press, 1971.

Schachter, S., & Singer, J. E. Cognitive, social and physiological determinants of emotional state. *Psychological Review*, 1962, *69*, 379–399.

Schaefer, H. H., Tregerthan, G. J., & Colgan, A. H. Measures and self-estimated penile erection. *Behavior Therapy*, 1976, *7*, 1–7.

Schiavo, R. S., Alexander, J. F., Barton, C., & Parsons, B. V. Systems-behavioral intervention with families of delinquents: Therapist characteristics, family behavior and outcome. *Journal of Consulting and Clinical Psychology*, 1976, *44*, 656–664.

Schill, R., Evans, R., Monroe, S., & Ramanaiah, N. V. *The effects of self verbalizations on performance: A test of the rational-emotive position*. Unpublished manuscript, Carbondale, 1976.

Schleifer, M., & Douglas, V. Effects of training on the moral judgment of young children. *Journal of Personality and Social Psychology*, 1973, *28*, 62–68.

Schmeck, H. M. Effects of early deprivation on children found reversible. *New York Times*, December 27, 1972, 15.

Schmickley, V. G. *A self-managed program for overcoming debilitating depression*. Unpublished manuscript, Eaton Company Counseling Center, Charlotte, Mich., 1976.

Schopler, E., & Loftin, J. Thinking disorders in parents of young children. *Journal of Abnormal Psychology*, 1969, *74*, 281–287.

Schopler, J., & Compere, J. S. Effects of being kind or harsh to another on liking. *Journal of Personality and Social Psychology*, 1971, *20*, 135–139.

Schroeder, H. E., & Rich, A. R. The process of fear reduction through systematic desensitization. *Journal of Consulting and Clinical Psychology*, 1976, *44*, 191–199.

Schumsky, D. A. Prior information and "awareness" in verbal conditioning. *Journal of Personality and Social Psychology*, 1972, *24*, 162–165.

Schwartz, G. E. Biofeedback as therapy: Some theoretical and practical issues. *American Psychologist*, 1973, *28*, 666–673.

Schwartz, R., & Gottman, J. *A task analysis approach to clinical problems: A study of assertive behavior*. Unpublished manuscript, Indiana University, 1974.

Schwartz, S. Effects of sex, guilt, and sexual arousal on the retention of birth control information. *Journal of Consulting and Clinical Psychology*, 1973, *41*, 61–64.

Sears, R. R. *Survey of objective studies of psychoanalytic concepts*. New York: Social Science Research Council, 1943.

Segal, B., & Sims, J. Covert sensitization with a homosexual: A controlled replication. *Journal of Consulting Psychology*, 1972, *39*, 259–263.

Seligman, M. E. P. Phobias and preparedness. *Behavior Therapy*, 1971, *2*, 307–320.

Seligman, M. E. P. Fall into helplessness. *Psychology Today*, 1973, *7*(1), 43–48.

Seligman, M. E. P. *Helplessness: On depression, development and death*. San Francisco: W. H. Freeman, 1975.

Semans, J. H. Premature ejaculation new approach. *Southern Medical Journal*, 1956, *49*, 353–358.

Sergio, Y., Brahm, G., Charnes, G., Jacard, L., Picota, E., & Rutman, F. The extinction of phobic behavior as a function of attention shifts. *Behaviour Research and Therapy*, 1975, *13*, 173–176.

Shaffer, D. R., & Hendrick, C. Dogmatism and tolerance for ambiguity as determinants of differential reactions to cognitive inconsistency. *Journal of Personality and Social Psychology*, 1974, *29*, 601–608.

Shapiro, M. B., Litman, G. K., & Hendry, E. The effects of context upon the frequency of short-term changes in affective states. *British Journal of Social and Clinical Psychology*, 1973, *12*, 295–302.

Sharma, K. L. *A rational group therapy approach to counseling anxious underachievers*. Doctoral dissertation, University of Alberta, 1970.

Shaw, M. E., & Margulis, S. T. The power of the printed word: Its effect on the judgment of the quality of research. *Journal of Social Psychology*, 1974, *94*, 301–302.

Shean, G., Faia, C., & Schmaltz, E. Cognitive appraisal of stress and schizophrenic subtype. *Journal of Abnormal Psychology*, 1974, *83*, 523–528.

Sheehan, P. W., & Bowman, L. Peer model and experimenter expectancies about appropriate response as determinants of behavior in the hypnotic setting. *Journal of Abnormal Psychology*, 1973, *82*, 112–123.

Sheehan, P. W., & Marsh, N. C. Demonstration of the effect of faking subject knowledge that others are aware of their pretense on perception of role playing performance: A methodological comment. *International Journal of Clinical and Experimental Hypnosis*, 1974, *22*, 62–67.

Shelton, J. L., & Ackerman, J. M. *Homework in counseling and psychotherapy: Examples of systematic assignments for therapeutic use by mental health professionals*. Springfield, Ill.: Charles C Thomas, 1974.

Sherman, A. R. Real life exposure as a primary therapeutic factor in the desensitization treatment of fear. *Journal of Abnormal Psychology*, 1972, *79*, 19–28.

Sherman, A. R., Mulac, A. & McCann, M. J. Synergistic effect of self-relaxation and rehearsal feedback in the treatment of subjective and behavior dimensions of speech anxiety. *Journal of Consulting and Clinical Psychology*, 1974, *42*, 819–827.

Sherman, A. R., & Plummer, I. L. Training in relaxation as a behavior self-management skill: An exploratory investigation. *Behavior Therapy*, 1973, *4*, 543–550.

Shibles, W. *Emotion: The method of philosophical therapy*. Whitewater, Wis.: Language Press, 1974.

Shortell, J., & Biller, H. B. Extended version of a brief report. *Developmental Psychology*, 1970, *3*, 1–10.

Shrauger, J. S., & Terbovic, M. L. Self evaluation and assessments of performance by self and others. *Journal of Consulting and Clinical Psychology*, 1976, *44*, 564–572.

Si, I. The unconscious in the anthropology of Claude Lévi-Strauss. *American Anthropologist,* 1973, *75,* 20–48.

Silverman, B. I., & Cochrane, R. Effect of the social context on the principle of belief congruence. *Journal of Personality and Social Psychology,* 1972, *22,* 259–268.

Singer, J. L. Era of cognition. *New York State Psychologist,* 1972, *24*(1), 4–5.

Singer, J. L. *Imagery and daydream methods in psychotherapy and behavior modification.* New York: Academic Press, 1974.

Singerman, K. J., Borkovec, T. D., & Baron, R. S. Failure of misattribution therapy manipulation with a clinically relevant target behavior. *Behavior Therapy,* 1976, *7,* 306–313.

Sirota, A. D., Schwartz, G. E., & Shapiro, D. Voluntary control of human heart rate: Effect on reaction to aversive stimulation. *Journal of Abnormal Psychology,* 1974, *83,* 261–267.

Skinner, B. F. *Science and human behavior.* New York: Macmillan, 1953.

Skinner, B. F. *Beyond freedom and dignity.* New York: Knopf, 1971.

Slater, E., & Cowie, V. *Psychiatry and genetics.* London: Oxford University Press, 1971.

Sloane, B., Cristol, A. H., Pepernik, M. C., & Staples, F. R. Role preparation and expectation of improvement in psychotherapy. *Journal of Nervous and Mental Disease,* 1970, *150,* 18–26.

Smith, J. *The effect of self-instructional training on children's attending behavior.* Unpublished doctoral dissertation, University of Toledo, 1975.

Smith, M. L., & Glass, G. V. *Meta analysis of psychotherapy outcome studies. American Psychologist,* 1977, *32,* 752–760.

Snyder, C. R., & Larson, G. R. A further look at student acceptance of general personality interpretations. *Journal of Counseling and Clinical Psychology,* 1972, *38,* 384–388.

Snyder, M., Schulz, R., & Jones, E. E. Expectancy and apparent duration as determinants of fatigue. *Journal of Personality and Social Psychology,* 1974, *29,* 426–434.

Sobell, L. C., & Sobell, M. B. Case histories and shorter communications. *Behaviour Research and Therapy,* 1973, *11,* 237–238.

Sogin, S. R., & Pallak, M. S. Bad decisions, responsibility and attitude change: Effects of volition, foreseeability, and locus of causality of negative consequences. *Journal of Personality and Social Psychology,* 1976, *33,* 300–306.

Spanos, N., Horton, C., & Chaves, J. F. The effects of two cognitive strategies on pain threshold. *Journal of Abnormal Psychology,* 1975, *84,* 677–681.

Sparks, L. *Self-hypnosis: A conditioned-response technique.* New York: Grune & Stratton, 1962.

Speisman, J. C., Lazarus, R. S., Nordkoff, A., & Davison, L. Experimental reduction of stress based on ego defense theory. *Journal of Abnormal Psychology,* 1964, *68,* 367–380.

Sperry, R. W. Science and the problem of values. *Zygon: Journal of Religion and Science,* 1975, *1,* 7–21.

Spiegler, M. D., Cooley, E. J., Marshall, G. J., Prince, H. T., Puckett, S. P., & Skenazy, J. A. A self control versus a counterconditioning paradigm for systematic desensitization: An experimental comparison. *Journal of Counseling Psychology,* 1976, *23,* 83–86.

Spielberger, C. D. (Ed.). *Anxiety: Current trends in theory and research* (2 volumes). New York: Academic Press, 1972.

Spielberger, C. D., & Gorsuch, R. L. Mediation process in verbal conditioning. *Report of the United States Public Health Service Grants,* MH 7229, September 1966.

Spinoza, B. D. *Improvement of the understanding, ethics and correspondence.* New York: Dunne, 1901.

Spivack, G., & Shure, M. *Social adjustment in young children.* San Francisco: Jossey-Bass, 1974.

Staats, A. W. Letters to the editor. Language behavior therapy, a derivative of social behaviorism: New principles, analyses, procedures. *Behavior Therapy,* 1975, *6,* 407–410.

Staats, A. W., Gross, M. C., Guay, P. F., & Carlson, C. C. Personality and special systems and attitude reinforcer-discriminative theory. *Journal of Personality and Social Psychology*, 1973, *26*, 251–261.

Staby, R., Keefe, R., & Frey, K. *Verbal regulation of aggression and altruism in children*. Unpublished manuscript, University of Washington, 1975.

Stadter, M. *In vivo* facilitation as a variable in the effectiveness of taped flooding. *Behaviour Research and Therapy*, 1973, *11*, 239–242.

Stampfl, T. G., & Levis, D. J. Phobic patients: Treatment with the learning approach of implosive therapy. *Voices*, 1967, *3*, 23–27.

Start, K. B. Relationship between intelligence and the effect of mental practice on the performance of a motor skill. *Research Quarterly*, 1960, *31*, 644–649.

Steber, J. E. Effects of decision importance on ability to generate warranted subjective uncertainty. *Journal of Personality and Social Psychology*, 1974, *30*, 688–694.

Steele, C. M. Name-calling and compliance. *Journal of Personality and Social Psychology*, 1975, *31*, 361–369.

Steele, C. M., & Ostrom, T. M. Perspective mediated attitude change: When is indirect persuasion more effective than direct persuasion? *Journal of Personality and Social Psychology*, 1974, *29*, 737–741.

Steinmark, S. W., & Borkovec, T. D. Active and placebo treatment effects on moderate insomnia under counterdemand and positive demand instructions. *Journal of Abnormal Psychology*, 1974, *83*, 157–163.

Stekel, W. *Technique of analytic psychotherapy*. New York: Liberight, 1950.

Stephan, W. G., Lucker, G. W., & Aronson, E. The interpersonal consequences of self-disclosure and internal attributions for success. *Personnel and Social Psychology Bulletin*, 1976, *2*, 252–255.

Straus, M. A. Leveling, civility and violence in the family. *Journal of Marriage and the Family*, 1974, *36*, 13–29.

Strickland, B., Hale, W., & Anderson, L. Effect of induced mood states on activity and self reported affect. *Journal of Consulting and Clinical Psychology*, 1975, *43*, 587.

Strong, S. T., & Gray, B. L. Social comparison, evaluation and influence in counseling. *Journal of Counseling Psychology*, 1972, *19*, 178–183.

Stuart, R. Operant-interpersonal treatment for marital discord. *Journal of Consulting and Clinical Psychology*, 1969, *33*, 675–682.

Suchotliff, L. C. Relation of formal thought disorder to the communication deficit in schizophrenics. *Journal of Abnormal Psychology*, 1970, *76*, 250–257.

Suinn, R. M., & Richardson, F. Anxiety managment training: A nonspecific behavior therapy program for anxiety control. *Behavior Therapy*, 1971, *2*, 498–510.

Sullivan, R. Experimentally induced somatagnosis. *Archives of General Psychiatry*, 1969, *20*, 71–78.

Suls, J. M., & Miller, R. L. Humor as an attributional index. *Personnel and Social Psychology Bulletin*, 1976, *2*, 256–259.

Suzuki, D. T. *Zen Buddhism*. New York: Doubleday Anchor Books, 1956.

Suzuki, D. T., Fromm, E., & DeMartino, R. *Zen Buddhism and psychoanalysis*. New York: Grove Press, 1963.

Sydel, A. *A study to determine the effects of emotional education on fifth-grade children*. M.A. thesis, Queens College, New York, 1972.

Szpiler, J. A., & Epstein, S. Availability of an avoidance response as related to autonomic arousal. *Journal of Abnormal Psychology*, 1976, *85*, 75–82.

Taffel, S. J., O'Leary, K. D., & Armel, S. Reasoning and praise: Their effects on academic behavior. *Journal of Educational Psychology*, 1974, *66*, 291–295.

Taylor, M. H. A rational emotive workshop on overcoming study blocks. *Personnel and Guidance Journal*, 1975, *53*, 458–462.

Tesser, A., & Conlee, M. C. Some effects of time and thought on attitude polarization. *Journal of Personality and Social Psychology*, 1975, *31*, 262–270.

Theisen, J. C. *A case study of a psychotherapist: Albert Ellis*. M.A. thesis, U.S. International University, 1973.

Thomas, A., Chess, S., & Birch, H. G. *Temperament and behavior disorders in children.* New York: New York University Press, 1968.

Thomas, A., Chess, S., & Birch, H. G. The origin of personality. *Scientific American,* 1970, *223*(3), 102–109.

Thomas, E. J. A case application of a signaling system to the assessment and modification of selected problems of marital communication. *Behavior Therapy,* 1973, *4,* 629–645.

Thorne, F. C. *Principles of personality counseling.* Brandon, Vt.: Journal of Clinical Psychology Press, 1950.

Thorne, F. C. *Personality: A clinical eclectic view.* Brandon, Vt.: Journal of Clinical Psychology Press, 1961.

Thorpe, G. L. Desensitization, behavior rehearsal, self instructional training and placebo effects on assertive refusal behavior. *European Journal of Behavior Analysis Modification,* 1975, *1,* 30–44.

Thorpe, G. L., Amatu, H., Blakey, R., & Burns, L. *Contributions of overt instructional rehearsal and "specific insight" to the effectiveness of self-instructional training: A preliminary study.* Unpublished manuscript, 1975.

Tolman, E. C. *Purposive behavior in animals and men.* New York: Appleton-Century-Crofts, 1967.

Tori, C., & Worell, L. Reduction of human avoidant behavior: A comparison of counter-conditioning, expectancy and cognitive information approaches. *Journal of Consulting and Clinical Psychology,* 1973, *41,* 269–278.

Tosi, D. J. *Youth: Toward personal growth.* Columbus: Merrill, 1974.

Trotter, R. T. Transcendental meditation. *Science News,* 1973, *104,* 376–378.

Trotter, S. Biofeedback helps epileptics control seizures. *APA Monitor,* 1973, *4*(12), 5.

Truax, C. B., Fine, H., Moravec, J., & Millis, W. Effects of therapist persuasive potency in individual psychotherapy. *Journal of Clinical Psychology,* 1968, *24,* 359–362.

Ullman, L., & Krasner, L. (Eds.). *Case studies in behavior modification.* New York: Holt, Rinehart, & Winston, 1965.

Usher, B. *The teaching and training of interpersonal skills and cognitions in a counselor education program.* Unpublished doctoral dissertation, University of Toronto, 1974.

Valins, S. Cognitive effects of false heart-rate feedback. *Journal of Personality and Social Psychology,* 1966, *4,* 400–408.

Valins, S. Emotionality and information concerning internal reactions. *Journal of Personality and Social Psychology,* 1967, *6,* 458–463.

Valins, S. The perception and labeling of bodily changes as determinants of emotional behavior. In P. Black (Ed.), *Physiological correlates of emotion.* New York: Academic Press, 1970.

Valins, S., & Ray, A. A. Effects of cognitive desensitization on avoidance behavior. *Journal of Personality and Social Psychology,* 1967, *7,* 345–350.

Vandell, R. A., Davis, R. A., & Clugston, N. A. Function of mental practice in the acquisition of motor skills. *Journal of General Psychology,* 1943, *20,* 243–350.

Van den Berg, J. H. *Dubious maternal affection.* Pittsburgh: Duquesne University Press, 1972.

Vantress, F. E., & Williams, C. B. The effect of the presence of the provocator and the opportunity to counteraggress on systolic blood pressure. *Journal of General Psychology,* 1972, *86,* 63–68.

Vargas, J. M., & Adesso, V. J. A comparison of aversion therapies for nailbiting behavior. *Behavior Therapy,* 1976, *7,* 322–329.

Velten, E. A laboratory task for induction of mood states. *Behaviour Research and Therapy,* 1968, *6,* 473–482.

Vernallis, F., Holson, D., Shipper, J., & Butler, D. The treatment process in saturation group therapy. *Psychotherapy: Theory, Research and Practice,* 1972, *9,* 121–126.

Vidman, N. Effects of decision alternatives on the verdicts and social perceptions of simulated jurors. *Journal of Personality and Social Psychology,* 1972, *22,* 211–218.

Viernstein, L. *Evaluation of therapeutic techniques of covert sensitization.* Unpublished data, Queens College, Charlottesville, N.C., 1968.

Vincent, J. P., Weiss, R. L., & Birchler, G. R. A behavioral analysis of problem solving in distressed and nondistressed married and stranger dyads. *Behavior Therapy*, 1975, *6*, 475–487.

Wagner, A. C. Changing teaching behavior: A comparison of microteaching and cognitive discrimination training. *Journal of Educational Psychology*, 1973, *64*, 299-305.

Wagner, M. K. Reinforcement of the expression of anger through role playing. *Behaviour Research and Therapy*, 1968, *6*, 91-95.

Wallace, R. K. Physiological effects of transcendental meditation. *Science*, 1970, *167*, 1751-1754.

Wallace, R. K., & Benson, H. The physiology of meditation. *Scientific American*, 1972, *226*, 84-90.

Walster, E., Walster, G. W., Piliavin, J., & Schmidt, L. Playing hard to get: Understanding an elusive phenomenon. *Journal of Personality and Social Psychology*, 1973, *26*, 113-121.

Walton, D. R. Controlling classical conditioning with sentence structure. *Psychological Reports*, 1971, *29*, 328-329.

Wardell, D., & Royce, J. R. Relationships between cognitive and temperament traits and the concept of style. *Journal of Multivariate Experimental Personality and Clinical Psychology*, 1975, *1*, 244-266.

Warren, N. C., & Rice, L. N. Structuring and stabilizing of psychotherapy for low prognosis clients. *Journal of Consulting and Clinical Psychology*, 1972, *39*, 173-181.

Warson, S. R., & Huey, W. P. The role of intentionality in recovery: II. Operational concepts. *Psychosomatics*, 1969, *10*, 225-229.

Watson, D. L., & Tharp, R. G., *Self-directed behavior: Self-modification for personal adjustment* (2nd ed.). Monterey, Calif.: Brooks/Cole, 1977.

Watson, J. P., Gaind, R., & Marks, I. M. Physiological habituation to continuous phobic stimulation. *Behaviour Research and Therapy*, 1972, *10*, 269-278.

Weimer, W. B., & Palermo, D. S. (Eds.), *Cognition and the symbolic processes*. New York: Wiley, 1974.

Wein, K., Nelson, R., & Odom, J. The relative contributions of reattribution and verbal extinction to the effectiveness of cognitive restructuring. *Behavior Therapy*, 1975, *6*, 459-474.

Weiner, B. *Cognitive views of human motivation*. New York: Academic Press, 1974.

Weiner, B., Heckhausen, H., & Meyer, W. Causal ascriptions and achievement behavior: A conceptual analysis of effort and reanalysis of locus of control. *Journal of Personality and Social Psychology*, 1972, *21*, 239-248.

Weiner, M. J., & Samuel, W. The effect of attributing internal arousal to an external source upon test anxiety and performance. *Journal of Social Psychology*, 1975, *96*, 255–265.

Weinstein, E., Abrams, S., & Gibbons, D. The validity of the polygraph with hypnotically induced repression and guilt. *American Journal of Psychiatry*, 1970, *126*, 1159-1162.

Wender, P. H. Role of genetics in the etiology of schizophrenia. *American Journal of Orthopsychiatry*, 1969, *39*, 447-456.

Wenger, M. A., Averill, J. R., & Smith, D. D. B. Autonomic activity during sexual arousal. *Psychophysiology*, 1968, *4*, 468-478.

West, S. C., & Shultz, T. Liking for common and uncommon first names. *Personality and Social Psychology Bulletin*, 1976, *2*, 299-302.

Wexler, D. A cognitive theory of experiencing self-actualization and therapeutic process. In D. Wexler & L. Rice (Eds.), *Innovations in client-centered therapy*. New York: Wiley, 1974. (a)

Wexler, D. A. Self-actualization and cognitive processes. *Journal of Consulting and Clinical Psychology*, 1974, *42*, 47-53. (b)

Whalen, C. K., & Henker, B. Psychostimulants and children: A review and analysis. *Psychological Bulletin*, 1976, *83*, 1113-1130.

Whitehill, M., DeMeyer-Gapin, S., & Scott, T. J. Stimulation seeking in antisocial preadolescent children. *Journal of Abnormal Psychology*, 1976, *85*, 101-104.

Widom, C. S. Interpersonal and personal construct systems in psychopaths. *Journal of Consulting and Clinical Psychology,* 1976, *44,* 614–623.

Williams, G. J. Internal-external control as a situational variable in determining information seeking by Negro students. *Journal of Consulting and Clinical Psychology,* 1973, *39,* 187–193.

Williams, G. J., & Stack, J. J. Internal-external control as a situational variable. *Journal of Counseling Psychology,* 1972, *3,* 187–193.

Willner, A. E., & Struve, F. A. An analogy test that predicts EEG abnormality. *Archives of General Psychiatry,* 1970, *23,* 993–999.

Wilson, G. T., & Davison, G. C. Processes of fear-reduction in systematic desensitization: I. Animal studies. *Psychological Bulletin,* 1971, *76,* 1–14.

Wilson, G. T., & Thomas, M. G. W. Self- versus drug-produced relaxation and the effects of instuctional set in standardized systematic desensitization. *Behaviour Research and Therapy,* 1973, *11,* 279–288.

Wilson, M. N., & Rappaport, J. Personal self-disclosure: Expectancy and situational effects. *Journal of Consulting and Clinical Psychology,* 1974, *42,* 901–908.

Wine, J. Test anxiety and direction of attention. *Psychological Bulletin,* 1971, *76,* 92–104.

Winship, B. J., & Kelley, J. D. A verbal response model of assertiveness. *Journal of Counseling Psychology,* 1976, *23,* 215–220.

Wisocki, P. A. A covert reinforcement program for the treatment of test anxiety: Brief report. *Behavior Therapy,* 1973, *4,* 264–266.

Witkin, H. *Personality through perception.* New York: Harper, 1954.

Wittgenstein, L. *Philosophical investigations.* New York: Macmillan, 1958.

Wolberg, L. R. *The technique of psychotherapy* (2nd. ed.). New York: Grune & Stratton, 1967, 126–128.

Wolf, S. Effects of suggestion and conditioning on the action of chemical agents in human subjects: The pharmacology of placebos. *Journal of Clinical Investigation,* 1950, *29,* 100–109.

Wolf, S., & Pinsky, R. H. Effects of placebo administration and occurrence of toxic reactions. *Journal of American Medical Association,* 1954, *155,* 339–341.

Wolman, R. N., Lewis, W. C., & King, M. The development of the language of emotions: Conditions of emotional arousal. *Child Development,* 1971, *42,* 1291.

Wolpe, J. *Psychotherapy by reciprocal inhibition.* Stanford, Calif.: Stanford University Press, 1958.

Wolpe, J. The discontinuity of neurosis and schizophrenia. *Behaviour Research and Therapy,* 1970, *8,* 179–187.

Wolpe, J. *The practice of behavior therapy.* New York: Pergamon Press, 1973.

Wolpe, J., & Lazarus, A. *Behavior therapy techniques.* London: Pergamon Press, 1966.

Woodard, W., Burck, H. D., & Sweeney, P. Counselor's evaluation of Rogers-Perls-Ellis relationship skills. *Journal of Employment Counseling,* 1975, *12,* 108–111.

Wooley, S. Physiological versus cognitive factors in short term food regulation in the obese and non obese. *Psychosomatic Medicine,* 1972, *34,* 62–68.

Worchel, S., & Andreoli, V. A. Attribution of causality as a means of restoring behavioral freedom. *Journal of Personality and Social Psychology,* 1974, *29,* 237–245.

Wortman, C. B. Some determinants of perceived control. *Journal of Personality and Social Psychology,* 1975, *31,* 282–294.

Wright, D. M. Impairment in abstract conceptualization and Bannister and Fransella's grid test of schizophrenic thought disorder. *Journal of Consulting and Clinical Psychology,* 1973, *41,* 474.

Wyer, R. S., Jr. Category ratings as "subjective expected values": Implications for attitude formation and change. *Psychological Review,* 1973, *80,* 446–467.

Wyer, R. S., Jr. Effects of previously formed beliefs on syllogistic inference processes. *Journal of Personality and Social Psychology,* 1976, *33,* 307–316.

Yablonsky, L. *The tunnel back.* New York: Macmillan, 1965.

Yates, A. J. *Behavior therapy.* New York: Wiley, 1976.

Young, H. *Rational counseling primer.* New York: Institute for Rational Living, 1974.

Yulis, S. Generalization of therapeutic gain in the treatment of premature ejaculation. *Behavior Therapy,* 1976, *1,* 355–358.

Yulis, S., Brahm, G., Charnes, G., Jacard, L. M., Picota, E., & Rutman, F. The extinction of phobic behavior as a function of attention shifts. *Behaviour Research and Therapy,* 1975, *13,* 173–176.

Zajonc, R. B. Attitudinal effects of mere exposure. *Journal of Personality and Social Psychology,* 1968, *9.* (Monograph supplement.)

Zanna, M. P., & Cooper, J. Dissonance and the pill: An attribution approach to studying the arousal properties of dissonance. *Journal of Personality and Social Psychology,* 1974, *29,* 703–709.

Ziemelis, A. Effects of client preference and expectancy upon the initial interview. *Journal of Counseling Psychology,* 1974, *21,* 23–30.

Zimbardo, P. G. *The cognitive control of motivation.* Chicago: Scott, Foresman, 1969.

Zimbardo, P. G. A Pirandellian prison. *New York Times Magazine,* April 8, 1973, 38–60.

Zimbardo, P. G., & Ebbesen, E. Experimental modification of the relationship between effort, attitude, and behavior. *Journal of Personality and Social Psychology,* 1970, *16,* 207–213.

Zimbardo, P. G., Marshall, G., & Marlash, C. Liberating behavior from time-bound control: Expanding the present through hypnosis. *Journal of Applied Social Psychology,* 1971, *1*(4), 305–323.

Zimmer, J. M., & Cowles, K. H. Content analysis using Fortran: Applied to interviews conducted by C. Rogers, F. Perls, and A. Ellis. *Journal of Counseling Psychology,* 1972, *19,* 161–166.

Zimmer, J. M., & Pepyne, E. W. A descriptive and comparative study of dimensions of counselor response. *Journal of Counseling Psychology,* 1971, *18,* 441–447.

Zimmer, J. M, Wightman, L., & McArthur, D. *Categories of counselor behaviors as defined from a cross-validated factorial description.* Amherst, Mass.: Massachusetts University School of Education, 1970.

Zingle, H. W. *Therapy approach to counseling underachievers.* Unpublished doctoral dissertation, University of Alberta, 1965.

Zingle, H. W., & Mallett, M. *A bibliography of RET materials, articles and theses.* Edmonton: University of Alberta, 1976.

Dr. Ellis,
Please Stand Up

DONALD MEICHENBAUM

University of Waterloo

Perhaps, I should preface my reactions to Albert Ellis' article on "Research Data That Support Rational-Emotive Therapy" with a description of my first meeting with Dr. Ellis. Some 12 years ago as a graduate student in clinical psychology, I attended a meeting of the American Psychological Association in Philadelphia. At one of the sessions a group of psychotherapists (that is, a psychoanalyst, a Gestalt therapist, and a rational-emotive therapist) were demonstrating their respective therapy procedures with volunteer patients from the audience. Following the demonstrations the therapists entertained questions from the audience. As a somewhat naive clinical graduate student, I asked the therapists if the empirical basis for their therapy, and indeed the efficacy they achieved, derived from such factors as patient/therapist expectancy, general changes in the client's "assumptive world," and the nonspecific relationship factors common to each therapy approach. As you can surmise, I had just finished reading Jerome Frank's fine book *Persuasion and Healing,* and this meeting provided me with an opportunity to use this newly acquired information.

The psychoanalyst and Gestalt therapist, in their own fashion, attempted to answer my question, but it was the rational-emotive therapist whose answer left an indelible mark. He said "Please rise, young man." Dutifully I rose from the throng of several hundred people present. "That is complete bullshit!" He then went on to describe the specific ingredients inherent in rational-emotive therapy (RET).

As you can well imagine by now, the therapist was Albert Ellis, who in his inimitable fashion was forcefully presenting his approach. I always fantasized that some day, somewhere, when he least expected it, someone would say "Dr. Ellis, please stand up!"

Since that initial meeting I have had many opportunities to meet and benefit from contacts with Dr. Ellis. Indeed, the RET approach has been instrumental in influencing my research and clinical career, as described in Meichenbaum (1977).

But somehow the question I raised 12 years ago continues to bother me, especially as I read Ellis' paper on the purported research data that underlies an RET approach. Using Ellis' framework, I can analyze my reaction as follows: A is Ellis' manuscript; C are my feelings of awe, admiration, anger, frustration, and irritation that I experienced while reading the manuscript.

In order to understand these feelings, according to Ellis, I must discern the B—namely, the set of self-statements that underlie and contribute to these feelings. If my resultant behavior is maladaptive, then I should determine and then dispute the so-called underlying "irrational" beliefs that give rise to my feelings. Well, it doesn't seem to work that easily. For most of the internal dialogue to which Ellis refers seemed to have followed, not preceded, my affective experience. The so-called internal dialogue seemed to be more like a set of rationalizations designed to explain my reactions. The purpose of this review is to try to briefly describe the content of my internal dialogue, the B part of Ellis' approach.

For nearly 20 years Albert Ellis has been one of the few voices within the field of psychotherapy emphasizing the role of cognitions as playing a central role in the amelioration of psychological disturbances. When behavioral approaches were eschewing the importance of mediational concepts, Ellis held on tenaciously to his set of beliefs that behavior and emotion can be explained by a simplistic A-B-C theory. Indeed, over the 20 years RET has undergone little or no change. My awe and admiration derive from a general affinity that I have for a cognitive approach to therapy in the tradition of Dubois, Adler, Horney, Kelley, and others.

Ellis claims that the research backing for his system of psychotherapy is "immense—indeed almost awesome." That is quite a claim! To justify this claim, Ellis then bombards the reader with a citation of studies that vary immensely. If only one could prove something by mere citations! Unfortunately Ellis' fervor has gotten the better of him. Perhaps this is excusable for someone who is a progenitor of a particular therapeutic approach. At times when reading the manuscript, I had the image of an encyclopedia salesman who had somehow gotten his foot in the door and wasn't going to leave until I finally said "Yes, I'll buy it."

My defense against the salesman (in this case, Ellis) is the knowledge that many of the studies he cites have provided evidence contrary to the points he is trying to make and that his review is totally selective. As Ellis states, he has focused only on confirmatory studies and omitted nonconfirmatory critical studies. This strategy is very unfortunate, for a number of the studies Ellis cites have been appropriately criticized, and their data have been severely challenged. My impression is that Ellis has provided a useful service in the form of a valuable bibliography, but over and above that I would seriously question his conclusions, especially the final conclusion that RET is based on a strong empirical foundation. Instead, our interests as readers would have been more aptly served if Ellis had reviewed studies that disconfirmed his theory.

This brings me to the major issue, which is "What is the theory underlying rational-emotive therapy?" In considering this question, it is important to draw a distinction between the RET therapy approach and RET theory.

Exactly what is RET theory, and, moreover, what kind of data could Ellis point to that would lead him to alter his theory? I suspect the answer to this question would be more informative than the citation of innumerable studies.

In order to illustrate my concern, let me take a prototypic example. Ellis cites the work of Coué and Peale and suggests that two studies by Kanfer, Karoly and Newman (1975) and Suinn and Richardson (1971) provide a test of their hypothesis. The mental calisthenics required to see these studies as supportive of the Coué and Peale position is of Olympic magnitude. Unless one is operating under the generic notion that thought (or what one says to oneself) influences behavior, the experimental correspondence is quite imprecise.

But I think Ellis is indeed operating under such a generic framework. If one "boils down" the myriad number of cited studies, the common feature is that thinking is important to how people behave and feel. The issues of how best to conceptualize the thought processes or how they interact in a complex relationship with other ongoing processes such as one's feelings and behaviors are unexplored.

The data to support RET may be considered "awesome" and "confirmatory" only because the theory is imprecise and general. The concepts offered are too naive and simplistic. For example, the concept that one's "internal dialogue" causes emotion is likely incorrect and fails to take into consideration the complex relationship between facial proprioceptive feedback, physiological responses, cognition, and behavior. One clearly has to distinguish the potential usefulness (yet to be clearly demonstrated) of an RET therapy approach that uses a simplistic model, seduces, cajoles, and teaches the client to view his maladaptive feelings and behavior in an A-B-C framework *versus* the much more complex demand of explaining the origin and maintenance of maladaptive feelings, thoughts, and behaviors. It is only when these two sides of the coin become confused that any study that has cognitions in its title can be taken as evidence for an RET theory.

I can continue to share my other concerns about Ellis' review involving his notions that he has offered "hypotheses" or that empirical thinking is qualitatively different from nonempirical thinking, or Ellis' claim for the efficacy of desensitization a la the recent review of Kazdin and Wilcoxon (1976), or to question Ellis concerning the meaning of the innateness of irrational thinking—but I had best stop. I fear Dr. Ellis is getting tired of standing.

REFERENCES

Frank, J. *Persuasion and healing.* New York: Schocken, 1974.

Kanfer, F., Karoly, P., & Newman, A. Reduction of children's fear of the dark by competence-related and situational threat-related verbal cues. *Journal of Consulting and Clinical Psychology,* 1975, *43,* 251–258.

Kazdin, A., & Wilcoxon, L. Systematic desensitization and non-specific treatment effects: A methodological evaluation. *Psychological Bulletin,* 1976, *83,* 729–758.

Meichenbaum, D. *Cognitive-behavior modification: An integrative approach.* New York: Plenum, 1977.

Suinn, R., & Richardson, F. Anxiety management training: A nonspecific behavior therapy program for anxiety control. *Behavior Therapy,* 1971, *2,* 498–510.

A Critical Analysis of
Rational-Emotive Theory
and Therapy

MICHAEL J. MAHONEY
The Pennsylvania State University

Ellis' article on the data base of RET is both timely and heuristic. It draws attention to a rapidly expanding area of clinical psychology—one which can now claim more widespread practice than Carl Rogers' client-centered approach (Garfield & Kurtz, 1976). It also offers a valuable bibliography of contemporary research on cognitive processes in behavior change. Given the current interest in cognitive-behavioral hybrids, one might therefore welcome an integrated "state of the art" survey. However, I suspect that the review and conclusions offered by Ellis might well have been more conservative had they come from a less enthusiastic proponent of RET. This is not to slight Ellis' intentions or to overlook his pioneering contributions in our belated recognition of certain thought processes in human distress. As a review of the literature bearing on RET, however, Ellis' article is disappointing.

When I first sat down to review his article, I decided I would write down each of the 32 hypotheses and then evaluate whether Ellis had objectively reviewed and interpreted the evidence relevant to each. It soon became apparent that this rather straightforward task was virtually impossible. On the one hand, many of the hypotheses are never stated, and, when one tries to distill an hypothesis, the result is often unexciting. For example, is hypothesis 4 that "humans think" or hypothesis 5 that "humans can imagine and fantasize"? Surely this voluminous bibliography is not directed at such unchallenging targets. On the other hand, where Ellis does offer relatively clear hypotheses, their parentage is often disputable. Hypothesis 25, for example—"people tend to focus mainly on one thing at a time"—can be traced back as far as William James and is hardly an RET insight. After reading all 32 hypotheses, one does not come away with the sense of a model or theory at all. Instead, this is a collection of loosely related and poorly elucidated propositions.

My objections up to this point might be summarized by saying that Ellis' presentation of rational-emotive theory is disappointing. He offers no formal theoretical model suitable for empirical cultivation. Let us not, however, conclude that these conceptual problems—if they are real—must force a dichotomously negative verdict on RET. Ellis should be credited with clarifying the

177

possible role of irrational beliefs in behavior disorders and with stimulating research interest in cognitive processes. In fact, one of my major objections rests on Ellis' representation of his review as a survey of RET hypotheses rather than simply hypotheses linking cognition to behavior and affect. He makes two attempts to clarify the relationship between RET and other cognitive approaches (e.g., hypothesis 25), but the bulk of his review implies the assumption that any demonstration of influential cognitive processes necessarily strengthens the RET position. One gets the impression that RET is a superordinate class comprised of any theory, therapy, or technique that makes reference to thoughts, images, or fantasies. Ellis' review seems to be aimed at defending the viability of a cognitive approach to human behavior, with the implicit message that, if one accepts this view, then RET is the system of choice. An alternate view would place RET in a subordinate category with other therapeutic approaches which accept the general notion that cognitive processes (and changes therein) are important to human adjustment (cf. Beck, 1976; Mahoney, 1977; Meichenbaum, 1977; Mahoney & Arnkoff, 1978). From this latter perspective, the hypotheses and techniques of RET must be viewed as contenders among a large field. The model and hypotheses proposed by Bandura (1977a, 1977b), for example, address some of the same data and phenomena as RET and should be examined for their relative ability to predict and guide human behavior. At the present time, I think the cognitive social-learning model offers a more unified and adequate account of cognitive-behavioral interactions.

Turning from conceptual to empirical matters, one must note the voluminous citations enlisted in support of RET. Unlike tenure, however, truth cannot be judged by the bulk of a bibliography. In contrast to his statement that RET can claim "immense—indeed, almost awesome—research backing," consider an alternate summary:

> Experimental research evaluating the efficacy of [RET] has been sparse, methodologically poor, and summarily modest in its implications. . . . In short, the extent, quality, and findings of the existing experimental work . . . do not warrant an evaluative conclusion. This, of course, means that the clinical efficacy of RET has yet to be adequately demonstrated. . . . We are obliged to suspend a more confident judgment until further data are available [Mahoney, 1974, p. 182].

Despite this intentionally cautious summary, Ellis includes the above source as one of those corroborating the data base of RET. I do not here imply that my own evaluation is "correct" and that Ellis' should be rejected, but the divergence of our opinions suggests that the data base of RET may be less unequivocal than his article represents.

In addition to citing references which bear only remote relevance for orthodox RET, Ellis displays an unfortunate confirmatory bias in his review. That is, he selectively emphasizes those studies which (he claims) support RET and disregards the remainder. This leads to the practice of *affirming the consequent*—an illogical inference in which a true conclusion is used to defend a true premise (cf. Weimer, 1977; Mahoney, 1976). For example: "If rational-emotive theory is true (the premise), then RET will be effective" (the conclusion).

According to the rules of logic, there are only two forms of valid inference for this form of implication. In the first (*modus ponens* or "confirmation"), we are told that the premise is true and can then validly conclude that the conclusion is true. Since science seldom deals with questions in which the truth of the premise can be taken for granted, *modus ponens* is of little use to scientists. The only viable option left to the researcher is *modus tollens* (or "disconfirmation"), which figures prominently in the writings of Karl Popper (1972). For disconfirmation, we must determine that the conclusion is false, and from this we can validly infer that the premise is false. Ellis erroneously assumes that a true conclusion implies a true premise—an error which is all too common in the behavioral sciences:

> The writing of behavioral scientists often reads as though they assumed—what it is hard to believe anyone would explicitly assert if challenged—that successful and unsuccessful predictions are practically on all fours in arguing for and against a substantive theory. Many experimental articles in the behavioral sciences, and, even more strangely, review articles which purport to survey the current status of a particular theory in the light of all available evidence treat the confirming instances and the disconfirming instances with equal methodological respect, as if one could, so to speak, "Count noses," so that if a theory has somewhat more confirming than disconfirming instances, it is in pretty good shape evidentially.... This is ... grossly incorrect on purely formal grounds [Meehl, 1967, p. 112].

In the case of Ellis' review, he has not even counted the contrary noses let alone emphasized their epistemological priority.

There are a number of other points with which one might here take issue. For example, what is Ellis' definition of "rationality"? Can a behavior pattern be "rational," or does this qualifier apply only to thoughts? Can a thought be irrational but adaptive? Rational but maladaptive? What would constitute "irrational-emotive therapy"? How could one evaluate the "inborn" nature of irrational beliefs to the satisfaction of a geneticist? These are only a few of the many questions which require clarification. But perhaps the foregoing comments are sufficient. They should, in retrospect, reflect an agreement with Ellis on the importance of cognitive processes in human distress, as well as a respect for his prolific contributions to this area. On the other hand, I would prefer cautious optimism over his zealous enthusiasm and a clearer presentation of both the hypotheses and the evidence in this area. From my own reading of the available literature, the cognitive therapies offer a refreshing and promising avenue for future evaluation. They have in a sense shown enough mettle to merit our attention, but I don't think we can yet declare them unequivocally superior to other forms of therapy.

REFERENCES

Bandura, A. *Social learning theory.* Englewood Cliffs, N.J.: Prentice-Hall, 1977. (a)

Bandura, A. Self-efficacy: Towards a unifying theory of behavioral change. *Psychological Review,* 1977, *84*(2), 191–215. (b)

Beck, A. T. *Cognitive therapy and the emotional disorders.* New York: International Universities Press, 1976.

Garfield, S. L., & Kurtz, R. Clinical psychologists in the 1970's. *American Psychologist,* 1976, *31,* 1–9.

Mahoney, M. J. *Cognition and behavior modification.* Cambridge, Mass.: Ballinger, 1974.

Mahoney, M. J. *Scientist as subject: The psychological imperative.* Cambridge, Mass.: Ballinger, 1976.

Mahoney, M. J. Reflections on the cognitive learning trend in psychotherapy. *American Psychologist,* 1977, *32,* 5–13.

Mahoney, M. J., & Arnkoff, D. Cognitive and self-control therapies. In S. L. Garfield & A. E. Bergin (Eds.), *Handbook of psychotherapy and behavior change* (2nd ed.). New York: Wiley, 1978.

Meehl, P. E. Theory-testing in psychology and physics: A methodological paradox. *Philosophy of Science,* 1967, *34,* 103–115.

Meichenbaum, D. *Cognitive-behavior modification.* New York: Plenum, 1977.

Popper, K. R. *Objective knowledge.* London: Oxford University Press, 1972.

Weimer, W. B. *Psychology and the conceptual foundations of science.* Hillsdale, N.J.: Erlbaum, 1977.

Personal Reactions
with Some Emphasis on New Directions,
Application, and Research

DONALD J. TOSI
The Ohio State University

I commend Albert Ellis for his outstanding presentation on the empirical basis for cognitive behavior therapy and rational-emotive therapy. I am sure the readers of his article would agree that Ellis has systematically brought together a group of diverse researches that give encouraging support for the many hypotheses contained in rational-emotive therapy. It would be an awesome task for any of us to review the number of studies Ellis cited, let alone integrate them in such a way as to convince the reader that there is indeed more to RET than mere armchair philosophical speculation. My commentary on the Ellis article will address several aspects of RET: theory, practice, and research; conceptions and misconceptions of rationality in RET; extensions and applications of RET; and some future directions. I will also have some concluding remarks.

The test of a good theory, ultimately, is that it reflects reality or some phenomenon, organizes observations, generates meaningful statements that can be made operational, is testable through experience, and can lead to predictions. It would be very difficult to argue philosophically and empirically that Albert Ellis' theoretical formulations do not meet or approximate the criteria of a good theory. Moreover, the notions contained in RET have been shown to have therapeutic utility and value (Lazarus, 1971; Meichenbaum, 1974; Tosi & Reardon, 1976; Reardon, Tosi, & Gwynne, 1977; Tosi & Moleski, 1975).

If one is not inclined to take Ellis seriously, he or she may wish to refer to recent work of Dr. Gene Glass on meta-analysis in psychotherapy. Ellis, in his presentation, did indicate that Glass and Smith (1975) found RET to be more effective than other systems of counseling and psychotherapy that included psychodynamic, Adlerian, eclectic, transactional analysis, behavioral modification, implosion, client centered, and Gestalt. RET, however, was a close second to systematic desensitization. Of course, SD has been researched longer than RET, as Ellis has already mentioned.

In brief, Glass and Smith are what I would call methodologists in the true sense—ones who study method. Using a set of well-defined criteria regarding experimental design and outcome measures, such as school/work achievement,

181

self-esteem, adjustment, and fear and anxiety, Glass and Smith were able to apply statistical reasoning and principles to the two questions "Do counseling and psychotherapy really work?" and "Are some systems of counseling and psychotherapy more effective than others?" Meta-analysis of present counseling and psychotherapy research implies strongly that both questions can be answered in the affirmative. Moreover, the conclusions reached through Glass and Smith's meta-analysis using empirical and statistical methods and Ellis' philosophical analytic-synthetic methods converge impressively.

A most impressive feature of rational-emotive theory is that it has stimulated research while being extremely practical. Behavioral theorists, such as Ellis, have helped to simplify the language of personality and counseling and psychotherapy. Ellis has been accused by some that his system is far too intellectual and devoid of emotion and too far removed from the existential aspects of man. But Ellis' writings and counseling practice portray a very realistic, humanistic, and concrete view of man as a thinking, emoting, behaving, and social organism. RET, philosophically, places human beings at the center of the universe, in control of their destinies, and responsible for creating themselves.

The reader should not assume that the object of RET is to create a person in the image and likeness of Albert Ellis. Nowhere does Ellis emphasize what the ultimate man should be. Ellis, more than most contemporary psychological theorists, stresses the use of reason to minimize self-defeating emotions and behavior—*not just the mere replacing or substituting of rational ideas for irrational ones.* For Ellis, reason is a process a human being may apply to personal and innermost thoughts, feelings, bodily responses, overt behavior, and the environment. Reason isolated—or reason abstracted—from these other human processes and the environment may be for the rationalist, the scholastic, or the mentalist, not for the practitioner of rational-emotive counseling and psychotherapy. Although, I must admit, some of us at times may, for some uniquely human but irrational reasons of our own, fail to practice what we preach in this regard.

What does *rational* mean or imply in rational-emotive therapy? Rational has to do with logical correct thinking that gives full consideration to facts and their interrelationships according to commonly accepted rules. In counseling and psychotherapy the facts or data are behavioral and environmental in nature, in that they are both inside of the person and outside of the person or, if you will, subjective and objective. Rationality in counseling implies logical thinking and acting as a way of achieving some personal goal or set of goals. If rationality is construed as a cognitive process and an aspect of human existence, then it simply becomes a means through which persons can act on their innermost thoughts, emotions, physical reactions, behavior, and the environment for the purpose of achieving a sense of well-being and freedom of thought and action.

Rationality, in the context of RET, does not imply intellectualization or isolation of affect in the Freudian/neo-Freudian sense. Intellectualization, or pseudorationality, serves as a defense mechanism, suggesting an underlying intention for self-deception and distortion of reality. Rationality is that human dimension that allows one to move beyond awareness, insight, and reflective thought into meaningful, concrete, and productive action.

Counselors and psychotherapists are not above pseudorationality, regardless of their philosophical, theoretical, and practical orientations. RET emphasizes the value of active confronting, doubting, questioning, and challenging matters of human existence, whether personal or environmental. Criteria for rational thinking and acting have been described by Maultsby (1971), Ellis and Harper (1975), and Tosi (1974).

If rational-emotive therapy has but one goal, it is simply to help another human being minimize self-defeating thoughts, emotions, bodily responses, and behavior (i.e., depression, anxiety, psychosomatic disorders, unassertiveness) so that one may be free to choose more personally productive alternative ways of acting. In so doing, a person is more likely to understand, accept, and affirm these same processes in others.

Now, is it a reasonable assumption that human beings minimize self-defeating behavior through educational lectures on rationality, merely replacing old irrational ideas with new rational ones? Definitely not. Many forget that RET uses concrete experiential behavioral tasks (homework), as well as direct and forceful confrontation, to force persons to face themselves.

The emergence of rational-emotive therapy and cognitive-behavior therapy will undoubtedly stimulate many behavioral methodologists who have ignored subjective processes such as thinking to include these in their subsequent researches. Mahoney (1977), in a paper appearing in The American Psychologist, predicts that methodological behaviorism is ready to admit cognition into its field of variables for study.

EXTENSIONS OF RET AND COGNITIVE-BEHAVIOR THERAPY

I have personally found the views of Albert Ellis helpful and most stimulating in the practice of counseling and psychotherapy, in teaching counseling and psychotherapy, and in conducting research. Recently, at The Ohio State University, we have been combining the idea of cognitive restructuring with hypnosis and imagery. What emerged was a cognitive therapy enabling the client to connect various irrational/rational ideas with undesirable/desirable emotions, physiological responses, and behavior. In addition to cognitive restructuring and hypnosis, a staging concept was introduced. The result—Rational Stage-Directed Therapy (Tosi, 1974; Tosi & Marzella, 1975; Tosi & Reardon, 1976)—guides the client's use of rational restructuring through the developmental stages of awareness, exploration, commitment to rational thinking and acting, implementation of rational thinking and acting, internalization of these processes, and finally change. *In vivo* behavioral tasks approximating imagery content are routinely given.

Our research efforts found that hypnosis and imagery appear to magnify and amplify the process of rational restructuring and its emotional, physiological, and behavioral impact. The inclusion of hypnotic and sensory imagery modalities with some of the rudimentary methods of RET seems to have a facilitative influence on the therapy process.

In most of our research we have used multiple-criteria measures that include cognitive, affective, physiological, and behavioral indices of psychological growth. The use of multivariate statistical procedures (e.g., multivariate analysis of variance, discriminant function analysis, and factor analysis) has permitted us to examine many variables, including sets of independent and dependent variables at the same time. For example, a study on some of the basic theoretical constructs in RET was conducted by Tosi and Eshbaugh (1976). A hierarchical factor analysis was performed on the Personal Beliefs Inventory, a measure of irrationality (Hartman, 1968). The findings indicated that certain irrational ideas are related statistically to specific negative, emotional, and behavioral tendencies. The emergence of a higher-order factor implies that most of Ellis' irrational ideas and their affective and behavioral concomitants seem to suggest an overall attitude of low self-worth.

Our experimental research using combinations of cognitive restructuring, *in vivo* behavioral assignments, hypnosis and imagery, and susceptibility to hypnosis has produced some rather promising findings giving additional support to rational-emotive therapy. Boutin and Tosi (1977), in a multifactorial experiment using multivariate analysis of variance, found that cognitive restructuring combined with hypnosis was a significantly more effective treatment for test anxiety in nurses than was hypnosis alone, placebo, or control. Changes in subject behavior were evidenced along a set of cognitive, affective, and physiological-criterion measures. Also, test-anxious nurses experiencing cognitive restructuring and hypnosis were able to increase their GPA more significantly than nurses in the other experimental conditions. Reardon and Tosi (1977) found that cognitive restructuring combined with deep relaxation and imagery was more effective in modifying self-concept and emotional stress in delinquent girls than treatments consisting of cognitive restructuring alone, relaxation alone, placebo, or control. In a comparative study, Moleski and Tosi (1976) found rational-emotive therapy to be more successful than systematic desensitization in the treatment of stuttering. Both rational-emotive therapy and systematic desensitization were more effective than a comparable control group in modifying attitudes (irrational ideas) toward stuttering, emotional stress, and speech disfluences. The inclusion of *in vivo* behavioral tasks, in many instances, augmented treatment effects.

Case studies have also provided valuable clinical evidence of the efficacy of rational-emotive therapy with the added experiential dimension of hypnosis in treating guilt (Tosi & Reardon, 1976), depression (Reardon, Tosi, & Gwynne, 1977), test anxiety (Boutin & Gwynne, 1975), assertiveness (Howard & Tosi, 1977). In the systematic case studies, multiple-criterion measures of client cognitive, affective, physiological, and behavioral functioning were employed and submitted to behavioral analysis.

It is a known fact that RET has been criticized sharply by many relationship-oriented theorists in the field for deemphasizing the importance of the

counseling relationship. Giving full consideration to these critics, Tosi and Eshbaugh (1978) developed a cognitive-experiential approach to the training of
counselors. Cognitive-experiential counselor training attends to the development
of relationship skills (i.e., core conditions of empathy, genuineness, respect, confrontation, self-disclosure, and concreteness), rational self-management skills,
and systematic behavioral feedback. Tosi and Eshbaugh (1978), in an experimental study, found that groups of counselor trainees exposed to training in the
core conditions via various group exercises, behavioral feedback, and, additionally, to cognitive restructuring increased their levels of interpersonal functioning and intrapersonal functioning significantly more than subjects who
experienced training consisting of core conditions alone, core conditions plus
behavioral feedback, or behavioral feedback alone. A control group was also
included. Criterion measures were based on levels of interpersonal functioning
(Carkhuff, 1969) and intrapersonal functioning (Personality Orientation Inventory, Shostrom, 1972).

CONCLUSION

In conclusion, rational-emotive theory in particular and cognitive-behavior
therapy in general appear to be having a profound effect on the field of counseling and psychotherapy practice and research. Finally, cognition and brain processes can be the object of experimental investigation in counseling research as
well as psychophysiological research. Although Ellis' review of research was
indeed impressive, I do believe, however, that we are merely on the ground-
floor. Much research is yet needed.

I predict that in the future there will be increasing attempts along the
earlier lines of David Graham's research (Graham, 1972) to use and investigate
rational or cognitive therapy in relation to psychophysiological disorders (hives,
hypertension, gastrointestinal disorders, headaches). Investigations using biofeedback methods that include a systematic study of the role of cognitive
factors will begin to appear more frequently in the literature. Moreover, complex experimental designs and multivariate statistical procedures will be used in
such research.

Theorists such as Joseph Wolpe, Carl Rogers, and Albert Ellis in their
work demonstrate a deep commitment to the value of scientific method. In
effect this means that, whatever theoretical abstractions emerged out of their
counseling experiences, these men were willing to submit them to testing and
experimentation. And, as we have seen over these years and specifically in
relation to Ellis' article, such a commitment has forced a modification and expansion of their views. Whatever personal and subjective views one may hold
about Wolpe, Rogers, and Ellis, many of their basic formulations will stand
the empirical test. And as for those who criticize RET, and Ellis particularly,
for being authoritarian, let these same people submit their views to empirical
validation and public scrutiny. Moreover, I have come to believe personally that
some of us in the field of counseling and psychotherapy have had difficulty

making a distinction between authoritarian and authoritative. Ellis on that dimension, philosophically and empirically, is clearly in the direction of authoritative. Rational-emotive theory, as any other theory, consists of a set of hypotheses that need to be tested or verified under many different conditions. To the degree that the theory espoused by Ellis encourages research and constructive criticism from within and from without and considers empirical findings, it cannot be regarded as a closed system. The excellent review of research by Ellis most certainly will add to the scientific credibility of his views.

REFERENCES

Boutin, G., & Gwynne, P. *The treatment of test anxiety with rational stage-directed hypnotherapy.* Unpublished manuscript, Ohio State University, 1975.

Boutin, G., & Tosi, D. J. *The treatment of test anxiety with rational stage-directed hypnotherapy.* Unpublished research paper, Ohio State University, 1977.

Carkhuff, R. R. *Helping and human relations* (Vols. 1 and 2). New York: Holt, Rinehart & Winston, 1969.

Ellis, A., & Harper, R. *A new guide to rational living.* Englewood Cliffs, N.J.: Prentice-Hall, 1975. (Also, Hollywood, Calif.: Wilshire Books, 1975.)

Glass, G. V., & Smith, M. L. *Meta-analysis of psychotherapy outcome studies.* Paper presented at the annual meeting of the Society for Psychotherapy, Boston, June 18, 1975.

Graham, D. T. Psychosomatic medicine. In N. S. Greenfield & R. A. Sternbach (Eds.), *Handbook of psychophysiology.* New York: Holt, Rinehart & Winston, 1972.

Hartman, B. J. Sixty revealing questions for twenty minutes. *Rational Living,* 1968, *3,* 7-8.

Howard, L., & Tosi, D. J. *The effects of rational stage-directed imagery and behavioral rehearsal on assertiveness.* Unpublished paper, Ohio State University, 1977.

Lazarus, A. A. *Behavior therapy and beyond.* New York: McGraw-Hill, 1971.

Mahoney, M. J. Reflections on the cognitive learning trend in psychotherapy. *The American Psychologist,* 1977, *32,* 5-13.

Maultsby, M. C. *Handbook for rational self-counseling.* Madison, Wis.: Association for Rational Thinking, 1971.

Meichenbaum, D. H. *Cognitive behavior modification.* Morristown, N.J.: General Learning Press, 1974.

Moleski, R., & Tosi, D. J. Comparative psychotherapy: Rational-emotive therapy versus systematic desensitization in the treatment of stuttering. *Journal of Clinical and Consulting Psychology,* 1976, *44*(2), 309-311.

Reardon, J. P., & Tosi, D. J. The effects of rational stage-directed imagery on self-concept and reduction of psychological stress in adolescent delinquent females. *Journal of Clinical Psychology,* 1977, *33*(4), 1084-1092.

Reardon, J. P., Tosi, D. J., & Gwynne, P. The treatment of depression through rational stage-directed hypnotherapy: A case study. *Psychotherapy: Theory, Practice and Research,* 1977, *14*(1), 95-103.

Shostrom, E. The measurement of growth in psychotherapy. *Psychotherapy: Theory, Research and Practice,* 1972, *9,* 194-199.

Tosi, D. J. *Youth toward personal growth: A rational-emotive approach.* Columbus, Ohio: Merrill, 1974.

Tosi, D. J., & Eshbaugh, D. M. The personal beliefs inventory: A factor analytic study. *Journal of Clinical Psychology,* 1976, *32*(2), 322-327.

Tosi, D. J., & Eshbaugh, D. M. A cognitive experiential approach to the interpersonal and intrapersonal development of counselors and therapists. *Journal of Clinical Psychology,* 1978, *34*(2), 494-500.

Tosi, D. J., & Marzella, J. N. *Rational stage-directed therapy (RSDT)*. Paper presented at First National Conference on Rational Psychotherapy, Chicago, June 1975.

Tosi, D. J. & Moleski, R. *Rational-emotive crisis intervention therapy (RECIT)*, 1975, *10*(1), 32–37.

Tosi, D. J., & Reardon, J. P. The treatment of guilt through rational stage-directed therapy. *Rational Living,* 1976, *11*(1), 8–11.

Commentary on
Albert Ellis' Article

FREDRIC B. KLEINER
Prince George's County Health Department

I like rational-emotive psychotherapy. It is my experience that it works. It's worked for me personally in my life, and it's worked with clients of mine with whom I've worked in an RET mode. I also share Dr. Ellis' conviction that a person's beliefs about a particular situation determines his/her experience of that situation. I particularly like the way John Lilly states this concept in *Programming and Metaprogramming in the Human Biocomputer* (1974).

"All human beings, all persons who reach childhood in the world today, are programmed biocomputers. No one can escape one's own nature as a programmable entity. Literally, each of us may be his programs, nothing more, nothing less." Or, as Lilly states in *The Center of the Cyclone* (1972), "In the province of the mind, what one believes to be true either is true or becomes true within certain limits to be found experientially and experimentally." I also subscribe to the definition of belief system that Lilly presents in *Simulations of God: The Science of Belief* (1976).

> In a given person, a basic belief system is that conscious/unconscious set of basic beliefs, assumptions, axioms, biases/prejudices, models, simulations which determine, at a given instant, decisions, actions, thoughts, feelings, motives and a sense of the real and true.
> A given person usually has several belief systems, which may or may not overlap, may or may not generate paradoxes, agree/contradict, control/ be controlled by one another, be arranged/disarranged, logical/illogical, be fixed/shifting [pp. 19, 20].

One of my immediate reactions to Ellis' article is surprise that he is fighting so hard to convince people of a "fact" (that our beliefs determine our experience of reality) that I have accepted to be "true" for such a long time.

Part of the reason for being of Ellis' article seems to be to (1) dispute Arbuckle's (1975) contention that RET is authoritarian and (2) to argue against other critics (Ellis cites Wolpe as one) who see it as lacking empirical confirmation (Ellis & Wolpe, 1974). Ellis typically bombards us with enough data, whatever my particular quarrel or question is with some of them, that I can't see how one can reasonably maintain that there is a lack of empirical confirmation for

RET's being an effective therapy. Of the basic hypotheses of RET, the one that appears to me to have the least empirical validation is the hypothesis that unconditional self-acceptance or self-regard would better consist of no rating of one's self or essence. While I personally share this belief with Ellis and agree with him that more studies of this RET hypothesis would seem called for, the nature of the hypothesis leads me to wonder how this in fact could be done, since in my experience I have never met anyone who is totally devoid of rating him/ herself, and that includes Ellis himself. However, it does seem possible that an instrument measuring the degree to which a person rates him/herself or essence could be devised to measure this quality on a relative level.

A population of people that I would like to see tested on this self-rating continuum would be those "enlightened" masters such as Zen masters, yoga masters, Tibetan tulkus or lamas, and others who similarly to Ellis espouse the virtues of non self-judgment. I can't help but chuckle over the fact that confirmation for one of RET's major tenets might come from spiritual sources, knowing what I do about Ellis' negative views about religion and its effect on people's emotions. Actually, it is delightful for me to notice the great amount of confirmation for this hypothesis, at least consentaneously, that comes from spiritual or transpersonal sources. My hunch is that, if Ellis looked into some of these sources in a less biased manner than I have heard him do in the past, he might find his beliefs about the destructiveness of spiritual and/or transpersonal thought being modified in a positive direction.

As for the criticism of RET being authoritarian, it is my experience that RET could in fact be authoritarian depending on the degree of authoritarianism present in the RET therapist. Is that different for any other kind of therapy? As Ram Dass states in *The Only Dance There Is* (1974), "Therapy is as high as the therapist is" (p. 28). As I have gotten clearer as to my underlying beliefs and prejudices, I have been able to be a much less dogmatic or authoritarian therapist than I was when I first started out on my internship some nine years ago. For me, perhaps the most important or essential rule of RET or any other therapy that could ensure its lack of authoritarianism or at least mitigate any authoritarianism that is inherent in the system is that the client be instructed above all to trust him/herself. If what the therapist is saying doesn't make sense or doesn't ring true, the client should be encouraged to challenge the therapist and feel free to reject the therapist's notions. In my personal experience of being with Albert Ellis, I have found that he has in fact encouraged people to challenge him and particularly loves challenges and battles in this area. My own experience tells me that, while some clients are relatively self-confident and trusting in their own beliefs and willing to reject things that don't feel true to them, it is extremely important for the therapist to encourage less self-trusting clients to frequently question and challenge what the therapist says or implies to be "the truth." Naturally, the more open and secure the therapist is, the more he/she is likely to do so.

To me, the greatest safety device against the therapist's being dogmatic and authoritarian with his/her clients is for the therapist to unscrupulously examine his/her own basic beliefs and to do this on a regular basis. I have come across a number of different devices and systems that encourage therapists to examine their own basic beliefs and some of these, at least for me, are even more effective in this particular area than is RET. I find that John Lilly's books have particular value for me in questioning my basic beliefs and knowing that I have them. Another book that I have found useful is one by Ourobourus International called *Mind Magic: The Science of Microcosmology* (1976). I also find Bucky Fuller's *Operating Manual for Spaceship Earth* (1970) to be helpful in pointing out how we human beings so uncritically accept and tend to believe words rather than to assimilate our personal experience. Perhaps most valuable, powerful and important to me is Werner Erhard's est training (1976). Of all the experiences that I've had that encouraged me to look into my own experience and my own beliefs, this has been by far the most powerful. In terms of efficiency, I know of no other method for observing one's self that achieved for me and others that I know as profound results in this area as did the two weekends spent in the est training. That certainly is not to say that other methods don't exist—just that I have not experienced or heard of any experiences that purport to produce more profound or efficient results in this area. While it certainly could be argued that, if someone spent 60 hours (which is approximately how long the est training takes) and spent them in RET, one might achieve the same result; it seems to me to be a relatively rare occurrence that the "observing ego" that seems to be uncovered for most people experiencing the est training can be as profoundly activated by six sessions of any kind of psychotherapy. That certainly is not to say that it can't be done, or hasn't been done, or that it hasn't been done in even less time than two weekends. It's just that my experience as a psychotherapy practitioner and consumer comparing systems of psychotherapy hasn't found many people being able to achieve in six sessions (or at a cost of less than $300, figuring at $50 a session) the same degree of awareness of their basic thought processes, attitudes and beliefs as the est training appears to uncover in people in two weekends at a cost of $300.

I want to make clear that I am not saying that the est training is better as a psychotherapy than rational-emotive therapy or any other kind of therapy. It does not purport itself to be psychotherapy and should not be considered a replacement for psychotherapy for those individuals whose beliefs about themselves and reality are entrenched and solid enough to warrant particular individual attention. However, the est training is certainly experienced by the graduates with whom I've come in contact as being quite therapeutic in its impact on them.

From my observations of belief systems and consciousness that are shared by my fellow beings on this planet, I am aware of some particularly destructive beliefs in our society that I would like to see questioned, re-evaluated and altered to beliefs that I believe are more sane and more consistent with the "truth," as I experience it. Buckminster Fuller in particular points out that perhaps the major thing that has stopped us from ending starvation on this planet is the notion that there is not and cannot be enough to go around. I particularly urge those of us in the behavioral sciences to read some of Fuller's books. His *Operating Manual for Spaceship Earth* (1970), or Eric Perlman's (1977) article about Bucky's work seem to me to be particularly good places to start to experience his logical demonstration that we do in fact have enough to go around if we would be more systematic in utilizing and pooling our resources and present technology. One of the most destructive beliefs that keep people stuck in their hopelessness and despair is the belief that it is impossible for things to be done other than the way they presently are being done. I think as scientists and psychotherapists we owe it to ourselves and to our clients and to humanity in general to remain as open as we possibly can to thoughts and beliefs that can minimize human suffering and anguish and increase people's experience of satisfaction with themselves and with their lives. If I have any intention here, it is to open us all up to investigating nontraditional sources of information and to encourage us to suspend some of our long-held prejudices against spiritual or transpersonal data such as Jane Roberts presents in *The Nature of Personal Reality* (1974) and her other Seth books, or toward works by independent thinkers such as Buckminster Fuller.

I don't want to be misinterpreted as advocating that people give up their skepticism. I think it is incredibly important for people to hold on to and maintain their skepticism and to test for themselves those notions which seem to be valuable for them and to determine for themselves, by their own experience, the "truth" or falsity of those notions. The point I'm making is that I'd like to see us be a lot more open than we as a group have been to nontraditional sources of data. What I would like to do is to convince those of you who are investigating hypotheses about theories of psychotherapy that can aid in people's lives to open yourselves to nontraditional sources and apply the scientific method of investigation to these areas.

I would like to acknowledge Albert Ellis as a pioneer in modern psychology and psychotherapy's investigation of people's attitudes and beliefs and to acknowledge RET's contribution to my life and to the lives of many clients with whom I have successfully used RET methods. However, what this article brings up for me is my wish to see engendered in our field in general an attitude of looking and seeing what things work rather than trying to specifically prove one method over another or investigating minute points of theoretical difference that really result in little or no experience of satisfaction in people's lives. For me, at the state of the art and science of psychotherapy as it exists today, it feels much more appropriate to be doing investigative comparative research as to clients' perception of the satisfactions and gains they have made with different systems of psychotherapy than to be arguing about fine theoretical points. Not that theorizing is bad. It's just been my experience that the preponderance of research with which we engage ourselves consists of proving or disproving various theoretical points rather than checking with the clients or consumers of particular kinds of psychotherapy and finding out from them what works and doesn't work for them. I know that this is open to the criticism that the clients themselves may not know what in fact worked or was effective, and this may in fact be true. So what? I'd rather see research being done to check out our clients' ideas of what works and doesn't work in therapy for them. Perhaps we'd even learn something new. What about some of us developing a standard questionnaire or other format which we could voluntarily agree to use with our clients to evaluate the perceived effectiveness of our work and then pool the data? To me, client satisfaction has always been the single most important criterion of whether or not psychotherapy has been effective in doing its job. This was certainly so for me when I was a psychotherapy patient, and I have a pretty good hunch that this is also true for the vast majority of people who are into psychotherapeutic treatment these days.

One of the things that I've learned most since graduating from Ohio State's graduate program in counseling psychology is how little I really knew when I was there and how afraid I felt to acknowledge that at the time. While I've heard so many people share similar experiences about their graduate school training, there seems to be almost no attention paid to this phenomenon in most of the graduate school training programs that I've heard about. Perhaps the most important thing I've learned as a practicing psychotherapist is to distinguish between what I think I know and what I really know or experience. Unfortunately, most graduate schools and programs for training psychotherapists that I'm familiar with encourage young psychotherapists to pretend that they know what they don't know. I'd like to see an attitude encouraged in our graduate training programs where students and faculty could feel safe enough to admit what they don't know so they could stop pretending and find out. By the same token, I'd like to see those of us who practice psychotherapy be scrupulous in checking with ourselves to see if the things that we're saying to our clients and to ourselves are true in our experience or are just beliefs that we have uncritically accepted and are uncritically perpetuating.

REFERENCES

Arbuckle, D. S. Ellis on Ellis. *Counselor Education and Supervision,* 1975, *15,* 70–71.
Ellis, A., & Wolpe, J. The forum: Rational-emotive revisited. *Professional Psychology,* 1974, *5,* 111–112.
Erhard, W. *What is the purpose of the* est *training?* San Francisco: Erhard Seminars Training, 1976.
Fuller, R. B. *Operating manual for spaceship earth.* New York: Pocket Books, 1970.
Lilly, John C. *The center of the cyclone.* New York: Julian Press, 1972.
Lilly, John C. *Programming and metaprogramming in the human biocomputer.* New York: Bantam Books, 1974.
Lilly, John C. *Simulations of God: The science of belief.* New York: Bantam Books, 1976.
Ourobourus International. *Mind magic: The science of microcosmology.* New York: 1976.
Perlman, E. Fifty years later, the fuller universe. *New Age,* 1977, *2*(8), 41–47.
Ram Dass. *The only dance there is.* New York: Anchor Press, 1974.
Roberts, Jane. *The nature of personal reality: A Seth book.* Englewood Cliffs, N.J.: Prentice-Hall, 1974.

The Rational-Emotive Manifesto

CRAIG K. EWART
CARL E. THORESEN
Stanford University

Albert Ellis has done good things for the field of psychotherapy and counseling. He has alarmed and goaded psychodynamic therapists, challenging them to grapple with their clients' crazy ways of thinking. He has hammered radical behaviorists with the message that psychological processes of people are as real as the bar presses of rats. Further, he has created a well-known form of therapy that is consistent with a broad current of psychological theory and research, a therapy which highlights the role of cognitive processes in emotional and behavioral disorders. Now Ellis tells us that his rational-emotive procedures are supported not only by clinical data but by an "almost awesome" body of controlled empirical research. While we agree that empirical support for a cognitive learning approach has been growing, we are not convinced that the usefulness of RET is as well documented as is that of other cognitive therapies (e.g., self-instruction training). In fact, we find Ellis' arguments on behalf of his claims very difficult to evaluate.

The difficulty in evaluating the hypotheses Ellis offers involves three issues: (1) the confirmatory bias of the research review; (2) ambiguities and apparent inconsistencies in the hypotheses themselves; (3) uncritical citations of research evidence. Despite the impressive numbers of studies mentioned, few if any seem to have much bearing on some of RET's most distinctive and controversial claims. Before enlarging on these issues, we would like to point out a problem which constitutes the critical weakness in the article. The difficulty can be illustrated by citing a bit of "animal literature."

A FABLE FOR SCIENTISTS: THE OSTRICH
WHO WAS NEVER AFRAID

There once was an ostrich who was never afraid. In fact, he was the only ostrich in the zoo who was not always getting upset about something. When the sight-seeing helicopter flew over the zoo, or the warthog squealed,

Preparation of this manuscript was supported in part by grants from the Spencer Foundation and from the Boys Town Center for Youth Development at Stanford. The opinions expressed or the policies advocated herein do not necessarily reflect those of the Spencer Foundation or of Boys Town. We gratefully acknowledge the comments of John D. Krumboltz on an earlier version of this article.

or the hungry lions roared for their dinner, all the other ostriches went absolutely silly. They would stampede around the ostrich yard in mindless panic, flapping their useless plumes and flailing their long ungainly legs. But the ostrich who was never afraid had taken to heart the old saw that ostriches bury their heads when frightened: he thrust his head into a drain pipe at the corner of the ostrich yard and found peace of mind. The pipe quieted his nervous brain and gave him a look of tranquil self-assurance that set him apart from his companions.

So engrossed did he become in his contemplations, that he eventually devised a theory which he shared with the other ostriches one day over lunch:

"The reason why I lead a serene, untroubled life and the rest of you do not," he patiently began, "is nicely explained by my revolutionary new Drain Pipe theory. I have performed the experiment many times now and the results are invariably the same: *What you don't see can't hurt you!*"

He paused, wanting his words to have their full effect, but the sudden return of the helicopter prevented further discussion.

That night a hungry lion escaped from its cage and made its way into the ostrich yard. All the ostriches but one went mad with fear; they galloped in every direction, waving their silly plumage and kicking their great powerful legs. The lion, wishing to avoid a lethal blow, headed straight for the drain pipe where he found a quick and easy meal.

Moral: What you don't see not only can hurt you, it can also disprove your theory.

Popular theories of counseling and psychotherapy often enjoy a "drain-pipe" omnipotence. Unlike the hapless ostrich they repeatedly elude the hungry lions of experience. They may even live forever—provided they can be safeguarded against the lethal threat of disconfirmation (Thoresen, 1978). But to be of scientific value, a theory must be exposed systematically and repeatedly to the perils of unfriendly experience and the rigors of critical analysis. The fearless ostrich understandably yet fatally repeated the mistakes of many a scientist, erroneously believing that one's theory is "proved" by a set of confirming experiences or observations. The ostrich's reasoning followed a familiar but illogical course: every time I hide my eyes from danger, I feel better, and nothing terrible happens. Since my experience repeatedly confirms my "out of sight, out of danger" hypothesis, my theory must be true.

The main weakness of Ellis' defense of RET is that it is based entirely on this insulating strategy of selective confirmation. He tells us that he will mention only those studies that appear to support his theory, as "less than 10% gave negative or equivocal results." If one adopts this protective maneuver, even the conviction that "what you don't see can't hurt you" is rescued from its debacle at the zoo. One need only point to the fact that the ostrich had performed his experiment many times and that his theory had been proven wrong *only once*. From these statistics and on the basis of "almost uniformly favorable results" one might well utter Ellis' optimistic phrase in arguing that the drain-pipe hypothesis has "immense—indeed almost awesome—research backing." What is the roar of one lion to that of 99 helicopters?

In our effort to understand a phenomenon it is often the *unexpected* or *disconfirming* event that tells us most. For the Drain Pipe theory, the lion incident was the most important "experiment" of our ostrich's scientific career: it marked out the limits of a bold hypothesis. One unexpected outcome did more to clarify the nature of the relationship between "seeing" and the "thing seen" than did all those successful trials with warthogs and helicopters. By not looking at disconfirming instances, Ellis often misses data that might contribute to a better understanding of how our ways of thinking determine our sense of mental well-being. As a theoretician, Ellis is surely aware of this problem, yet his decision not to review negative findings weakens his arguments, even in the eyes of those who share many of his views and wish to advance them.[1]

Although we agree with much of what Ellis says, we find that most of the hypotheses he puts forward and the evidence he cites in their favor do not contribute a great deal to therapeutic theory or practice. This is because (1) some hypotheses are so vague they could not possibly be tested in their present form; (2) some, while testable, do not seem very informative; (3) important instances of negative findings are not explained; (4) the relationship of certain predictions to RET theory is ambiguous; (5) there are apparent inconsistencies among predictions; (6) several hypotheses seem indistinguishable from ones put forward by many other theories; and (7) in those few instances where distinctive and specific predictions are made, little or no research evidence is offered on their behalf.

We shall illustrate these criticisms with specific examples.

1. Untestable hypotheses. Some hypotheses are stated in terms so general that it would be very hard to test them—i.e., subject them to possible disconfirmation, the procedure by which scientific knowledge is advanced (cf. Popper, 1972). We invite the reader to try to devise experimental tests of the following hypotheses:

---

[1] The problem, of course, lies in the "truth" of the premise (the Drain Pipe theory). If the theory (call it A) were unquestionably true, then hypothesized outcomes or observations (call them B) would be true and consistent with the theory. For example, if we knew that *all* birds having two long powerful legs were ostriches (A) and we then observed a bird with two long powerful legs (B), we could conclude that this bird was an ostrich (A clearly implies B). However, if our theory (A) is only *assumed* or *believed* to be valid (but is not true for sure), then any observations (B) consistent with that theory ("When I stick my head into this pipe, scary things go away")—no matter how often experienced—do not prove or clearly confirm the theory. Obviously other "theories" may equally or even better account for the same observations (If A, then B; *or* If A_2, then B; *or* if A_3, then B . . .).

The history of science is a tale of yesterday's truths that have become today's ancient fictions. The Ptolemic universe revolving about a stationary earth and centuries of medical practice (e.g., boiling oil on wounds) based on the doctrines of Galen are but two examples of theories repeatedly "proven" true by countless observations until other theories appeared (e.g., Copernican and bacterial germ theory). If we only seek confirmation for our theories, we can often find it. But by only looking for supportive data we do not *prove* our theories beyond reasonable doubt. Instead we only isolate them (and ourselves) from the enlightening errors of experience (cf. Popper, 1972; Thoresen, 1978; Weimer, 1976).

Hypothesis 8 (Innate influences on emotions and behavior): Humans appear to have very strong innate as well as acquired tendencies to think, emote, and behave in certain ways, although virtually none of their behavior stems solely from instinct and just about all of it has powerful environmental and learning factors that contribute to its "causation."

Hypothesis 12 (Irrational thinking): Humans have strong innate and acquired tendencies to set up basic values (especially the values of survival and happiness) and to think and act both rationally (abetting the achievement of their basic values) or irrationally (sabotaging the achievement of such values).

Hypothesis 15 (Low frustration tolerance): People have an innate and acquired tendency to have low frustration tolerance (LFT)—to do things that seem easier in the short run even though they often bring poor results in the future; to go for immediate gratification and stimulation seeking that offer highly specious rewards; and to procrastinate and avoid behaviors and disciplines that would bring them greater ultimate rewards.

How might one demonstrate that human emotions are not both innately and environmentally determined? That people do not act in ways that are inconsistent with the ends they strive for? That they do not do things that bring immediate benefits and long-term distress? Who would care to attempt such "proofs"? The extreme poles of the nature/nurture controversy are sparsely populated. Assuming these statements enjoy the status of truths too self-evident to be denied, how do they alter the way one does therapy? All major systems of psychotherapy, philosophy, and religion endorse these earnest truisms; taken in themselves, they do not prescribe one course of action over another. The important and divisive questions arise when one tries to specify the *limits* of nature or environment in given instances (e.g., intelligence) or the precise "mechanisms" that cause our irrational actions. While all theories contain assumptions that cannot be subjected to direct experimental test, these are more appropriately viewed as basic premises for which "research data" would not be pertinent. Adducing experimental evidence on behalf of hypotheses which cannot be tested is not a very informative exercise.

2. Hypotheses that are testable but uninformative. Some hypotheses *could* be tested, but in their present form they are so general that, even if true, they would not tell us a great deal. Consider the following:

Hypothesis 1 (Thinking creates emotion): Human thinking and emotion do not constitute two disparate or different processes, but significantly overlap. Cognition represents a mediating operation between stimuli and responses. What we call emotions and behaviors do not stem merely from people's reactions to their environment but also from their thoughts, beliefs, and attitudes about that environment.

Hypothesis 2 (Semantic processes and self-statements): People invariably talk to themselves (and others), and the kinds of things they say to themselves, as well as the form in which they say these things, significantly affect their emotions and behavior and sometimes lead them to feel emotionally disturbed. Effective psychotherapy partly consists of helping them to talk to themselves more precisely, empirically, rationally, and unabsolutistically.

The statements that thoughts create emotions and that the things people tell themselves influence their feelings are testable assertions, but in their present form they do not tell us a great deal. It is not hard to find experimental data consistent with omnibus, unspecific generalizations of this sort. The problem is that therapeutic interventions may have different effects on physiological arousal, task performance, and subjective distress (Bandura, 1969; Mahoney, 1974). In the case of phobias, for example, cognitive restructuring advocated in RET may help relieve subjective anxiety without significantly improving an individual's ability to approach or interact with feared objects (D'Zurilla, Wilson, & Nelson, 1973). It is not enough to assert that effective psychotherapy "partly" consists of helping clients to talk to themselves differently. Under what conditions should client self-talk become a *central* focus of therapy? A more specific formulation using the available research evidence would render RET claims easier to evaluate.

3. Failure to account for negative evidence. There are important instances in which a failure to recognize and discuss "negative" or disconfirming data seriously limits the usefulness of Ellis' theory. Three examples deserve comment. In defense of hypothesis 4 (awareness; insight; self-monitoring) Ellis claims that studies of self-observation "almost uniformly tend to show that when people monitor their own behavior . . . they frequently change their dysfunctional habits without employing any other kinds of reinforcements or penalties." But one can just as easily argue from available evidence that effects of self-observation on behavior are *not* terribly impressive. The most unequivocal evidence for self-monitoring effects derives from short-term laboratory studies of *nonclinical* behaviors (Kazdin, 1974a). Undesirable or dysfunctional behaviors often do not change when self-observed in clinical contexts (Bayer, 1972; Hall, 1972; Jackson, 1972; Kazdin, 1974b; Mahoney, 1971; Mahoney, Moura, & Wade, 1973). Where changes do occur, the extent to which they persist may be strongly related to certain environmental factors (Ewart, 1978). In many cases, self-awareness seems to exert only a very slight effect on behavior. Unless RET formulations can account for negative findings of this sort, the theory's claims concerning self-awareness will be of limited value to clinicians and researchers alike.

Some bypassing of negative facts may be an oversight. Although Ellis appears to know otherwise (cf. his discussion of hypothesis 19), his comment that "the most popular and effective of all the conventional behavior-therapy techniques used in psychotherapy consists of Wolpe's systematic desensitization method" in the context of snake phobias is clearly contradicted by Bandura's widely known research in precisely this area (Bandura, 1969, 1977). Bandura found that an *in vivo* method—live modeling with guided participation—was far superior to *symbolic* desensitization procedures in reducing subjects' fear of snakes (Bandura, 1969, 1977; Bandura, Blanchard, & Ritter, 1969). Shaw and Thoresen (1974) also demonstrated that modeling with guided practice was much more effective than symbolic desensitization with persons suffering from extreme fears of dentists and dental work. The finding that direct exposure is more powerful than imaginal presentation alone is highly relevant to any therapy that relies heavily on cognitive restructuring. Ellis does advocate the use of direct practice and homework assignments (hypothesis 19), but his discussion makes it difficult to know what relative emphasis he would place on these procedures. This in turn makes it harder to evaluate the adequacy of RET in relation to current research evidence.

A third and equally serious oversight occurs where research data are cited without noting that they contain weaknesses that have been widely documented. The defense of hypothesis 11 (attribution errors) contains an important example of this problem. Ellis cites research by Valins and Ray (1967) in which subjects were presumably cured of snake phobias when, while watching slides of snakes, they heard falsified feedback of their heart rate. He fails to note, however, that this research has never been successfully replicated despite numerous attempts (e.g., Rosen, Rosen, & Reid, 1972; Stern, Botto, & Herrick, 1972; Wilson, 1973) and that, because the fearfulness of subjects in the original study was not objectively assessed, it is difficult to determine whether the attribution treatment had much effect (Bandura, 1969). It would be irrational of us to expect Ellis, more than any other researcher, to detect and expose every weakness in data that favors his own position. Yet it seems careless to cite reviews by Bandura (1969) and Mahoney (1974) in defense of attribution theory without noting that these authors conclude that evidence for the theory is weak.

4. "Free-floating" predictions. In some cases it is not clear how Ellis derives specific predictions from his theory. While potentially testable and worthy of attention, they would be more informative if they were tied to a theoretical analysis. For example, in hypothesis 17 (active-directive therapy) Ellis appears to derive his preference for a "highly active-directive" approach over a "passive and unobtrusive" one from the observations that (1) self-defeating tendencies are innate and acquired, (2) dysfunctional patterns persist from early childhood, and (3) positive changes are not always maintained over time. Yet these observations in themselves provide no reason to choose a "directive" approach over a "passive" one. A psychoanalyst, for example, could find them quite compatible with a decision to pursue a more passive, reflective strategy, focusing on recollections of early childhood experiences. The choice of a therapeutic approach is not based just on a problem behavior's history or tenacity *per se;* it rests more on an analysis of a problem's possible causes. A passive approach assumes that the factors causing dysfunctional behavior are not entirely susceptible to conscious or direct manipulation. More directive approaches assume that they are. Presumably the RET techniques would be justified on an assumption that problem thoughts, feelings and behaviors are a function of variables that can be manipulated directly, although the hypothesis does not specify this.

The same difficulty is seen in the case of hypothesis 18 (disputing and persuasion). This hypothesis seems to assert that, because people hold self-defeating ideas that cause them to feel bad, a therapist can help them feel better by challenging the logic of these ideas and pointing out their self-hurtful nature. Again, the preference for logical disputation and persuasion would seem to be justified not on the grounds that people have irrational ideas that cause them pain but on the assumption that individuals will abandon these ideas in the face of a therapist's forceful arguments. Further, if these ideas are given up, it is assumed that desired behavioral and emotional changes will occur. These assumptions are based, in turn, on an analysis of the conditions under which cognitions control behaviors and emotions—an analysis which RET does not clearly provide.

The problem with statements of this sort is that they seem to tell us more than they really do. There is an implication that, should these predictions hold up under repeated tests, one could argue that the premises from which they are supposedly derived are "true" or valid. Hence the success of a disputative approach with clients would presumably encourage us to endorse the premise that peoples' problems are the result of irrational thinking.

But there is a major logical problem with this line of reasoning. If the prediction (disputation is therapeutic) was not entailed by the premise (people's self-defeating ideas cause their distress), the argument would be invalid. Thus a finding that rational argument led to a reduction in clients' difficulties would be clinically useful but would *not* provide support for Ellis' contention that emotional problems are the product of irrational thoughts. Ellis thus makes a prediction (hypothesis), the test of which could neither help nor harm his basic theory. Disputation could be effective for reasons totally unrelated to the rationality of clients' thoughts. Or clients' problems might indeed result from irrational thought patterns, but using disputation and persuasion may not be effective ways to change these. Lacking is some kind of plausible account of just how disputation acts to influence irrational thoughts and behavior. Unless a mechanism is specified by which disputation affects thinking and, in turn, influences behavior, evidence that supports the prediction itself (e.g., the client got better after being confronted) contributes little to the theory. Thus, while RET is more useful than theories of therapy that make no predictions at all, it is less adequate than ones which attempt to predict *and* explain (Bandura, 1977).

5. Inconsistencies among predictions. Another difficulty in evaluating RET arises from what looks like an inconsistency between assertions made in relation to hypothesis 5 (imaging and fantasy) and hypothesis 19 (homework). Ellis' prediction that *in vivo* practice will prove more effective in eliminating fears than will *imaginal* techniques, such as systematic desensitization, seems to contradict his earlier claim (itself contradicted by a great deal of experimental evidence) that systematic desensitization is the most effective treatment. We suspect that this really was just an oversight on Ellis' part and not a self-contradiction, yet it is another ambiguity that makes his defense of RET difficult to evaluate. Again, the confusion might not arise if Ellis were to be more specific about what kinds of treatments are likely to work best for which problems and clients and why.[2]

6. *Many RET hypotheses are shared by all therapies.* A number of hypotheses, even if they withstood evaluation, would have little impact on theory or practice because they are endorsed by most popular systems of therapy. The very general assertions that thoughts are related to moods (hypothesis 3), that effective therapy requires some unspecified combination of "cognitive, emotive, and behavioral techniques" (hypothesis 6), and the oft repeated reminder that human actions are a product both of nature *and* nurture (hypothesis 8) are commonplaces to which diverse theories might easily subscribe. The problem is not that these "background assumptions" play no useful role in a theory but that RET does not offer a formulation distinctive enough to improve therapeutic practice or advance our understanding beyond current levels. Instead of suggesting new approaches or lines of investigation, they sound more like cheerful slogans chanted over and over in an effort to wear down the opposition.[3]

7. *Where distinctive hypotheses are advanced, few supportive data are offered.* RET offers several distinctive and possibly valuable assertions concerning the cause of emotional distress and its treatment. These include the statement that irrational and absolutistic thinking produces defensiveness (hypothesis 14), that people are happier if they refuse to "rate" themselves against *any* standard (hypothesis 13), and that disputation and rational argument are highly effective ways to help clients change problem feelings and behaviors (hypothesis 18). Unfortunately, as Ellis himself notes, there are few if any controlled investigations of these assumptions.

MORE LIONS PLEASE

By mentioning a number of criticisms we may sound as if we do not think highly of Ellis' ideas or are pessimistic about the value of RET. This is not the case. We find the *clinical* evidence quite encouraging. There is good reason

[2]We well appreciate the difficulty of this kind of task. Yet not to attempt it is to leave theory and practice at the starting block. The time is past when we could be content with a demonstration that *any* version of counseling or therapy is better than no treatment at all. Even pitting one approach against another tells us little, since the variability of individual clients' responses to a given treatment obscures clear-cut interpretations. We encourage the reader to read Cronbach (1975), Glass (1976), Cronbach and Snow (1977) and Thoresen (in preparation) on these issues.

[3]See Thoresen (1977) for a critical discussion of a similar problem involving "empathic understanding."

to think that cognitive restructuring of the kind Ellis advocates might, in certain cases, prove a very useful clinical technique. On these grounds the approach deserves further experimental scrutiny. The problem is that we simply cannot accept Ellis' claim that his methods are supported by large numbers of well-designed, scientific studies. While this can be said for *some* of the hypotheses he offers (e.g., effects of modeling and guided practice, relevance of self-perceived competencies in skill training), most of the RET statements offered are very ambiguously related to research data or are not supported at all. This is particularly true for those aspects of RET that do *not* overlap other cognitive behavior therapies (e.g., the emphasis on rational disputation as the primary means to effect change). Before RET can be properly evaluated as a theory and as a therapeutic procedure, the fundamental assertions involved must be formulated more precisely in light of the *negative* as well as the positive research data.

For the clinical researcher, it would be helpful if Ellis were to frame his hypotheses not so much to persuade as to explain. Irrefutable statements may be very persuasive, but they do not stimulate the generation of new knowledge. While we share Ellis' enthusiasm for the use of cognitive techniques in therapy, we believe it is important to keep in mind the distinction between a scientific theory and a programmatic manifesto. Strong forceful advocacy plays a valuable part in therapy and in professional discourse. But an understanding of the fundamental phenomena addressed by RET will require more than the persuasive rhetoric which has helped bring them the attention they rightly deserve. A more critical, systematic skepticism will be needed if we are to move from persuasion to explanation.

REFERENCES

Bandura, A. *Principles of behavior modification.* Englewood Cliffs, N.J.: Prentice-Hall, 1969.

Bandura, A. *Social learning theory.* Englewood Cliffs, N.J.: Prentice-Hall, 1977.

Bandura, A., Blanchard, E. B., & Ritter, B. Relative efficacy of desensitization and modeling approaches for inducing behavioral, affective, and attitudinal changes. *Journal of Personality and Social Psychology,* 1969, *13,* 173-199.

Bayer, C. A. Self-monitoring and mild aversion treatment of trichotilomania. *Journal of Behavior Therapy and Experimental Psychiatry,* 1972, *3,* 139-141.

Cronbach, L. G. Beyond the two disciplines of scientific psychology. *American Psychologist,* 1975, *30,* 116-127.

Cronbach, L. G., & Snow, R. E. *Aptitudes and instructional methods.* New York: Irvington, 1977.

D'Zurilla, T. J., Wilson, G. T., & Nelson, R. A preliminary study of the effectiveness of graduated prolonged exposure in the treatment of irrational fear. *Behavior Therapy,* 1973, *4,* 672-685.

Ewart, C. K. Self-observation in natural environments: Reactive effects of behavior desirability and goal setting. *Cognitive Therapy and Research,* 1978, *2*(1), 39-56.

Glass, G. V. Primary, secondary, and meta-analysis of research. *Educational Researcher,* 1976, *5*(10), 3-8.

Hall, S. M. Self-control and therapist control in the behavioral treatment of overweight women. *Behaviour Research and Therapy,* 1972, *10,* 59-68.

Jackson, B. Treatment of depression by self-reinforcement. *Behavior Therapy,* 1972, *3,* 298-307.

Kazdin, A. E. Reactive self-monitoring: The effects of response desirability, goal-setting and feedback. *Journal of Consulting and Clinical Psychology*, 1974, *42*, 704–716. (a)

Kazdin, A. E. Self-monitoring and behavior change. In M. J. Mahoney & C. E. Thoresen, *Self-control: Power to the person*. Monterey, Calif.: Brooks/Cole, 1974. (b)

Mahoney, M. J. The self-management of covert behavior: A case study. *Behavior Therapy*, 1971, *2*, 575–578.

Mahoney, M. J. *Cognition and behavior modification*. Cambridge, Mass.: Ballinger, 1974.

Mahoney, M. J., Moura, N. G., & Wade, T. C. The relative efficacy of self-reward, self-punishment, and self-monitoring techniques for weight loss. *Journal of Consulting and Clinical Psychology*, 1973, *40*, 404–407.

Popper, K. *Objective knowledge*. Oxford: Oxford University Press, 1972.

Rosen, G. M., Rosen, E., & Reid, J. B. Cognitive desensitization and avoidance behavior: A reevaluation. *Journal of Abnormal Psychology*, 1972, *80*, 176–182.

Shaw, D. W., & Thoresen, C. E. Social modeling and systematic desensitization approaches in reducing dentist avoidance. *Journal of Counseling Psychology*, 1974, *21*, 415–420.

Stern, R. M., Botto, R. W., & Herrick, C. D. Behavioral and physiological effects of false heart rate feedback: A replication and extension. *Psychophysiology*, 1972, *9*, 21–29.

Thoresen, C. E. Constructs don't speak for themselves. *Counselor Education and Supervision*, 1977, *16*, 296–303.

Thoresen, C. E. Making better science, intensively. *Personnel Guidance Journal*, 1978, *56*, 279–282.

Thoresen, C. E. *Let's get intensive: Studying change over time*. Englewood Cliffs, N.J.: Prentice-Hall, in preparation.

Valins, S., & Ray, A. A. Effects of cognitive desensitization on avoidance behavior. *Journal of Personality and Social Psychology*, 1967, *7*, 345–350.

Weimer, W. B. *Psychology and the conceptual foundations of science*. Hillsdale, N.J.: Erlbaum, 1976.

Wilson, G. T. Effects of false feedback on avoidance behavior: "Cognitive" desensitization revisited. *Journal of Personality and Social Psychology*, 1973, *28*, 115–122.

The Relationship of Rational-Emotive Therapy to Other Psychotherapies and Personality Theories

ROBERT H. DOLLIVER

University of Missouri—Columbia

Albert Ellis places the origin of rational-emotive therapy (RET) in 1955. Ellis practiced orthodox psychoanalysis from 1949 to 1952 and psychoanalytically oriented therapy between 1952 and 1955 (Ellis, 1957b). His publications during this period indicate considerable reviewing, reflecting upon, and reformulating of therapies and theories. Ellis (1950) attempted to bring psychoanalysis into the realm of science, citing a number of dangers which he identified in psychoanalytic theorizing. Ellis (1956) reformulated some of the basic principles of psychoanalysis along the line of operationism. Ellis did an exhaustive review of psychotherapeutic practices reflected in professional journals from 1950 to 1953. That review was divided into two parts: for neurotic patients (Ellis, 1955a) and for psychotic patients (Ellis, 1955b). Ellis (1957b) provided a short account of RET when he compared his therapeutic effectiveness using three methods of psychotherapy at different times in his career. The first complete description of RET was published following a convention presentation in 1956 (Ellis, 1958). This description of RET is quite similar to the most recent descriptions which Ellis has made.

Ellis frequently acknowledges indebtedness to other theorists, although he usually does so in a sketchy manner. For instance, Ellis (1973c, pp. 173-175) mentions his relationship to Freud, neo-Freudians, Adler, Jung, Rogers, existentialists and conditioning-learning or behavior-modification approaches. By drawing on Ellis' comments and the present author's reading of Ellis and other sources, the present article delineates similarities and differences between RET and views espoused by other authors beginning with Stoic philosophers.

Many colleagues read, reacted to, identified additional references, and made suggestions concerning this article. Special contributions were made by De Laura Lobenstein of the University of Missouri Library, who secured bibliographic materials, by Janet Wollersheim Smith, who initiated my interest in RET, by Ben Ard, who broadened my view of RET, and by Everett Worthington, who added helpful ideas to this paper.

STOIC PHILOSOPHY

Ellis frequently notes that he has drawn upon Stoic philosophers in developing his psychotherapeutic techniques. He especially cites Epictetus: "Men are disturbed not by things but by the views that they take of them." This is, of course, the basis of Ellis' A-B-C theory of emotions. Ard (1967) identifies additional connections to Stoic philosophers. Sahakian (1969, p. 32) notes

> According to the psychology of the Stoics, what cannot be changed should be accepted or else treated with philosophical indifference. A fact which is not accepted by a person may cause him great distress; that is, if he is confronted with a problem or situation which he cannot change but nevertheless strives doggedly to dispel, he will merely succeed in intensifying the emotional tension and stress, causing him more misery than the problem that he is seeking to resolve. Actually, what is most distressing to many neurotics and others is the emotional stress exerted to combat their problem, creating an emotional exhaustion, a state of doubt and insecurity that readily stimulates or triggers anxiety at the slightest provocation [p. 35].

Rollo May (1969, p. 295) focuses on another aspect in his comment about the Stoics: "An attitude of 'unshakability' toward life, a passionless calm [was] attained . . . by an effort of strong will and by a refusal to let one's self be touched by the ordinary emotions of grief, hardship, and loss of life." Ellis comments how he was impressed very early in his life with Stoic philosophy, but Abraham Low was a probable aid in Ellis' translation of the Stoic philosophy into a psychotherapeutic method.

ABRAHAM LOW

Low's book *Mental Health through Will-Training* was first published in 1950. The description of his therapy method is quite limited and (perhaps because Low is a physician) is mostly oriented to physical sensations and upsets. Nevertheless, important points of similarity can be recognized between RET and Low's will-training used in Recovery, Incorporated.

Low's approach to patients is to have them first recognize their tendency to overreact to situations. Patients are then instructed how to dispute that tendency with the phrase that a particular sensation is "merely distressing but not dangerous." Low used the term "temper" to label the overreaction to situations. He said "You know . . . that temper will neither burn nor boil unless you form the idea that you have been wronged. From this we conclude that prior to releasing your temper you thought or decided that the boss was wrong and you were right" (Low, 1952, p. 365).* ". . . temper has two divisions. The one comes

---

*This and all other quotations from this source are from *Mental Health through Will-Training*, by A. A. Low. Copyright 1950, 1978 by A. A. Low and Phyllis Low Cameron. Reprinted by permission of The Christopher Publishing House.

into play when I persuade myself that a person has done me wrong ... The other variety of temper is brought into action when I feel that I am wrong" (p. 22). (Those two components can be recognized as central in Ellis' list of irrational ideas.) Low was highly attuned to the ways in which patients label their experiences: "She formulated the familiar philosophy of nervous patients which can be condensed in two sentences: I *feel* tired; hence I *am* tired; and I *think* my muscles are exhausted, hence they *are*" (p. 73). "The judgment 'he is wrong' cannot be passed except by a duly appointed judge" (p. 153).

Specific similarities to RET can be seen in the following quotations. "If you were a realist you would give first consideration to the actual facts of the prevailing situation and would not hesitate to suppress your thoughts or shelve your feelings if you found they conflicted with the realities of the situation" (p. 74). "A total has parts and the total experience has its part experiences. ... They are thoughts, feelings, sensations, impulses. ... Control one dominant part—for instance, confused thoughts—and the rest of the team (feelings, sensations and impulses) will follow suit" (p. 131). Ellis (1958) identifies the basic processes as perception, movement, thinking, and emotion. Ellis (1967), in reviewing Low's *Lectures to Relatives of Former Patients,* says "Although the outlines for correcting emotionally disturbed behavior are definitely there, the details are often sketchy and could be amplified." Low's *Lectures* book may have been a stimulus for *How to Live with a Neurotic* (Ellis, 1957a).

KAREN HORNEY

Ellis gives a nod of recognition to Karen Horney, but she seems to be a highly important source for Ellis' views. (Ellis was in therapy with a Horneyian analyst in the early 1950s, which would have been a time of Ellis' exposure to Horney's ideas.)

Ellis (1957a) especially shows resemblance to Horney (1937) in (1) his description of the overall characteristics of neurotics and in Ellis' specific comment (p. 55) "Most neurotics have an inordinate desire to receive and an infinitesimal ability to give, love." (2) Ellis (1957a, p. 49; 1966b, p. 81; 1972a, p. 184; Ellis & Blum, 1967, p. 1281; Ellis & Harper, 1961, pp. 33 and 108) employs Karen Horney's term "vicious circle" and uses the concept in description of clients (e.g., the shy person tending to become more socially awkward, thus more shy.) (3) Horney's definition of neurosis as "a discrepancy between potentialities and actualities" bears some similarity to Ellis' definition of "stupid behavior by a non-stupid person." (4) Horney's comment "realizing that they [the demands for love] are irrational is the first step in giving them up" (1937, p. 134) is certainly in keeping with Ellis' views.

(5) Horney (1942) notes that neurotics have "mottos" or "maxims," about which she says (p. 229) "It is as if the neurotic thought along these lines." Thus Ellis' "statements with which the neurotic propagandizes himself" has antecedents from Karen Horney. Ellis (1957a, p. 59) used the term "motto" concerning a client. (6) Similarity can be seen in Horney's "tyranny of the

should" (Ellis, Note 1), which may have been a source for Ellis' 11 irrational ideas, many of which counter the belief about the way things should be (how others should behave, how oneself should be, how others should be, what should happen, etc.). Several of Horney's (1942, pp. 54–59) "neurotic trends" resemble some of Ellis' (1962, ch. 3) "irrational ideas which cause disturbance." (a) Horney's identification of "neurotic need for affection and approval" and "neurotic need for personal admiration" resembles Ellis' first-listed irrational idea that "it is essential that one be loved or approved by virtually everyone in his community." (b) Horney's views on "neurotic ambition for personal achievement" and the "neurotic need for perfection and unassailability" resemble Ellis' second irrational idea that "one must be perfectly competent, adequate, and achieving to consider himself worthwhile." (c) Horney's "neurotic need to restrict one's life within narrow borders" bears some resemblance to Ellis' seventh irrational idea that "it is easier to avoid certain difficulties and self-responsibilities than to face them." (d) Horney's "neurotic need for a 'partner' who will take over one's life" resembles Ellis' eighth irrational idea that "one should be dependent on others and must have someone stronger on whom to rely."

The major difference is between Ellis' intrapersonal and Horney's interpersonal focus. Ellis emphasizes the self-statements with which the neurotic propagandizes himself (e.g., how horrible it would be for me if a particular thing happened). Horney's "mottos" reflect trying to figure out how others will act or how they ought to act if the neurotic does something toward that person. Horney suggests that neurotics are insufficient in relying on their own strength and in taking responsibility upon themselves, a view shared by Ellis. But Horney indicates that such tendencies can be carried too far when she speaks of "the neurotic need for self-sufficiency and independence" and "the neurotic need to control self and others through reason and foresight." Ellis would appear to differ from Horney on the extent it is profitable to go in those directions.

ALFRED ADLER

In two articles Ellis (1957b, 1971) considers the relationship of RET to the Individual Psychology of Alfred Adler. Most recently, Ellis comments "Adler was certainly one of my main mentors; and it is highly probable that without his pioneering work I would have never arrived at the main elements of RET." Ellis says that he was "essentially duplicating" Adler in some respects. The similarities to Adler which Ellis describes are: (1) the stress upon cognition, (2) the observation that many clients believe that they are inadequate, inferior, or worthless, (3) never making judgments concerning the moral worth of an individual, (4) that anger is not a useful emotion, (5) disturbed people ask too much of those around them, (6) meaning is not determined by the situation but by the meaning we give to the situation, which is the essence of Ellis' A-B-C description—i.e., in Adler's words, "Man makes one thing the cause and another thing the effect, then joins the two" (Ansbacher & Ansbacher, 1956, p. 91), and (7) "He [Adler] correctly saw that sexual drives and behavior . . . are largely the result rather than the cause of man's nonsexual philosophies" (Ellis, 1970d, p. 11).

The main differences which Ellis identifies with Adler are (1) Adler's primary concern with social interest versus Ellis' primary concern with self-interest (which Ellis claims includes an important dimension of social interest), (2) Adler's showing "human beings how to esteem themselves in spite of their innate and acquired limitations" versus Ellis' "effort to induce the individual not to rate or esteem himself at all" (Ellis, 1971, p. 50), and (3) the Adlerian view that the disturbed person has basic premises and goals which are false but that he proceeds logically and Ellis' belief that the disturbed person uses *both* false premises and illogical deductions.

SIGMUND FREUD

Ellis' relationship to Freud is somewhat difficult to delineate. Ellis received psychoanalytic training and considered himself, for a period of time, to be a psychoanalyst. Ellis, in 1950, published a book-length manuscript entitled *An Introduction to the Principles of Scientific Psychoanalysis* in which Ellis concluded that psychoanalysis (or psychoanalytically oriented therapy) "holds the best promise for the understanding and treatment of personality disorders- providing that its theories and procedures are formulated in truly scientific terms" (p. 205). Ellis (1957c) acknowledged that RET "owes an inestimable debt to the thinking of Sigmund Freud." Ellis (1971, p. 51) credits Freud with originating the view that neurosis is basically *ideogenic* (italics in the original), a view which Ellis says got lost in Freud's later theorizing.

Many of Ellis' views can be described in terms of agreement or disagreement with Freud's views. The following major elements in RET seem in essential agreement with Freud: (1) both Ellis and Freud would place rationality in the position of control over emotion. This orientation is represented in Freud's statement "Where id was, there shall ego be." (2) Ellis' view of "short-term self-interest" versus "enlightened self-interest" closely resembles Freud's view of the Pleasure Principle versus the Reality Principle (Ellis, 1966b, p. 130). (3) Ellis' view of religion seems similar to Freud's view presented in *The Future of An Illusion.* Both men criticize religion for not being scientific (although their definitions differ) and view religion as childish dependence. (4) Ellis has indicated his agreement with Freud's statement that the goal of life is to "love and to work," agreeing that these apparently diverse activities also appear to Ellis to come from the same source. (5) Both Ellis and Freud see man as hedonistic, specifically in pursuit of sexual pleasure. Fromm (1959, p. 104) describes Freud in a way which also seems to fit Ellis: "Reduction of tension constitutes the nature of pleasure. In order to arrive at this satisfaction, men and women need each other. They become engaged in mutual satisfaction of their libidinous needs, and this constitutes their interest in each other. However, they remain basically isolated beings, just as vendor and buyer on the market do."

The following elements are in opposition to Freud's views: (1) Ellis is antideterministic; he does not view other people or events as causing behavior. (An interesting light is cast on the issue of childhood determinants in Ellis' autobiography [Ellis, 1972c].) (2) Ellis believes that the psychoanalytic goal of insight into the origin of behavior is neither necessary nor sufficient to change behavior. (Ellis may have been influenced in this view by Allport's [1937] concept of "functional autonomy," which relates to this same issue.) (3) Ellis (1963b) indicates that the psychoanalytic concept of "emotional" insight (as opposed to the intellectual kind) would be better described as insight which is believed and which makes a difference in behavior.

Ellis (1968b) asks the rhetorical question "Is psychoanalysis harmful?" He identifies these major reasons why he believes psychoanalysis does more harm than good: (a) sidetracking (promoting the consideration of irrelevancies), (b) fostering dependency, (c) emphasis on feelings, (d) bolstering conformism, (e) strengthening irrationality, (f) sabotaging health potential, (g) holding the wrong therapeutic goals—i.e., to understand the history of his disturbances.

ALFRED KORZYBSKI

In Ellis' concern about the way in which concepts are employed, he draws on the orientation of general semantics. General semanticists have called attention (1) to the influence of labeling on feeling and behavior (e.g., Ellis replacing "awful, castastrophic" with "unpleasant, inconvenient") and (2) to the unique capacity of humans to endlessly react to their reactions (e.g., Ellis' view that people get upset about being upset, have problems about having problems). (3) Ellis' application of the semantics notion that "the word is not the thing" is evident in the frequent Ellis statement that being called a fool does not make one a fool. This is sometimes illustrated with the statement that if someone called you a giraffe that would not make you a giraffe. (4) An additional application of semantics is Ellis' concern with overly inclusive categorizing. Ellis (1965) goes so far as to argue that Leonardo da Vinci was not a genius, because he did some stupid and uncreative things in his personal life. Ellis also manifests concern with categorizations projected into the future (e.g., "Where is your proof that you cannot attract a mate in the future, simply because you have not done so in the past?"). Ellis (Note 2) makes the extreme comment "Even if I say that I can't flap my hands and fly, that's a nutty statement." Ellis goes on to say that flying under such circumstances is highly improbable because up to now it has not occurred, but the use of the word "can't" is inappropriate. Ellis' intent is to demonstrate how clients limit themselves by the way they use words. (This concern is also a part of Gestalt therapy.) Payne (1971) describes applications of Korzybski's (1933) ideas in a way which shows the similarity to RET principles.

General semantics is receiving increasing recognition recently within RET. Ellis (Note 3) said "Rational-emotive therapists practice one of the few truly semantic therapies that now exist" and "I stick fairly closely to principles of general semantics as originally laid down by the brilliant Alfred Korzybski." Two standard works within RET (Ellis, 1975; Ellis & Harper, 1975) have been revised in new editions using "E-prime" where all forms of "to be" (e.g., is, am, are, were) have been removed. This mode of writing comes from D. David Bourland (*The Un-isness of Is,* 1969), a Korzybski follower. Ellis (Note 3) indicates that problems do not come from the id, as Freud thought, but from the *is,* which "makes your id urges sacred and almost forces you to foolishly upset yourself about them." Moore (Note 4) notes that the sentence "This is awful" would formerly have been shifted to "This is inconvenient." Now, however, the word "is" would also be questioned since it frequently reflects overgeneralization. Actually only certain aspects of the situation are probably inconvenient and only for me and not for other people, or only immediately does "this" appear inconvenient while later "this" may seem to hold some advantage not presently observed. The standard RET sentence "I am a fallible human being" would be shifted to "I behave fallibly" or some other sentence. The use of E-prime is considered to lead to statements that are more specific, clearer, and more limited. These qualities promote the consideration of whether or not the statements are true. The introductions to the revised editions (Ellis, 1975; Ellis & Harper, 1975) provide more detail on the theory and application of E-prime and other uses of general semantics in RET.

BERTRAND RUSSELL

Russell's book (1930) *The Conquest of Happiness* contains elements which Ellis has incorporated into RET, as may be noted in the following examples from Russell's book. "When you have looked for some time steadily at the worst possibility and have said to yourself with real conviction, 'Well, after all, that would not matter so much,' you will find that your worry diminishes to a quite extraordinary extent" (p. 47). "The proper course with every kind of fear is to think about it rationally and calmly, but with great concentration, until it has been completely familiar. In the end familiarity will blunt its terrors" (p. 48). "Public opinion is always more tyrannical towards those who obviously fear it than towards those who feel indifferent to it" (p. 76). Gossack (1966) identifies these additional similarities between Ellis and Russell: beliefs determine actions, striving for approval above all else is sick, enjoying rather than evaluating what you do is appropriate, and pleasure which does no harm is to be valued.

SELF THEORY

The major tenet of self theory is that how people view themselves becomes itself a source of behavior. Ellis shows concern for how clients view themselves. Ellis reasons that, if clients think poorly of themselves, they will lack the confidence to attempt behavioral changes. For Ellis, personal worth is considered to be intrinsic, separate from behavior or accomplishment. Thus Ellis argues that failure to accomplish something does not mean that the person is no good. RET protects client self-esteem through insulating against derogation of clients by themselves or by other people. Ellis' views on sin and guilt can be readily interpreted in the same self-theory perspective. If clients see themselves as having sinned, that perception becomes burdensome in their effort to change.

William James' (1907) chapter on the self is an early classic presentation. He notes the paradox that some people who objectively are quite successful feel they are a failure, while some people who are not successful do not feel they are failures. James (p. 187) concludes that "Self-esteem = Success ÷ Pretentions." Ellis' views can be seen in this framework. Ellis notes that many people go to excessive lengths to avoid being foolish, making mistakes or failing at something. Ellis says to these people that they should expect to fail at times, that failure is an inevitable part of living. Ellis thus seeks to reduce the denominator (Pretentions) in the ratio which James presents.

Epstein's (1973) presentation of self-concept is in keeping with Ellis' views: "The most fundamental purpose of the self-theory is to optimize the pleasure/pain balance of the individual over the course of a lifetime. Two other basic functions, not unrelated to the first, are to facilitate the maintenance of self-esteem, and to organize the data of experience in a manner that can be coped with effectively" (p. 407).

CARL ROGERS

Ellis and Rogers seem about as dissimilar as it is possible to be in the conduct of their interviews. Ellis (1973c, p. 174) identifies RET as more persuading, more didactic, and more information-giving than Rogers would be. Ellis wrote two articles specifically directed to Rogers' writings. In the first, Ellis (1948) indicates that what Rogers has said about "non-directive therapy" applies to many forms of therapy and that Rogers' theoretical view is at many points simply an extension of psychoanalytic theory. In the second (1959), Ellis answers Rogers' article on the "necessary and sufficient conditions for psychotherapeutic personality change." Ellis concludes there are *no* absolutely necessary conditions for personality change to occur.

Ellis (1966a, p. 164) says "I partially go along with Carl Rogers' contention that the therapist's unconditional positive regard for the patient is a necessary condition for good therapy, because I believe that most patients only accept themselves very conditionally, and blame themselves mercilessly for their shortcomings. Therefore, they are considerably helped by a therapist who shows them ... that he believes that people can be of value to themselves and lead happy lives just because they exist, and not because they do anything well or to mutually please others." Ellis (1972b, p. 103) indicates that he has dropped the use of the term "unconditional positive regard" because it implies that the individual must rate or measure himself in some way. He says that he now uses the terms "self-acceptance" or "self-choosing," which seems a more neutral word and does not imply any rating of the self.

Ellis has indicated that his major disagreement with Rogers is that Rogers strengthens rather than disabuses clients of their views that they need close, appreciative relationships with people, whereas Ellis would label such a belief as "irrational." Patterson (1973, p. 74) says "I would suspect that Ellis' results are more influenced by the relationship he has with clients than he is willing to admit. His genuine interest and concern for the client are apparent and must be important factors." Ellis has commented—correctly, I think— that the kind of relationship which a Rogerian might seek is not present in RET.

ERIC BERNE

A number of similarities stand out between Berne's Transactional Analysis (TA) and RET. (1) Ellis is very concerned about client self-esteem, as discussed in the self-concept section. This concern seems much akin to the TA "I'm OK" as a goal for therapy. (2) RET and TA share an emphasis on the analysis of recent events with the purpose of changing nonfunctional client responses. (3) RET and TA share the emphasis on direct attempts to change behavior. Rozsnafszky (1974) terms this "stress on appropriate, realistic behavior, rather than insight, as the criterion of mental health" (which she indicates originated with Adler). (4) Rozsnafszky also notes "a renewed belief in the patient's responsibility for his behavior" as part of RET and TA (also originally from Adler). (5) Ellis points to the destructiveness of "shoulds" (from Horney). These "shoulds," in TA terms, come from the Parent ego state. Sometimes in TA treatment, the Parent state is temporarily "decathected," which is very similar to Ellis' getting rid of the "shoulds." (6) Both RET and TA (along with Freud) see adult maladjustment as stemming from the perpetuation of childish modes. Holland (1969) notes the possibility of a rapprochement between Ellis and TA in the view taken of emotion.

Three major differences stand out. (1) Though both are analytic, RET focuses mainly on the intrapersonal, while TA focuses mainly on the interpersonal dialogue. (2) In TA, awareness of needs is encouraged, along with the consideration of how these needs might be met. In RET, needs are typically viewed as mislabeled "wants," which are largely inappropriate since they are the outgrowth of an irrational philosophy and should be dispensed with. (3) In TA, stress is placed on the integration of all of the ego states as part of the total personality, while in RET use of the adult ego state (using data to come to decisions) is emphasized. Ellis (Note 1) comments that TA is a fairly good cognitive system but that it uses bad terminology and is unclear.

FRITZ PERLS

Ellis (Note 1) was asked about the relationship between RET and Gestalt therapy. He replied that he regarded the Gestalt *philosophy* as similar on the following points: (1) get rid of the shoulds, (2) be individualistic, (3) take care of yourself first, (4) take responsibility, and (5) stay largely in the here and now (as opposed to 20 years ago). Ellis (Note 1), however, indicated that Gestalt *techniques* are dissimilar from RET because they: (1) tend to obscure the issues in an emotionalized manner, (2) don't promote thinking through problems, and (3) are overweighted on the emotive aspects. He notes that Gestaltists would probably regard RET as overintellectualized ("mind-fucking").

Gestalt therapy and RET are similar in their stress on autonomy for clients rather than on relationships. The therapy relationship in either does not serve as a model for the kind of relationships the clients would seek in their personal lives. A number of additional differences exist between RET and Gestalt therapy: (1) Gestalt theorists describe people as unable to "let go" of an experience because they have not gone completely into the experience. Thus Gestalt therapy includes, as an important part, the going into (and thus through) old experiences. Ellis, on the other hand, believes that people do not "let go" of an experience because they have overreacted through recycling the experience or destructively misapplying the experience to themselves, as noted in the self-concept section. (2) Ellis and Perls take quite different views of emotion. Perls sees emotion as pointing to something which should be attended to: "Nature does not just create emotions to be discharged" (Perls, 1970, p. 31). Ellis sees emotion, especially prolonged, negative emotion, as the product of irrational sentences—something to be disposed of. (3) The net effect of Gestalt is additive: clients go away thinking that they are more complex and more interesting than they realized and probably desire to reflect on and learn more about their processes. Ellis' approach, in contrast, seems largely subtractive: clients get mainly the impression that some of their processes should be gotten rid of. (4) There seems to be a substantial difference in the individual quality of Gestalt as opposed to a rather stereotypical view of RET. In order to exaggerate the contrast, one might say that in Gestalt only the person is able to know the meaning of his/her behavior, whereas in RET only the therapist is able to know the meaning of the behavior which he/she then teaches to the client.

OTHER THEORISTS AND THERAPISTS

Since its beginning, RET has included a behavioral emphasis (e.g., homework assignments), and a number of behavioral techniques have been employed. Recently, there are indications of an increasing rapprochement between behavioral techniques and RET theory, which has been termed "cognitive behavior therapy" (Ellis, 1969; 1973a), "cognitive behavior modification" (Meichenbaum, Note 5), or "cognitive desensitization" (Wollersheim, 1974). Maxie Maultsby, Jr., a prominent RET practitioner, has consistently used the term "rational behavior training." Arnold Lazarus has also been a key figure in relating RET and behavioral techniques. Ellis (1973a) concludes that RET and cognitive behavior therapy significantly overlap in goals and methods but are not synonymous. Meichenbaum (Note 5) offers a complete description of group procedures designed to change the self-statements of speech-anxious college students. Meichenbaum (1972) outlines methods for modifying client self-statements, as does Lazarus (1971).

Phillips' (1956) interference theory bears similarity to RET in attending to clients' cognitive processes which contain dubious assumptions. Phillips notes four steps: assertion of an expectation, disconfirmation that the expectation will be met, tension over the disconfirmation, and redundancy (a redoubling of effort in keeping with the original assertion). The major difference is that Phillips sees considerable variability in the assertions which clients make, whereas Ellis believes that his clients' irrational ideas usually fall within his list of eleven.

In her description of assertiveness training for women, Jakubowski-Spector (1973) has employed Ellis' conceptualization of irrational ideas. She notes that nonassertive behavior is sometimes difficult to change because of beliefs or irrational fears about what would happen if the client were assertive. Ellis (1963 a, Chapter 4) discusses assertion without aggression, which is a major theme in assertion training. (Ellis defines the terms in a somewhat different way, however.)

Provocative therapy (Farrelly & Brandsma, 1974) employs some of the conceptualizations in Ellis' RET by mirroring the ways clients seem to be viewing themselves and the world (including the irrational ideas, as in RET). An important difference exists in the methods used: Ellis is largely rational, informative, and argumentative; Farrelly uses humor, belittling, sarcasm, exaggeration, and caricature. Another difference is in Farrelly's goal for clients to assert and appropriately defend themselves against the therapist. Ellis, on the other hand, clearly places clients in the position of being taught, as he corrects their errors or provides information.

Ellis sets forth the claim that most therapies contain a cognitive component which constitutes a major element, even in therapies which seem to stress emotive components. This is the thesis in Ellis (1970b), where Eugene Gendlin's (1964) therapy methods are the focus. The same thesis is maintained in Ellis (1974b), where comments are directed to Gestalt therapy (Perls, 1969), orthodox Reichian therapy (Reich, 1972), Lowenian bioenergetics (Lowen, 1967), Janov's (1970) primal therapy, Stampfl's implosive therapy (Stampfl & Levis, 1967), Malamud's (1973) self-confrontation, Shorr's (1973) imagining technique, and Brown's (1973) body therapy. The presence of cognition in conventional behavior therapy is described in Ellis (1969).

Ellis (1973b, p. 4) identifies RET as "a revolutionary humanistic approach to psychotherapy" on the basis that RET "squarely places man in the center of the universe and of his own emotional fate and gives him almost full responsibility for choosing to make or not make himself seriously disturbed." Ellis goes on to list ten reasons why he believes RET to be one of "the most humanistic of psychological treatment procedures," one of which is the promoting of acceptance of human fallibility and encouraging maximum understanding of and tolerance for human frailty.

Ellis (1974a) comments that Janov's primal therapy (1970) encourages clients to become bigger babies than they were. Ellis is highly antagonistic to the premise shared by Freud, Berne (1972), and Janov that children need certain experiences with parents to promote healthy adult functioning. But Ellis comments that primal therapy does some good because of behavioral and philosophical undercurrents. When primal clients yell and scream unashamedly, they are, in RET terms, engaging in an "antishame exercise." This experience in Ellis' view broadens some of the confines on the client's behavior and promotes his/her esteeming himself/herself whether other people do or not. Ellis (1974a) is critical that Janov promotes clients finding evidence of the accuracy of his therapeutic hypothesis. (Ellis, [1950] had made the same criticism of psychoanalysis regarding "proofs" of childhood trauma.) Such criticism is puzzling, given Ellis' comment (1957c, p. 41) that the rational therapist "knows, even before he talks to the client, that this client *must* believe some silly, irrational ideas—otherwise he/she could not possibly be disturbed. And, knowing this, the rational therapist deliberately looks for these irrationalities, often predicts them, and soon discovers and explains them." Movies and tapes of Ellis doing RET give ample evidence that Ellis promotes the client's buying into an RET view of psychological processes.

The objectivist philosophy of Ayn Rand (1961) and Nathaniel Branden (1969) (no longer associated with Ayn Rand) receives critical analysis in Ellis (1968a). Ellis' main complaint is that objectivism is not a truly rational approach although it may appear to be so. Ellis (1970a) is again antagonistic toward Branden's writing.

REFLECTIONS

My impression is that most counseling psychologists have underestimated the importance of Ellis' writings in defining and clarifying issues in personality theory and psychological treatment because they disagreed with his resolution of these issues. My hope is that my having done some "spade work" will encourage others to "dig in." I am impressed by Ellis' scholarship (especially Ellis, 1950, 1955a, 1955b, 1956, 1966a, 1968a, 1970c, 1974a, and 1974b). There is no question that Ellis is well informed about the views of other therapists. While I disagree with many of Ellis' views, I am glad to have gained more in-depth understanding of his views.

REFERENCE NOTES

1. Ellis, A. Rational-emotive psychotherapy. Lecture given to The Missouri Institute of Psychiatry, February, 1973.
2. Ellis, A. Experiential therapy versus rational therapy. Paper presented at the meeting of the American Psychological Association, New Orleans, September 1974. Reprinted by the Institute for Rational Living, New York, 1975.
3. Ellis, A. RET as a personality theory/therapy approach/philosophy of life. Paper presented at the First National Conference on Rational Psychotherapy, Glen Ellyn, Illinois, June 1975.
4. Moore, R. H. E-prime: A new language for improved self-communication. Paper presented at the First National Conference on Rational Psychotherapy, Glen Ellyn, Illinois, June 1975.
5. Meichenbaum, D. Therapist manual for cognitive behavior modification. Unpublished manuscript, University of Waterloo, 1974.

REFERENCES

Allport, G. W. *Personality: A psychological interpretation.* New York: Holt, 1937.

Ansbacher, H. L., & Ansbacher, R. R. (Eds.), *The individual psychology of Alfred Adler.* New York: Basic Books, 1956.

Ard, B. N., Jr. The A-B-C of marriage counseling. *Rational Living,* 1967, *2*(2), 10–12.

Berne, E. *What do you say after you say hello?* New York: Grove Press, 1972.

Branden, N. *The psychology of self-esteem.* Los Angeles: Nash, 1969.

Brown, M. The new body psychotherapies. *Psychotherapy: Theory, Research and Practice,* 1973, *10,* 98–116.

Ellis, A. A critique of the theoretical contributions of nondirective therapy. *Journal of Clinical Psychology,* 1948, *4,* 248–255.

Ellis, A. An introduction to the principles of scientific psychoanalysis. *Genetic Psychology Monographs,* 1950, *41,* 147–212.

Ellis, A. New approaches to psychotherapy techniques. *Journal of Clinical Psychology Monograph Supplement,* 1955, no. 11, 207–260. (a)

Ellis, A. Psychotherapy techniques for use with psychotics. *American Journal of Psychotherapy,* 1955, *9,* 452–476. (b)

Ellis, A. An operational reformulation of some of the basic principles of psychoanalysis. *Psychoanalytic Review,* 1956, *43,* 163–180.

Ellis, A. *How to live with a neurotic.* New York: Crown, 1957. (a)

Ellis, A. Outcome of employing three techniques of psychotherapy. *Journal of Clinical Psychology,* 1957, *13,* 344–350. (b)

Ellis, A. Rational psychotherapy and Individual Psychology. *Journal of Individual Psychology,* 1957, *13,* 38–44. (c)

Ellis, A. Rational psychotherapy. *Journal of General Psychology,* 1958, *59,* 35–49.

Ellis, A. Requisite conditions for basic personality change. *Journal of Consulting Psychology,* 1959, *23,* 538–540.

Ellis, A. *Reason and emotion in psychotherapy.* New York: Lyle Stuart, 1962.

Ellis, A. *The intelligent woman's guide to man-hunting.* New York: Lyle Stuart, 1963. (a)

Ellis, A. Toward a more precise definition of "emotional" and "intellectual" insight. *Psychological Reports,* 1963, *13,* 125–126. (b)

Ellis, A. Showing the patient that he is not a worthless individual. *Voices,* 1965, *1,* 74–77.

Ellis, A. Continuing personal growth of the psychotherapist: A rational-emotive view. *Journal of Humanistic Psychology,* 1966, *6*(2), 156–169. (a)

Ellis, A. *How to raise an emotionally healthy, happy child.* Hollywood: Wilshire, 1966. (b)

Ellis, A. Book review of *Lectures to relatives of former patients. Rational Living,* 1967, *2*(2), 29–30.

Ellis, A. *Is objectivism a religion?* New York: Lyle Stuart, 1968. (a)

Ellis, A. Is psychoanalysis harmful? *Psychiatric Opinion,* 1968, *5,* 16–25. (b)

Ellis, A. A cognitive approach to behavior therapy. *International Journal of Psychiatry,* 1969, *8,* 896–899.

Ellis, A. Book review of *The psychology of self-esteem. Rational Living,* 1970, *4*(2), 31–32. (a)

Ellis, A. The cognitive element in experiential and relationship psychotherapy. *Existential Psychiatry,* 1970, *7*(28), 35–52. (b)

Ellis, A. Rational-emotive therapy. In L. Hersher (Ed.), *Four psychotherapies.* New York: Appleton-Century-Crofts, 1970. (c)

Ellis, A. Tributes to Alfred Adler on his 100th birthday: Humanism, values, rationality. *Journal of Individual Psychology,* 1970, *26,* 11–12. (d)

Ellis, A. Reason and emotion in the Individual Psychology of Alfred Adler. *Journal of Individual Psychology,* 1971, *27*(1), 50–64.

Ellis, A. *The civilized couple's guide to extramarital adventure.* New York: Wyden, 1972. (a)

Ellis, A. *Executive leadership: A rational approach.* Secaucus, N.J.: Citadel Press, 1972. (b)

Ellis, A. Psychotherapy without tears. In A. Burton & Associates, *Twelve therapists.* San Francisco: Jossey-Bass, 1972. (c)

Ellis, A. Are cognitive behavior therapy and rational therapy synonymous? *Rational Living,* 1973, *8*(2), 8–11. (a)

Ellis, A. *Humanistic psychotherapy: The rational-emotive approach.* New York: Julian Press, 1973. (b)

Ellis, A. Rational-emotive therapy. In R. Corsini (Ed.), *Current psychotherapies.* Itasca, Ill.: Peacock, 1973. (c)

Ellis, A. Cognitive aspects of abreactive therapy. *Voices,* 1974, *10*(1), 48–56. (a)

Ellis, A. Rational-emotive theory: Albert Ellis. In A. Burton (Ed.), *Operational theories of personality.* New York: Brunner/Mazel, 1974. (b)

Ellis, A. *Three approaches to group therapy.* Part II: Rational-emotive therapy. Orange, Calif.: Psychological Films, 1974. (Film) (c)

Ellis, A. *How to live with a neurotic at home and at work* (Rev. ed.). New York: Crown, 1975.

Ellis, A. *A comprehensive bibliography of materials on rational-emotive therapy and cognitive-behavior therapy.* New York: Institute for Rational Living, 1980.

Ellis A., & Abrahms, E. *Brief psychotherapy in medical and health practice.* New York: Springer, 1978.

Ellis, A., & Blum, J. L. Rational training: A new method of facilitating management and labor relations. *Psychological Reports,* 1967, *20*(3, Pt. 2), 1267–1284.

Ellis, A., & Grieger, R. *Handbook of rational-emotive therapy.* New York: Springer, 1977.

Ellis, A., & Harper, R. A. *A guide to rational living.* Englewood Cliffs, N.J.: Prentice-Hall, 1961.

Ellis, A., & Harper, R. A. *A new guide to rational living* (Rev. ed.). Englewood Cliffs, N.J.: Prentice-Hall, 1975.

Epstein, S. The self-concept revisited or a theory of a theory. *American Psychologist,* 1973, *28*, 404–416.

Farrelly, F., & Brandsma, J. *Provocative therapy.* Fort Collins, Colo.: Shields, 1974.

Fromm, E. *Sigmund Freud's mission.* New York: Grove Press, 1959.

Gendlin, E. A theory of personality change. In P. Worchel & D. Byrne (Eds.), *Personality change.* New York: Wiley, 1964.

Gossack, M. M. Bertrand Russell on rational therapy. *Rational Living,* 1966, *1*(2), 44.

Holland, G. A. Book reviews. *Rational Living,* 1969, *4*(1), 28–30.

Horney, K. *The neurotic personality of our time.* New York: Norton, 1937.

Horney, K. *Self-analysis.* New York: Norton, 1942.

Jakubowski-Spector, P. Facilitating the growth of women through assertive training. *The Counseling Psychologist,* 1973, *4,* 75–86.

James, W. *Psychology.* New York: Holt, 1907.

Janov, A. *The primal scream.* New York: Delta, 1970.

Korzybski, A. *Science and sanity.* Lancaster, Penn.: Lancaster Press, 1933.

Lazarus, A. New techniques for behavioral change. *Rational Living,* 1971, *6*(1), 2–7.

Low, A. A. *Mental health through will-training.* Boston: Christopher, 1952.

Lowen, A. *The betrayal of the body.* New York: Macmillan, 1967.

Malamud, D. Self-confrontation methods in psychotherapy. *Psychotherapy: Theory, Research and Practice,* 1973, *10,* 123–130.

May, R. *Love and will.* New York: Norton, 1969.

Meichenbaum, D. Ways of modifying what clients say to themselves. *Rational Living,* 1972, *7*(1), 23–27.

Murphy, R., & Simon, W. *An annotated bibliography on rational-emotive therapy and cognitive-behavior therapy.* New York: Institute for Rational Living, 1980.

Patterson, C. H. *Theories of counseling and psychotherapy* (2nd ed.). New York: Harper & Row, 1973.

Payne, B. Uncovering destructive self-criticism: A teaching technique. *Rational Living,* 1971, *6*(2), 26–30.

Perls, F. S. *Gestalt therapy verbatim.* Lafayette, Calif.: Real People Press, 1969.

Perls, F. S. Four lectures. In J. Fagen & I. L. Shepherd (Eds.), *Gestalt therapy now: Theory, techniques, applications.* New York: Harper & Row, 1970.

Phillips, E. L. *Psychotherapy: A modern theory and practice.* Englewood Cliffs, N.J.: Prentice-Hall, 1956.

Rand, A. *For the new intellectual.* New York: Random House, 1961.

Reich, W. *The function of the orgasm.* New York: Orgone Institute Press, 1972.

Rozsnafszky, J. The impact of Alfred Adler on three "free-will" therapies of the 1960's. *Journal of Individual Psychology,* 1974, *30,* 65–80.

Russell, B. *The conquest of happiness.* New York: New American Library, 1930.

Sahakian, W. S. Stoic philosophical psychotherapy. *Journal of Individual Psychology,* 1969, *25,* 32–35.

Shorr, J. E. Imagine, in what part of your body your mother resides? *Psychotherapy: Theory, Research and Practice,* 1973, *10,* 131–134.

Stampfl, P. G., & Levis, D. J. Essentials of implosive therapy. *Journal of Abnormal Psychology,* 1967, *72,* 496–503.

The un-isness of is. *Time,* May 23, 1969, p. 69.

Wollersheim, J. P. Cognitive desensitization: Explication of a new technique via a case report. *Journal of Contemporary Psychotherapy,* 1974, *6,* 146–153.

A Review of
Rational-Emotive Psychotherapy
Outcome Studies

RAYMOND A. DiGIUSEPPE

Institute for Rational-Emotive Therapy
and Long Island Jewish-Hillsdale Medical Center

NORMAN J. MILLER

Institute for Rational-Emotive Therapy
and Southeast Nassau Guidance Center

LARRY D. TREXLER

Camden County Psychiatric Hospital

In his article at the beginning of Section 2 of this book, Albert Ellis presents numerous "clinical and personality" hypotheses related to that form of therapy which he developed and for which he continues to serve as the very active leading proponent. For each of those hypotheses he refers the reader to studies in the mental-health literature supporting it.

After all is said and done, the practicing clinician or counselor may well still have one overriding question: but does it work? Because of the importance of this hypothesis (that it does), we decided to present a separate article, giving some depth and detail information about studies—mainly experimental and controlled —supporting it. More specifically, such a hypothesis needs to be broken down into more meaningful parts, so that it would read: RET works (a) better than no treatment, (b) better than nonspecific treatment effects, such as attention-placebo, and (c) at least as well, if not better than, other competing approaches to psychotherapy.

As with psychotherapy and counseling methods in general, outcome research with RET was slow in coming and has not always achieved high standards methodologically speaking. The recent trend has been toward both increased quality and quantity. Rational-emotive therapy, as a cognitive-behavioral procedure, lends itself readily to hypothesis testing. The definitive "critical" study remains to be done (if it ever will!), and the weight of the research we shall present decreases in impressiveness as we proceed from the above (a) through (c). Nevertheless, as we shall discuss more fully later, we believe it does overall show considerable support for the effectiveness and efficiency of this form of treatment. We shall make every effort to view the studies and their data objectively, frequently pointing out methodological shortcomings. Rational-emotive therapy advocates scientific thinking as opposed to that based on faith or authority. It would be a travesty not to apply rigorous scientific tests to RET itself.

Some of the papers included in this review are not, strictly speaking, rational-emotive therapy outcome studies. They fall under a variety of rubrics, such as "cognitive therapy," "self-instructional training," "cognitive-behavior therapy," and "cognitive restructuring." Their overall similarity to rational-emotive therapy, or emphasis upon key elements thereof, makes it necessary in our opinion to include them as relevant to the test of rational-emotive therapy principles.

Research stimulated by rational-emotive theory has been focused in three main areas: (1) the influence of cognitions and beliefs on emotional arousal, (2) attempts to correlate endorsement of Ellis' 11 irrational ideas and psychopathology, and (3) studies concerned with the efficacy of RET.

The results of research in the first category are discussed by Ellis in his article and are quite extensive; therefore they will not be discussed here.

The amount of research in the second category has mushroomed. The number of scales to measure irrational thinking has also increased. The results lend support to the hypothesis that endorsement of Ellis' 11 irrational beliefs is positively correlated to emotional disturbance. These results are reported in studies by Argabite and Nidorf (1968), Bard (1973), Fox and Davies (1971), Goldfried and Sobocinski (1975), Jones (1968), Kassinove, Crisci, and Tiegerman (Note 2), Laughridge (1975), MacDonald and Games (1972), Newmark (1972), Newmark, Frerking, Cook, and Newmark (1973), Trexler and Karst (1973), Waugh (1975), and Zingle (1976). Because of space limitations this research shall not be discussed in more detail. The following will be concerned with outcome studies of the effectiveness of RET.

NONCOMPARATIVE OUTCOME STUDIES

Our discussion of specific RET outcome studies begins with those in which this form of therapy is not compared, in a controlled manner, with others. The reason for beginning with this category is in part historical, for that is where the early RET outcome studies fall.

The initial study documenting the effectiveness of rational-emotive (then called "rational") therapy was published by Ellis in 1957. Ellis evaluated his own effectiveness as a therapist during three periods of his professional practice. According to his own rating at the time of termination, Ellis found that, with the patients receiving orthodox psychoanalysis, 50% showed little or no improvement, 37% some distinct improvement, and only 13% considerable improvement. With the analytically oriented therapy the respective figures were 37%, 45%, and 18%. The patients treated with rational-emotive therapy showed the greatest trend towards success: 10%, 46%, and 44%. An additional finding of the study was that Ellis saw considerable improvement in 22 patients treated by rational-emotive therapy in one to five sessions, as compared to only seven analytically oriented cases, and no orthodox analysis cases, receiving the same small range of sessions.

Ellis, however, remarks that these results may be somewhat suspect because they may reflect his own enthusiasm for rational-emotive therapy and his relative lack of the same for the other treatment modalities. Meltzoff and Kornreich (1971) criticized the study additionally for its lack of controls and inadequate dependent variables. They state: "The data from a single therapist are not representative and lack generality, especially when he is the sole judge of his own case records and the founder of the approach that shows up best" (p. 185).

Bibliotherapy as an adjunct to therapy is frequently employed among rational therapists. Ellis and his colleagues almost routinely assign clients *A New Guide to Rational Living* (Ellis & Harper, 1975), as well as other materials to be read after the first session. An attempt to isolate and evaluate the effectiveness of bibliotherapy as an adjunct to rational-emotive therapy in the reduction of speech anxiety was made by Jarmon (1972). The results showed that on all of the dependent measures the bibliotherapy rational-emotive therapy groups demonstrated a significant decrease in anxiety relative to the other three groups.

These differences were not maintained at follow-up. In any case, more research into the effectiveness of adjunct bibliotherapy is needed before its usefulness can be ascertained. It is possible that being given therapeutic readings carries a placebo effect. Experimental designs controlling for this effect have not yet appeared in studying the role of adjunct bibliotherapy.

In addition to bibliotherapy, rational therapists frequently assign cognitive and behavioral homework as a standard procedure. Maxie Maultsby (1971), who helped pioneer systematic homework, investigated the effectiveness of utilizing written homework sheets as therapy. He assigned 87 psychiatric outpatients to a homework therapy condition for ten weeks. Results demonstrated that 85% of the patients who were judged most improved rated the assignments as an effective adjunct to their therapy.

Although these results were statistically significant, one cannot be certain of whether or not the patients' expressed support of the homework sheets was just an artifact of their improvement. Adequate controls were lacking, the written homework was an isolated variable, and, since no control groups were used which included homework assignments in addition to therapy, the effects of such assignments could not be assessed.

Jacobs (1971), who studied the effectiveness of rational-emotive therapy with college students, also included reading assignments and homework sheets. After treatment, the rational-emotive group differed significantly from the two control groups in the predicted direction on the Irrational Beliefs Inventory (Jones, 1968), the trait scale of the State-Trait Anxiety Inventory, and the Mooney Problem Check List.

Keller, Crooke, and Brookings (1975) investigated the use of rational-emotive therapy in reducing irrational thinking and self-reported anxiety in a geriatric population. The members of the experimental group showed significant reductions in the dependent measures at the posttest, while the control group showed no change.

The Keller et al. and Jacobs studies suggest that rational-emotive therapy can be effective in a short period of time, with only a few therapy sessions. Unfortunately, the Keller et al. study did not include a placebo control, neither study reported any follow-up, and only self-report measures were used. In addition, no attempt was made to determine the extent to which the various treatment components (i.e., the rational-emotive discussion, readings, or the homework sheets) contributed to, or were necessary for, effective treatment results.

Wine (1971) did attempt to investigate separate components of rational therapy. Results indicated that the behavior-rehearsal-plus-modeling group improved significantly more than the insight-only group. Wine concluded that a rational-emotive therapeutic approach that focuses on the exploration of the irrational beliefs through insight, without rehearsing the appropriate rational self-statements, would not achieve its goals in reducing self-defeating emotions and behaviors.

A recently published paper by Yu and Schill (1976) presents support for the ability of rational-emotive therapy to reduce vulnerability to criticism and rejection. Results favored RET on the three self-report measures, with these gains maintained at three-week follow-up.

Unfortunately, no behavioral measure was employed, and the RET subjects had an initially higher level on the "Fear of Disapproval" measure. Nevertheless, as the authors state (p. 14), "these results are encouraging since they suggest RET can be effective in helping people overcome an inordinate sensitivity to the opinions and criticisms of others and do so with relatively few treatment sessions."

Trexler and Karst (1972), in a partial replication and expansion of an earlier study (Karst & Trexler, 1970), investigated the efficacy of rational-emotive therapy as compared to attention-placebo and no-treatment control groups in the treatment of public-speaking anxiety. The results demonstrated, on self-report and behavioral measures (with trained independent raters), that RET was more effective than the placebo or no-treatment conditions. A subsequent self-report follow-up six months after completion revealed that the improvement had been maintained.

In a study patterned after the Trexler and Karst (1972) experiment, Straatmeyer and Watkins (1974) investigated the effects of rational-emotive therapy on public-speaking anxiety. The combined rational-therapy group showed a significant decrease in anxiety on all measures. On the generalization measure, both rational-emotive therapy groups showed transfer-of-training effects. The importance of this study seems limited by the failures to find any significant differences in the analysis of covariance. The use of a second statistic increased the probability of a type-1 error.

These studies demonstrate some support for the efficacy of rational-emotive therapy. However, methodological problems (such as a subject pool which is not representative of a typical clinical population) limit their generalizability.

RATIONAL-EMOTIVE EDUCATION AS PRIMARY PREVENTION

Ellis has claimed that, in addition to reducing inappropriate, excessive negative emotions and maladjusted behavior patterns, the principles of rational-emotive therapy can also be applied to the prevention of psychopathology. Maultsby (1974) has developed a program with rational-emotive therapy (which he terms "Rational Behavior Therapy") that is essentially designed for use in high schools and college classrooms. The program was originated primarily for use as a preventive mental-health tool. His goal was to teach students to utilize rational-emotive therapy in analyzing their emotional upset and to give them an effective method for solving personal conflicts.

Maultsby, Knipping, and Carpenter (1974), through a series of studies, investigated the efficacy of the above program. In an initial study (not preventative), two groups of already emotionally disturbed high school students were used as the sample population. One group received the rational-emotive therapy course, and the other served as a control group. Dependent measures included several personality-assessment scales—the Rotter Internal-External Scale (Rotter, 1966), the Personal Orientation Inventory (Shostrom, 1964), and the Maultsby Common Trait Inventory (Maultsby, Note 3). Results indicated significant differences in the positive direction on all three measures in the group receiving rational-emotive therapy.

A replication of the above (described in the same article) but using "normal" college students again demonstrated that the group receiving the rational-emotive course showed more pre-posttest improvement on the same dependent variables.

Maultsby, Costello, and Carpenter (Note 4) again attempted to validate the efficacy of rational-emotive therapy as a preventive mental-health program with college students. The results, as measured by the scores on a mental-health adjustment scale, yielded more positive results with the rational-emotive-therapy group than with the control group.

Thus, these studies demonstrate that a course based on principles can be used effectively as a preventive mental-health educational model with "normal" populations and that its effectiveness is not limited to the amelioration of clinical problems. That is, it was effective in producing immediate benefits to the participants. Despite these claims, the above studies failed to demonstrate that their educational programs reduced the incidence of psychopathology. That would require incorporation of a follow-up measure indicating that the experimental groups have a lower incidence of emotional disturbance than control groups. Such studies have not yet been forthcoming.

RATIONAL-EMOTIVE EDUCATION WITH CHILDREN

Since the elementary school environment may be an important setting for instituting preventive efforts, there has been increasing interest in developing mental-health programs in the classroom that would promote emotional and behavioral adjustment (Ivery & Alchuler, 1973; Spivack & Shure, 1974). In accordance with their views, Ellis (1971) has recommended that the principles of rational-emotive therapy be taught to elementary school children.

Rational-emotive education is a direct extension of rational-emotive therapy. Anecdotal studies have demonstrated that rational-emotive-therapy principles can be effective with both disturbed and nondisturbed children (Ellis, 1969, 1972; Ellis, Wolfe, & Moseley, 1966; Glicken, 1968; Hauck, 1967; Knaus, 1974). However, there is a paucity of well-controlled studies investigating whether children can acquire the cognitive principles of rational-emotive therapy and whether such acquisition will result in a generalized improvement in adjustment.

A series of rational-emotive education modules for use with a group of elementary school children was designed by Knaus (1974). Knaus and Boker (1975) investigated its effectiveness with children. Results indicated that the children receiving rational-emotive education scored significantly lower on the anxiety measure and higher on the self-esteem measure than the control groups.

Albert (1972) also investigated the effectiveness of a rational-emotive education program with "normal" fifth-graders, utilizing the same experimental procedures and measures as Knaus and Boker (1975). The children receiving rational-emotive education showed less anxiety on the Anxiety Scale for Children.

Both of these studies lend some support to the hypothesis that rational-emotive education can be effective in reducing anxiety and in the promotion of emotional adjustment. A number of deficiencies in the studies, however, limit their internal and external validity: (1) no pretest was administered to assess any initial differences; (2) an attention-placebo group was lacking to control for the "Hawthorne" effect; and (3) only self-report dependent measures were used.

A study that is described by its authors, Warren, Deffenbach, and Broding (1976), as "rational-emotive therapy" appears sufficiently close in the procedures employed to rational-emotive "education" to be included in this section. Both the RET and no-treatment groups improved their scores on subsequent testing, but the former subjects did significantly better than the latter on this measure. No treatment differences were found, however, on posttreatment-only measures of general anxiety and arithmetic performance. The authors acknowledge methodological shortcomings, including a relatively inexperienced therapist, short therapy time, and irregularly held sessions. Additionally, there was no control for attention-placebo effect, significant results only with one of the self-report measures, and no follow-up. There is, furthermore, no indication of whether or not—and, if so, how—the rational-emotive education-treatment procedures were adapted for the children.

Katz (1974) attempted to control for some of the experimental problems noted above. He studied the efficacy of rational-emotive education with "nondisturbed" fifth-graders. Students were randomly assigned to one of four different treatment conditions. Positive significant differences for the rational-emotive-treatment group were found on the Coopersmith Self-Esteem Behavior Rating

Form but not on measures of self-concept or locus of control. These results may be biased by the fact that the three groups were different not only in the kind of treatment they received but in their level of reading as well. This methodological limitation was further compounded by the fact that only one teacher-therapist was used to teach the rational-emotive education program, thus increasing the possibility of experimenter bias.

DiGiuseppe and Kassinove (1976) also compared the efficacy of rational-emotive education with an alternate mental-health program and a no-contact control group. The children who received rational-emotive education scored significantly higher and endorsed fewer irrational beliefs than either the alternate-treatment or the control group on both content-acquisition measures. On the measures of emotional adjustment, only the fourth-grade rational-emotive education condition showed less neuroticism and anxiety than either the alternate-treatment or the control group.

An interesting yet unexpected finding, in opposition to the original hypothesis, was that the younger children benefited more from the rational-emotive-therapy program than the older ones. DiGiuseppe and Kassinove explain this contradictory finding by suggesting that the younger children have not yet established a well-ingrained belief system, while the older children have been inculcated with the irrational beliefs of society.

Brody (1974) investigated the effects of a similar rational-emotive affective education program on the anxiety, self-esteem, and tolerance for frustration of fifth-graders. While there was no significant effect on the children's self-esteem scores, the rational-treatment groups differed significantly from the controls on measures of anxiety and tolerance for frustration. These differences were not present at the eight-week follow-up. The same pattern of results occurred in the replication of the experiment.

Although the Brody study reports positive findings, the failure to maintain these results at follow-up questions the long-range effectiveness of rational affective education programs. Possibly more teaching sessions, distributed over a longer period of time, would result in more persistent gains.

The DiGiuseppe and Kassinove (1976) and Brody (1974) studies both utilized the posttest-only design. There are practical advantages and disadvantages to this. The assumption of randomization is difficult to make, and it is possible to have initial group differences; on the other hand, the utilization of a design that requires pretesting may confound the treatment effects. While it appears that the use of this design is justified, the results must be interpreted with caution. Also, both studies utilized one instructor for both the experimental and control groups, which allows for the possibility of experimenter bias. However, using different instructors for different groups in future studies would also present problems in that instructor and treatment effects could then be confounded. Future research in the effectiveness of rational-affective education could avoid these problems by using several different instructors for both experimental and control groups.

The studies described in this section provide support for the hypothesis that elementary school children are capable of acquiring knowledge of rational-emotive principles and that the modification of a child's self-verbalizations or irrational self-statements can have a positive effect on emotional adjustment and behavior. Certain critical factors relevant to rational-emotive-therapy procedures with children have not been thoroughly investigated. These include specification of the relative contributions of the behavioral components within rational-emotive therapy (i.e., behavioral rehearsal and written homework assignments) and the degree to which a child's intellectual ability is related to his acquisition of the cognitively oriented principles of rational-emotive therapy.

The studies do not support the efficacy of rational-emotive therapy with emotionally disturbed children, although it could be hypothesized that RET would be effective with such children.

COMPARATIVE STUDIES

The majority of the comparative outcome studies have compared rational-emotive therapy with some form of behavior therapy, particularly systematic desensitization or behavior rehearsal. Studies comparing RET with these types of behavioral techniques will be discussed separately. (A few of them have compared rational-emotive therapy with client-centered therapy as well.) No studies have appeared in the literature comparing the efficacy of RET with such other major schools as Gestalt, transactional analysis, psychoanalytic or reality therapy.

RATIONAL-EMOTIVE PSYCHOTHERAPY AND
SYSTEMATIC DESENSITIZATION

DiLoreto (1971) investigated the effectiveness of rational-emotive therapy, systematic desensitization, and client-centered therapy in the treatment of subjects with interpersonal anxiety. The results indicated that all the treatment conditions significantly differed from both control conditions on all the dependent measures, except that the client-centered group did not achieve significance on the interpersonal activity scale. Systematic desensitization achieved the greatest amount of anxiety reduction with both personality types; rational-emotive therapy produced more significant decreases in anxiety with introverts than did client-centered; and client-centered was more effective than rational-emotive therapy with extroverts.

DiLoreto's results appear overall to indicate that systematic desensitization was the most effective treatment. A follow-up assessment three months later, however, indicated that students who received rational-emotive therapy reported more change in their behavior at that time than students receiving either desensitization or client-centered therapy. Specifically, they exhibited more interpersonal interactions and assertive behavior. Thus, while systematic desensitization was most effective in reducing anxiety at termination, rational-emotive therapy was most successful in changing behavior after treatment. This result appears to be of the utmost importance for psychotherapy outcome research. Its validity would have been strengthened if behavioral measures had been included in the follow-up.

The DiLoreto study is one of the most advanced comparative studies to date in psychotherapy. Bergin and Strupp (1972, p. 511) commented that "the phenomena and processes involved were somewhat closer to the real thing." The results were, nevertheless, limited due to the nature of the subjects and therapists. The interpersonally anxious college students are not exactly equivalent to psychotherapy clients, and graduate students, regardless of training, are not the equivalent of experienced therapists. Another major criticism appears to be the nature of the "placebo" treatment. This group met for discussions of university life, academic problems, and study skills for only three sessions. Thus, they could have been cued that this was not "treatment" and that they were not expected to change.

Ellis (DiLoreto, 1971), in his review of this study, noted that the therapist used a "watered down" RET approach. According to Ellis, the therapists did not demonstrate why the students' beliefs were irrational, did not give enough stress to the necessity for work and practice, and tended to be too generally didactic and lecturing.

Rational-emotive therapy, client-centered therapy, and systematic desensitization were also compared by Maes and Heinman (1970), this time in the treatment of test-anxious high school students. There were no significant differences between the four groups on the state anxiety measure. However, significant differences were found on the galvanic-skin and heart-rate measures, supporting the effectiveness of RET and systematic desensitization over the client-centered and no-treatment control groups.

While this study is important as one of the pioneer efforts in comparing RET with other treatment modalities, it has methodological limitations—the failure to match subjects on initial level of anxiety; the small number of subjects, which prevented use of more powerful statistical tests; lack of a placebo control group; and the .10 significance level for the post-hoc analysis.

Meichenbaum, Gilmore, and Fedoravicus (1971) investigated the effectiveness of group rational-emotive therapy and group systematic desensitization on the treatment of speech anxiety in college students. Subjects receiving systematic desensitization only, or rational-emotive therapy only showed the greatest improvement in reducing speech anxiety. Their level of speech performance following treatment matched that of an additional group of low speech-anxious subjects, included so as to provide a standard for adaptive responding in group speech situations. Self-report follow-up measures at three months indicated that improvement had been maintained.

A post-hoc analysis found that desensitization and rational-emotive therapy had differential effects depending upon the type of speech anxiety the students displayed. Desensitization appeared to be more effective with students for whom speech anxiety was confined to situationally specific stimuli; conversely, rational-emotive therapy was more effective with students who suffered anxiety in a variety of social situations. This finding is consistent with previous research (Lazarus, 1974; Meichenbaum, 1973) which suggests that systematic desensitization is a more effective treatment of persons with monosymptomatic phobias or the "classical phobias"; a cognitive approach such as rational-emotive therapy works better with those who demonstrate more general anxiety or the "social phobias."

Meichenbaum (1972) compared the relative efficacy of "cognitive modification," systematic desensitization, and a waiting-list control group with test-anxious college students. The "cognitive-modification" procedure was found to be significantly more effective in reducing test anxiety than either standard systematic desensitization or the control conditions on self-report measures, an analog test situation, and grade-point average. This improvement was maintained in a one-month follow-up.

In an attempt to separate the relative contributions of the components in Meichenbaum's cognitive-modification treatment package, Thompson (1974) conducted a study using standard systematic desensitization, desensitization plus coping imagery, and cognitive modification.

Thompson found that the cognitive-modification group showed the most significant improvement on self-report and test-anxiety inventories. He concluded that the results found in the Meichenbaum (1972) study were due to the cognitive components of his cognitive-modification treatment rather than the relaxation or coping imagery.

Kanter's (1975) investigation of the outcome of therapy is closer to the "real thing" than most studies in the field. It is equaled only by DiLoreto's (1971) in complexity and thoroughness. Kanter attempted to compare the effectiveness of systematic desensitization to systematic rational restructuring and a combined treatment.

Kanter predicted that the combined-treatment condition would be the most effective and that the desensitization and restructuring treatments would be equally effective. While all treatments showed significant reductions in anxiety from pre- to posttests and were significantly more effective than the control condition, the rational-restructuring approach fared best. These results were maintained at the follow-up. The prediction of differential effectiveness at various levels of anxiety, specifically that the cognitive therapy would be least effective with subjects with high degrees of anxiety, was not supported.

For all its sophistication and thoroughness, the Kanter study has some shortcomings. The possibility of experimenter bias arises from the experimenter's having led all treatment groups. There was no attention-placebo control. A longer follow-up with more valid measures than self-report scales would have strengthened the results. Despite these deficiencies, this study comes closer than analog studies to an actual test of psychotherapy, since the subjects were people seeking help with anxiety problems and thus approximate an outpatient population. Its results add strong support for the efficacy of rational-emotive and related therapies.

In a very well-controlled study, Wein, Nelson, and Odom (1975) investigated the effectiveness of cognitive restructuring with phobias. The results for the behavioral measure indicated that cognitive restructuring was as effective as systematic desensitization in increasing approach behavior, while both were superior to the verbal extinction treatment and the two control conditions. Cognitive restructuring was the only effective treatment as measured by self-report. These results support the effectiveness of cognitive therapy and indicate that, in comparison with desensitization, it is equally, if not more, efficacious. Unfortunately, the lack of follow-up measures leaves unclear the long-term effectiveness of the interventions employed by Wein et al. (1975). The comparison between the restructuring and extinction groups confirms that it is cognitive reappraisal, not extinction, that accounts for the therapeutic gains of rational-emotive and similar cognitive therapies. These results are similar to those of Wine (1971), who demonstrated that providing the client with alternate cognitions while viewing a situation is a critical component of therapy.

The first published rational-emotive study to include an actual patient population was that of Molesky and Tosi (1976). The authors hypothesized that RET would be more efficient than systematic desensitization in the treatment of adult stutterers. The results of this study strongly support the effectiveness of rational-emotive therapy over systematic desensitization in reducing stuttering behavior as well as the accompanying anxiety and irrational attitudes concerning stuttering. These results were sustained at follow-up.

The inclusion of behavioral homework assignments did not have consistent effects across all dependent measures. However, the results confirm that rational-emotive therapy, without *in vivo* assignments, was more efficacious than both systematic-desensitization conditions (i.e., with and without homework). The addition of the assignments enhanced the effectiveness of the rational approach on one behavioral measure. These results suggest, overall, that cognitive interventions alone are sufficient to change behavior; although the behavioral components may be beneficial, they are not necessary. This conclusion should be considered tentative until more investigations systematically isolate the behavioral and cognitive components of rational-emotive therapy.

Molesky and Tosi's (1976) study offers the strongest support to date for rational-emotive therapy. The inclusion of multiple therapists and raters is strongly recommended for all future studies. While follow-up measures were also employed here, it is suggested that they be administered at progressively longer intervals after the conclusion of treatment.

Of particular interest would be an experimental test of Meichenbaum et al.'s (1971) post-hoc findings that desensitization was most effective with subjects with more situationally specific anxiety, whereas cognitive therapy was more efficacious with subjects with more generalized social anxiety. In addition, research is needed to explore the relationship between other patient characteristics and the relative effectiveness of these approaches. This could, for example, include replication of DiLoreto's (1971) study concerning introversion and extroversion.

RATIONAL-EMOTIVE PSYCHOTHERAPY AND
ASSERTIVE TRAINING

Recently there has been a large number of studies in the treatment of interpersonal anxiety by means of assertive training. Results have shown that assertive training is useful in reducing such anxiety and promoting assertive behavior (Lazarus, 1966; McFall & Lillesand, 1970; McFall & Marston, 1970; Young, Rimm, & Kennedy, 1973). This section will review the comparative effectiveness of assertive training with and without rational-emotive therapy in the reduction of interpersonal anxiety.

Wolfe (1975) investigated the efficacy of modeling and behavioral rehearsal as an adjunct to rational-emotive therapy in increasing assertive responses in women. It was hypothesized that the combination of rational-emotive therapy and behavioral rehearsal/modeling would be more effective than behavioral rehearsal/modeling alone. It was also predicted that the combined approach would show greater generalization of treatment effects. Dependent measures included self-reports of assertiveness and situational and general anxiety. The results indicated that both modeling/behavioral rehearsal and the combined treatment showed significantly more improvement on measures of assertiveness than the control groups.

Tiegerman (1975) compared rational-emotive therapy, assertive training, and a combined treatment of both with an attention-placebo group and a no-contact control group in reducing interpersonal anxiety in college students. Results provided partial support for the relative efficacy of all three treatment approaches in promoting assertion over the control groups. The most consistent gains were achieved by the assertive-training groups, followed by the combined approach and the rational-emotive-therapy group. Postexperimental interviews revealed that the students in the combined treatment thought that "too much material was presented in a small amount of time." The relative failure of the rational-emotive therapy was considered to be a function of the missing behavioral component. These subjects received only the cognitive component of the rational-emotive-therapy approach. This is in direct contrast to the usual rational-emotive-therapy procedure, which relies heavily on behavioral components such as behavior rehearsal and homework assignments, in addition to cognitive restructuring.

Additional methodological limitations included failure to use behavioral measures, no follow-up data, and a small sample ($n = 5$ per cell). Finally, an analysis of the pretest measures indicated that the students had a low degree of interpersonal anxiety and a high degree of assertiveness, thus reducing the chances for treatment effect.

Thorpe (1975) designed a study comparing the merits of self-instructional training, systematic desensitization, behavior rehearsal, and a placebo control group in increasing assertiveness in college students. Results indicated the general superiority of self-instructional training, followed by behavior rehearsal. However, one cannot singularly attribute the success of the self-instructional group to the cognitive components of rational-emotive therapy, since Thorpe did not isolate the behavioral and cognitive components of self-instructional therapy.

In sum, the research in the area of assertive training as an adjunct to rational-emotive therapy has thus far been scant and at best equivocal. Three essentially unresolved problems remain: (1) inadequate isolation of the behavioral and cognitive components of the rational-emotive-therapy procedure; (2) limited duration of the treatment period; and (3) no adequate follow-up data. It is only when the above requisite conditions are met that the beneficial effects of a combined cognitive-behavioral approach to assertive training will be demonstrated.

RATIONAL-EMOTIVE THERAPY AND FIXED-ROLE THERAPY

Karst and Trexler (1970) investigated the comparative effectiveness of rational-emotive and fixed-role therapy (Kelly, 1955), which is also highly cognitive-behavioral, in the reduction of speech anxiety in college students. While results showed no difference between the two methods, both were significantly higher than no treatment. This relationship, however, was found only in the self-report measures and not in the behavioral measure. Karst and Trexler attribute the failure to find significance on the behavioral measure to its low reliability. An additional criticism of the study is its lack of a placebo control group in the experimental design.

Since there is only one study comparing these two therapies, and considering its limitations, it is premature to draw conclusions as to which method may be more effective.

COGNITIVE-THERAPY STUDIES ON DEPRESSION

As mentioned earlier in this article, Aaron T. Beck (1970, 1976) has independently devised a systematic approach called *cognitive psychotherapy* that is very similar to rational-emotive therapy. Both are based on the premise that emotional disturbances are caused by cognitive distortions and that the therapist's principal task is actively and directly to teach the client to recognize and change those belief systems. Beck's "cognitive therapy," like RET, also employs behavioral procedures, such as graded-task and *in vivo* desensitization activity. Because of these similarities, research in one is seen as supporting the other. Beck developed his ideas while doing research in the area of depression (Beck, 1967), and thus the outcome studies of cognitive therapy have primarily been done with depressed subjects.

An important and impressive paper has just come out of the work of Beck and his associates at the Depression Research Unity of the University of Pennsylvania. Rush, Beck, Kovacs, and Hollon (in press) found cognitive therapy to be superior to pharmacotherapy in the treatment of depressed outpatients. These results contrast with a number of other studies that have reported the superiority of pharmacotherapy over various forms of psychotherapy. Methodologically the study is also noteworthy for its use of an actual clinical population of neurotic depressed patients, professional-level therapists, and a relatively extended period of treatment.

The results of the study were that both groups significantly decreased in both depression and anxiety. Cognitive therapy was found to be significantly superior to pharmacotherapy on all three measures. Furthermore, approximately 80% of cognitive-therapy patients showed marked improvement or complete remission of symptoms, compared with 23% for imipramine. Follow-up data are being collected but were not available for this report. There are a number of methodological problems, such as the independent raters' not being blind to patient condition and the Raskin scales' being completed by the therapists, with no interrater reliability data for the latter. The authors openly acknowledge and discuss such potential drawbacks, pointing out, for example, that what might appear to be experimenter bias was probably mitigated because the original predisposition of most of the therapists lay in favor of pharmacotherapy. Rush et al. conclude that "the results of our study indicate that cognitive therapy may hold great promise as a short term for depressed outpatients."

Beck's cognitive-therapy approach was also employed in a study by Brian Shaw (1977) comparing it with Lewinsohn's behavioral treatment for depression, nondirective therapy, and a waiting-list control group. The results indicated that the cognitive treatment was the most effective overall in reducing depression immediately posttreatment. The behavioral and nondirective groups were not significantly different: both were more effective than the waiting-list control. Unfortunately these results were not maintained at one-month follow-up (at which time only the two treatment groups were assessed). The results of this study are encouraging, given the degree of control and the elaborate means of data collecting. Persistent results would be difficult to sustain, given the small number of sessions as compared with typical clinical practice. It is possible that more extensive, longer-term treatment could have maintained the positive results in follow-up. (It is interesting, however, that follow-up results actually improved for the cognitive-behavior therapy group, despite less treatment time, in the Taylor & Marshall study.)

Cognitive therapy based on the ideas of Beck, Ellis, Kanfer, and Todd was compared by Taylor and Marshall (in press) with a behavioral approach derived from Ferster and Arnold Lazarus, a treatment combining these two strategies, and a waiting-list control group. Results showed that all therapy groups did better, on all measures, than the no-treatment group. There were no differences between cognitive and behavior therapy on any measure. The combined-treatment group did significantly better than the average effect of the two separate treatments on the Beck Depression Inventory (at both posttreatment and follow-up), the Dempsey D-30 Scale, a measure derived from the MMPI "D" scale (at follow-up only), and also on a measure of self-acceptance. Taylor and Marshall conclude that their findings "support the current move toward an integration of behavioral and cognitive approaches"—which is what both the Ellis and Beck approaches are when employed fully rather than piecemeal.

DISCUSSION

In looking over this fairly extensive collection of studies investigating rational-emotive therapy outcome, perhaps the most encouraging aspect is its increasing quantity and improving quality. Much work remains to be done on both dimensions. Nevertheless, progress has been made in terms of scientific RET-hypothesis testing since two earlier, yet recent, reviews of this literature (Mahoney, 1974; Meichenbaum, 1975).

In a review paper presented at the 1976 meeting of the Society for Psychotherapy Research, Glass and Smith (Note 1) provided data supporting our view that rational-emotive therapy appears to have earned some scientific credibility as a relatively effective form of treatment. Examining 375 psychotherapy outcome studies (35 of them involving rational-emotive therapy) employing control groups, they found that rational-emotive therapy ranked second among 10 types of therapy (including psychodynamic, Gestalt, Transactional Analysis, Adlerian, client-centered, behavior modification, implosion, eclectic, and systematic desensitization), with a "mean effect" size of .77 standard deviations higher than control group outcome. Only systematic desensitization, with a "mean effect" size of .91, fared better. Behavior modification (.76) was close behind rational-emotive therapy, but the authors in further analysis concluded that the superior showing of the behavioral therapies tended to be in part the result of experimental artifacts, such as susceptibility to bias of the outcome measures used in the behavioral studies. (It is interesting that here again rational-emotive therapy poses a problem of categorization, since it was classified as "nonbehavioral" when in fact it employs both cognitive and behavioral procedures.) The authors in this paper were more interested in evaluating a number of variables characteristic of controlled studies, in terms of their relationship to outcome, and did not attempt to judge the merits or demerits of individual studies.

The earlier qualifications and skepticism of Mahoney (1974) and Meichenbaum (1975) concerning rational-emotive and related therapy outcome research still basically hold true. Both the scientific attitude and the still early stage of inquiry require this. While the results, as we see them now, appear generally positive and promising, they remain far from conclusive. Within the limits of our ability to be objective, we have attempted to both encourage the RET scientist-practitioner by giving credit for work done and challenge him/her to address further research to some of the problems and questions raised here. The goal is not to "prove" RET but to test it.

REFERENCE NOTES

1. Glass, G., & Smith, M. L. *Meta-analysis of psychotherapy outcome studies.* Paper presented at the annual meeting of the Society for Psychotherapy Research, Boston, June 1976.
2. Kassinove, H., Crisci, R., & Tiegerman, S. Personal communication, 1976.
3. Maultsby, M. *Eleven common irrational ideas.* Mimeographed paper. University of Kentucky Medical School, 1970.

4. Maultsby, M., Costello, P. T., & Carpenter, L. *Classroom rational self-counseling.* Mimeographed paper, University of Kentucky Medical Center, 1974.

REFERENCES

Albert, S. *A study to determine the effectiveness of affective education with fifth-grade students.* Unpublished master's thesis, Queens College, 1972.

Argabite, A. H., & Nidorf, L. J. Fifteen questions for rating reason. *Rational Living,* 1968, *3,* 9–11.

Bard, J. A self-rating scale for rationality. *Rational Living,* 1973, *8,* 19.

Beck, A. T. *Depression: Clinical, experimental and therapeutic aspects.* New York: Harper & Row, 1967.

Beck, A. T. Cognitive therapy: Nature and relation to behavior therapy. *Behavior Therapy,* 1970, *1,* 184–200.

Beck, A. T. *Cognitive therapy and the emotional disorders.* New York: International Universities Press, 1976.

Bergin, A. E., & Strupp, H. H. *Changing frontiers in the science of psychotherapy.* Chicago: Aldine, 1972.

Brody, M. *The effect of the rational-emotive affective education approach on anxiety, frustration tolerance and self-esteem with fifth-grade students.* Unpublished doctoral dissertation, Temple University, 1974.

Coopersmith, S. *The antecedents of self-esteem.* San Francisco: Freeman, 1967.

DiGiuseppe, R., & Kassinove, H. Effects of a rational-emotive school mental health program on children's emotional adjustment. *Journal of Community Psychology,* 1976, *4,* 382–387.

DiLoreto, A. *Comparative psychotherapy.* Chicago: Aldine, 1971.

Ellis, A. Outcome of employing three techniques of psychotherapy. *Journal of Clinical Psychology,* 1957, *13,* 344–350.

Ellis, A. *Reason and emotion in psychotherapy.* New York: Lyle Stuart, 1962.

Ellis, A. Teaching emotional education in the classroom. *School Health Review,* November 1969, 10–13.

Ellis, A. *Growth through reason.* Palo Alto: Science and Behavior Books, 1971.

Ellis, A. Emotional education in the classroom. *Journal of Clinical Child Psychology,* 1972, *1,* 19–22.

Ellis, A. Are cognitive behavior therapy and rational therapy synonymous? *Rational Living,* 1973, *8*(2), 8–11.

Ellis, A., & Harper, R. *A new guide to rational living.* North Hollywood, Calif.: Wilshire, 1975.

Ellis, A., Wolfe, J. L., & Moseley, S. *How to prevent your child from becoming a neurotic adult.* New York: Crown, 1966.

Fox, E., & Davies, R. Test your rationality. *Rational Living,* 1971, *5,* 23–25.

Glicken, M. Rational counseling: A new approach to children. *Journal of Elementary School Guidance and Counseling,* 1968, *2,* 261–267.

Goldfried, M. R., & Sobocinski, D. The effect of irrational beliefs on emotional arousal. *Journal of Consulting and Clinical Psychology,* 1975, *43,* 504–510.

Hauck, P. A. *The rational management of children.* New York: Libra, 1967.

Ivery, A., & Alchuler, A. Getting into psychological education. *Personnel and Guidance Journal,* 1973, *51,* 682–691.

Jacobs, E. E. *The effects of a systematic learning program for college undergraduates based on rational-emotive concepts and techniques.* Unpublished master's thesis, Florida State University, 1971.

Jarmon, D. S. *Differential effectiveness of rational-emotive therapy bibliotherapy and attention placebo in the treatment of speech anxiety.* Unpublished doctoral dissertation, Southern Illinois University, 1972.

Jones, R. *A factored measure of Ellis' irrational belief systems with personality and mal-adjustment correlates.* Unpublished doctoral dissertation, Texas Tech College, 1968.

Kanter, N. J. *A comparison of self-control desensitization and systematic rational restructuring for the reduction of interpersonal anxiety.* Unpublished doctoral dissertation, SUNY at Stony Brook, 1975.

Karst, S., & Trexler, L. An initial study using fixed role and rational-emotive therapies in treating public speaking anxiety. *Journal of Consulting and Clinical Psychology,* 1970, *34,* 360–366.

Katz, S. *The effects of emotional education on locus of control and self-concept.* Unpublished doctoral dissertation, Hofstra University, 1974.

Keller, J., Crooke, J., & Brookings, J. Effects of a program in rational thinking on anxiety in older persons. *Journal of Counseling Psychology,* 1975, *22,* 54–57.

Kelly, G. *The psychology of personal constructs.* New York: Norton, 1955.

Knaus, W. *Rational-emotive education: A manual for elementary school teachers.* New York: Institute for Rational Living, 1974.

Knaus, W., & Boker, S. The effect of rational-emotive education on anxiety and self-concept. *Rational Living,* 1975, *10*(2), 7–10.

Laughridge, S. Differential diagnosis with a test of irrational ideation. *Rational Living,* 1975, *10*(2), 21–23.

Lazarus, A. A. Behavioral rehearsal vs. non-directive therapy vs. advice in effecting behavior change. *Behaviour Research and Therapy,* 1966, *4,* 209–212.

Lazarus, A. A. Desensitization and cognitive restructuring. *Psychotherapy: Therapy, Research and Practice,* 1974, *11,* 98–102.

Lewinsohn, P. M. A behavioral approach to depression. In R. J. Friedman & M. M. Katz (Eds.), *The psychology of depression: Contemporary theory and research.* New York: Wiley, 1974.

MacDonald, A., & Games, R. Ellis' irrational ideas: A validation study. *Rational Living,* 1972, *7*(2), 25–29.

Maes, W., & Heinman, R. *The comparison of three approaches to the reduction of test anxiety in high school students.* Final report project 9-1-040. Washington, D.C.: Office of Education, United States Department of Health, Education and Welfare, October 1970.

Mahoney, M. *Cognition and behavior modification.* New York: Ballinger, 1974.

Maultsby, M. Systematic written homework in psychotherapy. *Psychotherapy: Theory, Research and Practice,* 1971, *8,* 195–198.

Maultsby, M. The classroom as an emotional health center. *The Educational Magazine,* 1974, *31*(5), 8–11.

Maultsby, M., Knipping, P., & Carpenter, L. Teaching self-help in the classroom with rational self-counseling. *Journal of School Health,* 1974, *44,* 445–448.

McFall, R. M., & Lillesand, D. B. Behavioral rehearsal with modeling and coaching in assertive training. *Journal of Abnormal Psychology,* 1970, *77,* 313–323.

McFall, R. M., & Marston, A. R. An experimental investigation of assertive training. *Journal of Abnormal Psychology,* 1970, *76,* 295–303.

Meichenbaum, D. Cognitive modification of test-anxious college students. *Journal of Consulting and Clinical Psychology,* 1972, *39,* 370–380.

Meichenbaum, D. Cognitive factors in behavior modification: Modifying what clients say to themselves. In A. A. Lazarus (Ed.), *Advances in behavior modification* (Vol. 4). New York: Academic Press, 1973.

Meichenbaum, D. Towards a cognitive theory of self-control. In G. Schwartz & D. Shapiro (Eds.), *Consciousness and self-regulation: Advances in research.* New York: Plenum, 1975.

Meichenbaum, D., Gilmore, J., & Fedoravicus, D. Group insight versus group desensitization in treating speech anxiety. *Journal of Consulting and Clinical Psychology,* 1971, *36,* 410–421.

Meltzoff, J., & Kornreich, M. *Research in psychotherapy.* New York: Atherton, 1971.

Molesky, R., & Tosi, D. Comparative psychotherapy: Rational-emotive therapy versus systematic desensitization in the treatment of stuttering. *Journal of Consulting and Clinical Psychology,* 1976, *44,* 309–311.

Newmark, C. Professional opinions with regard to Ellis' irrational ideas. *Journal of Clinical Psychology,* 1972, *25,* 452–456.

Newmark, C., Frerking, R., Cook, L. K., & Newmark, L. Endorsement of Ellis' irrational beliefs as a function of psychopathology. *Journal of Clinical Psychology,* 1973, *29,* 300–302.

Rimm, D. C., & Litvak, S. B. Self-verbalization and emotional arousal. *Journal of Abnormal Psychology,* 1969, *74,* 181–187.

Rimm, D. C., & Masters, J. C. *Behavior therapy: Techniques and empirical findings.* New York: Academic Press, 1974.

Rotter, J. Generalized expectancy for internal versus external control of reinforcement. *Psychological Monographs,* 1966, *80,* No. 1 (Whole No. 609).

Rush, A. J., Beck, A. T., Kovacs, M., & Hollon, S. Comparative efficacy of cognitive therapy and pharmacotherapy in the treatment of depressed outpatients. *Cognitive Therapy and Research,* in press.

Shaw, B. F. Comparison of cognitive therapy and behavior therapy in the treatment of depression. *Journal of Consulting and Clinical Psychology,* 1977, *45*(4), 543–551.

Shostrom, E. L. A test for the measurement of self-actualization. *Educational and Psychological Measurement,* 1964, *24,* 207–218.

Spivack, G., & Shure, M. *Social adjustment of young children.* San Francisco: Jossey-Bass, 1974.

Straatmeyer, A. J., & Watkins, J. T. Rational-emotive therapy and the reduction of speech anxiety. *Rational Living,* 1974, *9*(1), 33–37.

Taylor, F. G., & Marshal, W. L. A cognitive behavioral therapy for depression. *Cognitive Therapy and Research,* in press.

Thompson, S. *The relative efficacy of desensitization, desensitization with coping imagery, cognitive modification, and rational-emotive therapy with test-anxious college students.* Unpublished doctoral dissertation, University of Arkansas, 1974.

Thorpe, G. L. Desensitization, behavioral rehearsal, self-instruction training and placebo effects on assertive-refusal behavior. *European Journal of Behavior Analysis and Modification,* 1975, *1,* 30–44.

Tiegerman, S. *Effects of assertive training and cognitive components of rational therapy on the promotion of assertive behavior and the reduction of interpersonal anxiety.* Unpublished doctoral dissertation, Hofstra University, 1975.

Trexler, L., & Karst, J. Rational-emotive therapy, placebo and no-treatment effects on public speaking anxiety. *Journal of Abnormal Psychology,* 1972, *79,* 60–67.

Trexler, L., & Karst, J. Further validation for a new measure of irrational cognitions. *Journal of Personality Assessment,* 1973, *37,* 150–155.

Warren, R., Deffenbach, J., & Broding, P. Rational-emotive therapy and the reduction of test anxiety in elementary school students. *Rational Living,* 1976, *11*(2), 28–29.

Waugh, N. M. *Rationality and emotional adjustment: A test of Ellis' theory of rational-emotive therapy.* Unpublished doctoral dissertation, Case Western Reserve University, 1975.

Wein, K. S., Nelson, R. O., & Odom, J. V. The relative contribution of reattribution and verbal extinction to the effectiveness of cognitive restructuring. *Behavior Therapy,* 1975, *6,* 459–474.

Wine, J. *Investigations of attentional interpretations of test anxiety.* Unpublished doctoral dissertation, University of Waterloo, 1971.

Wolfe, J. L. *Short-term effects of modeling/behavior rehearsal, modeling/behavior rehearsal plus rational therapy, placebo.* Doctoral dissertation, New York University, 1975.

Wolfe, J. L., & Fodor, I. G. A cognitive/behavior approach to modifying assertive behavior in women. *The Counseling Psychologist,* 1975, *5*(4), 45–52.

Young, E. R., Rimm, D. C., & Kennedy, T. D. An experimental investigation of modeling and verbal reinforcement in the modification of assertive behavior. *Behaviour Research and Therapy,* 1973, *11,* 317–319.

Yu, A., & Schill, T. Rational-emotive therapy as a treatment in reducing vulnerability to criticism. *Rational Living,* 1976, *11*(2), 12–14.

Zingle, H. *Bibliography of RET articles and theses.* Edmonton: University of Alberta, 1976.

Can RET Become a Cult?

ARNOLD A. LAZARUS

Rutgers—The State University

When Albert Ellis formulated his basic cognitive hypotheses in the 1950s, not only was he ahead of his time; he was also a scientist-practitioner intent on testing the value and limitations of "rational psychotherapy." At a time when people like Wolpe (1958) were arguing that human emotion emanates from sub-cortical hypothalamic brain centers, with little or no connection to cognitive processes, Ellis held the (now widely accepted and neurophysiologically valid) view that cognitive and affective processes are not at all disparate but essentially interactive. The cornerstone of rational psychotherapy—that people largely create their own emotional reactions by the ways they interpret or evaluate their environments—represented a crucial hypothesis that was open to verification or disproof. Indeed, the manner in which Ellis (1958) couched his basic premises 20 years ago readily permitted one to test them through controlled experimenta-tion. This cannot be said about many of the current hypotheses of "rational-emotive therapy" (RET).

As soon as "rational psychotherapy" gave way to "rational-emotive ther-apy," we witnessed the emergence of an overinclusive philosophy. The central theme of Ellis' earlier writings was that self-fulfilling, creative, and emotionally satisfying living was contingent on organized and disciplined *thinking*. Therapy was then a process of controlling and changing human emotion by reason and intellect. Disordered emotions were to be ameliorated by repudiating faulty thinking. But rational-emotive therapy has compounded these pristine ideas beyond recognition.

When a system is so pliable that almost any method can be incorporated into its purview, it has few meaningful boundaries and few distinctive parameters. Apart from transpersonal dogma and downright mystical ideologies, RET can accommodate the entire gamut from "humanism" to "behaviorism." Whereas RP (rational psychotherapy) was a system based on the virtues of cognitive restructuring or rational disputation, RET (rational-emotive therapy) also employs rational-emotive imagery, behavior rehearsal, *in vivo* assignments,

My thanks to Cyril M. Franks for his help with some of the more subtle nuances of this paper.

antishame exercises, assertiveness training, graded assignments, operant conditioning, and many other such strategies in addition to several innovative semantic interventions. Far from remaining a distinctive and testable theory and therapy, RET is now almost indistinguishable from most action-oriented eclectic disciplines. (I say this despite Ellis' protestation that RET is distinctly different from cognitive-behavior therapy and other types of therapy.)

It would seem that Ellis found rational psychotherapy too narrow and too limited to induce long-lasting and meaningful change. Cognitive restructuring alone was obviously insufficient. Other modalities had to be incorporated. But Ellis has not capitulated. Although he relies on methods of modeling, relaxation training, behavioral assignments, skills training, role playing, self-management, contingency contracting, and so forth, he still adheres to a theory of cognitive supremacy, if not cognitive exclusivism.

Freud (1919/1924) resorted to similar Procrustean maneuvers. "Insight" was to Freud what "reasoning" is to Ellis. But when Freud failed to help his phobic patients by insight alone, he actively induced them to encounter their feared situations; this often produced "a considerable moderation of the phobia." This deviation from the standard psychoanalytic procedure did not lead Freud to doubt the omnificent powers of insight. He simply "explained" that *in vivo* exposure aroused "richer associations," which, in turn, permitted the proper insights to prevail. And so it is with Ellis. Why is modeling effective? Because it significantly changes peoples' thoughts. What do new skills and abilities accomplish? They lead to better patterns of evaluation and self-perception. What really lies behind the success of biofeedback? Changes in reasoning and thinking!

Ellis is correct in asserting that many affective reactions are fueled by cognitive mediation. But is thinking the *sine qua non* of feeling? Woolfolk (1976) ably argues that "no one class of factors is both necessary and sufficient to account for all emotionality in all human beings . . . only multiple-factor theories of emotion can account for the research data across situations and individuals."

Scientists cannot proselytize. To review research data that support one's pet hypotheses and to ignore those that yield equivocal or negative results is decidedly antiscience. The essence of any scientific endeavor is to challenge if not refute established theories. A true scientist is more interested in disconfirming hypotheses than in substantiating them. Let us remember that one negative finding is sufficient to discredit a general hypothesis. Does Ellis actively question, challenge, and attempt to refute his favored theories and practices? On the contrary, he seeks only to confirm them.

Notwithstanding all the aforementioned criticisms, I regard Albert Ellis as one of the most significant thinkers and perhaps the most creative theorist of our times. By underscoring the crucial (but not exclusive!) role of cognitions and specific thought patterns in human feeling and interaction, Ellis has provided us with a pragmatic philosophy, with profound keys for self-understanding, and with elegant methods of psychological change. But in his zeal to underscore the often critical role played by cognitive factors, Ellis is inclined to ignore "noncognitive" processes. By citing what I regard as a typical RET failure that responded well to broader-based "multimodal" methods (Lazarus, 1976), my general criticisms may gain specific substance.

G. A., a 32-year-old male high school teacher, was overconcerned about his health ("I think I'm a bit of a hypochondriac!") and suffered from several psychosomatic complaints (gastrointestinal distress, intermittent tachycardia, light-headedness, and undifferentiated chest pains). Medical tests and examinations revealed no organic pathology. After seeing a psychiatrist for several years, he changed therapists and received RET. He worked hard at eliminating his categorical imperatives, at disputing catastrophic cognitions, and at challenging other false and irrational thoughts. While some significant improvements accrued, his psychosomatic complaints receded only very slightly.

When he consulted me, I immediately embarked on a course of intensive relaxation and meditation techniques. There are data showing that deep muscle relaxation and clinically standardized meditation (Carrington, 1977) produce *physiological* reactions that have a significant (positive) *biological* impact in most cases. While "placebo" or "suggestion" (cognitive factors) may be part of the variance, there can be little doubt that the very act of letting go and the altered state of consciousness that usually follows the repeated chanting of a mantra evoke a change in lower-brain centers that cannot be reached by reason alone.

In addition to relaxation and meditation, I discussed diet and exercise with G. A. and his physician. This decidedly noncognitive modality was especially important. By increasing his intake of roughage and by decreasing his intake of milk (in many people, lactose intolerance causes severe gastrointestinal distress after drinking milk), his stomach problems cleared up. And through jogging and other exercise regimens, his general level of physical fitness reached an unprecedented peak. Tachycardia, chest pains, and light-headedness soon became things of the past.

As a multimodal therapist, I constructed a "modality profile." That is, I assessed G. A.'s significant behavioral strengths and deficiencies; I delved into his main affective reactions, sensations, images, cognitions, and interpersonal relationships. The RET approach had done an excellent job of modifying salient affective-behavioral-cognitive processes. To some extent, G. A.'s poor self-image had been incorporated into the therapy, but not as pointedly as I deem necessary. But his sensory and interpersonal dimensions had been largely overlooked. Indeed, as I explored the interpersonal consequences of his psychosomatic symptoms and as we searched specifically for associated imagery (Lazarus, 1978), it became apparent that the mainstay of his problems amounted to a massive fear of rejection from women (a fact that had eluded the scrutiny of the rational-emotive therapist). Subsequently, as we entered into several "dating assignments," the problem of premature ejaculation came to the fore. Here again, I used a *sensory* exercise. He had become somewhat attached to a particular young woman, and I instructed the couple how to employ *threshhold training* for overcoming his rapid ejaculation (Semans, 1956).

There is nothing to prevent RET practitioners from employing multimodal methods; at this stage of our psychological development, it is foolhardy not to be technically eclectic. But multimodal therapy is an approach, not a system. Systems are too narrow and too self-limiting to assuage the suffering of the people who ask for our help. My major criticism of Ellis is that he began with a system (rational therapy) but has added so much to it that rational-emotive therapy has become an approach while Ellis still regards it as a system.

I hope that Ellis will not argue that the case of G. A. simply shows that a particular rational-emotive therapist, not RET in general, may be brought into question. Since Ellis lumps behavioral and interpersonal processes together, since he does not separate imagery and cognition, and since he also regards affect and sensation as one and the same (Ellis, 1977), it is my contention that he does not delve sufficiently deeply into the subtle personal ties and relations that tend to maintain certain neurotic hang-ups. Similarly, by viewing imagery as one of many cognitive activities (together with self-talk, decision making, problem solving, and so on), he does not pay enough attention to pure imagery. In short, by glossing over certain dimensions of the BASIC ID (Lazarus, 1976), he is likely to overlook significant aspects of a client's psychological disturbances.

Psychotherapists of any persuasion have yet to provide acceptable facts concerning the necessary and sufficient procedures for optimal change to occur. Rational psychotherapy (Ellis, 1958) was obviously insufficient, and it was therefore expanded into rational-emotive therapy (Ellis, 1962). But the 1962 RET vintage and the present-day version (Ellis & Grieger, 1978) cannot be compared. The technical armamentarium has expanded beyond recognition, but the theoretical underpinnings remain unchanged. When a theory can account for anything and can explain away everything, one grows wary that a once good theory might turn into a cult.

REFERENCES

Carrington, P. *Freedom in meditation.* New York: Doubleday, 1977.
Ellis, A. Rational psychotherapy. *Journal of Genetic Psychology,* 1958, *59,* 35–49.
Ellis, A. *Reason and emotion in psychotherapy.* New York: Lyle Stuart, 1962.
Ellis, A. Workshop on "Cognitive behavior therapy." Institute for Rational Living, New York City, January 16, 1977.
Ellis, A., & Grieger, R. *Handbook of rational-emotive therapy.* New York: Springer, 1978.
Freud, S. Turnings in the ways of psychoanalytic therapy. In *Collected Papers,* 1924, *2,* 392–402. (Originally published, 1919.)
Lazarus, A. A. *Multimodal behavior therapy.* New York: Springer, 1976.
Lazarus, A. A. *In the mind's eye.* New York: Rawson Associates, 1978.
Semans, J. H. Premature ejaculation: A new approach. *Southern Medical Journal,* 1956, *49,* 353–361.
Wolpe, J. *Psychotherapy by reciprocal inhibition.* Stanford, Calif.: Stanford University Press, 1958.
Woolfolk, R. L. A multimodal perspective on emotion. In A. A. Lazarus, *Multimodal behavior therapy.* New York: Springer, 1976.

Rejoinder: Elegant
and Inelegant RET

ALBERT ELLIS
Institute for Rational-Emotive Therapy

I want to thank all the authors of the critiques of my article on RET research data, particularly those who have taken me somewhat severely to task,
because this kind of criticism is particularly helpful in encouraging me to rethink
some of my own views and to come up with more precise and more effective
formulations. Every time I write something on psychotherapy, it naturally seems
crystal clear to me—otherwise I wouldn't send it to the printer. But critics often
do manage to misunderstand my meaning; and although this misunderstanding
may well have something to do with their misperceptions (as RET theory would
postulate!), it also probably has something to do with my errors of omission and
commission—which these critics then give me a better chance to correct in my
future expositions. So, as a result of writing my article and of having it criticized,
I shall probably do better at formulating and delineating RET theory and practice in the future. At least, let us hope so!

Even more importantly, the field of psychotherapy seems divided today
into two main aspects: the "scientific" therapies, such as classical behavior
therapy and RET, which attempt to validate both their theory and their practice and to discard or replace elements of both that prove invalid or lead to poor
results, and the "nonscientific" therapies, such as psychoanalysis, faith healing,
and transpersonal (or mystical) therapy, whose results can be, and sometimes
are, experimentally tested but whose basic theories contain vague or untestable
assumptions and at least partially unconfirmable or disconfirmable hypotheses.
If RET is to remain in the "scientific" class, it is good that it be continually
reassessed and criticized by sound researchers and theoreticians and especially
by outstanding people like Mahoney and Meichenbaum, who are cognitive-
behavioral therapists and who therefore tend to have favorable rather than
unfavorable biases about some of the main RET-oriented hypotheses. If they
and people like them have serious objections to some aspects of RET, I and
my associates had better watch out! And perhaps change.

Let me first deal with some of Mahoney's objections. As far as I can tell
(though I am not sure about this), they are largely based on his conception of
what RET should be rather than what it really is; and this is perhaps as much
my fault as anyone's for not making it more clear what it really is. Meichenbaum,

too, objects to some aspects of RET, because he sees rational-emotive therapy rather differently from the way I see it; and this, once again, may be because of my own lack of clarity when I sometimes present the RET viewpoint.

Both Mahoney and Meichenbaum, and especially the former, seem to claim that the 32 hypotheses in my RET data article (1) are not really RET hypotheses but apply to cognitive therapy or cognitive-behavior therapy in general, and (2) do not constitute, as they would like to see me constitute, an elegant or comprehensive theory of RET that could be tested against other theories of cognitive-behavior therapy. They therefore find my paper, for all its confirmatory data, disappointing or relatively trivial.

Much of the disagreement between Mahoney and Meichenbaum on the one hand and myself on the other hand seems to arise from the notion, which both of them have now held for a number of years, that RET is, and is only, a *special* kind of cognitive-emotive-behavioral (CEB) therapy and that, as such, it cannot legitimately employ or preempt hypotheses or data from *other* CEB therapies. They are, of course, entitled to this view; but, as the founder and chief proponent of RET, I heartily disagree with it; and, presumably, I really *know* something about what RET truly is!

Mahoney and Meichenbaum's view seems to have been largely distilled from reading my early RET writings (Ellis, 1957a, 1957b, 1958, 1962), which stressed mainly one particular mode of RET—rational disputing or logical persuasion—and which only barely hinted at many other cognitive methods—such as those independently created by Beck (1976)—but which are also in fact part of RET and which were often used by me as far back as 1955, when I originated the system. They thus take a highly limited view of what RET is and criticize me for not sticking with that view.

What Mahoney and Meichenbaum do not seem to take into account is that, although RET did emphasize (and perhaps overemphasize) cognitive disputing in its early years, as my own experience with RET increased and as other therapists all over the world began to employ it and revise and add to its procedures, our joint efforts produced a good many other cognitive (not to mention emotive and behavioral) procedures—such as rational-emotive imagery (Maultsby & Ellis, 1974; Maultsby, 1975); referenting and other semantic procedures (Ellis & Harper, 1975); and emphatic self-statements (Ellis, 1977a). Sparked largely by my own writings, as well as those of Mahoney (1974), Meichenbaum (1977b), Goldfried and Davison (1976), Lembo (1976), Beck (1976), and other cognitive-behavior therapists, many cognitive methods of therapy have now been added to those I originally stressed; and these have often been incorporated into RET. As I noted in a conference on cognitive-behavior-therapy research (Ellis, 1976), probably 50 or 60 different kinds of cognitive procedures in therapy now exist, and more appear all the time. RET tries to use, in various ways, almost all these methods, or at least those that seem effective and that do not contradict other important aspects of its theory. Although this was not so in 1955 or in my classic book *Reason and Emotion in Psychotherapy* (Ellis, 1962), it is true today.

In other words, although RET was once a special kind of rational-persuasive therapy, it no longer really is only of that nature. It has grown significantly in recent years, as a comparison of the 1961 *A Guide to Rational Living* (Ellis & Harper, 1961) and the 1975 *A New Guide to Rational Living* (Ellis & Harper, 1975) will show. In many respects, RET is now synonymous with what is often called cognitive-behavior (CB) therapy or cognitive-behavior modification, and that is why I entitled my article "Rational-Emotive Therapy: Research Data That Support the Clinical and Personality Hypotheses of RET and Other Modes of Cognitive-Behavior Therapy." Mahoney and Meichenbaum often do not seem to be taking my title very seriously and seem to be objecting (1) to old-time RET, which really does not exist anymore and (2) to my including in my article many hypotheses which are not *distinctively* old-time RET but which most definitely now are part of RET.

Does RET, then, have *no* distinctive features in its own right that would tend to set it clearly apart from other cognitive-emotive-behavior therapy systems? That depends on whether we consider what I now call "general," or "inelegant," RET or whether we consider what I call "elegant" RET. General, or "inelegant," RET stems from my original formulations, as stated in *A Guide to Rational Living* (Ellis & Harper, 1961):

> We function, then, as a single organism—perceiving, moving, thinking, and emoting simultaneously and interrelatedly. These four basic life processes are *not* distinctly different ones, each of which begins where the others leave off. Instead, they all significantly overlap and are in some respects aspects of the *same thing.*
>
> Thus, thinking, aside from consisting of bioelectric changes (which are, of course, motor processes) in the brain, and in addition to consisting of remembering, learning, comparing, and problem-solving, also is—and to some extent has to be—sensory, motor, and emotional behavior.
>
> Instead, therefore, of saying, as we usually vaguely say, "Jones thinks about this puzzle," we could more accurately note that Jones perceives-moves-feels-*and*-THINKS about the puzzle. Because, however, Jones' motives in regard to the puzzle may be *largely* focused upon solving it, and only *incidentally* on seeing, manipulating, and emoting about it, we may justifiably state that he thinks about the puzzle without our specifically mentioning that he *also* perceives, moves, and feels in relation to it. But we should never forget that Jones (like everyone else) is not really able, except for a split-second or two, *just* to think about the puzzle [pp. 17–18].*

Because of the consciously holistic, cognitive-emotive-behavioral emphasis of RET, its general theory and practice (as Meichenbaum and Mahoney often seem to forget) just about always include a good number of varied CEB methods;

*From *A Guide to Rational Living*, by A. Ellis and R. A. Harper. Copyright©1961 by The Institute for Rational Living. Reprinted by permission of Prentice-Hall, Inc., Englewood Cliffs, New Jersey.

sometimes 30 or 40 of them are used with a given client. General RET, as I may not have always made very clear but as I now specifically affirm, therefore really is first synonymous with cognitive-behavior or cognitive-emotive-behavior therapy and, as I have written and said on many occasions, even makes use of many specialized emotive methods (such as encounter exercises, Gestalt therapy or psychodrama techniques, and unconditional acceptance of clients with their poor behavior) which were originally devised on the basis of highly "emotive" psychotherapeutic theories that RET by no means goes along with. RET therapists can and do often employ all kinds of techniques—including various kinds of cognitive methods.

Does RET, then, have any *distinctive* features that would tend to set it apart from other cognitive-emotive-behavioral therapies? Yes it does—in its *elegant* or *preferential,* version. Suppose, for example, I were to see a client who fails to get or maintain erections the way he would like to do. I might well employ with him, especially if he were of dull-normal intelligence, an inelegant CEB approach. Cognitively, I would show him that, because he sometimes fails, he need not always do so; that he can "succeed" by giving women pleasure with his hands and tongue as well as with his erect penis; and that, with the techniques I shall bring to his attention, he can expect or hope to do better at sex in the future than he has up to the present time. Emotively, I would accept him with his failing and perhaps identify with him as one who, too, has been at times impotent but who has managed not to down himself for it. Behaviorally, I would teach him the sensate focus and other extravaginal methods made famous by Masters and Johnson (1970) and, even before that, promulgated by myself and other early sexologists (Ellis, 1954). This CEB procedure would very probably work very well, and he might fairly easily and quickly become more potent.

In the elegant, or preferential, version of RET, however, I would go distinctly beyond the methods I have just listed and *also* try to show this sexually malfunctioning male that, even if he *never* became fully potent, that would be very inconvenient but not "awful" or "horrible"; that he could fully accept himself no matter *what* his sex partners or anyone else thought of him; and that there is no reason why he *must* or *has to* succeed sexually—or, for that matter, *should* succeed in any other goal that he *wishes* or *prefers* to succeed at. In the elegant version of RET, therefore, I would try to help him change his *fundamental* disturbance-creating philosophies, about sex or any other aspect of his life, and try to show him how to deal fairly comfortably, unneurotically, and non-self-downingly with *any* present or future difficulty that might arise. Therefore, although elegant RET is invariably done in a general or inelegant RET framework, the reverse is not true: inelegant RET may well, particularly with certain types of clients, omit or treat lightly some of the goals and methods employed in elegant RET.

If Mahoney and Meichenbaum, therefore, want me to delineate a *special* set of hypotheses that are concerned with RET, I could probably do so in terms of its elegant aspects. This set of hypotheses might possibly or temporarily be stated as follows.

Elegant RET is a form of therapy that consciously uses cognitive, emotive, and behavioral techniques to help clients change their dysfunctional (or self-defeating) thoughts, emotions, and behaviors. It is done within the framework of general RET or of cognitive-emotive-behavioral (CEB) therapy; but it tends to differ from most other CEB therapies—e.g., those of Adler (1927), Beck (1976), Kelly (1956), and Glasser (1965)—in that:

1. It stresses especially (but never solely) the achievement of a profound cognitive or philosophic change in clients' basic assumptions, especially their absolutistic, demanding, *must*urbatory, irrational ways of viewing themselves, others, and the world.

2. It strives, where feasible, for an elegant therapeutic solution to emotional disturbance rather than for mere symptom removal. It tries to help clients not only to change their existing disturbances but also to acquire an antiawfulizing, anti*must*urbating attitude that will (a) help them cope with and eliminate new symptoms if and when they arise and (b) help them prophylactically ward off or minimize their chances of creating new emotional disturbances in the future.

3. It holds that cognitions do not by themselves cause "emotional" disturbances (since environmental and biological factors also significantly *contribute* to their creation) but that in most humans most of the time cognitions are (a) the most important source of such disturbances and (b) the most useful processes for clients to employ to achieve elegant, pervasive, lasting improvement.

4. It hypothesizes that changes in cognitions that lead to profound and lasting emotive and behavioral modification usually (not always!) require considerable behavioral practice; especially, they require repetition, forceful or vigorous self-presentations, and reinforcing (or penalizing) consequences.

5. It views most clients as having powerful (though hardly unlimited) capacities to significantly change their own dysfunctional thoughts, emotions, and behaviors and the ability to do this largely (or most importantly) through cognitive processes—e.g., through self-consciousness, willing, determination, deciding, planning, self-control, and self-acceptance.

6. It strongly encourages (though does not deify) the use of the scientific, logico-empirical method by both therapists and clients. This means that not only it tries to substantiate its own hypotheses and clinical procedures by empirical and experimentally gathered data (as also does classical behavior therapy) but that it also highly evaluates this method as a means of assessing and uprooting emotional disturbance. Therefore, RET teaches clients, in its elegant form, how to think in a more logico-empirical, problem-solving manner and uses such teaching as one of its most important therapeutic methods.

I think (though I am not sure) that critics like Mahoney and Meichenbaum want me to define RET almost exclusively in the above "elegant" terms and then show experimental data that would substantiate these "elegant" RET hypotheses. The reason why I have not done so in my RET data article is that RET is frequently, and perhaps more frequently than not, done *in*elegantly— as, for example, Meichenbaum (1977b) himself frequently seems to do. Where I would usually "elegantly" show clients how to logically and empirically challenge their own "wrong" assumptions (e.g., that they can't cope with difficult situations because they are pretty worthless individuals), Meichenbaum would often "inelegantly" teach them "better" assumptions or self-statements (e.g., that they can cope and that the world won't come to an end if they don't). We both, in my view, would thereby be practicing cognitive-emotive-behavioral therapy or general RET; but I would be striving for a more "elegant" solution than his.

Another reason why my article does not focus on elegant RET hypotheses is that very little research has yet been done to test them out. A number of experimental studies have shown, for example, that my "elegant" type of RET produces significantly better results than no therapy or non-RET therapy; and a number of studies have shown that the "inelegant" type of RET used by Meichenbaum and others has also produced significantly better results when compared to those obtained with no-therapy or non-RET-therapy groups. But no studies seem to have tested "elegant" versus "inelegant" RET. This seems to be a fertile field for investigation.

Mahoney and Meichenbaum really seem to be defining RET only in one way—mainly in the "elegant" way—and then asking me and other researchers to test out this way against less elegant forms of RET. Fine! And I agree with them that this had better eventually be done. But I still insist—and, again, as the founder of RET, I presumably know something about this—rational-emotive therapy includes *both* "elegant" and "inelegant" procedures, and defining it in the monolithic way that they seem to define it is hardly legitimate. Mahoney states that after reading my 32 RET hypotheses, "one does not come away with a sense of a model or theory at all." Right! In the sense that he would like a well-integrated model or theory that, in relatively few words, would incorporate all the major RET ideas. It would be nice to have such a model, and someday I or someone else may come up with it. But probably not—just as it is improbable that someone may come up with a well-integrated model of what we now call behavior therapy. For general RET, or cognitive-behavior therapy, is even *more* comprehensive than behavior therapy (although the latter term may be used, if one wishes, generically, with cognitive-behavior therapy as a subheading), in that it employs practically all the usual behavior-therapy methods and *also* a number of cognitive methods (e.g., fantasy, persuasion, problem solving, semantic analysis, and the teaching of logic).

As I think about this matter some more, I am beginning to see that defining what psychotherapy is seems to be the nub of some of my differences with Mahoney, Meichenbaum, and various other critics and supporters of RET. And such a definition is much more difficult than it might at first appear. Thus, psychotherapy itself can be defined as any kind of personality change or behavior modification—including even drug treatment, which Lazarus (1976) includes in "multimodal therapy"—or it can be defined in more limited terms as any form of personality change or behavior modification that stresses verbal or instructional interchange between clients and therapists. The latter definition would presumably not include some forms of behavior modification, such as token economies controlled almost exclusively by the modifier without almost any kind of a relationship or persuasive influence between him/her and the clients.

Once psychotherapy is defined, we could then say that it has fairly clear subheadings—such as cognitive, emotive, and behavioral methodologies—but also that these "forms" of therapy are never quite pure but significantly overlap. Then we could label one form of therapy cognitive-emotive-behavioral (CEB), in that it consciously and on theoretical as well as practical grounds normally employs all three major modalities. Then, under CEB therapy, we could include a kind of treatment called rational-emotive-behavioral therapy that includes all the methods employed under general CEB therapy but *also* stresses a good deal of rational-persuasive logic or persuasion under its cognitive heading. If we define psychotherapy in the above manner, then what we now call RET would *first* consist of cognitive-emotive-behavioral therapy in general and *also* consist of rational-emotive-behavioral therapy in particular. If we wanted to be still more precise, we could define an RET therapist as one who *generally* does CEB therapy and who also *specifically* does rational-emotive-cognitive therapy.

Mahoney and Meichenbaum strongly object to my stating hypotheses and supportive data backing them for CEB therapy in general and seem to want me to stick *only* to more specific or "elegant" RET hypotheses and the supportive data backing these theories. In the final analysis, they may be right; but at the present time much more evidence exists supporting the basic tenets of CEB therapy in general than of elegant RET therapy. And I have therefore reviewed this evidence in my article, and deliberately included in the title of the article, "Research Data That Support the Clinical and Personality Hypotheses of RET and Other Modes of Cognitive-Behavior Therapy." Once the hypotheses stated in my article seem reasonably confirmed by sufficient data and once enough evidence appears backing the rational-persuasive aspects of CEB therapy, another review article can list and assess this kind of data. But it does not exist yet, and Mahoney and Meichenbaum are rightly saying, perhaps in a somewhat whining (and irrational!) tone, that I should present it.

They also seem to be complaining that I am claiming the efficacy of rational-emotive *therapy* by presenting evidence for the validity of some of its main personality and clinical theories. But, as far as I can see, I make no such claims in my article. I deliberately say virtually nothing about outcome studies of RET, since these are ably covered by DiGiuseppe, Miller, and Trexler (in this book) and in another article by Murphy (Murphy & Simon, in press). If I were to summarize the findings presented in those articles, I would say that they give fairly good evidence that RET works quite well with certain tested populations when compared to no-therapy group controls but that its superiority over other types of therapy has by no means yet been proven, nor has it been shown that "elegant" forms of RET work better than "inelegant" forms. Studies of *all* kinds of psychotherapy have to date been fairly poor and contain the same kind of sampling, methodological, and other shortcomings that DiGiuseppe, Miller, and Trexler clearly reveal exist in most RET outcome studies that have been thus far done. Therefore, I am personally gratified that RET has come off as well as it has in these respects. For, although the "not proven" verdict of its effectiveness previously noted by Mahoney (1974) and Meichenbaum (1977a) still largely stands, their verdicts could much better apply to virtually all the other well-known psychotherapies (e.g., psychoanalysis, transactional analysis, Gestalt therapy, and client-centered therapy) and could equally well apply, as Kazdin and Wilcoxon (1976) and other recent reviewers have shown, to most classical forms of behavior therapy, such as systematic desensitization. So, in terms of outcome studies, RET's effectiveness has been reasonably well attested today in comparison to the proven effectiveness of other forms of therapy, as, again, a reading of the DiGiuseppe, Miller, and Trexler article will show.

But—again!—my article is not about outcome studies or the clinical effectiveness of RET with clients; Mahoney insists that, at least implicitly, it is and that I strongly imply that, if a cognitive approach to human behavior is viable, RET is the therapeutic system of choice. Maybe that is the message he received; but it was certainly not the one I meant. I meant to imply that, if a cognitive approach to human behavior is viable and, more specifically, if human personality and behavior can change significantly when people change their cognitions (as I think both Mahoney and I agree my review article fairly clearly shows), then it is highly probable that CEB therapy in general (or inelegant RET) will produce better therapeutic results than less cognitive-oriented therapies. I did not mean to say that rational-persuasive-cognitive-therapy (or elegant RET) has proven validity because many general CEB hypotheses have a great deal of empirical substantiation.

Mahoney thinks that I make the logical error of affirming the consequent by inferring that, if RET theory is true, then RET will be effective. But I did not state or imply in my article that RET is an effective treatment method. As noted above, if this conclusion has any validity, it would have to be based on the data presented in the article by DiGiuseppe, Miller, and Trexler. I quite agree with Mahoney that, even if RET personality and clinical theory has empirical backing, RET as a treatment procedure could still be ineffective. For one thing, its personality theory might have little to do with its theory of personality *change*—for what human personality *is* and how we can help *change* what it is may be two theories that are not very well related (Ellis, 1978). For another thing, even if RET clinical theory has validity, this might show, at best, that RET is likely to be more effective than other therapies—but still fairly ineffective. So I agree with Mahoney that, *if* I implied that RET's theoretical validity indubitably proves its superior effectiveness for treatment, I would definitely be wrong. I just don't see that I made any such implication.

Mahoney quotes Meehl's (1967) remark that "if a theory has somewhat more confirming than disconfirming instances" it is wrong to assume that "it is in pretty good shape evidentially." Correct! But I pointed out in my article that RET (or, if you will, CEB) personality and clinical theory seems to have *over*whelming data behind it—literally hundreds of empirical studies, over 90% of which present confirmatory data. I think that even Paul Meehl (who, incidentally, is a card-carrying professional member of the Institute for Rational-Emotive Therapy and has been primarily an RET therapist for about 15 years) would not seriously object to my opinion that RET personality and clinical theory, in view of the enormous amount of empirical evidence behind it, is in pretty good shape evidentially.

Mahoney is certainly entitled to his preference for "cautious optimism" over my presumably "zealous enthusiasm" for the importance of cognitive processes in human distress. Like Beck (1976), another fairly enthusiastic cognitive therapist, I don't consider myself exactly zealous; and if I am, I agree with Mahoney's implication that this is unscientific—and irrational! But I am really glad that Mahoney finds me enthusiastic about RET and other forms of cognitive-emotive-behavior therapy. For I am frequently accused of having created a form of psychological treatment that helps people get over their serious emotional problems and behavioral dysfunctioning but, alas, robs them of their spontaneity and enthusiasm. Perhaps Mahoney will agree with me that, after using RET on myself and others for almost a quarter of a century, it has hardly wreaked this kind of havoc on me yet!

Mahoney concludes that "from my own reading of the available literature, the cognitive therapies offer a refreshing and promising avenue for future evaluation. They have in a sense shown enough mettle to merit our attention, but I don't think we can yet declare them unequivocally superior to other forms of therapy." Right! Nor did I imply any unequivocal superiority in my article. I merely presented a great deal of evidence that cognition is a very powerful element of personality and behavioral change and implied that CEB or RET therapy therefore *probably* has distinct advantages over therapies that neglect cognitive factors and strongly favor "pure" emotive and/or behavioral techniques.

Meichenbaum's critique of my paper is somewhat similar to that of Mahoney's, except that it seems a bit more emotive than rational! He also seems to think that I am supporting RET practice in my article, when I am merely stating some important RET (and CEB) personality and clinical hypotheses and citing empirical evidence in *their* support. Like Mahoney, Meichenbaum objects to my "final conclusion that RET is based on a strong empirical foundation." I didn't exactly make that conclusion; but more precisely, and I believe more cautiously, I concluded that many (not all) *theories* on which RET is founded have strong empirical backing. Like psychoanalysis and most other therapies, RET is comprised of both a set of theoretical assumptions and a set of clinical practices. It is largely its *assumptions* that I list in my article, and it is these for which I cite favorable evidence. The efficacy of its practice had better be much more solidly established than it has been so far; but I still think that my article shows that most of its main theories have considerable—and, to repeat an admittedly bad term, even "awesome"—empirical support.

Meichenbaum objects to my citing studies by Kanfer, Karoly, and Newman (1975) and Suinn and Richardson (1971) to support the hypotheses of Coué and Peale that positive thinking helps people do better than negative or neutral thinking. Although it is true that neither of these research teams specifically mention Coué, Peale, or positive thinking, the former researchers showed that sentences emphasizing children's active control or competence proved generally superior to sentences concentrating on reducing aversive qualities of a stimulus situation and to neutral sentences. The latter researchers also showed that anxiety management training involving training clients to react to anxiety with success feelings proved better than desensitization procedures using anxiety hierarchies and relaxation or reciprocal inhibition responses. Both Coué and Peale emphasize cognitions favoring competence and success; so I think it quite legitimate to cite the Kanfer, Karoly, and Newman and the Suinn and Richardson studies as researches that at least partly support the Coué and Peale hypotheses. I am not sure why Meichenbaum is so scandalized by my "imprecise" citation of these two studies (which I easily, of course, could have put under other headings of cognition-supported researches rather than under the heading of positive-thinking-supported researches) when he himself states that RET and my A-B-C theory of disturbance and of personality change are "a cognitive approach to therapy in the tradition of Dubois, Adler, Horney, Kelly, and others." He is certainly right about this—but also, of course, wrong. For, although *some* elements of my practice are (as I have said myself on many occasions) in the tradition of the cognitive approach to therapy of Dubois and Adler, many other things I do (including the strong use of operant conditioning and other behavioral methods) are quite unlike those that Dubois and Adler did. And although many of my ideas overlap with those of Horney and, especially, Kelly (as again I have often pointed out), my practice of psychotherapy is usually very different from their practice. The point is that, although Meichenbaum rightly accuses me of some amount of fitting facts into the procrustean bed of theory when I cite the Kanfer, Karoly, and Newman and the Suinn and Richardson studies to back up the theories of Coué and Peale, he nitpickingly also forgets the relevance and correctness of my citations. Very few experimental studies *exactly* test a given psychological hypothesis; and yet most of them give some significant evidence for or against different theories.

Meichenbaum notes that "a number of the studies Ellis cites have been appropriately criticized, and their data have been severely challenged." True, if by "a number of" he means "a few of" the hundreds of studies I cite. But the same can be said of a number of the studies in virtually every notable review article in the *Psychological Bulletin*. In fact, almost *all* published psychological studies, today, are severely criticizable, since they tend to use inadequate samples, highly selected subjects, faulty statistical procedures, etc. But that hardly stops reviewers—including Meichenbaum and myself—from making *some* conclusions from these studies, especially when we consider scores of them in certain areas. Once again, it seems to me, Meichenbaum is doing some fancy nitpicking!

Ironically, Meichenbaum states that "an RET therapy approach . . . uses a simplistic model, seduces, cajoles, and teaches the client to view his maladaptive feelings and behavior in an A-B-C framework *versus* the much more complex demand of explaining the origin and maintenance of maladaptive feelings, thoughts, and behaviors." This is ironic because, first of all, as I state above, RET does consistently (and almost compulsively) deal with the origin (that is, the creation) and the maintenance (that is, the constant repetition) of maladaptive feelings, thoughts, and behaviors—and it uniquely gives incisive and detailed scrutiny to the role of cognitions in creating and maintaining feelings and behaviors. No other form of therapy seems to be as thoroughgoing as RET in these regards.

Even more ironically, "simplistic" RET usually strives to help clients not merely to see and understand their irrational beliefs (B in the RET A-B-C framework) but to actively and thoughtfully dispute them (at D)—that is, to question and challenge them and use the logico-empirical methods of science to eviscerate them. Thereby it strives to help these clients to stop creating a new set of irrational beliefs (and dysfunctional emotions and behaviors) in the future. *This* is what the RET therapist "seduces, cajoles, and teaches" most clients to do—to think for themselves, to learn the scientific method and to actively use it for the rest of their lives, and thereby to make themselves less conditionable, less reinforceable, and less suggestible to external stimuli, including social approval.

One of Meichenbaum's main cognitive methods, on the other hand, is fairly close to Coué and Peale's "positive thinking." For it consists of forcefully indoctrinating clients with more "rational" beliefs, self-statements, or coping philosophies instead of helping them (as in the elegant form of RET) to arrive at such beliefs through their own thinking and problem-solving processes. This method of presenting positive, rational, or coping self-statements to clients, for the efficacy of which Meichenbaum and others have presented some convincing empirical confirmation (Meichenbaum, 1977b), certainly often works. It even works with very difficult clients, such as schizophrenics and overly impulsive children, with whom more "rational," logico-persuasive techniques like RET might do more poorly. But it is, of course, much more "simplistic" and less occupied with understanding the maintenance and the creation of maladaptive feelings, thoughts, and behaviors than the usual kind of RET to which Meichenbaum seems to object. It is also much more liable to the accusation of brainwashing or indoctrinating than is the "seductive," "cajoling," and "teaching" form of RET, which I tend to more heavily espouse. Another irony: Meichenbaum, in his present criticism and in other comments on RET, often views it as a "selling" approach. But the giving of self-statements to the client in the approaches of Coué, Peale, Meichenbaum, and others seems to me to be a much higher-pressured type of salesmanship and one which the relatively unthinking client may much more suggestibly accept.

Dolliver's article, "The Relationship of Rational-Emotive Therapy to Other Psychotherapies and Personality Theories" (in this section of the book) is unusually accurate and in an amazingly brief space gives a good summary of many of my views on psychotherapy and personality. I found it quite helpful to see these views objectively laid out and compared to those of other therapists and theorists. I found only a few relatively minor points with which to disagree, including the following:

1. As far as I know, I learned very little from Abraham Low in developing the principles and practice of RET, since I read his book, *Mental Health through Will-Training* (Low, 1952) only in the late 1950s, a few years after I had given several talks on RET and had written my original papers on it, as well as my book, *How to Live with a "Neurotic" at Home and at Work* (Ellis, 1957). But Low, somewhat like Claire Weekes (1969, 1972), seems to have independently created many of the ideas that I also independently created in RET. All three of us, I think, largely got our "rational" ideas mainly from observing clients and not from other therapists or writers; and Low, having started his work a good decade before I arrived at RET formulations, was a real pioneer and an outstanding original thinker.

2. Dolliver puts me in the same class as Fromm put Freud—as one who believes that "men and women need each other. They become engaged in mutual satisfaction of their libidinous needs, and this constitutes their interest in each other." This is definitely not my view, since I think that love, and especially one-to-one relationships between men and women, is an innate tendency, and a strong one at that, in its own right and that it may be enhanced by but is rarely created out of the human sex drives.

3. Dolliver states that "in RET, needs are typically viewed as mislabeled 'wants,' which are largely inappropriate since they are the outgrowth of an irrational philosophy and should be dispensed with." First of all, I hold that needs are not exactly "mislabeled" wants but are absolutistic demands or commands *about* wants. Humans unfortunately believe that they *must* have what they want, and they thereby irrationally create unrealistic "needs." Secondly, Dolliver's sentence, because of its peculiar wording, may seem to imply that I think wants are inappropriate or should be dispensed with. No, I think that almost all wants, desires, or preferences are appropriate and very much help to make life worthwhile. Only the escalation of such wants into "needs" is inappropriate and had better be surrendered.

4. "Ellis sees emotion, especially prolonged, negative emotion, as the product of irrational sentences, something to be disposed of." No, I see emotion as largely the product of rational sentences—e.g., "I like music and would like to hear more of it," or "I hate golf and never want to play it again!" Even

negative emotions, such as sorrow, regret, annoyance, and irritation, stem largely from rational sentences—e.g., "I loathe your behavior and hope to get you to stop it!" Almost the only inappropriate or self-defeating emotions that we have arise from *must*urbatory sentences—e.g., "I *must* not hear the music I dislike and *can't stand* it when I do!" or "I *must* be better at golf than you are, and I am a rotten person if I am not!"

5. "Ellis' approach, in contrast [to Gestalt therapy], seems largely subtractive: clients get mainly the impression that some of their processes should be gotten rid of." I hope not! RET therapists like myself try to give clients the impression that they had better get rid of some of their irrational ideas and self-defeating emotions *in order to live better and enjoy themselves more.* The very frank and honest goal of RET is quite hedonistic: longer life and greater enjoyment!

6. "In Gestalt only the person is able to know the meaning of his/her behavior, whereas in RET only the therapist is able to know the meaning of the behavior which he/she then teaches to the client." Only partially so! In RET, the therapist largely teaches clients to discover for themselves what they really want and what they foolishly think they need and to keep discovering this and to keep working at retaining their wants and surrendering their "needs" for the rest of their lives. RET also teaches that the therapist can do very little for clients except show them how to understand and to change themselves. RET strongly teaches client and not therapist responsibility for change; therapies like Gestalt therapy are also very instructive, hence cognitive.

7. "Another difference is in Farrelly's goal for clients to assert and appropriately defend themselves against the therapist. Ellis, on the other hand, clearly places clients in the position of being taught, as he corrects their errors or provides information." Almost, but not quite, right! I try to show clients that they need not defend themselves, especially their egos, against anyone, including the therapist, but, instead, to fight like hell against their own self-defeating philosophies. I do correct their errors and provide information—but only when they are defeating themselves and failing to get what they want. I am much more interested in their interest in themselves and their potential enjoyment than (as Farrelly may indeed be) interested in their relationship with *me*.

8. Dolliver shows that I criticize Janov and the psychoanalysts for training clients or even hypnotizing clients to find "evidence" for these therapists own biased views of human behavior. And then he says that "such criticism is puzzling, given Ellis' comment (1957b, p. 41) that the traditional therapist 'knows, even before he talks to the client, that this client *must* believe some silly, irrational ideas—otherwise he/she could not possibly be disturbed. And, knowing this, the rational therapist deliberately looks for these irrationalities, often predicts them, and soon discovers and explains them.' Movies and tapes of Ellis doing RET give ample evidence that Ellis promotes the client's buying into an RET view of psychological processes."

Dolliver is quite right in calling me to task here, since my 1957 quotation is dogmatically overstated, and I would not subscribe to it any longer. I would change it to "The RET practitioner knows on theoretical grounds, even before he talks to the client, that this client most probably has some silly, irrational ideas—particularly, that he holds some absolutistic shoulds and musts—otherwise he would very likely not be disturbed. And, knowing this, the rational therapist deliberately looks for these irrationalities, often predicts them, and most often is able to discover them, to get the client to agree that they exist, and to show the client how to logico-empirically dispute and surrender them." What I am "selling" in the movies and tapes that Dolliver refers to largely is the scientific method of looking at one's own hypotheses or assumptions and questioning and challenging them. I do this very similarly to the way in which a physics or biology or psychology professor teaches this same scientific method. I contend, on the other hand, that primal therapists, psychoanalysts, and many other therapists strongly attempt to teach their clients the *un*scientific method— try to help them be more gullible than they naturally are. It seems to me that a therapist's "selling" gullibility and "selling" a logico-empirical, problem-solving method of thinking are quite different kinds of "salesmanship"! I think it very sad that rational therapists are practically forced to teach or "sell" scientific thinking to their clients. But if many or most of these clients, because of their innate and acquired tendencies to think crookedly, eschew scientific methodology and had better be helped to attain more proficiency in this kind of thinking and thereby be induced to ultimately think for themselves, so be it!

I greatly enjoyed reading Tosi's "Personal Reactions with Some Emphasis on New Directions, Application, and Research" and am delighted to have it included in this book, because it adds supplementary data to those included in my article and in that of DiGiuseppe, Miller, and Trexler. Although the latter article is quite thorough, it does omit several important outcome studies of RET, including several, which Tosi mentions, by himself and his associates. The particular ones described by Tosi, as well as about 40 other studies not mentioned at all in these articles, present even more confirmatory data on the clinical efficacy of RET. All this evidence, including Tosi's, is hardly definitive; but I am still prejudiced enough to think that it is somewhat convincing!

I am also happy that Tosi stresses the humanistic emphasis of RET, since it often gets lost in the shuffle, and the other articles in this book, including my own, tend to neglect it. As he notes, what we call "rational" in RET does not mean some abstract kind of rationality, in its own right, but reason used in the service of human happiness and particularly in the service of personal as well as social happiness. I think it most significant that Tosi, one of the main researchers and methodologists in RET, not only highlights its scientific outlook in his paper but also stresses its humanistic framework. His orientation nicely encompasses both of these aspects.

Kleiner's commentary on my article brings in another important vector of psychotherapy—the personal experience of the client. He also nicely expounds the virtue of openness and stresses the Eastern attitudes toward somewhat "unusual" and "unpopular" therapeutic methodologies. I quite agree with him that "as scientists and psychotherapists, we owe it to ourselves and to our clients and to humanity in general to remain as open as we possibly can to thoughts and beliefs that can minimize human suffering and anguish and increase people's experience of satisfaction with themselves and with their lives."

Openness, however, does not amount to uncriticalness or gullibility, and I wonder whether Kleiner is somewhat too uncritical of some of the teachings of Werner Erhard, Ouroborus International, and Jane Roberts, not to mention even John Lilly and Buckminster Fuller. Many such writings have doubtless proved helpful to various people; and, as I have said for many years, so have the highly dubious statements of Mary Baker Eddy and a large number of other religionists and mystics. But immense harm is also probably done by such philosophies.

Thus, est graduates often do experience their training as being quite therapeutic. But virtually all of those to whom I have spoken and who claim benefit from it also have become devoutly—and I truly mean devoutly—dedicated to Erhard and to est and in that sense, I would personally say, distinctly more disturbed than before they took Erhard Seminars Training. As Hoffer (1952) pointed out many years ago, the fact that true believers swear by a certain philosophic or religious system hardly means that they do so in a healthful or undisturbed manner!

So I am highly delighted that est has made a significant contribution to Kleiner's life and the lives of many of his clients; but that kind of experience for him and for them hardly proves its validity. I would side, in this respect, more with the scientific scepticism of Mahoney and Meichenbaum than with the experiential enthusiasm of Kleiner. Also, there is increasing evidence that, although many people believe devoutly that they benefit from forms of "therapy," like est, and in some ways they of course do, many are also significantly harmed and, as recent evidence has shown, even have psychotic breaks apparently as a result of this kind of religious experience (Glass, Kirsch, & Parris, 1977).

The critique of my article by Ewart and Thoresen overlaps significantly with some of the points made by Mahoney and Meichenbaum but makes these points in a more objective manner and merits a thoughtful discussion. They also assume that I am "proving" the clinical effectiveness of RET in my article, which I am not trying to do, and they rightly point out that the hypotheses I include in my article do not include some of RET's most distinctive and controversial claims. This is true; but, again, the most distinctive and controversial RET claims seem to be the most difficult to investigate and have not been researched yet. Therefore, I cannot very well give any pro or con evidence regarding them.

The most valuable point in Ewart and Thoresen's critique, I think, is their contention that "to be of scientific value, a theory must be exposed systematically and repeatedly to the perils of unfriendly experience and the rigors of critical analysis" and that "by not looking at disconfirming instances, Ellis often misses data that might contribute to a better understanding of how our ways of thinking determine our sense of mental well-being." Mahoney and Meichenbaum essentially hint at this point, too, and they are right. I would make their point even stronger: not only had I and other cognitive-behavior theorists better look at disconfirming instances, but we had better also look at confirming studies which include contradictory or disconfirming (as well as substantiating) data. Virtually no theorists tend to do this; but Ewart and Thoresen (as well as Mahoney and Meichenbaum) are still on solid grounds, and they have convinced me, as critiques of this kind may well usefully do, that I had better give more attention to disconfirming data—and to contradictory theories as well.

Accordingly, I shall spend the next year or so collecting this kind of material and shall review it in a later paper to see what important lessons about RET (and other forms of therapy) can be learned from it. I already have a good deal of material to sort through in this respect. But, if any readers of this article can suggest other material, I would appreciate their sending me complete references and, preferably, reprints of empirical and theoretical findings that seem to go against RET hypotheses.

Ewart and Thoresen point out that some of the hypotheses in my article are stated in terms so general that it would be very hard to test them. They are right about this; and I'd better insert some modifying words in these particular hypotheses. Thus, I had better restate hypotheses 8, 12, and 15 as follows:

> *Hypothesis 8* (Innate influences on emotions and behavior): Humans appear to have very strong innate as well as acquired tendencies to think, emote, and behave in certain ways, although virtually none of their behavior stems solely from instinct and just about all of it has powerful environmental and learning factors that contribute to its "causation." Their innate tendencies quite often contribute much, and even most, of the "causative" variance to their thinking, emoting, and behaving.

> *Hypothesis 12* (Irrational thinking): Humans have strong innate and acquired tendencies to set up basic values (especially the values of survival and happiness) and to think and act both rationally (abetting the achievement of their basic values) or irrationally (sabotaging the achievement of such values). Although they manage to survive with their irrational tendencies, they frequently and importantly sabotage their desires for happiness.

> *Hypothesis 15* (Low frustration tolerance): People have an innate and acquired tendency to have low frustration tolerance (LFT)—to do things that seem easier in the short run even though they often bring poor results in the future, to go for immediate gratification and stimulation seeking that offer highly specious rewards, and to procrastinate and avoid behaviors and disciplines that would bring them greater ultimate rewards. Even when they seem quite conscious of their low frustration tolerance and resolve to do something about it, they often continue to go for short-range instead of long-range gains.

By adding a final sentence to each of the above hypotheses, I think that I have now made them testable. Ewart and Thoresen correctly indicate that, in their original versions, they are too general and therefore relatively untestable.

On the other hand, Ewart and Thoresen are probably wrong about their implication that, if these hypotheses, especially in the form just restated, are confirmed, they have little relevance to therapy and do not help prescribe one course of action over another. If these RET-oriented hypotheses hold up, therapists had better face the fact that clients *easily* and *naturally* think crookedly and act self-defeatingly. and that in all probability most of them will find it exceptionally *difficult* to change significantly and to retain the cognitive, emotive, and behavioral changes they bring about in themselves. Consequently, a very hard-headed, directive, *in vivo* desensitizing approach may well be more fruitful with most clients, and particularly some of them, than a less elegant, less disputational RET approach.

Ewart and Thoresen object that some of my hypotheses—such as that thinking creates emotion and semantic processes, or helping clients talk to themselves more precisely, empirically, rationally, and unabsolutistically—"do not tell us a great deal." I strongly disagree! Granted that certain *kinds* of cognitive reconstruction may well be more effective for therapy than other kinds (as experimenters have *not* yet investigated and validated), I think it most valuable for therapists to realize that *some* kinds of cognitions (perhaps several different kinds) create disordered emotions and that "empirically, rationally, and unabsolutistically" oriented cognitions may well (if experimental data adds to our knowledge in this respect) constitute effective psychotherapy. Ewart and Thoresen on the one hand accuse me of too much generalization and vagueness, but when I specifically posit that "effective psychotherapy partly consists of helping [clients] to talk to themselves more precisely, empirically, rationally, and unabsolutistically," they insist that I am not specific, because I include the term "partly." Obviously, however, no method of therapy seems to *completely*, or merely and only in its own right, help people change; so I would resort to greater than necessary generalization if I did not include the term "partly" here. They ask "Under what conditions should client self-talk become a *central* focus of therapy?" Personally, I would reply "Under almost all conditions with average clients." But that hypothesis, of course, could be experimentally investigated.

Ewart and Thoresen quote Bandura's (1969, 1977) advocacy of *in vivo* modeling over symbolic desensitization procedures in reducing subjects' fear of snakes; acknowledge that I advocate *in vivo* rather than symbolic desensitizing procedures. They then complain that my "discussion makes it difficult to know what relative emphasis he would place on these procedures. This in turn makes it harder to evaluate the adequacy of RET in relation to current research evidence." First of all, I would often use, in RET, both *in vivo* and imaginal procedures and might well guide my relative emphasis on them in relation to (1) the client and his/her symptoms and (2) the client's reaction to both procedures. So I and other RET therapists do not have to take an either/or position here. Secondly, Bandura's live modeling with guided participation and Shaw and

Thoresen's (1974) modeling with guided practice for individuals fearing dentists and dental work show that *sometimes* such procedures seem distinctly better than symbolizing or imaginal procedures. But why do RET practitioners and theorists have to take a general stand in this regard or propose that one or the other of these methods had always better be given a relative emphasis with all kinds of clients? Isn't this a little too much to ask of RET—or any system of therapy?

Ewart and Thoresen accuse me of "free-floating" predictions because, in my hypothesis 17 (Active-directive therapy), I hold that a highly active-directive approach seems better than a passive and unobtrusive one because (1) self-defeating tendencies are innate, (2) dysfunctional patterns persist from early childhood, and (3) positive changes are not always maintained over time. They say that my choice of a therapeutic approach here should preferably be based on an analysis of a problem's possible causes rather than on its history or tenacity. Perhaps my hypothesis 17 is unclear in the manner I stated it; but I certainly meant it to state a possible cause of behavioral disorder—namely, an exceptionally strong innate tendency of humans to think, emote, and act in certain self-defeating ways. Because I do think that the main (though not only) cause here is clients' innate or biological predisposition to behave dysfunctionally, I think that a highly active-directive approach to therapy (as well as disputing and persuasion, which I include in my hypothesis 18, and homework, which I include in hypothesis 19) will bring significantly better results than a more passive or history-based approach. Of course, psychoanalysts might agree with my hypothesis about strong innate predispositions to emotional disturbance and still advocate their own kind of approach; but even if we both were right about the origins of disturbance, one of us would probably prove more effective in regard to therapeutic outcome.

Ewart and Thoresen's notion that "presumably the RET techniques would be justified on an assumption that problem thoughts, feelings, and behaviors are a function of variables that can be manipulated directly" is *not* my view, since I also believe that they can be manipulated indirectly. Thus, if one of my male clients irrationally believes that he has to succeed in sex-love affairs, that he is a worm when he doesn't, and that, being a worm, he will invariably fail, I will not hesitate to directly and strongly challenge his *must*urbatory, overgeneralized, and antiempirical ideas. But I will also try to give him *in vivo* homework assignments, such as that of encountering as many potential sex-love partners as feasible, so that he can prove behaviorally that he won't invariably fail. This behavioral assignment is an indirect way of disputing his antiempirical belief about his always and inevitably failing. Since I believe that both direct and indirect ways can be, and usually had better be, used to challenge clients' irrational beliefs, I do not, as Ewart and Thoresen think that I do, have to specify the assumption in hypothesis 17—that only or mainly direct ways must be used. Assuming that the hypothesis has some degree of validity, there are more ways than one of skinning a cat and, similarly, more ways than one of helping people change, even if their dysfunctional behavior has strong innate predispositions and *some* direct cognitive-behavioral methods may be *sometimes* preferable to others. Ewart and Thoresen seem so determined to get me to specify every last letter of my therapeutic hypotheses that, if I did what they seem to want me to do, I would end up with more easily confirmable and disconfirmable propositions—but ones that would not necessarily be very helpful for effective psychotherapeutic change!

Ewart and Thoresen rightly take me to task for stating that systematic desensitization is "the most effective treatment." But I did not say that. I said that systematic desensitization is "the most popular and most effective of all the conventional behavior-therapy techniques." Therefore, there is no contradiction, as they claim, between my pointing out the popularity and effectiveness of SD, an imaginal technique, and my later predicting that *in vivo* practice will prove more effective in eliminating fears than will imaginal techniques. I do not consider *in vivo* practice among "the most popular" behavioral methods and tend to consider it unconventional rather than conventional. Moreover, the research literature so far shows many more successful SD than *in vivo* studies. Ewart and Thoresen are probably right in saying that my statements might be less confusing if I were "to be more specific about what kinds of treatments are likely to work best for which problems and clients and why." But, as any reader of the clinical and research literature knows today, no one has been this specific, and I would even say that such specificity, as yet, may not even be desirable. I suspect that highly cognitive behavior methods, such as RET, and somewhat less cognitive behavior methods, such as *in vivo* homework assignments, work best for most types of clients most of the time, mainly because they are more efficient than many other types of therapy. But I must admit that it would be interesting to discover if *any* specific forms of therapy work best for certain types of clients even if not for the majority of disturbed individuals.

DiGiuseppe, Miller, and Trexler, in their article "A Review of Rational-Emotive Psychotherapy Outcome Studies," do an excellent job of summarizing most of the research material that has appeared in that area. As they point out, "While the results, as we see them now, appear generally positive and promising, they remain far from conclusive." What they fail to emphasize equally, however, is that the results of controlled studies of *all* contemporary psychotherapies are far from conclusive. Hans J. Eysenck pointed out, almost a quarter of a century ago, that very little evidence exists for the effectiveness of *any* psychotherapeutic procedure. Even though he has been one of the pioneer advocates of and publicists in the field of behavior therapy for some time, he has stuck mainly to this position in recent years (Eysenck, 1960, 1964).

The cautions, then, that DiGiuseppe, Miller, and Trexler point out in regard to the validity of outcome studies in RET apply just as well, and often more so, to outcome studies of other forms of psychotherapy. The kind of research that almost any scholar would like to see done in this area rarely, if ever, has been accomplished; and hell knows when it will be!

In the interim, RET fares unusually well. First of all, although it is still a relatively new form of psychological treatment, it is one of the most popular forms of therapy studied. In addition to the researches cited in the DiGiuseppe, Miller, and Trexler article, a good number of other RET outcome studies have been done, so that, at the present writing, the total number runs to over 100 controlled experiments (Ellis, 1980; Murphy & Simon, in press). This seems to be a much larger number of studies than exists for most other systems of psychotherapy, such as transactional analysis or Gestalt therapy, which have been practiced for a longer period of time than RET.

Of the experimental studies of RET, almost all of them have shown that rational-emotive therapy (or some important aspect of it) produces significantly better results than those achieved by a no-treatment control group, and the majority have shown that it produces significantly better and/or longer-lasting results than those achieved by a group being treated with another form of psychotherapy. These results are hardly unequivocal or overwhelming, and much more information about the efficacy of RET remains to be discovered than has already been disclosed.

When Mahoney (1974) states, therefore, that "the clinical efficacy of RET has yet to be adequately demonstrated," he is technically correct. For, as long as the term *adequately demonstrated* is employed, the same statement could easily be made about every known form of psychotherapy—including Wolpe's systematic desensitization, which has produced more favorable results than has any other therapeutic technique so far. As Kazdin and Wilcoxon (1976) have shown, a methodological evaluation of the outcome studies of SD fairly convincingly shows that its clinical efficacy has hardly, as yet, been *adequately* demonstrated.

Consequently, RET and the scores of researchers who have thus far worked hard at showing its validity or invalidity have by no means solved the problems of unarguable criteria for personality change or of unassailable methodology for evaluating psychotherapy studies. So much remains to be learned in these important areas that I suspect that virtually all the existing outcome studies of therapy will appear exceptionally naive and inadequate a decade or two from now.

This, of course, is no reason to give up studying RET and other forms of therapy. As DiGiuseppe, Miller, and Trexler again point out, "The goal is not to 'prove' RET but to test it." As the years go by and as testing methods improve, I would guess that certain methods of RET that are fairly popular today will be found to be relatively invalid or inefficient and that certain other methods that are rarely used—or, for that matter, have not yet been invented—will be more fully validated. So be it! Science seems to grow mainly by changing. If RET is to remain—as I stoutly hope it will remain—a truly scientific form of psychotherapy, it will drastically change too. How, as a presumably scientific methodology, could it not?

Arnold Lazarus' critique, "Can RET Become a Cult?" repeats some of the same points made by Meichenbaum, Mahoney, and Ewart and Thoresen.

Let me try to restate some of his main theses that do not completely overlap with theirs and to reply to these theses.

1. *Many of the current hypotheses of RET cannot be tested through controlled experiment.* Which ones? Granted that I postulate today more RET hypotheses than when I first originated the main one in 1955—namely, that people largely create their own emotional reactions by the ways they interpret or evaluate their environments—this hardly proves that the additional ones are untestable through controlled experimentation, which Lazarus alleges but makes no effort to prove. In fact, the main thesis of my article on research data that support the clinical and personality hypotheses of RET and other modes of cognitive-behavior therapy is that just about all the 32 propositions listed in this article *have* been experimentally tested—and with a vengeance! It is a mystery to me, therefore, how Lazarus can say that, although my original basic premises permitted ready testing, the additional ones do not. The somewhat immense bibliography of research studies appended to my article most convincingly contradicts his strange allegation!

2. *RET has compounded its pristine idea—that therapy is a process of controlling and changing human emotions by reason and intellect—beyond recognition.* Lazarus assumes that my original paper "Rational Psychotherapy" (Ellis, 1958) presented *all* the main elements in rational therapy (RT). Not so! It was written for an American Psychological Association symposium held in September 1956, in which I was to have only 20 minutes to present the RT view. Therefore, it deliberately emphasized only one *major* and *distinctive* aspect of rational-emotive therapy. The other two main aspects—the emotive and the behavioral sides—were employed by me right from the start and were more completely outlined in *Reason and Emotion in Psychotherapy* (Ellis, 1962). And even that book was somewhat sketchy, since I rushed it to press to have a text ready for a professional workshop in RET that I was giving in conjunction with the American Psychiatric Association meetings in Toronto in 1962.

Virtually all the RET hypotheses delineated in the article criticized by Lazarus were first propounded by me in the 1950s and were actively used in RET practice at that time. But since some of them were also held by other systems of therapy—especially early behavior therapy, à la Wolpe and Eysenck—I simply did not emphasize them in my early RT and RET writings. Lazarus, along with Mahoney and Meichenbaum, assume that only recently have I added a number of less cognitive hypotheses to RET; but this is simply not true.

3. *"RET is now almost indistinguishable from most action-oriented eclectic disciplines. (I say this despite Ellis' protestation that RET is distinctly different from cognitive-behavior therapy and other types of therapy.)"* General (or inelegant) RET, as I try to make clear in this Rejoinder, *is* indistinguishable from many action-oriented eclectic disciplines, such as multimodal therapy (Lazarus, 1971, 1976), cognitive behavior therapy (Meichenbaum, 1977b), reality therapy (Glasser, 1965), clinical behavior therapy (Goldfried & Davison,

1976), and cognitive therapy (Beck, 1976). Even specific or elegant RET is still "eclectic," in that it is virtually never used without a strong emotive and behavioral component added to its more unique cognitive-disputing and teaching component. Lazarus, somewhat like Meichenbaum and Mahoney, insists that RET *has to* confine itself *only* to the disputing of irrational ideas, while they and other cognitive-behavior therapists presumably have the right to use cognitive restructuring *and* a variety of other techniques. This is a peculiar view of what RET *has to* or *must* be! It is fascinating to see how they give it a highly limited definition when I, its originator, and virtually all the RET therapists I know do not use it in this limited and restricted manner. One wonders why!

I definitely do NOT protest that "RET is distinctly different from cognitive-behavior therapy and other types of therapy." It is, I clearly believe, radically different (though not *completely* different) from, say, psychoanalysis, Gestalt therapy, and Rogerian therapy. But it *is* cognitive-behavior therapy, and I have clearly said so for a number of years (Ellis, 1969, 1973). Eysenck, one of the main founders and proponents of behavior therapy, beat me to it in this respect, since in 1964, in his book *Experiments in Behavior Therapy,* he included RET as the only notable form of cognitive-behavior therapy. Lazarus himself, in his 1971 book *Behavior Therapy and Beyond,* included RET as a basic mode of CBT. So I say again: RET is distinctly different from many other types of therapy but is virtually synonymous with cognitive-behavior therapy.

4. *Lazarus states that "Ellis found rational psychotherapy too narrow and too limited to induce long-lasting and meaningful change. Cognitive restructuring alone was obviously insufficient."* Again, he implies that I *first* found cognitive restructuring sufficient and *later* found it insufficient. Untrue! I always found cognitive restructuring (or, in RET terms, disputing irrational Beliefs) insufficient. Even in the few years when I was getting away from psychoanalysis and developing RET, I espoused *in vivo* activity homework assignments—for example, in my book *The American Sexual Tragedy,* written in 1952 and published in 1954. This was partly as a result of a comprehensive review of techniques of psychotherapy that I published in 1953. In this review and in *The American Sexual Tragedy,* I definitely went along with Herzberg (1945) and Salter (1949) in espousing *in vivo* desensitization for sex, love, and other problems. I also pioneered in espousing assertion training and coaching (Ellis, 1956, 1962) as well as contingency management (Ellis & Harper, 1961).

5. *Lazarus says that I still adhere to a theory of cognitive supremacy, if not cognitive exclusivism.* Correct! As noted previously in this Rejoinder, I stated in 1961 that cognitive, emotive, and behavioral processes all significantly interact and that emotion and action affect thinking, as well as the latter influences the former. But I do believe that humans, unlike lower animals, *more* profoundly, *more* pervasively, and *more* importantly change their emotions and actions by changing their thinking than they modify their thoughts by changing their emotions or behaviors. Why? Because they are *especially* and *uniquely* symbolizing and philosophizing creatures, while rats, guinea pigs, and

even the great apes are not. As even Skinner (1971) freely admits, humans have language and verbal behavior and have a cerebral cortex much more complex and more efficient than do members of subhuman species. Therefore, I would contend, they communicate better not only with each other but—more importantly—*with themselves*. As I said in my very first paper on RET (Ellis, 1958), humans importantly *talk to themselves*. Consequently, their emotions and behaviors differ enormously, in some respects, from those of other animals.

I quite agree with Woolfolk (1976) that "no one class of factors is both necessary and sufficient to account for all emotionality in all human beings... only multiple-factor theories of emotion can account for the research data across situations and individuals." But a multiple-factor theory of emotion, such as that which is included in the basic principles of RET, doesn't gainsay the fact that cognition is a *more* potent or *more* important factor in emotion than any other known element. And many of the studies I cite in my main article on research data and RET would seem to confirm this hypothesis. Lazarus compliments me for underscoring "the crucial (but not exclusive!) role of cognitions and specific thought patterns in human feeling and interaction." I graciously accept his compliment. For that is exactly what I believe—that cognition plays a crucial but hardly exclusive role in human feeling and interaction.

6. *After criticizing me somewhat severely for relying on "methods of modeling, . . . role playing, self-management, contingency contracting, and so forth," Lazarus accuses me of being "inclined to ignore 'noncognitive' processes."* What a peculiar allegation! It looks like he damns me for being overly concerned about, and at the same time unduly ignoring, noncognitive processes! Apparently, I'm damned if I do and damned if I don't ignore them! Actually, following John B. Watson and his student Mary Cover Jones (1924), as well as Herzberg (1945) and Salter (1949), I am probably one of the main proponents of *in vivo* desensitization. And, along with Bach (1966), Perls (1969), Schutz (1967), and Yablonsky (1965), I am also one of the early advocates of evocative-emotive-humanistic psychotherapy (Ellis, 1962, 1969, 1972). If this amounts to my ignoring noncognitive factors in disturbance and in psychotherapy, I wonder what I would have to do to take them into account!

7. *Lazarus points out that, in a case he treated with RET, at first he failed but that later a multimodal approach worked with this same client. Although he cautions me against replying to this "failing" of RET, he clearly implies that this "failure" shows that what he considers the essence of RET—cognitive restructuring—is an insufficient method of therapy.* He stubbornly fails to note that RET *is* and has *always been* multimodal and that what he *calls* RET is merely one of its important *aspects*. None of the techniques that he used with his client—and several additional emotive and behavioral techniques that he apparently did not use—are at all incompatible with RET. The fact that he succeeded with his client where a previous "RET" therapist did not is—as he seems afraid I will point out—of no more importance than the fact that one

RET therapist frequently succeeds with the same client with which another RET therapist has failed and that one multimodal therapist frequently does well where another one does poorly with the same client. To my knowledge, I have succeeded with several of Arnold Lazarus' ex-clients—and he has also succeeded with several of my failures. So what? The case Lazarus cites proves nothing, except, perhaps, that he is a fine propagandist for multimodal therapy—he who, ironically, chides me for my own proselytizing!

8. *Lazarus claims that RET was once a "system" and now it is an "approach."* I am not clear how the two differ. If a "system" has several main tenets but uses various techniques of therapy that generally follow or at least do not seriously contradict these tenets, then I suppose that RET is more of a "system" than an "approach." I would imagine, in the same sense, that multimodal therapy is also a system and is not thoroughly eclectic, since it hardly includes voodooism, prayer, astrology, or orgone therapy among its many "approaches." But if Arnold Lazarus feels more comfortable in calling RET an "approach" rather than a "system," that is fine with me. I would rather call it a group of therapeutic theories and practices, some of which have been fairly well substantiated by empirical data, some of which have not yet been adequately tested, and some of which will ultimately, in all probability, prove to be essentially invalid. If so, the "system"—or "approach," if you will—like all scientific theories will keep changing.

Lazarus seems to be saying that (a) the RET "system" has changed much too much for his tastes, and (b) it therefore cannot legitimately be called a "system." But science itself has changed enormously over the last hundred years, and yet it is still a "system" or "method" that includes many "eclectic" techniques but is still quite different from, say, religion.

9. *Lazarus contends that I lump "behavioral" and "interpersonal" processes together, that I do not separate "imagery" and "cognition," and that I regard "affect" and "sensation" as one and the same.* Where he got these notions, I am not clear; but none of these "lumpings" is mine. I believe, for example, that, when humans relate interpersonally, they behave *and* think *and* emote and that to look at interpersonal relations as a *separate* human modality (as multimodal therapy and Sullivan's [1947] brand of psychoanalysis often seem to do) is not exactly accurate or precise. But I have no objection against specifically inquiring about clients' interpersonal relations, and I quite often do so—just as I inquire about their family, vocational, academic, recreational, and other relations or activities.

I think that Lazarus' multimodal or BASIC ID classification of psychotherapy into seven "separate" or "different" modalities is as good as anyone else's classificatory system. But the fact that I separate therapy techniques into three major categories—cognitive, emotive, and behavioral—with many subcategories and he distinguishes seven major categories—behavior, affect, sensation, imagery, cognition, interpersonal, and drugs—with no special subheadings hardly proves that he is rigorously precise or that I am unduly lumping disparate processes together. In the final analysis, both RET and multimodal therapy probably include almost all the major useful techniques of therapy. If RET glosses over certain dimensions of the BASIC ID—which, as far as I can see, it doesn't—multimodal therapy tends to compulsively include all of them in its therapeutic plans. But when RET is properly employed—which, I take it, is practically never true when it is used by those who take Mahoney's, Meichenbaum's, and Lazarus' limited view of what it "is"—it may well have differences of emphasis but hardly of basic practice from the employment of multimodal therapy.

10. *Lazarus concludes by stating that the technical armamentarium of RET has expanded "beyond recognition, but the theoretical underpinnings remain unchanged."* Not quite true! Although many specific techniques have been added to RET (as well as to classical behavior therapy) since its inception, they follow its original cognitive-emotive-behavioral orientation. And its theoretical underpinnings, again following its CEB orientation, remain largely unchanged. But the theory of RET also includes some highly important modifications, most of them made after the publication of *Reason and Emotion in Psychotherapy* in 1962. For example, the RET theory of human value or worth has undergone significant changes (Ellis, 1972b, 1973, 1977a; Ellis & Abrahams, 1978; Ellis & Grieger, 1977). Lazarus (as well as Mahoney and Meichenbaum) seems scandalized by these changes—and at the same time horrified that RET has not changed, to suit their personal tastes, enough. I wonder whether it will ever be possible to satisfy critics like these!

Let me give an answer to Lazarus' main question. Can RET become a cult? Yes, if certain critics' limited *conception* of RET prevails. If RET were truly limited to restrictions such as those Mahoney, Meichenbaum, and Lazarus place on it, then it would probably never grow or develop and might well, as is the case with classical psychoanalysis, turn into a cult. But the relationship between their view of or beliefs about RET and my own less restricted view of RET seems very slight! As long as any scientific, and therefore constantly revised, concept of RET prevails, I think that RET will nicely survive the strong efforts of some of its critics to turn it into a cult!

If I were to sum up the critiques of my article on research data that support the clinical and personality hypotheses of RET and other modes of cognitive-behavior therapy, I would say that Tosi and Kleiner seem fairly enthusiastic about it, though for somewhat different reasons. Mahoney, Meichenbaum, Ewart and Thoresen, and Lazarus are distinctly unenthusiastic about many of its aspects, though endorsing the general tenets of cognitive-behavior therapy. Some of the legitimate points that they make are: (1) certain of my hypotheses are too vague and overgeneral; (2) I tend to be too enthusiastic and proselytizing in trying to get them across; (3) I ignore negative or disconfirming evidence; and (4) at times I seem to imply, if not actually state, that RET has already proved itself as an effective form of therapy.

Some of the points that these critics make and with which I would cavil include: (1) according to these critics, I do claim in my article that RET is an effective or superior form of treatment—when I actually make no such claims; (2) they demand supportive data for RET hypotheses which are distinctive but which have not yet been experimentally tested; (3) they see RET mainly in its "elegant" disputational form but fail to see that it also exists in an "inelegant" form which is virtually synonymous with cognitive-behavior therapy; and (4) they are sometimes as enthusiastically pejorative about my formulations as they accuse me of being hortatively promotional about RET. Anyway, I enjoyed all the commentaries, want to thank the authors for taking the time and trouble to respond to my views, and am determined to use their critiques to sharpen up the hypotheses presented in my article and thereby aid the further scientific investigation of cognitive-behavior therapy.

REFERENCES

Adler, A. *Understanding human nature.* Greenwich, Conn.: Fawcett World, 1927.

Bach, G. R. The marathon group: Intensive practice of intimate reaction. *Psychological Reports,* 1966, *18,* 995–1002.

Bandura, A. *Principles of behavior modification.* Englewood Cliffs, N.J.: Prentice-Hall, 1969.

Bandura, A. *Social learning theory.* Englewood Cliffs, N.J.: Prentice-Hall, 1977.

Beck, A. T. *Cognitive therapy and the emotional disorders.* New York: Grune & Stratton, 1976.

DiGiuseppe, R. A., Miller, N. J., & Trexler, L. D. A review of rational-emotive psychotherapy outcome studies. *The Counseling Psychologist,* 1977, *7*(1), 64–72.

Dolliver, R. H. The relationship of rational-emotive therapy to other psychotherapies and personality theories. *The Counseling Psychologist,* 1977, *7*(1), 57–63.

Ellis, A. *The American sexual tragedy.* New York: Twayne, 1954.

Ellis, A. An operational reformulation of some of the basic principles of psychoanalysis. *Psychoanalytic Review,* 1956, *43,* 163–180.

Ellis, A. *How to live with a "neurotic" at home and at work.* New York: Crown Publishers, 1957. (Rev. ed., New York: Crown Publishers, 1975.) (a)

Ellis, A. Rational psychotherapy and individual psychology. *Journal of Individual Psychology,* 1957, *13,* 38–44. (b)

Ellis, A. Rational psychotherapy. *Journal of General Psychology,* 1958, *59,* 35–49.

Ellis, A. *Reason and emotion in psychotherapy.* New York: Lyle Stuart, 1962.

Ellis, A. A cognitive approach to behavior therapy. *International Journal of Psychiatry,* 1969, *8,* 896–900.

Ellis, A. *The sensuous person: Critique and corrections.* New York: Lyle Stuart and New American Library, 1972.

Ellis, A. Are cognitive-behavior therapy and rational therapy synonymous? *Rational Living,* 1973, *8*(2), 8–11.

Ellis, A. Paper presented at the Conference on Cognitive-Behavior Therapy Research, New York City, April 3, 1976.

Ellis, A. *How to live with—and without—anger.* New York: Reader's Digest Press, 1977. (a)

Ellis, A. Rational-emotive therapy: Research data that support the clinical and personality hypotheses of RET and other modes of cognitive-behavior therapy. *The Counseling Psychologist,* 1977, *7*(1), 2–42. (b)

Ellis, A. Toward a theory of personality. In R. J. Corsini (Ed.), *A sourcebook of personality theories.* Itasca, Ill.: Peacock, 1978.

Ellis, A. *A comprehensive bibliography of articles and books on rational-emotive therapy and cognitive-behavior therapy.* New York: Institute for Rational Living, 1980.

Ellis, A., & Abrahams, E. *Brief psychotherapy in medical and health practice.* New York: Springer, 1978.

Ellis, A., & Grieger, R. *Handbook of rational-emotive therapy.* New York: Springer, 1977.

Ellis, A., & Harper, R. A. *A guide to rational living.* Englewood Cliffs, N.J.: Prentice-Hall, 1961. (Also, Hollywood, Calif.: Wilshire Books, 1961.)

Ellis, A., & Harper, R. A. *A new guide to rational living.* Englewood Cliffs, N.J.: Prentice-Hall, 1975. (Also, Hollywood, Calif.: Wilshire Books, 1975.)

Ewart, C. K., & Thoresen, C. E. The rational-emotive manifesto. *The Counseling Psychologist,* 1977, *7*(1), 52–56.

Eysenck, H. J. *Behavior therapy and the neuroses.* New York: Macmillan, 1960.

Eysenck, H. J. (Ed.). *Experiments in behavior therapy.* New York: Macmillan, 1964.

Glass, L. L., Kirsch, M. A., & Parris, F. N. quoted in J. Brody, Reports of psychosis after Erhard course. *New York Times,* April 24, 1977, 23.

Glasser, W. *Reality therapy.* New York: Harper, 1965.

Goldfried, M., & Davison, G. *Clinical behavior therapy.* New York: Holt, Rinehart & Winston, 1976.

Herzberg, A. *Active psychotherapy.* New York: Grune & Stratton, 1945.

Hoffer, E. *The true believer.* New York: Harper, 1952.

Jones, M. C. The elimination of children's fears. *Journal of Experimental Psychology,* 1924, *7*, 382–390.

Kanfer, F., Karoly, P., & Newman, A. Reduction of children's fear of the dark by competence-related and situational threat-related verbal cues. *Journal of Consulting and Clinical Psychology,* 1975, *43*, 251–258.

Kazdin, A., & Wilcoxon, L. Systematic desensitization and non-specific treatment effects: A methodological evaluation. *Psychological Bulletin,* 1976, *83*, 729–758.

Kelly, G. L. *The psychology of personal constructs.* New York: Norton, 1956.

Kleiner, F. B. Commentary on Albert Ellis' article. *The Counseling Psychologist,* 1977, *7*(1), 49–51.

Lazarus, A. A. *Behavior therapy and beyond.* New York: McGraw-Hill, 1971.

Lazarus, A. A. *Multimodal therapy.* New York: Springer, 1976.

Lembo, J. M. *The counseling process: A rational behavioral approach.* New York: Libra, 1976.

Low, A. A. *Mental health through will-training.* Boston: Christopher, 1952.

Mahoney, M. J. *Cognition and behavior modification.* Cambridge, Mass.: Ballinger, 1974.

Mahoney, M. J. A critical analysis of rational-emotive theory and therapy. *The Counseling Psychologist,* 1977, *7*(1), 44–46.

Masters, W., & Johnson, V. E. *Human sexual inadequacy.* Boston: Little, Brown, 1970.

Maultsby, M. C., Jr. *Help yourself to happiness.* New York: Institute for Rational Living, 1975.

Maultsby, M. C., Jr., & Ellis, A. *Technique for using rational-emotive imagery.* New York: Institute for Rational Living, 1974.

Meehl, P. E. Theory-testing in psychology and physics: A methodological paradox. *Philosophy of Science,* 1967, *34*, 103–115.

Meichenbaum, D. Dr. Ellis, please stand up. *The Counseling Psychologist,* 1977, *7*(1), 43–44. (a)

Meichenbaum, D. *Cognitive-behavior modification: An integrative approach.* New York: Plenum Press, 1977. (b)

Murphy, R., & Simon, W. *An annotated bibliography of research on rational-emotive therapy and cognitive-behavior therapy.* New York: Institute for Rational Living, in press.

Perls, F. S. *Gestalt therapy verbatim.* Lafayette, Calif.: Real People Press, 1969.

Salter, A. *Conditioned-reflex therapy.* New York: Creative Age, 1949.

Schutz, W. C. *Joy.* New York: Grove Press, 1967.

Shaw, D. W., & Thoresen, C. E. Social modeling and systematic desensitization approaches in reducing dentist avoidance. *Journal of Counseling Psychology,* 1974, *21*, 415–420.

Skinner, B. F. *Beyond freedom and dignity.* New York: Knopf, 1971.

Suinn, R., & Richardson, F. Anxiety management training: A nonspecific behavior therapy program for anxiety control. *Behavior Therapy,* 1971, *2*, 498–510.

Sullivan, H. S. *Conceptions of modern psychiatry.* Washington, D.C.: Wm. Alanson White Foundation, 1947. (Also, New York: Norton, 1961.)

Tosi, D. J. Personal reactions with some emphasis on new directions, application, and research. *The Counseling Psychologist,* 1977, *7*(1), 46–49.

Weekes, C. *Hope and help for your nerves.* New York: Hawthorne Books, 1969.

Weekes, C. *Peace from nervous suffering.* New York: Hawthorne Books, 1972.

Woolfolk, R. L. A multimodal perspective on emotion. In A. A. Lazarus (Ed.), *Multimodal behavior therapy.* New York: Springer, 1976.

Yablonsky, L. *The tunnel back.* New York: Macmillan, 1965.

INDEX